Effective Reports for Managerial Communication

Effective Reports for Managerial Communication

THIRD EDITION

Malra Treece
Memphis State University

Larry D. Hartman
Brigham Young University

ALLYN AND BACON
Boston   London   Toronto   Sydney   Tokyo   Singapore

Copyright © 1991, 1985, 1982 by Allyn and Bacon
A Division of Simon & Schuster, Inc.
160 Gould Street
Needham Heights, Massachusetts 02194

In its first and second editions, this book was published under the title *Effective Reports*
(Malra Treece).

Library of Congress Cataloging-in-Publication Data

Treece, Malra.
   Effective reports for managerial communication / Malra Treece,
Larry D. Hartman.—3rd ed.
     p. cm.
   Rev. ed. of: Effective reports. 2nd. ed. c1985.
   Includes bibliographical references and index.
   ISBN 0-205-12358-9
   1. Business report writing. 2. Report writing. 3. Business
communication. I. Hartman, Larry D. II. Treece, Malra. Effective
reports. III. Title.
HF5719.T73 1991
658.4'5—dc20   90-41167
                                         CIP

Printed in the United States of America

10 9 8 7 6 5 4 3 2 1   95 94 93 92 91

Contents

Preface

Effective Reports for Managerial Communication, Third Edition, is planned for use in undergraduate and graduate classes that include the preparation of written and oral reports. It is also useful for in-house training seminars and as a reference book for libraries and offices.

Emphasis is upon effective management through communication, especially through various kinds of reports. Instruction is provided about efficient report preparation, including word processing, editing, graphics, and page design.

Two chapters, 17 and 18, describe the job-seeking process and illustrate resumes and letters of application.

Approach

Although professional in approach, content, organization, examples, and problems, *Effective Reports for Managerial Communication* is planned for easy and interesting reading. Readability and interest are considered important from four major standpoints:

- To enable readers to understand and apply principles discussed throughout the eighteen chapters and four appendix sections.
- To enable readers to enjoy the book.
- To serve as an example of readable business and professional writing.
- To exemplify, by the book itself, one of the most important attributes of written and oral communication: consideration for the receiver of the message.

Succesful writers and speakers must have an understanding of the process of communication and of the effects of perceptions and emotions upon the reception of meaning. In addition, they are knowledgeable about their subject matter, and their messages are sincere. They are skillful technicians, using words as tools to bring about change.

New to the Third Edition

An important change in the third Edition is the addition of a co-author, Larry Hartman.

Also new to the Third Edition is an increased emphasis on managerial communication and the use of computers in preparing reports, resulting in a title change from *Effective Reports* to *Effective Reports for Managerial Communication.*

Chapter 13, "Using Computers to Prepare Reports," and Chapter 14, "Drafting and Editing Reports," describe computer capabilities in relation to report preparation, including collection, organization, and analysis of data. Other uses of computers, as described in Chapters 13 and 14, include writing with word processors and using editing software, laser printers, and developing desktop publishing skills. This section of the textbook also contains a list of commercial computerized databases.

Chapter 12 illustrates footnotes and other elements of documentation in leading styles: MLA, APA, and the Chicago Manual of Style.

Appendix D: A computer disk, "Basic English Tutor," for use with IBM or IBM-compatible personal computers, and a student handbook, "Basic English Guide" is provided.

Appendix C includes an additional collection of group and individual incident cases. Additional case guides, theory statements, examples, and analysis tools using two deductive approaches are new to the Third Edition. Computer-directed cases and computer-managed cases are explained for application to integrative cases.

Simulations have been added to several chapters in order to enable students to role-play in small group meetings in order to build arbitration and compromise skills. These simulations also require practice in group writing and editing.

Acknowledgments

Special thanks is expressed to Guy Treece and Diane Hartman, spouses of the authors, for their patience and encouragement.

Sincere appreciation is expressed to teachers and students at Memphis State University and Brigham Young University who contributed their ideas and suggestions for improvement.

Valuable advice came from reviewers and from users of the two previous editions. These users contributed particularly helpful ideas and suggestions because their evaluations were based on practical experience in classrooms and in business offices.

Other dedicated teachers and publishing professionals contributed to the success of this text:

Benjamin C. Johnson, Brigham Young University
Ronald C. Barwick, Arthur Andersen and Company
Steve Kuphner, Ernst and Young and Company
Mark Krammer, Mrs. Field's International Incorporated
Bryan A. McNatt, KPMG, Peat, Marwick and Company
Wallace A. Johnson, Brigham Young University Law School
Ann Denton, Memphis State University
Judy Baird, Memphis, Tennessee

The following firms and individuals provided materials included in *Effective Reports for Managerial Communication*, Third Edition. Thank you.

Apple Incorporated, California
Judy G. Cox
First Baptist Church, Memphis
Dr. Ed Goodin, University of Nevada, Las Vegas
Lotus Incorporated, Massachusetts
Microsoft Incorporated, Washington
Sloan Management Review Incorporated
Standard Chartered Review Incorporated
Tennessee Valley Authority
Dr. Jean W. Vining
Francis W. Weeks, University of Illinois, Champaign
David R. Weigel and Energy Management Consultants
Nina Whitehead, Press Center Supervisor, Brigham Young University
WordPerfect Corporation, Utah

Additional appreciation is expressed to Editor Jack Peters and Assistant Editor Carol Alper, Allyn and Bacon, and to Elydia Davis, Superscript Associates, for their encouragement and technical assistance.

Further appreciation goes to members of the Association for Business Communication, who for many years have made valuable contributions to the field of business communication. Colleagues in this worthy organization have provided information, ideas, and inspiration that are reflected in this book and in other communication textbooks and supporting materials released by Allyn and Bacon.

M. T.
L. D. H.

*Effective Reports for
Managerial Communication*

CHAPTER 1

An Introduction to the Study of Reports

Chapter Outline

Welcome to your study of communication through reports. Your career, whatever your business or profession, will depend upon your success in communicating, perhaps more than upon any other ability. In addition, effective communication is essential to a satisfying personal life.

Your ability to excel in communicating is one of the most valuable assets you will ever have. Perhaps more than any other accomplishment, your knowledge and skill in communication demonstrate your intellectual capacity for advancement to responsible positions. As you move up the ladder of responsibility, communication becomes even more important. Lack of skill in communicating can act as a barrier to professional growth.

All Elements of Communication Are Interrelated

The elements of communication are not separate ones at all, but parts of the whole. Principles of effective writing also apply to effective speech. Nonverbal communication enters into both oral and written messages. Communication in any form is affected by the many and varied influences that enter into human behavior. Although the emphasis in this book is on reports, all instruction in communication must be interdisciplinary. Thus your study will include instruction in language, research sources and methods, individual and organizational behavior, organizational management, personnel management, business ethics, logic, public speaking, and several other areas of knowledge.

Most written messages are far more similar to other written messages than they are dissimilar. Competent writers learn to adapt from one format to another and to readers with differing needs and preferences. Regardless of your background and study in other areas of communication, however, you are not likely to excel in business research and report writing unless you have studied the subject and applied this knowledge to the preparation of reports.

Communication Is Always Imperfect

Your communication efforts will always be less than perfect, as they are for all of us. Perhaps the most important principle to keep in mind, as you strive to speak and write effectively, is that all communication is imper-

2

fect. This truth applies to report writing or any other area of communication, including the many methods of nonverbal communication.

Perfect communication cannot occur because the transmission of a message depends on both the sender and the receiver. We can never be sure of the effect of our words or nonverbal messages on the receivers of these messages. We cannot predict an individual's reactions to our words because of such factors as his or her emotions of the moment, previous understandings, or unique connotations of words based on individual experiences. Many other factors act as barriers to understanding and acceptance of our intended messages. But we can do much to improve our skills in both sending and receiving communication. This learning must be a continuing process, based on a foundation of knowledge, understanding, and skills developed by concentrated study of communication theory and techniques.

Communication Must Be Sincere

The term *communication* should not be used—as it sometimes seems to be—as merely a front, a facade, a glossing over. An accountant, physician, politician, teacher, or anyone else who covers up a lack of knowledge or conviction by the skillful use of words, or ''packaging,'' is not really an effective communicator. *The most important quality of communication is sincerity.*

Techniques of effective writing and speech are vastly important, but mastery of these techniques is not enough. The thoughts we are trying to convey must be based on a sound background of information and understanding. A fuzzy and indecisive mind cannot send out clear, correct, and convincing words. In addition, readers and listeners must have confidence in the integrity and sincerity of the writer or speaker in order for information and ideas to be trusted and accepted. To communicate, we must be trustworthy and sincere. We must have meaningful messages to send forth, and we must have the ability to put these messages into words that will be believed, accepted, and acted upon by the receivers of the message.

Reports Differ in Nature and Purpose

A report is a written or oral message planned to convey information or to present a solution to a problem. Using this broad and simple definition, many letters, memorandums, telephone calls, and personal conversations are forms of reports, as are notes on memorandum pads or the backs of envelopes. A report may consist of hundreds of pages, on which many persons have worked for months or years, or of a few paragraphs written in ten minutes.

Reports consist of written and spoken words, columns of figures, charts, computer printouts, or a combination of all these and of other forms. We speak of news reports, weather reports, stock market reports, accounting reports, and the very broad term, business reports. Although any kind of report conveying business information is a "business report," the definition must be narrowed.

In the definition that follows, the word *effective* has been inserted to describe what reports should be, not necessarily what they are. Even a poor report is still called by that name, and, thus, the wording of the exact definition of the term is complicated by semantic factors.

> An effective business report is an orderly, objective presentation of factual information, with or without analysis, interpretation, and recommendations, planned to serve some business purpose, usually that of making a decision.

Other descriptions of a report are that it

- is a management tool;
- may be described by many names and in varying ways according to purpose, format, subject matter, scope, length, readership, and other factors;
- varies widely in form, length, and content;
- may merely relate information, or may relate information and, in addition, analyze it and make recommendations;
- may be planned only to analyze existing information;
- is usually written for one reader or for a small group of readers;
- often moves up the chain of command;
- tends to be written in a more formal style than some other types of business communication;
- ordinarily is assigned;
- may be prepared at specified, regular intervals or only for a special need;
- requires careful planning and organization;
- answers a question or solves a problem.

The basic qualities of effective reports are the same, for the most part, as those of effective communication of any kind. Clarity, coherence, conciseness, a wise choice of arrangement in order to achieve readability and the desired psychological approach, correctness, neatness, consideration of the reader, exactness—these considerations apply to all types of communication.

When planning reports, however, we must give special attention to organization and to an objective, unbiased approach. Because reports are often longer than most letters or memorandums, they must be especially planned for readability and an orderly progression of thought.

Reports Must Be Specific and Objective

We are especially concerned about *objectivity* in a report; that is, we must gather and analyze data without letting our preconceived opinions or personal biases influence our efforts in finding and presenting truthful and complete information and interpretations. Although, because we are human, it is impossible to be completely objective, we should strive to base conclusions on facts, not on emotions or desires. No other element in the report-writing process is more important.

We tend to see what we expect to see or what we want to see. The recognition of this natural human weakness, with an effort to avoid it, is essential to unbiased research and reporting. We also tend to overgeneralize and to interpret inferences and value judgements as facts. Although such "twisting of the truth," even though unconscious, is harmful in all facets of life, it is obviously a definite barrier to objective research and impartial interpretation of data.

Readers of reports are influenced by specific details that provide a complete answer to the stated problem, not by emotional, persuasive language planned to bring readers to the writer's point of view. The same considerations apply to oral reports and, to a great extent, to all other written or oral messages, even to sales presentations. The reader or listener is convinced by *evidence*, not by *persuasion*, as the term is ordinarily used. True persuasion consists of specific, factual evidence effectively presented in the light of the reader's or listener's interests.

An objective approach, based on correct and concrete information, is emphasized throughout this textbook, especially in chapters on evaluating and presenting data. Such an approach is discussed in this introductory chapter because it forms the basis for true reporting of all kinds.

Reports Are a Fact of Life

Reports of some kind are necessary in all occupations. Whether you prepare them well or poorly, easily or with difficulty, almost surely you will prepare them. You will save much time if you learn to do them well.

Report preparation is not always stimulating, exciting, or entertaining. Dedicated researchers, however, consider the "search for truth" as one of their most exciting and fulfilling activities. Any kind of work is creative when we give it our best, approach it in our own way (there will always be restrictions), and carry it through to successful completion.

Your written and oral reports bring your ability and hard work to the attention of your superiors. Reports are not only responsibilities; they are opportunities! Various reports are used daily in business and in all professions to make decisions.

In addition, your ability to write effective, readable reports will be an invaluable aid in many of your other classes, both at the undergraduate and the graduate level.

Determining Objectives Is an Aid to Progress

At the beginning of your study, as in any endeavor, it is good to determine goals and to decide upon methods of reaching these goals. If you are enrolled in a class, no doubt your instructor's course outline includes specific objectives to be attained during the term or semester. To be worthwhile, these goals must truly be your own. You may wish to set goals for yourself that are higher than the required ones. Do you have objectives for this course in addition to the ones below?

1. To consider the ethics of communication in business situations and to develop an ethical approach to solving business problems.
2. To understand the theory and concepts of the communication process, particularly as they apply to business research and reporting.
3. To increase your ability to inform and convince through the use of language.
4. To learn the forms and purposes of frequently used business reports.
5. To improve your ability to make decisions involving the selection and organization of content, media, and format.
6. To learn to communicate information and ideas in written form by
   a. developing a clear, concise, convincing, and objective writing style that is adapted to the readers of the message.
   b. learning and applying high standards of physical presentation in preparing written messages.
7. To learn the basic techniques of report preparation, including how to collect, evaluate, analyze, organize, and interpret information and to present it in written and oral reports.
8. To strengthen your ability to analyze written and oral communications.

9. To develop an understanding of how computers and other technological developments can aid report preparation.
10. To utilize computer graphs and statistical software in preparing reports and reinforcement visual tools.

If you have specific objectives of your own, such as how to prepare special-purpose reports in your area of knowledge or for a particular job, no doubt these more specific objectives are included in the general ones listed above. If you do have specialized goals, let your instructor know about them, perhaps in the form suggested in the first problem at the end of this chapter.

All Effective Reports Can Be Described by the Following Terms

Communication does not consist of one quality, but of several qualities woven together. Even when communication is limited to the medium of written business reports, many principles of effective communication enter into consideration throughout the process, from the beginning of the planning stage to the transmittal of the finished report.

Writing or speaking cannot be completely effective if it is weak in any area, regardless of how strong it is in other areas. For example, even though a report is carefully planned, researched, and objectively analyzed, it is less than effective if the writer does not know the principles of sentence construction or of correct language usage. On the other hand, correct language alone is far from enough, although it is extremely important.

Your work in the world is likely to be judged somewhat differently from the papers you prepare in school. If a report is not good from all standpoints, it will not be considered as fair or average, based on its strong points. If it is weak in one respect, it is weak overall.

The terms in the following list are not exclusive in meaning, and some are quite similar; for example, *clear* and *readable.* As these words apply to written material, they often are used synonymously, although *readable* is likely to mean *clear without reading effort.* Other terms with similar meanings are *courteous* and *considerate. Considerate is the broader term. Courteous* has more to do with phrasing, and, when applied to business research and report writing, effective communication throughout the report process. We cannot be considerate without also being courteous, but courteous phrasing does not guarantee true consideration.

Appropriate in Tone and Approach.   Communication differs in tone and approach according to the message, the listeners or readers, and the occasion. As much as possible, each message should be adapted to the individual reader. The tone of some reports differs from that of usual business letters. Writers must consider the purpose of the communication and, among other factors, organizational precedent for similar reports.

Attractive in Appearance.   Your business messages should be neatly typewritten or printed and arranged attractively on the sheet. The typewriter keys must be clean. Use an electric typewriter with a film ribbon or a letter-quality electronic printer. Choose an appropriate format that is easily readable. Leave plenty of white space. Use good quality paper.

Businesslike.   The term *businesslike* does not mean that reports or other business messages are written in any specialized or particular language. Good business language is the same language that is correctly used elsewhere in life. You are not being businesslike, but old-fashioned, if you use such stereotyped phrasing as "Please find enclosed herewith," "in your hands, " and "We beg to call your kind attention to. . . . " Business writing should not be stuffy, stiff, or pompous, but simple, natural, and direct. It should be polite and matter-of-fact, much as you would address associates in your office, particularly those at a higher level.

Clear.   Business writing must be immediately clear. *Readability* is another term used in this book to mean clarity, especially from the standpoint of adaptation to varying groups of readers.

Clarity can be achieved by using (1) concrete, specific words, including active verbs; (2) correct and appropriate sentence structure planned to convey the desired emphasis; (3) short, well-organized paragraphs, most of which begin with a topic sentence; (4) conventional punctuation, which is used not only to follow "accepted rules," but to convey meaning; (5) coherent phrasing and organization; and (6) readable formats.

Clear thinking must precede clear writing or speech. If the sender of the message does not know exactly what he or she wants to say, and does not keep the reader in mind, the message is likely to be inexact and ineffective.

Coherent.   Sentences and paragraphs should "hang together"; that is, the thought should flow naturally and freely from the beginning of the message to the end. If a message is well organized and contains well-chosen words, including necessary and appropriate transitional words, phrases, and paragraphs, it will be coherent.

Complete.   The message must be complete in that it answers fully all the reader's questions and gives all the needed or desired information. A report must fulfill its stated purpose which, in a report arranged in the inductive order, is stated early in the introduction.

Concise. Conciseness means a written or oral message is no longer than it needs to be to accomplish its particular purpose or purposes. Conciseness is not necessarily brevity. A one-hundred-page report and a ten-page letter are concise if every word is necessary to convey the information, to be considerate, and to be convincing. The lack of conciseness often occurs because of unnecessary repetition; rambling; wordy phrases, especially trite phrases of business jargon; and long, complicated words and phrases instead of simple, direct wording.

Considerate. Consideration goes one step further than courtesy. The terms are not exactly synonymous. Consideration is the broader term and includes what you actually say in your message or the solution to your particular problem. Consideration is simply another name for one aspect of the *you-attitude*, which is often discussed in relation to business letters but is also applicable to business reports and all other business messages.

Constructive. Constructive writing is positive, specific, helpful, convincing, and effective.

Convincing. Convincing writing is written in specific, concrete words that lead logically to a reasonable conclusion. Readers are convinced by evidence, not by persuasion.

Correct. A message should be correct in information given, in the form and approach chosen, and in English usage. Being grammatically correct in every detail, as important as this feature is, is not enough for good business writing. A report that includes inaccurate, incomplete, or biased, nonobjective interpretations causes more havoc than erratic punctuation or misspelled words.

Courteous. All business writing and speech should be courteous. Good manners are necessary in all business and professional communication. When writing reports, you show courtesy by submitting them on or before scheduled deadlines. You are courteous when you exemplify all the characteristics of effective communication, as discussed in this summary and throughout the text: clarity, completeness, conciseness, correctness, objectivity, and all the rest. A cover, title sheet, and transmittal letter are other courteous, considerate touches to a formal report.

Creative. Business writing is not usually referred to as "creative writing," a term most often used to describe novels, poetry, short stories, and, perhaps, some advertising copy. All our work, however, is creative if we have put our best into it, if we have looked at the situation and tried to solve it in the best possible way, not necessarily in the way it has always been solved before.

Effective.   Effective writing or speech accomplishes its particular purpose or purposes.

Emphatic.   Emphasis should be used to call attention to the most important parts of the message. Proper use of the methods of emphasis is the most important aid to clarity. Methods of achieving proper emphasis and clarity are approximately the same: position, space, word choice, sentence construction, format, and mechanical means of emphasis.

Ethical.   Business reports, like all other business communication, should be sincere, honest, and truthful. All communication should be based on a sincere interest in the reader and upon loyalty to the writer's employing organization.

Forceful.   Good writing is not forceful from the standpoint that it is dictatorial or demanding. It is forceful in that it is strong and vivid, written mostly in the active voice. Forceful writing is usually concise, for it is not weighted down with unnecessary, wordy phrases. Because it moves, it is likely to have good sentence construction. Forceful writing is also emphatic writing, and it is likely to be convincing.

Formal.   The word *formal*, when used to describe reports, describes both format and writing style. The word *formal*, like many other words, is relative and far from exact. As it concerns format, the greatest distinction between formal and informal reports is the inclusion of preliminary and appended parts. A formal writing style, as contrasted to an informal one, contains no contractions, casual, conversational expressions, or slang. All writing, regardless of formality, should be simple and natural.

Informal.   The word *informal*, when used to describe reports also refers to both format style and writing style. The term participative communication also refers to informal formats and styles. Today informal or *participative* styled messages refer to ease of access of decision-making data. The language is active and happening now, as if a casual conversation is recorded as a written message. Typically, informal messages use first names and personal pronouns when directing messages to individuals or specific groups. Selected jargon may be acceptable if both senders and receivers know the terminologies.

Goodwill Building.   In all business writing or speech, we must be concerned with goodwill, both with persons outside the organization and with other employees. In the case of reports, which are likely to move upward within the organization, the term *goodwill* is perhaps better expressed as recognition of your competence that you display by the overall quality of the finished report and your demonstrated ability throughout the report process. In addition, some reports are read by persons outside the organization; for example, annual reports are factual material to prospective employees or stockholders. For such reports, you must be concerned with building and maintaining goodwill toward your employing organization.

Interesting.   Your business reports and other business writing will be interesting if they answer the reader's questions in an easily readable, concise form. Anecdotes and jokes, although suitable for a few kinds of business writing, are ordinarily out of place in factual reporting.

Objective.   Business writing should be objective, or nonbiased, in that it is based upon facts. Objective writing is especially stressed in report writing, but it is important in all forms of communication. In reports, when opinions are stated, they should be clearly identified as opinion. Material expressed in the impersonal tone and formal writing style seems more objective to some readers than material written more informally with the use of personal pronouns, particularly *I* and *you*.

Original.   Not every business report can be completely different from every other business report, for often the situations are the same or similar. Your reports should be original in that they are written in your own words, not copied from some manual or handbook. Reports and other kinds of writing often lack originality because they are worded in trite, stereotyped business jargon or other stale clichés.

Positive.   The positive approach accents the pleasant aspects of a situation, not the unpleasant. It tells what *can* be done, not what *cannot* be done. Negative words such as *fail, criticize,* and *reject* are minimized, if not completely eliminated. The several methods of emphasis and subordination can be used to construct the message in a positive, pleasant, and diplomatic way.

Professional.   Report writers make their work professional by continuing study of the use of language, research methods, logic, and the art and skill of writing.

Specific.   Specific writing is the opposite of vague, general writing. It is concrete, not abstract or general. Specific writing is more forceful and vivid than general, abstract writing. Specific writing is usually the better choice. At times, however, in order to be tactful and courteous, you cannot be completely specific.

Tactful. Real courtesy and consideration, combined with careful word choice, should make all your messages tactful.

Summary   Success in your professional and personal life depends to a great extent upon the ability to communicate, perhaps more so than upon any other ability. Oral and written communication, including reports, is a vital and frequent employment responsibility, whatver your specialization or employing organization.

The most important element of all communication is sincerity.

At the beginning of your study of report preparation or of any other subject, it is good to determine goals and to decide upon methods for reaching these goals.

A report is a written or oral message planned to convey information or to present a solution. Reports are essential in all businesses and professions. Basic principles and considerations are the same for all.

Because all elements of communication are interrelated, the most important qualities of effective reports are the same, for the most part, as those of all effective messages. When preparing reports, however, we must give special attention to organization and to an objective, factual evaluation and presentation. Recommendations must be based on evidence.

Questions and Problems

1. Look back at the objectives listed for this course. Which ones interest you the most and the least? Why? In which areas referred to by these various objectives do you feel that you are now the strongest? The weakest? Express the answers to these questions in a letter or memorandum addressed to your instructor. (See Chapter 3 for suggested formats.)

2. Write a letter, memorandum, or other report to your instructor in which you give the following information:
   a. Your major and your expected date of graduation.
   b. The kind of work you hope to enter or continue after you complete your college work.
   c. Whether you have a part-time job, and, if so, what you do, particularly as your work relates to report writing or other communication.
   d. Your previous work experience, especially your experience in communication of any kind.

3. Interview one or more persons who are working in your area of specialization. For example, if you are majoring in personnel management, interview one or more persons already employed in this field. Ask them for their

advice about the skills and knowledge that you should try to obtain during your study of reports. Write a summary of the information you obtain in the format specified by your instructor. Be prepared to present this summary in the form of a short oral report to other class members.

4. Look in the *Business Periodical Index* under ''Communication in Management'' to find two articles that have been published within the past two years. Try to find articles that relate directly to your major field of study. For example, if you are majoring in accounting, find articles about communication as it relates to accountants. Write a one-page summary of one or both of these articles in the format that your instructor suggests. Be prepared to present this summary, or these summaries, orally to the class.

5. Step to the front of the classroom. Introduce yourself to your instructor and to your classmates. Tell them about your major field of study and your career goals. Describe your present employment, if any, especially as it relates to written or oral communication. Tell them anything else about yourself that you wish, provided you keep your remarks to no more than the time limit set by your instructor.

6. This assignment can be substituted for Number 5. Form into groups of two. Meet with someone with whom you are not already acquainted, preferably someone you have never seen before entering this class. Spend five to ten minutes (or the time limit set by your instructor) in becoming acquainted with your classmate.

7. Introduce your friend (Problem 6) to your instructor and to your classmates, much as you would introduce a speaker at a conference or at another speaking engagement. Tell the class something about this person, perhaps some of the information described in Problem 2.

8. If you are now employed, describe your communication activities in relation to the discussion in this chapter. Examples of topics to be discussed or questions to be answered are these:
   a. Do you spend more time in written communication or in oral communication?
   b. What kinds of reports do you prepare?
   c. What kinds of reports do you receive?
   d. What other kinds of written messages do you prepare?
   e. By which methods (telephone, conversation, group discussion, or public speaking) do you communicate orally? What are the purposes of these forms of oral communication?

9. Write a letter, memorandum, or other report to your instructor and to your classmates about databases that are available for immediate use in your college or university library. These databases are stored on compact disks. ABI/INFORM includes an index, with abstracts, of thousands of journal articles. Is this database available? If so, where is it located? (NOTE: This assignment may be substituted for or used in addition to Problem 4.)

CHAPTER 2

Classifications and Characteristics of Reports

Chapter Outline

Every oral or written report is different is some way from all others, yet in many ways similar to every other. Reports vary according to the reader, writer, subject matter, purpose, and many other factors. They are described by different terms in different organizations.

Although the terminology used elsewhere may differ from that in this book, understanding the report classifications given in this chapter will help you plan and prepare reports of various kinds because you will know the many ways in which they *can* be prepared. After learning basic principles, you can adapt to specialized and differing terminology, forms, and techniques.

In addition to the terms used in this chapter, reports are classified according to their specialized uses. Like individuals, they sometimes go by nicknames. For example, they may be called by special names, such as the "2001 Report," for which the descriptive term is only the number of the printed form on which data are recorded, or "the green sheet," to describe the color of the paper used for the report. Reports may also be classified according to product name or according to a company department or division or described by the purpose for which the report was prepared.

All these classifications you will learn on the job. Like other specialized terms you use in your daily work, they will soon become familiar to you. For example, Social Security claims representatives refer dozens of times a day to the "101" or the "201," which are the numbers given to special forms on which information is recorded. Accountants, as well as many other people at income-tax time, refer routinely to the "1040" or "1040E," as well as to other reports, by a number that serves as a name.

Reports are basically classified and arranged in the following ways, even if no one in a particular organization, including the writer, refers to them in this way. These terms describe factors common to all reports.

Classification by Readership

As is true with all effective communication, reports should be prepared and presented from the standpoint of the receiver or receivers of the message. Some reports differ from most letters and memorandums, however, in that you as the report writer cannot always be sure who your readers will be, even when the report is authorized and addressed to one individual.

For example, if you prepare a report for your supervisor, he or she may then use your report as a basis for a recommendation to someone higher in authority in the organization. In addition, your report may be filed away and referred to when other reports on the subject are prepared, perhaps years hence. In most instances, however, you *will* know who the principal readers of your report will be and can plan your approach accordingly.

If you believe that your report may be used in various ways, including publication, you will be wise to use a more traditional, formal approach than if you were writing routine memorandums to co-workers you know well. (See the terms *formal* and *informal* later in this chapter. Do not misinterpret the meaning of the word *formal*. All good writing, regardless of readership, should be simple, straightforward, and easy to read.)

Reports also are classified by readership in that they are *internal* or *external*. As the term indicates, internal reports are prepared for readers within your own organization, ordinarily someone higher in the chain of command. Many internal reports are prepared as memorandums. External reports go to someone outside an organization; for example, consultants submit reports to organizations other than their own. Another example of an external report is one to a government agency, perhaps to report the results of a research grant.

Although you will be guided by your expected readers, you can be sure that if your report is professionally written—that is, if it can be described by the characteristics of effective reports listed in Chapter 1—it will be well received by almost all readers, regardless of their background or position. A major consideration, however, is what your readers already know about the subject you plan to discuss. If at all possible, in the planning stage of your report, determine your readership and their needs and present knowledge of the subject.

Classification by Time Intervals

Periodic reports are prepared at regular intervals, such as daily, weekly, monthly, or annually. The annual corporate report is a periodic report, as is the daily sales report that consists only of rows of figures.

Special reports are not prepared at regular intervals, but only as the need arises. For example, a president of a bank with several branches learns that energy costs vary widely for the branches, which are located in buildings of similar size and construction. The president asks qualified bank personnel or an outside consulting firm to produce needed research and submit a report.

Progress reports, as the name indicates, relate the past and expected progress of an assigned project, often of a long, analytical report. These progress reports can also be described as periodic if, for example, a weekly progress report is expected until the project is completed. A consulting firm employed to find the reasons for the differing energy costs of the bank branches may be asked to make periodic reports to the president, perhaps weekly or as each branch bank is inspected. Progress reports are usually brief.

Classification by Authorization

Most reports are *assigned*. Even if the report writer wishes to initiate a project, it is ordinarily authorized by someone higher in authority, especially if the project is one that will necessitate much company time and expense. This authorization may be in written form and incorporated into the final report.

Justification reports usually are unassigned. Because they are usually, but not always, short and simply prepared, they seldom require written or oral authorization. As the name implies, they are prepared for the purpose of justifying a purchase, a procedure, or a change in the method of operation. Such reports are also prepared as *proposals* and described as such, as discussed in Chapter 7.

Classification by Subject Matter

Classification by subject matter is obviously one that will apply to all reports. (As you have no doubt noticed, the same report can be classified in several different ways.) Reports can be classified according to their particular subject matter or on the basis of a grouping of subjects.

Such a grouping is also described as classification by departments, if, within an organization, we refer to accounting, sales, management, research and development, credit, and other similar subject fields. To classify more narrowly, each of these broad subject areas could be divided into more specific descriptions; for example, accounting reports may be described as cost, audit, tax, and finance reports.

Classification by Purpose and Function

Every report should fulfill one, two, or three of the following purposes:

to inform,
to analyze,
to recommend.

Informational reports simply present data with no attempt to analyze or interpret the meaning of the data nor to make the recommendations for action.

Analytical reports also provide information but, in addition, include analysis and interpretation.

Informational reports are usually, but not always, shorter than analytical ones. Informational reports can be of any length, depending upon the amount of information to convey. Conversely, an analytical report can be short. (Long and short are relative terms, in reports as well as in everything else.) We do, however, often hear the terms *long analytical report* and *complete analytical report. Complete*, when used as a descriptive term, may mean that the report contains various preliminary and supplementary parts, which are discussed in depth in Chapter 15. The word may also be used to signify that the report and the investigation that preceded it are broad in space.

Analytical reports are sometimes further classified by such terms as *examination, recommendation,* or *improvement*. These distinctions are usually made between analytical reports that include stated recommendations and those that do not. An *examination* report includes an analysis of the data but no recommendations for improvement. Whether or not recommendations are definitely stated, an analysis of relevant data implies certain recommendations. For example, if a study of why a certain product is not selling well shows that customers do not like the color, obviously the report implies, or ''recommends,'' that the color be changed.

The distinction between informational and analytical reports will be important to you as you consider a proposed project. One of your first steps, particularly if you are a new employee, will be to determine exactly what is expected, not only from the standpoint of whether to analyze the data but from all other aspects of the problem.

Another term that is sometimes used in connection with an analytical report is *research report* or *research study*. A definition of research is ''to make a diligent and systematic inquiry or investigation into a subject in order to discover or revise facts, theories, applications, . . .''[1] Using this definition, we see that an analytical report is not necessarily based on data gathered by the report writer, who may prepare an analytical report from data already accumulated. In addition, a research report is not necessarily an analytical one, as research may be done only to gather information and to relay it, not to analyze the information and make recommendations.

An analytical report may consist of many combined informational reports from the standpoint that the data from these reports are combined and analyzed, often with the aid of a computer, and, from these combined data, analyses and recommendations are made for the solution of an existing problem.

---

1. *Random House Dictionary of the English Language* (New York: Random House, 1967), p. 1219.

Classification by Degree of Formality

Purpose and readership determine the degree of formality. The words *formal* and *informal,* as when used elsewhere, are relative terms when applied to reports; there is no exact and distinct dividing line. Reports that are not definitely and conclusively formal are best described as informal, a description that fits most business and professional writing and speech. In written messages, the words *formal* and *informal* are used to describe format, writing style, or both.

Format

A completely formal written report includes preliminary and supplementary parts that are omitted from the more informal arrangements. Such a report, as previously mentioned, is also described as a complete report. Some of these preliminary parts are *letter of transmittal, letter of acceptance, table of contents, list of tables, executive summary,* and *synopsis.* Supplementary parts include a *bibliography, appendix section,* and perhaps an *index.*

Informal reports may be presented in letter or memorandum format or in the various other short-form arrangements illustrated in Chapter 4. In addition, informal reports are prepared on numerous kinds of pre-printed forms in order to simplify preparation and reader comprehension.

A long report is likely to be arranged in the formal (complete) format, and a short report is likely to be presented as a memorandum or in some other informal report arrangement. This distinction, however, does not always apply. A fairly short report—six or seven pages, for example—may appropriately include preliminary and supplementary parts.

Writing Style

Formal writing includes no contractions, expressions that could be considered slang, or abbreviated sentences or sentence fragments. An informal writing style may include contractions and casual, conversational phrases or modes of expression.

Regardless of how the writing is described or how formal the situation, it should not appear unnatural, stilted, or pretentious. Some reports are written more formally than routine memorandums, but all business and professional writing should be interesting, natural, and easy to read. Both formal and informal writing should be grammatically correct, and both should be arranged and worded with the reader in mind.

Actually, neither classification, formal or informal, is completely exact as it pertains to most business and professional writing. ''Semiformal'' is more descriptive. *Ordinarily, you need not worry about degrees of formality but should merely write in a correct, natural, direct, simple, and respectful manner.* If you are not sure of the personality and the preference of your readers, and usually you won't be, you are wise to lean more toward the formal style than to be overly casual and familiar. Words that we put on paper, especially in the form of reports, are, at the least, semipermanent. We can never be sure how our written material will be used or when it will be used. A report that you write today could be filed away and used as a reference source ten or fifteen years from now.

The passages below are examples of formal writing, at least from the standpoint that they do not include contractions, colloquial language, or other evidences of extremely informal approach. They also illustrate the fact that a casual, colloquial approach is *not* required for easy readability or a natural style.

> The primary concern of American education today is not the development of the appreciation of the ''good life'' in young gentlemen born to the purple. . . . Our purpose is to cultivate in the largest possible number of our future citizens an appreciation of both the responsibilities and the benefits which come to them because they are Americans and are free.[2]

> Those who favor advertising make a strong argument when they say that the majority of lawyers will continue to abide by the Canons of Ethics and provide honest service. This argument becomes stronger when it is asserted that it is, and always will be, in the best interests of the members of the Bar who strive to uphold the honor and integrity of the profession to police their own members on this issue.[3]

An example of extremely informal writing, on the same subject as the second passage quoted, is as follows:

```
Okay, fellow barristers, we've decided to advertise. That historic
decision doesn't mean that we have to do so-it's up to you. But-
please-no flashing neon signs, singing commercials, or half-price
sales. It's not true, as some of you pessimists and idealists have
bemoaned, that the legal profession has at last hit rock bottom. That
happened a long time ago.
```

The following short business letter is also written in an informal style:

2. James Bryant Conant, Annual Report to the Board of Overseers, Harvard University, January 11, 1943. Quoted by John Bartlett in *Familiar Quotations*, 14th ed. (Boston: Little, Brown, 1968), p. 1026.

3. Jeffry A. Garrety, ''The Advertising Decision Facing the Practicing Attorney'' (unpublished report, 1977).

```
Thank you, Joan, for your blow-by-blow account of the annual sales
meeting. Before I received your letter, I was sorry that I was forced
to remain here in the main office.

Even so, I'm looking forward to seeing you at next year's meeting.
```

Your choice of writing style—light or serious, informal or formal—must be influenced by your relationship with the reader and the subject matter of your message. A light, humorous tone, no matter how clever, is inappropriate in some situations. On the other hand, business and professional communications are often concerned with subjects of less than immortal impact—although they are desirable or necessary for whatever purpose they are planned to accomplish.

Classification by Personal or Impersonal Writing Style

Most business writing, including many reports, is written in the *personal tone;* that is, the writer is free to use *I, we, you,* and other first- and second-person pronouns so long as they are not used to excess. The *impersonal tone* includes no first- or second-person pronouns. This style of writing is also referred to as the *third-person objective.*

An advantage of using the impersonal tone in reports is that it seems more objective and nonbiased. References are to facts and interpretations, not to the writer. The choice of writing style does not affect real objectivity; nevertheless, because it appears to do so, many writers and readers prefer the impersonal tone.

Another important advantage is that by using no first- or second-person pronouns, more emphasis is given to the facts and analyses being presented, where the emphasis should be. You should emphasize the results, not what you did as the researcher.

Some traditionally minded readers of business reports judge a report written in the impersonal tone to be more professional, more objective, more scientific, and more carefully prepared than one written in the personal tone. If you are likely to encounter this reaction, you are decreasing the likelihood of the acceptance of your ideas by using the personal tone. The use of *I, we,* and other first- and second-person pronouns may distract the reader's mind from whatever it is that you are trying to say.

The impersonal writing style is, in itself, more formal than the personal. It is ordinarily used when the report, according to format and wording, is described as formal. Written material, however, can convey formality even with the use of first- and second-person pronouns. Hence, the terms *formal writing style* and *impersonal tone* are not synonymous, although they are often used together in the same report.

Although opinions of the writer may be expressed, emphasis should be upon conclusions based upon the findings of the report, not upon what the researcher believes. The use of *I* and *we* in a formal report may lead readers' thoughts away from the information being reported to the person who did the reporting. This undue emphasis is often reason enough for wording some types of writing in the impersonal tone.

Opinions can be stated impersonally, without the use of *I,* as illustrated below:

```
The results of the study indicate that electricity consumption could
be reduced approximately 20 percent by the installation of
fluorescent lights throughout the plant and offices.

The study indicates that the company should install fluorescent
lights throughout the plant and offices.

Fluorescent lights should be installed throughout the plant and
offices.
```

That it is the report writer who is making the recommendation is apparent in most cases, since he or she has done the research and is writing the report.

The preceding sentences, if written in the personal tone, might read as follows.

```
We could decrease electricity consumption approximately 20 percent by
the installation of fluorescent lights throughout the plant and
offices.

The results of the study indicate that we should install fluorescent
lights throughout the plant and offices in order to decrease
electricity consumption by approximately 20 percent.

I recommend that we install fluorescent lights throughout the plant
and offices.
```

Notice that the personal tone results in a more natural and informal approach. In the third example the words *I recommend* emphasize the writer of the report and not the recommendation, as these words are in the emphatic sentence beginning. The second sentence includes the word *we* but uses the important and emphatic first position to mention results and the emphatic closing position to state benefits of the recommendation. In the first example, as well as the third, *we* refers to the organization, not to the report writer.

You are likely to do much more writing in the personal tone that in the impersonal, and appropriately so. *The expert writer, however, can write well in either style and can choose wisely between the two for differing kinds of material, readership, and situations.* Try to judge each bit of writing according to what you have to say and who will read it.

Classification by Arrangement of Ideas

Reports can be arranged in *direct* (or *deductive*) order or in *indirect* (or *inductive*) order. They can also be arranged in chronological ("as-it-happened") order.

Basically, the difference between direct and indirect order is this: The direct arrangement begins with the most important part of the message and then expands upon this central message by giving details, examples, or added information or explanations. The indirect arrangement builds up to the most important part of the message by beginning with an introductory section, presenting findings, and ending with conclusions and recommendations. These two arrangements can be used in written works of all lengths, including letters, memorandums, and reports.

For the most part, basic considerations as to which order should be chosen are the same for both writing and speech. Direct order is usually the best choice unless there is a definite, obvious reason for using indirect or chronological arrangement.

The direct arrangement of any written work is advantageous in that it is easy to read because the most important part of the message is presented first. The reader knows immediately what the communication is about. The emphatic beginning is used as it should be, to emphasize something important. The direct arrangement, however, has a psychological disadvantage in some instances. The reader may not be prepared for "the answer," especially if it is a disappointing one or something that the reader is not prepared to believe or accept.

In such a situation, the indirect arrangement should be used to prepare the reader to accept or to believe the conclusions of the letter or report. For example, if reasons are given first or if information is included to show how the final decision was reached, the reader is more likely to accept the decision. In addition, explanation of circumstances and background material are often necessary to make clear the most important part of the message, even though the reader is willing to accept the message.

News stories and news releases are usually written in the direct order; the main facts of the story are given in the first paragraph, facts of lesser importance are given in the second, and so on. This plan is used in news releases so that condensing, necessary sometimes because of limited space, can be done from the bottom up. Even when the article or release appears in its complete, original form, the direct arrangement of ideas, from the most important to the least, increases reader interest and understanding. Business letters, memorandums, and reports, like newspapers, are often read hurriedly; any arrangement that will increase quick and easy understanding should be used.

The inductive report arrangement, so traditional in some organizations in past years that it is sometimes described as the "traditional" arrangement, is no longer mandatory or routinely expected even for long analytical reports. Overall, the trend in report writing is toward informality and conciseness. Many readers prefer the "answer" at the beginning, even if this answer is not particularly pleasant. Other readers still prefer the inductive arrangement, saying it is more "logical" because it tells *why* (purpose) and *how* (methods) before presenting *what* (findings) and arriving at the *answer* (recommendations).

Not all material, including reports, can be written in the direct order, even when there is no psychological aspect to consider or precedent to follow. To do so would decrease, not increase, reader understanding. The reader (or listener) must have an idea of the subject to be discussed before understanding conclusions. You may need introductory paragraphs or sections to lead to comprehension of the most important facts.

A paragraph is also arranged in direct or indirect order, or perhaps in chronological order. A paragraph arranged in direct order begins with a topic sentence. A paragraph that builds up to the topic sentence is arranged in indirect order. The direct arrangement of paragraphs should ordinarily be preferred because of increased readability, although paragraphs, like sentences, should be varied in order to improve style, flow of thought, and the exact expression of ideas.

The two immediately preceding paragraphs illustrate the use of topic sentences as first sentences, resulting in the direct order of paragraph arrangement. The following paragraph illustrates the topic sentence at the end of the paragraph, as well as the informal writing style.

Are you thinking by this time that all these terms are just too much? Do you believe that the most important principle of writing is just to sit down and write—or, if you prefer, to stand up and write? (Thomas Wolfe, the six-foot-six-inch novelist, wrote while standing at his refrigerator, with the manuscript on top of the refrigerator.) You are at least partially right— it does no good whatsoever to talk about writing a report, or anything else, if you never get around to writing one. On the other hand, it's possible just to sit down and start writing, dictating, or composing at the keyboard, and come out with a jumbled mess. Like other abilities, successful report writing is based on an understanding of principles and concepts that are best described by exact terminology.

Figures 2–1 and 2–2, excerpts from a report in letter form, illustrate the use of the direct and the indirect order of arrangement. For a short report similar to the one on Saladmix in these two figures, many readers and writers prefer the direct order. This letter as shown in these figures, however, could serve as a summarizing transmittal letter to accompany a long comprehensive report. The notation about accompanying charts and graphs would be omitted and reference would be made to the complete report. For this particular subject, many readers would prefer far more detailed analysis on such matters as competing brands, types of advertising,

Figure 2–1.

Illustration of contents of letter report presented in the direct order of arrangement. (Based on a report prepared by Al Lyons.)

> Saladmix should be introduced into the market during March of next year.
>
> This recommendation is based on marketing data that show seasonal sales of other salad dressings and mixes, ours and those of our competitors. The highest volume months are June and July, followed by April and May. February and March are the months with the lowest volume in sales, with only a slightly higher total reported for December and January, as shown on the attached tables and charts.
>
> Because we cannot get Saladmix on the market before September of this year, we will have missed the highest volume months. Although introduction in September would give Saladmix a possible advantage over potential competition, I do not believe such an advantage warrants the additional cost. Sales from October to March are only 31 percent of the total annual sales, while sales from March to October are 69 percent of the total.
>
> By introducing Saladmix in March, preferably during the first week, we can take advantage of the highest volume months and benefit most from the increased advertising that will be necessary whenever Saladmix is released.
>
> Let's discuss any further questions about possible marketing strategies concerning Saladmix. Please call my office.

and other factors. The problem as stated should be discussed in far more detail unless the reader has complete confidence in the writer's decision. For a much longer report, on this subject or any other, the indirect order is often considered preferable.

Compare these direct and indirect arrangements:

Indirect arrangement	**Direct arrangement**
Introduction (purpose, methods, scope, other introductory material)	Recommendations (if stated) or conclusions, based on detailed findings
Detailed presentation of findings, usually divided into several sections	Purpose, methods, scope, and other necessary explanatory material (Sometimes these sections follow findings.)
Conclusions (based on findings) and recommendations, either stated or implied	Detailed presentations of findings, usually divided into several sections

Here is the report on the introduction of Saladmix. Marketing data that show seasonal sales of other salad dressings and mixes, ours and those of our competitors, are shown on the attached tables and charts.

The highest volume months are June and July, followed by April and May. February and March are the months with the lowest volume in sales, with only a slightly higher total reported for December and January.

Because we cannot get Saladmix on the market before September of this year, we will have missed the highest volume months. Although introduction in September would give Saladmix a possible advantage over potential competition, I do not believe such an advantage warrants the additional cost. Sales from October to March are only 31 percent of the total annual sales, while sales from March to October are 69 percent of the total.

By introducing Saladmix in March, preferably during the first week, we can take advantage of the highest volume months and benefit most from the increased advertising that will be necessary whenever Saladmix is released.

I, therefore, recommend that Saladmix be introduced into the market during March of next year.

Figure 2–2.

Illustration of contents of letter report presented in the indirect order of arrangement. (Based on a report prepared by Al Lyons.)

A more detailed illustration of the direct and indirect arrangements is shown in Figure 2–3.

As shown in Figure 2–3, the words *evidence* and *specific* describe requisites of all good reporting. The word *supporting*, however, includes both advantages and disadvantages of the recommendations. In a way, stated disadvantages are a form of ''evidence,'' or proof, in that a thorough analysis of both advantages and disadvantages, with an objective and complete presentation, indicates that you have considered all aspects of the situation before coming to your conclusions and making your recommendations.

Even though a report itself is presented in the indirect order, the use of a synopsis, which may be included in a transmittal letter similar to Figure 2–1 or 2–2, or as a separate preliminary part, combines features of both the direct and indirect arrangements in the overall report ''package.'' In the complete report format, the report package consists of preliminary parts, the report itself, and supplementary parts.

The synopsis is a greatly condensed version of the complete report. Because of the placement of the synopsis before the actual report, the re-

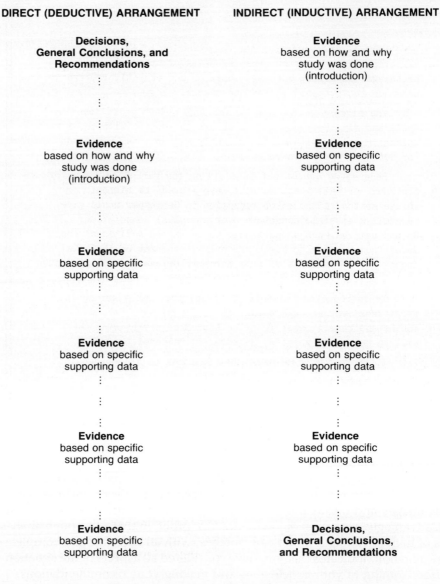

Figure 2–3.
Illustration of Direct and Indirect Arrangements.

DIRECT (DEDUCTIVE) ARRANGEMENT

**Decisions,
General Conclusions, and
Recommendations**
⋮
⋮
⋮

Evidence
based on how and why
study was done
(introduction)
⋮
⋮
⋮

Evidence
based on specific
supporting data
⋮
⋮
⋮

Evidence
based on specific
supporting data
⋮
⋮
⋮

Evidence
based on specific
supporting data
⋮
⋮
⋮

Evidence
based on specific
supporting data

INDIRECT (INDUCTIVE) ARRANGEMENT

Evidence
based on how and why
study was done
(introduction)
⋮
⋮
⋮

Evidence
based on specific
supporting data
⋮
⋮
⋮

Evidence
based on specific
supporting data
⋮
⋮
⋮

Evidence
based on specific
supporting data
⋮
⋮
⋮

Evidence
based on specific
supporting data
⋮
⋮
⋮

**Decisions,
General Conclusions,
and Recommendations**

port package is, in effect, arranged in direct order, even though the report proper is arranged in inductive order. In some reports we should prepare the reader to accept or to believe disappointing or startling conclusions. In such instances, the synopsis is better omitted unless to do so would be going against the expected or assigned format.

We realize, of course, that the reader of any message can look first at the conclusions and recommendations section no matter where it is placed.

Even so, the reader is not immediately given an unwelcome message without explanation or justification.

The synopsis and other parts of a formal report are discussed in more detail in Chapter 15.

Classification by Method of Presentation

Reports may be prepared both in *oral* and in *written* form. Many reports of considerable length and scope, or those involving extensive research, are prepared first in written form, then presented in oral form. The oral presentation may include only the highlights of the complete report.

The written report is often condensed for distribution or for publication. The synopsis, which is prepared as a preliminary to a formal report, may be used for this purpose.

The Role of Classifications in Report Planning

The conventional classifications given above are useful in planning, evaluating, and describing reports. Your study of report preparation, however, should not be based on these differing classifications. Instead, emphasis should be given to determining the problem, collecting and evaluating data, and presenting the report in oral or written form. Characteristics of all effective reports are similar, regardless of classification: readability; coherent organization; clear, concise, specific, diplomatic writing; correctness; and all the other attributes of effective written communication.

The following approaches to report writing are usually used together, although there can be exceptions:

1. Formal format WITH formal writing style WITH impersonal tone (third-person objective writing style) WITH the indirect (inductive) arrangement.
2. Informal format (letter, memorandum, or other short form; few if any preliminary or supplementary parts) WITH personal tone WITH direct arrangement (may be indirect, even if short, in order to attain a more persuasive psychological approach).

Summary

Although terminology differs widely, reports may be classified according to readership, time intervals, authorization, subject matter, function, degree of formality, the use of personal or impersonal tone, order of arrangement, and method of presentation.

The following classifications of reports are often used together:

- Formal format and writing style, impersonal tone, indirect (inductive) arrangement.
- Informal format, formal or informal writing style, personal tone, direct arrangement.

Most business and professional writing, with the exception of formal reports, is written in a rather informal (actually, "semiformal") style, using the personal tone.

Questions and Problems

1. Discuss the advantages and disadvantages of the personal and the impersonal tone; the formal and the informal writing styles; the direct and the indirect arrangements.

2. In what kinds of writing may *you* be used or implied, but not *I* or *we*? Explain.

3. Rewrite the following sentence, using the personal tone:

```
The results of the study indicate that more men's business suits
could be sold if they were manufactured in a wider range of colors.
```

4. Rewrite the following sentence, which is from the concluding section of an analytical research study, using the impersonal tone:

```
I recommend that the instructional emphasis now given to the
following types of written communication be increased.
```

5. Write a paragraph of at least four sentences on any subject. Use the personal tone and an informal (but grammatically correct) writing style. Write the paragraph in the direct order; that is, the first sentence is to serve as the topic sentence.

6. Write another paragraph of at least four sentences on any subject. Use the impersonal tone. Do not use contractions, slang, or anything else that is definitely informal, but write simply and naturally.

7. Assume that each of the following paragraphs is the first paragraph of a report planned to determine a suitable location for an addition to a chain of restaurants named Country Vittles. Consider all examples to be the first paragraph of the report body, not from any of the preliminary or supplementary parts.

   Example I: A Country Vittles restaurant should be built on Highway 20 West in Galena, Illinois.

Example II: I recommend that a Country Vittles restaurant be built on Highway 20 West in Galena, Illinois.

Example III: The purpose of this study is to determine possible locations for a Country Vittles restaurant and to determine which site should be chosen for the next addition to the Country Vittles chain.

Example IV: I've completed the study of possible locations for Country Vittles. Because everybody likes country cooking, I'm convinced that we need to build restaurants all over the world. But because we don't have the bread (cornbread or otherwise) for all these, I've picked out the best bet for our next restaurant. You'll find my recommendation at the end of this report. Everybody is going to be surprised.

   a. Which example(s) indicate(s) that the report is arranged in direct order? Indirect order?
   b. Which example(s) indicate(s) that the report is written in the personal tone? In the impersonal (third-person objective) tone?
   c. Which example(s) indicate(s) that the report is written in the informal writing style?
   d. Which example(s) is (are) likely to be taken from a complete and formal analytical report?
   e. Each of the four examples was taken from an analytical report. How can you tell?
   f. From the paragraphs given, do you think the report is a periodic one? Why or why not?
   g. Of the four passages, Example IV is likely to be the most undesirable. Why?

8. Assume that each of the following paragraphs is the first one of a report planned to determine which magazines, if any, should be added to those currently available in the teachers' reading room. Consider all examples to be the first one in the report body, not from any of the preliminary or supplementary parts.

Example A: The purpose of this study is to determine which magazine subscriptions, if any, should be added to the present collection available in the reading room.

Example B: With the assistance of the members of the Library Committee, I have completed a study of the magazines in the reading room. Although deciding whether or not we need anymore—and which ones—was quite a hassle, you'll find our recommendations at the end of this report.

Example C: I recommend that subscriptions to the *Journal of Business Communications,* the *Journal of Technical and Business Communications, PC World,* and *Info World* be added to the collection currently available in the reading room.

Example D: Subscriptions to the *Journal of Business Communication,* the *Journal of Technical and Business Communications, PC World,* and *Info World* should be added to the collection currently available in the reading room.

   a. Which example(s) indicate(s) that the report is arranged in the direct order? The indirect order?

  b. Which example(s) indicate(s) that the report is written in the personal tone? In the impersonal (third-person objective) tone?

  c. Which example(s) indicate(s) that the report is written in the informal writing style?

  d. Which example(s) is (are) most likely to be taken from a complete and formal analytical report?

  e. Each of the four examples was taken from an analytical report. How can you tell?

  f. Can you determine from the four examples whether or not the study was authorized? If it was not authorized, by what special term could it be described?

  g. From the paragraphs given, do you think the report is a periodic one? Why or why not?

9. Classify each of the following report situations according to the terms given in this chapter.

  a. A teacher reports students' absences to the Veterans Administration by circling the names of students with poor attendance. The report is made each month.

  b. An engineering consulting firm studies a church building and makes recommendations for the conservation of energy. The report is sixty pages long and includes various preliminary and supplementary parts. The last section of the report includes recommendations.

  c. A vice president of a business organization interviews applicants for employment and chooses the three who seem to be the best qualified. The vice president describes the three applicants in a memorandum to the president of the organization.

  d. A university prepares a "self-study"—a comprehensive report of more than a thousand pages, prepared by many committees and revised by an editor. Self-studies are made every ten years. All aspects of the educational program are analyzed. The report is presented to an accrediting committee, which studies the university and presents its own report to officials of the university, with suggestions for improvement. University officials make the suggested improvements, and report to the accrediting agency that they have done so.

  e. At the end of each month, the manager of an apartment complex submits a report of activities and occurrences throughout the month. The monthly reports are prepared from daily reports.

10. When is it wise to preface a formal report with a synopsis? It is good business and good communication strategy to send partial reports?

11. What advantages can an executive find in a report with the decision data and action statements in the "primary emphasis" section of a report?

12. What disadvantages exist in placing the decision data in the "primary emphasis" section for a report for a non-manager?

CHAPTER **3**

Letter and Memorandum Reports

Chapter Outline

Many letters and memorandums, widely used in business offices and organizations of all kinds, are, in effect, reports, although they are not always described as such.

The words *short* and *informal* are relative and inexact, as are many other words. A short report is not necessarily informal, and an informal report is not necessarily short.

A *short, informal* report, as it is considered in this book, is any reporting or analysis of information that is not presented in the complete, formal arrangement that includes preliminary and supplementary parts, as discussed and illustrated in Chapter 15. The report decreases in formality, as far as format is concerned, as each of the preliminary and supplementary parts is omitted.

Informal reports, whatever the format, are often presented in the direct order, but the choice of arrangement depends more upon the content of material to be conveyed than upon the degree of formality desired.

Choosing an Appropriate Format

The formats used for reports differ in many ways among organizations, as they should. No particular format is suitable for every purpose or for every organization, and sometimes no particular format is specified, with the choice left to the judgment of the report writer.

You, as a beginning report writer, may be free to use the format of your choice, although you are more likely to use a format already established by other writers in your organization. If this is the situation, you should conform exactly to the established arrangement and presentation. To do otherwise results in distraction for the reader, who expects to find certain information in a certain place in the report.

If you are free to use an arrangement of your choice, the examples in this chapter and in Chapter 15, with necessary and appropriate modifications, will be suitable for almost any report. Use care and judgment in format selection. A wisely chosen format is an aid to readability, organization, conciseness, and the proper use of emphasis.

Letter Reports

The term *letter report*, if used at all, refers only to a report presented in the form of a regular business letter. Using a broad interpretation of the definition of reports given in Chapter 1, "a report is a written or oral message planned to convey information or present a solution," many, if not most, of the millions of business letters written every day could be described as reports because they convey information. Although distinction is often made between factual and persuasive writing, such materials as sales letters and advertising copy must contain factual, specific information in order to be convincing and effective.

Illustrations of reports presented in letter form are shown in Figures 3–1 and 3–2. Figure 3–1 is an example of a letter written in direct order and arranged in the letter style described as the *modified block*.

Figure 3–2 is an example of a letter report written in indirect order. It is arranged in the letter style described as the *semiblock*. Both of these letters, as shown by the absence of an accounting firm's letterhead, are *personal business letters*. The Certified Public Accountant is acting as an individual consultant.

The information shown in Figures 3–1 and 3–2 could have been presented in various ways, In this particular instance, a letter seems to be the best choice because it is personal, friendly, and informal. Similar findings presented to another person within the writer's organization would ordinarily be in memorandum format. The material could have been presented to Mr. and Mrs. Hobbs in a short report accompanied by an individual letter transmitting the report, although such formality is not necessary in this instance.

Analyze these letters, Figure 3–1 and Figure 3–2, in relation to the terminology used earlier in Chapter 2. Notice that both letters illustrate these terms:

> *special,* in that similar reports are not made at periodic intervals;
> *assigned,* as indicated by the term "as you requested";
> *subject matter,* advice on real estate exchange;
> *function,* analytical;
> *degree of formality,* informal;
> *writing style,* personal, as indicated by inclusions of you, your, we;
> *format,* letter.

Even after you decide to use a letter format to transmit information, you still must determine the letter style to be used. The modified block style shown in Figure 3–1 and the semiblock style shown in Figure 3–2 are widely used letter arrangements. They are considered somewhat conservative. These letter arrangements are shown here for the purpose of illustration and to prepare you to use these styles, if you wish to do so and if your instructor directs, for assignments throughout the course.

These short letters, like Figures 2–1 and 2–2, illustrate in extremely abbreviated form the same principles as those of the much longer recom-

```
                                              7900 Creek Bend
                                              Houston, TX 77071
                                              October 14, 199-


Mr. and Mrs. Melvin Hobbs
2157 Rolling Water Cove
Houston, TX 77069

Dear Mr. and Mrs. Hobbs:

I recommend that you trade your house on Voss Road for the equity in Dungreen
Townhouses. This recommendation is based on the following factors:

1. By trading the house for the equity in the eight-unit townhouse complex, you
   will not be required to pay capital gains tax. If you sell the house, the
   difference between the purchase price and the selling price is taxable. Both
   the house and the townhouse complex are investment property.

2. Because of the greater overall value, the townhouse complex will appreciate
   more, in dollar value, than the single-family house.

3. Attractive, well-located rental property is becoming scarce.

4. The price of the townhouses is less than replacement costs.

5. The non-escalating interest rate of 8¼ percent is extremely low.

6. Because of allowable depreciation and other expenses, these townhouses will
   shelter some of your high taxable income.

Another factor, less advantageous, is the amount of time that must be devoted to
management. In addition, the complex could be hard to sell quickly should you need
to do so.

I was happy to make this study for you, as you requested. If you like, I will
investigate the possibility of part-time management services. Further explanations
and specifications are shown on the attached sheets.

                                              Sincerely,

                                              Robert Hutchinson

                                              Robert Hutchinson, CPA


wht
Attachments
```

Figure 3–1. *Letter report presented in direct order. Letter style:* modified block.

36

7900 Creek Bend
Houston, TX 77071
October 14, 199-

Mr. and Mrs. Melvin Hobbs
2157 Rolling Water Cove
Houston, TX 77069

Dear Mr. and Mrs. Hobbs:

As you requested, I have made a study of the advisability of trading your fully paid-for residence on Voss Road for the equity in Dungreen Townhouses. I was happy to make this study for you. Detailed explanations and specifications are given on the attached sheets.

Favorable factors are these:

1. By trading the house for the equity in the eight-unit townhouse complex, you will not be required to pay capital gains tax. If you sell the house, the difference between the purchase price and the selling price is taxable. Both the house and the townhouse complex are investment property.

2. Because of the greater overall value, the townhouse complex will appreciate more, in dollar value, than the single-family house.

3. Attractive, well-located rental property is becoming scarce.

4. The price of the townhouses is less than replacement costs.

5. The non-escalating interest rate of $8\frac{1}{4}$ percent is extremely low.

6. Because of allowable depreciation and other expenses, these townhouses will shelter some of your high taxable income.

Another factor, less advantageous, is the amount of time that must be devoted to management. In addition, the complex could be hard to sell quickly should you need to do so.

The proposed real estate exchange is a sound financial decision. Personal considerations must be left up to you, but I believe that part-time management services would be economical and convenient.

Sincerely,

Robert Hutchinson

Robert Hutchinson, CPA

wht
Attachments

Figure 3–2. *Letter report presented in indirect order. Letter style:* semiblock.

mendation reports discussed in following chapters. Except for more complicated and comprehensive research procedures and more formal arrangements, the overall process of both these short letters and the long reports is practically the same.

The letters shown in Figures 3–3 and 3–4 illustrate two additional letter styles, the *full-block* and the *simplified* arrangements. These letters can also be considered informational reports, using the term in a broad context, as they supply information to Mrs. Holcombe about the letter arrangements used for the letters themselves. (She had requested advice about the choice of a letter style for her company.) Because both letters end with recommendations, they can be described as being in the indirect, or inductive, order.

The *subject line* shown in Figure 3–4 is a required part of the simplified letter style. A subject line can be correctly used with any letter arrangement, although its use is optional except with the simplified style. It is placed a double space below the salutation in letters that include a salutation. The triple space that precedes and follows the subject line in the simplified arrangement gives added emphasis to the subject line. In the full-block or simplified styles, the subject line should begin at the left margin. In other letter styles, the subject line may be centered.

The letter shown in Figure 3–5 is a variation of the simplified letter style. In fact, it could be described as a simplified version of the simplified letter style. This letter arrangement is not widely used for the same reasons that the arrangement shown in Figure 3–4 is not widely used: Many writers are reluctant to break with tradition by omitting the salutation and complimentary close.

Figure 3–5 is designated here as the *functional* letter style to connote practical simplicity. At the present time, this letter format has no official name in widespread use.

The functional arrangement is in many instances more desirable than the simplified style illustrated in Figure 3–4. Not all letters benefit from the use of a subject line, which is a requirement in the simplified style. For instance, a subject line would add nothing to the short, simple letter shown in Figure 3–5 and would result in a more impersonal approach. In addition, the writer's name and title are typed in capitals and lower case instead of in all capitals, as ordinarily used in the simplified style.

Memorandum Reports

Memorandums are so frequently used that some writers apparently give little thought to their composition. No doubt some of the many thousands of memorandums written daily are unnecessary, as are many of the longer and more formal reports. On the other hand, too little internal com-

BOARD OF EDUCATION
Memphis City Schools
2597 Avery Avenue, Memphis, Tennessee 38112

Please reply to: Memphis Area Vocational
Technical School
620 Mosby Avenue
Memphis, Tn. 38105
Phone 901/527-8455

September 21, 199-

Mrs. Laura Holcombe, Office Manager
Holcome-Carr Insurance Agency
392 North Deer Creek Drive
Pikeville, KY 41501

Dear Mrs. Holcombe:

As you requested, I am sending you examples of letters that illustrate two of the newer letter styles, the full-block and the simplified arrangements. I am glad to help you in the preparation of your new correspondence handbook.

This letter illustrates the full-block arrangement. Because of the efficiency with which this letter style can be typewritten, it is growing in popularity.

Some persons object to this arrangement because everything is at the left; they believe that the date and the closing lines should be centered or backspaced from the right margin in order to give balance to the letter. Other persons prefer the crisp, businesslike appearance of the full-block style.

This letter differs from the modified block style you are now using only in the placement of the date and closing lines; they begin at the left margin instead of the center of the page. (They can also be backspaced from the left margin when using the modified block or semiblock style, but this position requires even more typing time.)

The semiblock arrangement is the same as the modified except that the paragraphs are indented.

This full-block arrangement would be an appropriate one for your insurance agency. It is more efficient than either the modified block or the semiblock.

Sincerely,

Fredna Vaughn

Mrs. Fredna Vaughn, Supervisor
Business Education Department

sn

Figure 3–3. *Example of letter arranged in full-block style.*

BOARD OF EDUCATION
Memphis City Schools
2597 Avery Avenue, Memphis, Tennessee 38112

Please reply to: Memphis Area Vocational
Technical School
620 Mosby Avenue
Memphis, Tn. 38105
Phone 901/527-8455

21 September 199-

Mrs. Laura Holcombe, Office Manager
Holcome-Carr Insurance Agency
392 North Deer Creek Drive
Pikeville, KY 41501

THE SIMPLIFIED LETTER

Mrs. Holcombe, do you like this arrangement? It has several advantages, but
possibly some disadvantages, too. It is the easiest letter of all to type. In
addition, it has a businesslike, no nonsense look about it.

Another advantage, at least in most letters, is the use of the subject line, which
is always a part of the simplified style. Notice that the subject line is preceded
and followed by a triple space.

Some writers believe that this letter arrangement is unfriendly and impersonal
because the customary salutation and complimentary close are omitted. These lines
are unnecessary if the letter is worded as it should be, so that the reader will
understand it is ''sincere,'' ''cordial,'' and ''very truly yours.'' Besides, many
of the readers we address as ''dear'' are not really dear to us, using the
ordinary meaning of the word.

Perhaps you will choose this letter arrangement to be the standard one for your
office. If not, I think the full-block would be a good choice. Either the
semiblock or the modified block is suitable for use in the office, but they are
more expensive because they require more time.

Mrs. Holcombe, I have enjoyed advising you about selecting a letter arrangement.
Will you let me know which one you choose for general office use?

Fredna Vaughn

Mrs. Fredna Vaughn, Supervisor
Business Education Department

sn

Figure 3–4. *Example of letter arranged in* simplified *style.*

MEMPHIS STATE UNIVERSITY
THE FOGELMAN COLLEGE OF BUSINESS AND ECONOMICS
Memphis, Tennessee 38152

Department of Management   *(901) 454-2466*

March 23, 199-

Department of Communication
The Royal Bank of Canada
Montreal, Quebec
Canada

Will you please add my name to your mailing list for your monthly newsletter to
employees about effective communication?

Your monthly newsletters will be helpful to my classes in business communication,
which include an undergraduate class, taught at the junior level and required of
all business majors, and a graduate class for Master of Business Administration
students. The Royal Bank of Canada will be given credit for all materials used in
class. If I should wish to use some of your material in future publications, I
will of course request specific written permission for every use.

You are to be commended for your continuing efforts to improve communication
throughout your organization. The writers of your material are excellent; please
give them my compliments.

Malra Treece

Malra Treece, Ph.D.
Professor

kf

Figure 3–5. *Example of letter arranged in functional style.*

munication results in inefficiency and poor morale. Employees want and need information in order to carry out their duties and to understand organizational strategy and purpose. They want to know what is going on and why. *Informed employees, who believe that they are valued and trusted by management personnel, are more likely to be cooperative and to devote their efforts to organizational goals.*

Suggestions for Writing Memorandums

Because memorandums are used so frequently and are used between workers in the same organization, at times they are not given the attention they deserve. Memorandums should not be considered unimportant because they are such a routine communication medium in business offices. Your ability to write clear, convincing, and persuasive memorandums will be important to your career, perhaps extremely so.

All the principles of effective writing discussed in Chapters 5 and 6 apply to memorandums. You will study approaches such as the positive versus the negative and the reader other than the writer approach. Other considerations are organization, clarity, principles of emphasis, and readability.

As in most business writing, with the exception of some formal reports, you will speak directly to the reader. Some writers, when writing to their co-workers or people they supervise, refer vaguely to "all employees" or "employees." Although memorandums often go to a group of people, not to one individual alone, your memorandum will be read by *one reader at a time.* That is, by means of your written memorandum you interact *individually* with each reader. As each person reads your words, he or she responds positively or negatively. It is to your advantage that your readers understand your memorandums and respond in a positive way. As much as possible, address your readers, regardless of the number, as *you.*

One major weakness of many memorandums can be corrected by the simple procedure of shortening paragraphs. Memorandums are likely to be read hurriedly. Short paragraphs help the reader to quickly grasp your meaning, provided you have chosen exact, specific words, placed these words in well-constructed sentences, and arranged the sentences in logical order.

Your memorandums should build and maintain favorable relationships with your readers, as with all people with whom you communicate. These favorable human relationships, however, cannot be maintained indefinitely through words alone if these words are not sincere. Sincerity is the basis for all successful communication, or for real communication of any kind.

Illustrations of Memorandums

Memorandums are usually typewritten on forms printed with these headings: *DATE:, TO:, FROM:,* and *SUBJECT:.* Although the printed headings are not necessarily in this exact order, *TO:* usually precedes *FROM:* as a matter of courtesy.

Figure 3–6 is a memorandum about memorandums. Although you are not likely to have occasion to write a message on this particular subject matter, the example is used here for two purposes: to illustrate format and to present information that you will need as you prepare memorandums, including reports arranged in memorandum form.

The memorandum shown in Figure 3–7 illustrates how the information in Figure 3–6 could be presented in a slightly different format, using side headings.

The memorandums shown as Figures 3–8 and 3–9 are short analytical reports. Notice the careful organization of each of these reports. Also no-

---

```
    Date:  November 19, 199-

      To:  All Office Employees

    From:  Isabella Rogers, Office Manager

 Subject:  SUGGESTED FORMAT OF INTEROFFICE MEMORANDUMS


Please observe the following instructions when preparing memorandums. A
consistent, uniform arrangement results in better organization, increased
readability, and savings of time for both writer and reader.

1. Use single or double spacing. Choose single spacing unless the memorandum
   is extremely short. Always leave an extra space between paragraphs of
   single-spaced typewritten material.

2. Use your choice of blocked or indented paragraphs. Some writers believe that
   indented paragraphs make a typewritten message easier to read, but this factor
   is not nearly so important as keeping paragraphs fairly short. One-sentence or
   one-line paragraphs are acceptable and often desirable, especially in the
   emphatic opening position.
```

Figure 3–6. *Example of memorandum format.*

SUGGESTED FORMAT OF INTEROFFICE MEMORANDUMS, page 2, November 19, 199-

3. Use a long line (6 inches, 60 spaces pica, 70 or 72 spaces elite) for all
memorandums, even short ones. This standard line length saves time in setting
margins and estimating message length. It also allows space for tabulations, as
illustrated in the memorandum you are reading. You need not attempt to center
the message vertically.

4. Use headings, as necessary or desirable, to introduce sections of the
memorandum. Ordinarily you will need headings of only one degree, or
''weight.'' They may be centered or placed at the left margin and typewritten
in one of several forms, including ALL CAPITALS; Capitals and Lower Case; or
Capitals and Lower Case, Underlined.

5. Sign or initial your memorandums to add authenticity and a personal touch. The
signature or handwritten initials may be placed by the typewritten name or at
the end of the last paragraph. A complimentary close (such as ''Yours
sincerely'' or ''Cordially yours'') should not be used on a memorandum.

6. Show your title or position unless your readers are sure of it already. Even if
your position is known to your readers, your title is necessary on important
memorandums or on those that will be filed for later reference.

7. Make sure that your memorandums, like all written messages, are neatly
typewritten and arranged. An attractive appearance is psychologically conducive
to the acceptance of your ideas as well as being a matter of common courtesy.

8. Identify the second and subsequent pages of memorandums by subject, page
number, and date. This heading may be shown in the method illustrated on this
page or in various other ways. For example, if you wish to ''stretch'' a short
second page, these items of information can be shown on three vertical lines at
the left margin. (If many of your routine memorandums are longer than one page,
make sure that they really need to be this long. Perhaps your writing can be
more effective and economical by being more concise. But do not omit material
necessary for the understanding or acceptance of your message.)

Your written messages to other employees in the organizations are as important, if
not more so, than those to readers outside the organization. Although format is
only one element of effective writing, it must be considered as one of the many
factors that work together for diplomatic, clear, and useful memorandums.

If you have further suggestions about the improvement of our interoffice
communication or messages going outside the organization, please tell me about
them. (Send me a memo.)

Figure 3–6. *continued*

```
      DATE:  November 19, 199-

        TO:  All Office Employees

      FROM:  James Brown

   SUBJECT:  YOUR INTEROFFICE MEMORANDUMS


   The following suggestions should help you plan and prepare your writings to other
   employees in this organization.

   SPACING

   Memorandums may be single or double spaced. If they are single-spaced, leave a
   double space between paragraphs, as you should do when single-spacing any
   typewritten material.

   PARAGRAPHS

   Paragraphs may be blocked or indented, as in letters. The blocked style saves time
   and, to many persons, presents a more modern appearance. Paragraphs in
   memorandums, as in letters, should be fairly short. Long, unbroken paragraphs are
   hard to read.

   MARGINS

   The long length (6 inches, which is 60 spaces pica, 70 elite) is ordinarily used
   in all memorandums, even short ones. The writing need not be centered vertically.
   (A 6-inch line, elite, is 72 spaces, as elite type contains 12 spaces per inch.
   For simplicity, this actual line is ordinarily rounded to 70 spaces. The six-inch
   line length allows side margins of slightly more than one inch.)

   SIDE HEADINGS

   Although side headings as shown here are not the only type that can be used in the
   memorandum, this all-capital side heading is easy to see and, if properly worded,
   immediately tells the reader something of the content of the following section.
   Compared to centered headings, side headings are quicker to type.

   SECOND-PAGE IDENTIFICATION

   The second page of a memorandum should be identified by subject, date, and page
   number as shown on the following page. This identification may also be shown
   in this order: subject, date, and page number.
```

Figure 3–7. *Another example of memorandum format.*

```
Your Interoffice Memorandums  2     November 19, 199-

SIGNATURE

No signature is required or expected on most memorandums, although they may be
signed. They should be signed if the contents are of special importance or if the
writer wants the reader to know that he or she personally wrote or dictated the
message. A complimentary close is not ordinarily used on a memorandum. The
signature may consist only of the writer's initials, placed at the end of the
memorandum or by the writer's typewritten name at the top. The complete signature
may also be placed in one of these two positions.

TITLES

The writer should show his or her title or position unless the readers are already
sure of it. A woman does not usually show a Miss, Mrs., or Ms. before her name in
a memorandum, although it is not considered incorrect to do so. A man never shows
Mr. before his name in a memorandum or elsewhere. Often a courtesy title should
appear before the name of the addressee, particularly if the addressee is in a
position of higher authority than the writer. Although there is no rule to this
effect, the writer is slightly discourteous to do otherwise.

NEATNESS

As in all written communications, an attractive appearance is psychologically
conducive to the acceptance of ideas. In addition, neatness is a matter of common
courtesy.
```

Figure 3–7. *continued*

tice the displayed headings that are used as an aid to organization, readability, and emphasis.

The data shown in Figure 3–8 were gathered and reported by an electrical engineer employed as an energy consultant. (This illustration is an actual report.) The "answer" is given in the first sentence. In addition, the recommended choice is repeated with the discussion of Table 2, which provides the basis for the choice.

Note: Figure 3–8 is a variation of the same report shown in Figure 15–8, Chapter 15. The report is *intentionally* shown in two versions to illustrate different approaches for the same report situation.

Figure 3–9 also is arranged, basically, in the direct order, as recommendations are given early. The preliminary paragraph serves as a short introductory statement, much like short introductory remarks preceding a speech. This paragraph also serves the same function as a transmittal letter

May 1, 19--

TO: Tom Anderton
    Project Director

FROM: David R. Weigel
      Energy Consultant

SUBJECT: Recommendation for Gymnasium Lighting at Christian
         Brothers High School

RECOMMENDATION

The gymnasium should be illuminated with metal halide lamps and luminaires, as my calculations show that these will provide the best possible fit to the design criteria supplied by the client and chief design engineer. Metal halide lighting will give the optimum mix of economy and color rendition when compared with incandescent, fluorescent, mercury vapor, high pressure sodium, and low pressure sodium.

DESIGN CRITERIA

The design criteria arrived at by the client and the chief design engineer are as follows, in order of assigned priority:

1. Maintenance of 75 footcandles on the playing floor and at least 30 footcandles on the bleacher seats,

2. Minimum life cycle cost, assuming a 20-year life, and,

3. Color rendition suitable for television broadcast.

The first of these is the illumination design, and cannot be changed. I was told by the client that the second (life cycle cost) should be weighted twice as heavily as the third (color).

Figure 3–8. *Short recommendation report.* (**Note:** *The same report is presented in a more formal format in Figure 15–8.)*

Tom Anderton   2   May 1, 19--

CALCULATION RESULTS

The following table depicts results of my calculations for six different light
sources. First cost is a function of the number of lamps and luminaires required
to achieve the specified light levels; maintenance cost is related to the number
of lamps, rated lamp life, and cost per lamp replacement (including labor). Energy
cost is derived from the efficiency of the light source, and the color rendering
index is taken from the IES standards. Life cycle cost assumes a 12 percent energy
inflation rate, a 10 percent capital inflation rate, and zero percent discount
rate.

Table 1
Calculation Results

Source	First Cost	Annual Energy Cost	Annual Maintenance	Life Cycle Cost	CRI*
Incandescent	$5,000	$9,800	$1,200	$780,000	100
Fluorescent	3,500	1,800	85	140,000	70
Mercury Vapor	6,000	2,500	180	195,000	65
Metal Halide	5,400	1,400	180	115,000	75
High Pressure Sodium	4,550	1,100	130	90,000	49
Low Pressure Sodium	6,600	800	250	78,000	12

* Color rendering Index

Figure 3–8. *continued*

Tom Anderton   *3*   May 1, 19--

DECISION

For each light source, I have assigned points for cost and color. Cost points are
proportional to the life cycle cost as shown in Table 1, with the lowest receiving
ten points and the highest receiving one point. Color points are assigned
according to the color rendering index, with the highest receiving five points and
the lowest receiving one-half point. The source with the highest resulting point
total is the one which most closely complies with the design criteria and client
weighting, and it should be selected. Table 2 displays these point assignments and
totals.

Table 2
Point Assignment

Source	Cost Points	Color Points	Total
Incandescent	1.0	5.0	6.0
Fluorescent	9.0	2.9	11.9
Mercury Vapor	8.3	2.7	11.0
Metal Halide	9.4	3.2	12.6
High Pressure Sodium	9.8	1.4	11.2
Low Pressure Sodium	10.0	0.5	10.5

Based on this table, I suggest illuminating the gymnasium with metal halide lamps
and luminaries, as they received the highest point total.

After these results are approved by the client and chief design engineer, please
notify my office so that work on the necessary drawings and specifications can
begin.

Figure 3–8. *continued*

```
     TO:  Mr. Lawrence Cole, Manager

   FROM:  William H. Ford, Jr., Assistant Manager

SUBJECT:  REPORT, WITH RECOMMENDATIONS, OF TRUCK ACCIDENT

   DATE:  April 7, 199-
```

Mr. Cole, I have investigated this accident thoroughly and talked with everyone concerned. I shall be happy to discuss the matter with you or to assist in implementing the suggested policy changes.

RECOMMENDED ACTIONS

1. The Car-Wash Division should pay Milltown Ford $752.50 for charges incurred for the delivery truck wrecked by Hugh Jones.
2. Mr. Jones should be permanently removed from the payroll because of causing the accident and because of previous traffic violations.
3. All employees should be informed of the company policy of not carrying collision insurance on fully depreciated (four-year-old) vehicles.
4. Only the assistant manager should be authorized to approve expenditures for damaged vehicles.
5. No charges of more than $500 should be incurred on fully depreciated vehicles.
6. The truck should be removed from Milltown Ford and sold for scrap.

INVESTIGATION OF ACCIDENT

On Friday, March 1, Hugh Jones, driver employed at the Delaware Street Car-Wash, skidded on wet pavement and struck a telephone pole at the Delaware and Third Avenue intersection. Mr. Jones was on the way to the Delaware Street Car-Wash to deliver supplies. He was not injured, but the truck, a 1983 Ford pickup, received extensive damage that left it inoperable.

Ray Cole, dispatcher, instructed a wrecker to take the truck to Milltown Ford for repairs. Mr. Cole, an employee for only eight weeks, was unaware of the policy of not insuring vehicles four or more years old. He is not to blame for authorizing the work.

By the time the insurance company claims adjuster notified us that the truck was not covered, expenses of $737.50 had been incurred. These charges are $700 for labor and $37.50 for wrecker service. Milltown Ford has added $15.00 for storage fees so that the total amount owed is $752.50. This amount is increasing by $7.50 a day.

Figure 3–9. *Short analytical report.*

```
REASONS FOR RECOMMENDATIONS

     The charges incurred must be paid to Milltown Ford, but the truck should not
be further repaired, as about $3,500 would be needed to make it operable. It is
already fully depreciated.

     Mr. Jones has a poor driving record for the six months he has worked for the
company. The police officer charged him with failure to keep the truck under
control. He had already received a citation for speeding three months ago. On two
other occasions, James Broom, his supervisor, warned him about speeding. The
Car-Wash Division should not retain such a potential liability.

     If the dispatcher had been aware of the policy of not insuring depreciated
vehicles, the company would have saved $715, plus continuing storage fees. Further
losses may occur if all employees are not notified.

     Dispatchers and other personnel should not be forced to make decisions about
expenditures for damaged vehicles, even if a definite policy of limiting costs to
$500 for depreciated vehicles is established. Such decisions are outside their
area of responsibility.
```

Figure 3–9. *continued*

in a longer report arranged in the traditional format, as illustrated in Chapter 15.

Figures 3–8 and 3–9, as well as other illustrations throughout this book, are included to emphasize the variety of arrangements in which information and recommendations can be presented. Organization of information and recommendations, wording and arrangement of headings, and choice of format should be considered as aspects of the composing and reporting process.

Arrange your own reports in the most readable and attractive way you can, regardless of whether you find a similar format illustrated in a textbook. *Remember, however, to follow exactly a specified arrangement whenever you are instructed or expected to do so.*

Summary

The term *short, informal report,* although relative and inexact, is ordinarily used to mean all reports that are not prepared in the complete formal arrangement that includes preliminary and supplementary parts. Many informal reports are presented in letter or memorandum format.

Informal reports are often, but not necessarily, arranged in the direct order, with recommendations given first. They frequently are worded in the personal tone, with the use of the pronouns *I* and *you*.

Frequently used letter styles are the modified block, semiblock, and full block. Less frequently used styles are the simplified and, as designated in this chapter, the functional.

Memorandums should be carefully written with the reader in mind. The writer must be concerned with building and maintaining favorable human relationships.

Paragraphs in memorandums should be fairly short. Readers should be addressed directly, not as members of a group.

Cases and Problems

Note: When writing solutions to the following problems and all other problems and cases in this textbook, do *not* lift sentences or phrases from the problem itself. Write in your own words.

1. *Informing personnel of chosen letter style.* Assume that you are the owner of an insurance agency, a manufacturing company, or any other company of your choice. Letters from writers in your organization are arranged in several differing styles, including all those illustrated in Chapter 3, the indented style, and mixtures of arrangements that seem to be of no particular origin other than the writer's originality. (The indented style, now seldom used in the United States, includes indentations of each opening and closing line in the inside address and signature block, as well as indented paragraphs. This letter arrangement is extremely time-consuming, even with automated typewriters and word processors. Because it requires more keyboarding time, it is more expensive.)

   Although you encourage freedom of thought and original thinking, you believe that efforts toward creativity should be directed into areas other than unusual letter styles, at least for routine letters. Choose one of the illustrations in Chapter 3 as the standard letter arrangement to be used throughout your organization. Write a letter to your employees asking that they use this style in all correspondence except direct sales messages or other specialized letters.

   Provide instructions about the specified letter style in your own letter. Mention that you are using your letter as an illustration of the desired format and arrangement. Explain that unconventional appearance is likely to attract the reader's attention to the format itself and, thus, away from the intended message. As when giving other instructions, readers are more likely to understand and to accept your ideas if adequate explanations and reasons for the change in procedure are given.

2. Look in *Business Periodicals Index* or the ABI/Inform database to find an article, or articles, about writing letters. Present your summary of data given in the

article, or articles, in a letter addressed to your instructor, using one of the letter arrangements illustrated in this chapter.

3. Look in *Business Periodicals Index* or the ABI/Inform database to find an article, or articles, on writing business memorandums. Present your summary of information in a memorandum addressed to your instructor or to members of your class. Use headings as shown in Figure 3-7.

4. Assume that you are the personnel manager of an organization located near your college or university. Write a memorandum to your employees telling them of the availability of the course in business report writing (or business communication) in which you are presently enrolled. Assume that the company will pay all expenses and that the employees will be excused from work. Give all necessary details. You hope that all who receive the memorandum will attend during the next two terms or semester, provided that they have not previously completed this course or a similar one. You hope that about one-half the number will enroll during the coming term or semester, and the remainder during the following term or semester, as you do not want them all to be away from the office at the same time.

5. Obtain copies of actual business memorandums. Analyze them to determine whether they can be described by the classifications of reports given in Chapter 2. Analyze them further as to clarity, consideration of reader, and attractive appearance. Present your analysis in a memorandum addressed to your instructor. Be prepared to present your analysis in a short oral report to your class.

6. Obtain one or more actual business letters; evaluate and present your findings as instructed in Problem 5.

7. In a memorandum addressed to your instructor, describe a hobby, extracurricular activity, or area of interest or study that is of interest to you, in addition to your present job, if you have one. Include information about the length of time you have been interested in this activity, the accomplishments you have made or the awards you have won, and anything that describes the activity of your involvement in it. Do you believe that this outside interest could result in a full-time career? Does this interest relate to your major field of college instruction or to your present employment?

8. Assume that you are Laura Holcombe, to whom the letters shown in Figures 3-3 and 3-4 are addressed. You have decided to adopt the full-block letter arrangement for use in your insurance agency. Write to Mrs. Vaughn. Tell her that you have made your choice and thank her for her assistance.

9. As chairperson of the committee to arrange a retirement dinner for Mrs. Margaret Lee, write a memorandum to all other employees of your organization. Tell them that Mrs. Lee is retiring on December 31, after thirty years with your organization. Your committee has planned a dinner party to be held at the Knickerbocker Inn, 1917 East Hudson Road, at 7:30 P.M., Satur-

day, December 11. (It is now November 17.) Cost for each person is $17.50, which includes the price of the dinner (menu is not yet chosen), wine, and a $2.50 contribution for a gift (also not yet chosen) for Mrs. Lee.

Mrs. Lee recently donated $5,000 for recreational facilities, including a jogging path, to be made available to all employees.

Employees are urged to bring their spouses and friends as guests. The cost for each additional person is $15. Reservations, with checks, must be received by November 27. Tell your readers where and how to make their reservations.

10. It is now December 10. Reservations for the dinner party of problem 9 total 217, about one-third of all employees, plus 152 guests. Your city is covered with eighteen inches of new snow. Write a memorandum to employees who have reservations and tell them that because of the snow you will cancel the banquet. Ask their permission to hold their checks and reservations for a dinner to be scheduled later. Explain you could not even buy the gift because of the snow.

11. It is now Monday morning. The Knickerbocker Inn refuses to return your $500 deposit for the dinner of problems 9 and 10, saying that major thoroughfares were cleared of snow by Saturday evening.

Mrs. Lee, you learned this morning, is using her accumulated sick leave to retire on December 15. She is leaving for Spain on December 16, and she will be busy all remaining evenings with preparations for her trip, according to her secretary. What should you do? What will you tell employees? Decide, and write a memorandum to those who have made reservations.

Note: Additional problems which pertain particularly to this chapter are given in Appendix C. Problem numbers 6, 7, 8, and 9 are based on Figures 3–1 and 3–2.

Short Reports in Manuscript Form

Chapter Outline

Reports described and illustrated in Chapter 4 are very much like the longer ones described and illustrated in Chapter 15. Short reports are included here, early in the text, to provide a basis for your own reports throughout the term or semester.

The most important difference between short reports illustrated in this chapter and the longer "complete" report described in Chapter 15 is the omission or inclusion of preliminary and supplementary parts. Many short reports, however, may require some preliminary and supplementary parts. Figure 4-2 includes a title page, a page of reference sources, and an appendix. (The appendix is not illustrated because of space limitations in this book.) In addition, a table of contents is helpful in many short reports.

Short reports and long reports, apart from their relative length, are quite similar. Nevertheless, long, "complete" reports by their very nature require more planning, research, and interpretation. Thus Chapter 15 is placed after the intervening chapters on business research.

Illustrations of Short Report Arrangements

Figure 4-1 is the first page of a short, informal report in manuscript form. Its subject is report format and arrangement, for which more discussion is given in a following section of this chapter.

The information in the report illustrated in Figure 4-2 could have been presented in various other ways, including the formal report arrangement illustrated in Chapter 15. In a more formal arrangement, the supporting evidence now included as an appendix, referred to in the report but not illustrated in Figure 4-2, would have been presented as a part of the report itself. Some traditionally minded readers would prefer that all supporting information be in the report itself and that the report include the expected preliminary and supplementary parts.

Geraldine Cone, the writer of the report shown in Figure 4-2, is obviously an employee of a rather small accounting firm. The reader of the report can be assumed to have confidence in the writer's judgment and not be overly influenced by an informal report arrangement.

The method of documentation illustrated in Figure 4-2 is also appropriate for other kinds of reports, including those described as "formal." As when deciding upon other facets of report presentation, you should consider any stated or implied preferences of the reader or readers, the

```
                        AN INFORMAL REPORT


        The format illustrated here is a good choice for informal

    reports, term papers, and other similar manuscripts unless you

    are expected to follow differing instructions because of company

    precedent or a specified style manual.


        Headings

        When you need only one or two levels of division, you need

    not take them in the order that would be necessary if your work

    required greater division. Other variations of the underlined

    side heading shown here are centered underlined headings, and

    headings in all capitals.


        Spacing

        Double-space the body of the manuscript unless cost and

    time considerations indicate that it should be single-spaced, or

    unless the format you are expected to follow is in the single-

    space arrangement. Triple-space (leave two blank lines) after

    the main title and before each side heading.


        Paragraph Division

        Leave at least two lines of a paragraph at the bottom of

    the page and carry over at least two lines.
```

Figure 4–1.

Format of first page of manuscript report.

format of similar reports prepared in the particular organization, and the kind and complexity of data to be discussed and analyzed. (Documentation is discussed further in Chapter 12.)

The method of documentation shown in Figure 4–2 is convenient in

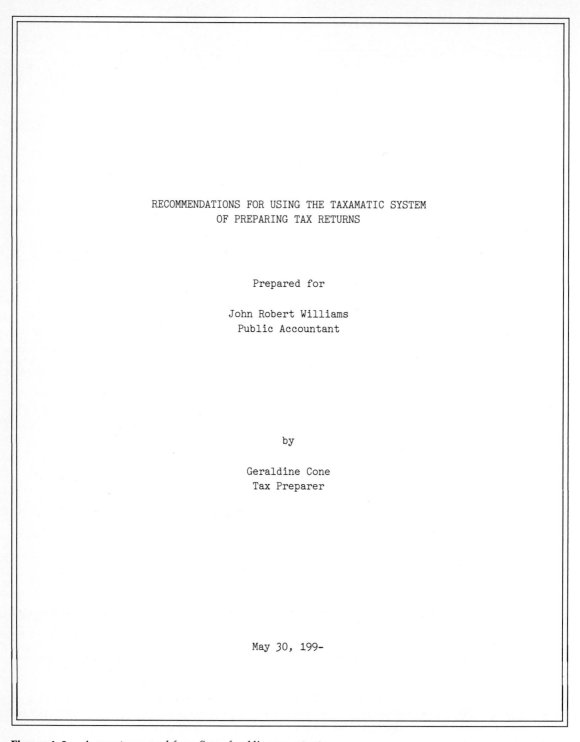

RECOMMENDATIONS FOR USING THE TAXAMATIC SYSTEM
OF PREPARING TAX RETURNS

Prepared for

John Robert Williams
Public Accountant

by

Geraldine Cone
Tax Preparer

May 30, 199-

Figure 4–2. *A report prepared for a firm of public accountants.*

RECOMMENDATIONS FOR USING THE TAXAMATIC SYSTEM
OF PREPARING 1040EZ TAX RETURNS

Summary

I recommend that the Taxamatic system be used in the Williams Accounting Firm for preparing 1040EZ tax returns. This recommendation is based on information obtained from tax preparers for the firm (7,9), secretaries employed by the firm (11,12), representatives of the Taxamatic Publishing Company (5,10), three present users of the Taxamatic system (4,6,8), and secondary sources (1,2,3). In addition, time studies were done of manual and Taxamatic preparations of tax returns.

Purpose of Study

The purpose of the study was to determine the cost and time required to prepare income tax returns with the Taxamatic Publishing Company System (TPC) and to compare them to the cost and time of preparing returns manually. This study is necessary because of rising costs of labor, the difficulty of finding dependable and efficient tax preparers and clerical workers, and the need to accept more clients than in previous years. For the past several years, numerous potential clients have been turned away because no employees were available to help them (7,9).

Findings

1. Using the Taxamatic system of preparing returns, the preparer enters information collected from the client on the forms provided. These forms are then picked up or mailed to the computer center, which determines the tax and returns the completed forms for the client's signature (3,5,10).

2. TPC was one of the first companies to computer process a tax return. Over one million Federal tax returns were processed in 1990 by Taxamatic (3). According to company representatives, the system is widely used in this geographic area, as well as throughout the country (5,10).

Figure 4–2. *continued*

3. The system provides two forms: one for present clients and one for new clients. For previous clients, the preparer is not required to re-enter names, addresses, social security numbers, dependents, or other year-to-year entries. The total number of entries made on Taxamatic interview forms are usually half that on manually prepared forms (3,5,10).

4. TPC provides numerous training aids at no extra charge. Local representatives provide individual assistance in accounting offices (5,10).

5. The benefits of computerization have been explained in accounting literature for more than fifteen years. Saul Berkowitz, in his article published in THE CPA JOURNAL made this statement:

> The variety of services offered by companies doing income tax returns by computer makes one of them beneficial to almost every accountant who does any amount of tax preparation. (1:933)

The use of computers in preparing tax returns has continued and is a standard in accounting firms and, according to Taxamatic representatives, forms and procedures have become more simplified and useful each year (5,10). Computerized tax systems were recommended in a recent edition of West Falls Accountants' Newsletter (3:2).

6. Under the present system of 1040EZ preparation, the firm finds it necessary to hire part-time checkers and typists during the tax season. These positions would be totally eliminated through the use of Taxamatic, as each return comes back fully printed, ready for the client's signature (5,10).

7. Representatives from three accounting firms that presently use the Taxamatic system were interviewed to determine whether they agree with statements of TPC representatives and material in sales literature. All agreed that the system has been beneficial to their companies (4,6,8).

8. About one hour of a tax preparer's time and one-half hour of secretarial time are saved on each return by using the Taxamatic system. Labor costs, plus copying and paper, total $25.40 for a manually prepared return. Cost of a Taxamatic prepared return is $18.58, which includes the time of a preparer and the charge for each return paid to Taxamatic. No secretarial time is required.

Figure 4–2. *continued*

Complete calculations showing the amount of time saved, based on experimental studies with five of our tax preparers, are included as an appendix to this report.

9. Total cost savings, with a resulting increase in net profit, cannot be determined because preparers will be released for more productive work, such as discretionary and decision-making functions for clients. They can examine the clients' entire tax picture and give advice about changes that could be made in the coming year to reduce taxes.

REFERENCES

Published Material

1. Berkowitz, Saul. ''Computer Prepared Income Tax Returns.'' The CPA Journal 42 (1972): 933-935.

2. ''Have You Considered Computerized Tax Systems?'' West Falls Accounting Newsletter, November 1989. (Four-page newsletter.)

3. ''Taxamatic, the Tax Return Processing System.'' Chicago: Taxamatic Publishing Company, 1989. (Twelve-page booklet)

Interviews

4. Blair, Clarence E., Public Accountant, 6433 Lincolnia Road, Alexandria, Virginia 22312. Telephone interview, May 2, 1990.

5. Dixon, James, Sales Representative, TPC. Personal and telephone interviews, February 10 to May 15, 1990.

6. Lloyd, Kenneth, Manager of Tax Associates, 7537 Lee Highway, Falls Church, Virginia 22202. Telephone interview, May 3, 1990.

7. Morris, Lee, Tax Preparer, Williams Accounting Firm. Personal interviews, February through May 15, 1990.

8. Sandbrook, Violet, Certified Public Accountant, 306 Glendale Avenue, Arlington, Virginia 22202. Telephone interview, May 2, 1990.

Figure 4–2. *continued*

---

9. Saliba, Jo, Tax Preparer, Williams Accounting Firm. Personal interviews,

   February through May 15, 1990.

10. Williamson, Elaine. Sales Manager, TPC. Personal interview, March 31, 1989.

11. Word, Kathy, Secretary, Williams Accounting Firm. Personal interviews,

   February through May 15, 1990.

12. Yearout, Martha, Secretary, Williams Accounting Firm. Personal interviews,

   February through May 15, 1990.

Figure 4–2. *continued*

reports in which you wish to refer to more than one source to support individual statements. For example, the *(3,5,10)* notation after Item 3 refers the reader to Numbers 3, 5, and 10 as they are numbered on the list of references. These three notations include one published source and two interviews. With Item 5, the *(1:933)* notation refers to Item 1, page 933.

This method of documentation is also convenient when you are using a great number of published sources that require rather lengthy descriptions, such as census reports and other government documents. Complete information need be given only once, in the bibliography—or on the corresponding page headed with *References, Sources,* or similar wording.

In addition, this illustrated method of documentation is far more convenient for the typist than the traditional bottom-of-page footnoting system. For many reports, however, bottom-of-page footnotes are preferable.

Compare the method of documentation used in Figure 4–2 with the methods illustrated in Figures 15–8 and 15–10, Chapter 15. Figure 15–8 is documented by bottom-of-page footnotes and followed by a bibliography. Figure 15–10 is prepared by the same method of documentation as Figure 4–2.

The report shown in Figure 4–3 is similar to that shown in Figure 4–2 in that attachments convey some of the supporting evidence. This report has no documentation presented in the form of footnotes or other methods of reference. The attachments include further evidence, including excerpts from journal articles. Complete information about the author, journal, place of publication, date, and page numbers should be given with the excerpts, as with other methods of documentation, for "giving credit where credit is due."

RECOMMENDATIONS FOR REPLACING PRESENTLY OWNED TYPEWRITERS
WITH PERSONAL COMPUTERS, WORD PROCESSING SOFTWARE,
AND PRINTERS

Prepared for

James T. Buchanan
Administrative Director

Countrywide Insurance Company

by

Mary Duncan
Office Manager

Chickasaw Branch Office

August 20, 199-

Figure 4–3. *Short recommendation report to be submitted with attachments containing supporting information.*

RECOMMENDATIONS FOR REPLACING PRESENTLY OWNED TYPEWRITERS

WITH PERSONAL COMPUTERS, WORD PROCESSING SOFTWARE,

AND PRINTERS

Purpose and Scope of Study

The purpose of this study was to determine whether the typewriters owned by Countrywide Insurance Company should be replaced by personal computers equipped with word processing software and letter-quality printers. Factors considered were cost of the equipment and all supporting materials, time and money to be saved after installation, and typists' efficiency and morale.

Not considered in this study were Countrywide offices outside the United States and Canada or possible changes in word processing centers now in use in the home office and in seventeen major cities. Research following the present study will determine the particular choice of computer, software, and printer most desirable for Countrywide offices. Still further research will indicate the cost and time necessary to provide training for the users of the new equipment.

Findings

1. Except for twenty-four IBM personal computers used in executive offices in the home office, all secretaries and typists throughout the Countrywide organization use electric typewriters. (Centralized word processing centers in the home office and seventeen other major cities are not considered here. Even in these offices, however, numerous typewriters are in use.)

2. According to Inventory Control, Countrywide Insurance Company owns 5,120 electric typewriters, 3,220 of which are self-correcting with memory capacity and 1,200 are self-correcting without memory capacity. For the past twenty years, Countrywide has routinely replaced typewriters after five years.

Figure 4–3. *continued*

Attachment A is a list of typewriters of each kind, with the purchase price and date of purchase.

3. An experiment conducted by Ms. Rita Richards, secretary in the Chickasaw Branch Office, indicated that letters and other materials are more attractive when prepared using word processing and a letter-quality printer. Attachment B includes examples of letters prepared on typewriters used in the Chickasaw office and examples of letters prepared with a demonstration Zenith personal computer and word processing software.

4. According to Ms. Richards' experiment, one-fifth to one-fourth of a typist's time is saved by the use of word processing. In addition, the secretary who participated in the experiment had only three weeks' experience with the Zenith computer and the software package. As typists become thoroughly familiar with word processing, even more time will be saved. One of the most important advantages of word processing is that corrections of all kinds can be made without retyping the entire page. See Attachment C.

5. According to estimates reported by three sales representatives and two journal articles (See Attachment D), within five years 90 percent of all offices will be equipped with some kind of word processors.)

6. Another important advantage of word processing, among others, is that material can be stored on disks, rather than in file cabinets. This time saving feature also saves office space and makes material easier to find.

Recommendations

I recommend that personal computers, with word processing software and letter-quality printers, be purchased to replace typewriters in all Countrywide Insurance Company offices.

Figure 4–3. *continued*

Physical Presentation of Reports

The physical presentation of a report or manuscript of any kind will depend upon these factors:

1. The expected or required form and arrangement, based on organizational precedent or a specified handbook. Footnotes, headings, indentations, and other kinds of format and arrangement differ from authority to authority. If you have no specified handbook or guide to follow, use readability, simplicity, and consistency as your guides.
2. The complexity of the material and the need for breakdown into various divisions. For example, if a report outline includes headings to correspond to *I, A, 1,* and *a,* the text of the report must include four types of headings. But if the report contains only the main heading (the title) and one level of division, only one form of heading is necessary in addition to the title.
3. The readers of the material, with their known or likely preferences.

Headings

Headings, which are also referred to as *captions,* are useful in reports of any length, even letter, memorandum, and one-page manuscript reports. The longer the written message, the more essential headings become. Regardless of the length of the communication in which they are used, exactly worded and arranged headings show immediately the organization of the writing, the weight of each heading, and its relationship to all the other headings and the entire content of the message.

Headings act as "dividers" of written communication and serve as titles for the material given below. *Each heading describes and includes the contents of all subheadings that come below it; for example, "A," "B," and "C" headings combine to equal the heading above them.*

Word headings carefully, not only from the standpoints of readability and organization, but to direct the flow of thought and the exact progression of ideas. Try to word headings so that they provide information instead of merely indicating the kind of information that is below them. Headings also improve the transition of information from one section to the next.

No single arrangement and format of headings can be said to be the only correct one. If you are using a particular reference manual as a guide, follow its specific instructions exactly. Most reference books, however, provide for a choice of style and arrangement, as does this textbook.

Headings can be varied by both type style and position. Headings may be typed in the following ways:

<u>SOLID CAPITALS UNDERSCORED</u>
SOLID CAPITALS

<u>Capitals and Lowercase Underscored</u>
Capitals and Lowercase

Headings may be positioned:

CENTERED
AT THE LEFT MARGIN, FREESTANDING

<u>At the Paragraph Indentation, Run-In and Underlined.</u> The first sentence follows.

<u>At the Paragraph Indentation, Underlined,</u> in which the heading begins the sentence.

Headings can be set up in several other ways, especially in print or with the use of special typewriter elements. Headings are most likely to be centered or placed in a freestanding position at the left margin.

The traditional outline arrangement includes headings preceded by roman and arabic numerals and by alphabetic letters in capitals and lower case, as shown below.

FIRST-DEGREE HEADING (TITLE)

  I. Second-Degree Heading
    A. Third-Degree Heading
    B. Third-Degree Heading
      1. Fourth-Degree Heading
      2. Fourth-Degree Heading
        a. Fifth-Degree Heading
        b. Fifth-Degree Heading
 II. Second-Degree Heading

These divisions of the report outline, which are also shown in the table of contents (often in revised form), can be shown in the report according to the method shown below.

FIRST-DEGREE HEADING

The first-degree heading (title) is centered and typed in all capitals. When the title consists of more than one line, usually these lines are double spaced; the first line is longer than the second, and the second is longer than the third. (Titles should be as short as possible, but they should also be exact and descriptive.)

Second-Degree Headings

Second-degree headings, using the arrangement shown here, are centered and underlined. They describe the major sections of the report and correspond to the headings preceded by roman numerals, as shown in the report outline.

Third-Degree Headings

Third-degree headings correspond to A, B, C, and following letters, as shown in the report outline. In this plan of arrangement, they are placed at the left margin, typed in capitals and lower case, and underscored.

Fourth-degree headings. Placement at the paragraph indentation on the same line with the text distinguishes fourth-degree headings from third-degree ones. The underscore and the period separate the heading from the remainder of the paragraph.

Fifth-degree headings are also placed at the paragraph indentation, on the same line as the text. These headings, however, are integral parts of beginning sentences.

The alternate plans described below, as well as other variations, may be used for headings within the text of a report.

Type the title as a spread heading, like this:

TITLE OF REPORT

One space is left between each two letters, and three spaces are left between words. Thus the first-degree heading is a spread heading, second-degree headings are centered in all capitals, third-degree headings are centered and underscored, and following headings of decreasing importance are moved up one level throughout the report.

When you need fewer divisions than those shown here, you need not follow exactly this suggested order of arrangement—unless a variation would consist of a departure from instructions in the handbook you are using as a guide. For example, if your report requires only one level of division, you might choose to use side headings instead of the centered ones described here as second-degree headings. And, as in the preceding example of a well-designed memorandum, these side headings may be displayed in all capitals. (See Figure 3–7, Chapter 3.)

Another widely used arrangement of headings is shown below:

MAIN HEADING (TITLE)
SECOND-DEGREE HEADINGS

Third-Degree Headings

Fourth-Degree Headings. These headings begin at the paragraph indentation.

See the examples of reports shown in Chapter 15 for other arrangements of headings.

A portion of a table of contents, shown in Figure 4–4, illustrates that headings should be grammatically parallel within each category. For example, the three major headings shown here (Parts III, IV, and V) are parallel in that they are noun phrases. Headings A, B, and C under Part III are complete sentences. Headings A, B, and C under Part IV are noun phrases. Headings A, B, and C under Part V are complete sentences in question form. The rest of the table of contents has headings that are similarly parallel.

```
III. BENEFITS OF CREDIT UNIONS TO PEOPLE UNDER AGE 22
       A. Young People Are Interested in Security, Especially
          Insurance
       B. Young People Want to Build Substantial Savings Accounts
       C. Young People Need to Borrow Money

 IV. DEMOGRAPHICS OF MAT CREDIT UNION ACCOUNTS
       A. Share Accounts, Classified by Age Groups Under 22
       B. Certificates of Deposit, Classified by Age Groups
          Under 22
       C. Loan Accounts, Classified by Age Groups Under 22

  V. MARKETING EFFORTS TOWARD BIRTH-TO-FIVE-YEAR-OLD GROUP
       A. How Can We Attract New Accounts?
       B. How Should We Promote These Accounts?
       C. How Should We Service These Accounts?
```

Figure 4–4.

Portion of table of contents

These headings are from the table of contents of a report on how to promote the services of a teachers' credit union to eligible young people. These headings are numbered here, for the purpose of discussion, with roman numerals and capital letters. They may be shown in this way in the table of contents, as in a tentative outline. These numbers and letters of the alphabet are also correctly omitted from a table of contents, as illustrated in Chapter 15.

Figure 4–4 is an illustration of an *acceptable* arrangement and wording of headings. Do not think that you *must* vary the grammatical construction of headings in the same report. Some writers and readers prefer that headings be consistent throughout, although most people consider headings to be sufficiently parallel if they are in the same form as others in the same group, as illustrated in Figure 4–4. The "requirement" that every heading in a report be grammatically consistent with every other heading throughout the report may prevent the best possible expression of ideas to be conveyed through headings.

If you use a table of contents, which can be helpful even in short, informal reports, make sure that the headings in the table of contents agree exactly with the headings in the text of the report itself.

An example of a complete report, including a table of contents with corresponding headings within the text, is shown in Chapter 15. In addition, wording of headings is considered with report organization in Chapter 10.

Margins

If the manuscript is to remain unbound, use a six-inch line (60 spaces pica, 70 spaces elite). These line lengths provide side margins of slightly more than one inch. Exceptions to this general rule include material to be published, for which you ordinarily should leave an additional half inch on each side. Another exception is that in some situations you should consider using a longer line in order to save duplicating expense, filing space, and paper.

For manuscripts to be bound on the left, move side margins an additional one-half inch to the right.

On the first page of a report manuscript, leave a two-inch top margin. On following pages, leave a top margin of approximately one inch. On all pages, leave a bottom margin of one to one and one-half inches.

Spacing

Formal reports are traditionally double-spaced, but many organizations are now preparing all keyboarded work in single-space form to economize. Your choice will depend on organizational policy, purpose and readership of the report, and cost considerations.

Pagination

The first page of the report itself (the "report proper") is considered as page 1. This page number is centered at the bottom of the page or omitted. Page numbers of following pages are placed in the upper right-hand corner, on line 5 to 7 from the top. Thus the "approximately one inch" top margin refers to the "white space" above the page number. Triple-space after the page number before beginning the first line of type.

Additional Guides to Report Appearance

1. Use sturdy bond paper.
2. Use standard-size paper, 8½ by 11 inches.
3. Use a self-correcting typewriter or word processing equipment with a letter-quality printer or laser printer.
4. If a self-correcting typewriter or word processing equipment is not available, make all corrections neatly with an eraser, correction tape, or correction liquid. Do not leave strikeovers, obvious erasures, or white spots made with correcting tape or liquid.
5. If a self-correcting typewriter or word processing equipment is not available, prefer an electric model equipped with a film ribbon that turns through the typewriter and is used only once. (Self-correcting typewriters also are equipped with film ribbons.) If your typewriter is not equipped with a film ribbon, replace ribbons regularly so that they do not become worn.
6. Make sure that typewriter keys, printing heads, or ink jets are completely clean.
7. Leave at least two lines of a paragraph at the bottom of each page and carry over at least two lines to the next page. Thus, three-line paragraphs cannot be divided. The minimum bottom margin of at least one inch can be increased by enough lines to allow for appropriate paragraph division.
8. A subheading (caption) near the bottom of a page should be followed by at least two lines of type, preferably more. A wider-than-average bottom margin is preferable to a subheading with insufficient following material.
9. Indent paragraphs in all double-spaced material. Paragraphs are usually indented five spaces, but they may be indented eight or ten spaces. Single-spaced material may also be indented. Leave a blank line between paragraphs of all typewritten material.
10. Avoid long paragraphs; they are hard to read.

Summary   Memorandums and reports typewritten in manuscript form may be single-spaced or double-spaced. Ordinarily double-spacing is preferred, but single-spacing is being used more frequently because it saves paper and copying costs.

Subheadings, also referred to as captions, are useful in reports of any length or format. The longer the report, the more essential subheadings become. They should be worded and arranged in a format that shows the organization of the entire written work. They should indicate the importance of each part in relation to the whole.

Short reports, in comparison to longer ones, are less likely to include preliminary and supplementary parts, although some preliminary and supplementary parts are desirable or necessary in reports of any length.

The physical format and arrangement of a report will depend on the expected or required form and arrangement, plus the purpose and complexity of the material.

Headings in a table of contents should agree exactly with headings in the text of a report itself.

Cases and Problems   **Note:** No cases or problems are given with this chapter because of the numerous ones in Appendix C. According to the directions of the instructor, students may prepare solutions to the cases in Appendix C in various report formats and arrangements, including those illustrated in Chapters 3, 4, and 15. Chapters 3 and 4 are presented early in the text to provide illustrations for reports to be prepared throughout the course. (Naturally, students and teachers may choose to study textbook chapters in some other order than the one in which they are presented.)

CHAPTER **5**

Choosing the Proper Emphasis and Approach

Chapter Outline

Regardless of the changing methods of recording, reproducing, and transmitting information, words will remain of prime importance, as they have been since the beginning of civilization. We shall continue to use spoken and written language because we must.

Although you may not be a professional writer or speaker, as the terms are ordinarily used, language is essential to your profession, whatever it is. In this sense, the use of words is a professional knowledge and skill, even more important than specialized education in accounting, management, engineering, law, or any other field. Aside from its benefits to your career and social life, growth in language ability will be a source of personal pride and accomplishment, perhaps your most worthwhile goal.

Appendix D, "Computer Based Basic English Tutor," relates to this chapter. If you have not already done so, study these learning tools as you study this chapter.

Accuracy and Knowledge: The Vital Ingredients

The techniques of communication are vastly important, but mere mastery of these techniques does not ensure effective communication. If the thoughts we are trying to communicate are not based on a sound background of information and understanding, expert expression is of little value. A fuzzy and indecisive mind cannot send clear, correct, convincing messages. In addition, the confidence of the writer or speaker is affected by the knowledge, or the lack of knowledge, of company policies and procedures and of the particular situation.

Obtaining the necessary knowledge and understanding upon which to prepare effective reports can be a tedious process. To a certain extent, it depends on your entire background. If you are knowledgeable in many areas because of an inquiring mind, varied experiences, and wide reading, you are already far better informed about many specialized business problems than you may think. Even without an excellent background of general knowledge, you can become well informed in your field by consistent and dedicated effort.

Because data are copied and transmitted by computers and other forms of mass reproduction, one error can become thousands of errors. Incorrect information in a letter, memorandum, or report sent to one reader is bad enough, but a message sent to thousands of people greatly multiplies whatever difficulties will be encountered because of the error.

74

The overall amount of information available in all fields is increasing at a tremendous rate. Much of what you learn in school will be at least partially obsolete in a few years or months. In your business or profession, by the time you have learned one procedure, set of instructions, or group of "facts," they are likely to be supplanted by others, and then more and more. To be a good leader (or even a good follower) you must be aware of change, expect it, accept it, and use it to your advantage and that of your employing organization. To be a good report writer requires even more knowledge, judgment, and decisiveness.

Conservative, Businesslike Standards of Correctness

Correct writing and speech, from the standpoints of grammatical correctness and accuracy of information, is not necessarily effective communication, nor is it necessarily easily understood, interesting, or diplomatic. Correctness is only one of the many components of effective communication, but reports and other business and professional communications cannot be completely effective if they are not correct grammatically and if they do not supply correct information.

Although grammatical errors do not always result in misunderstanding, they are likely to weaken the reader's confidence of the writer's overall competence. At times, also, the wrong word and omitted or misplaced punctuation change the intended meaning. Notice the differences in meaning in these sentences:

```
All salesmen who have exceeded their quotas will receive a 10 percent
bonus.

All salesmen, who have exceeded their quotas, will receive a 10
percent bonus.

The old publications that originally sold for $2 or less are to be
destroyed.

The old publications, which originally sold for $2 or less, are to be
destroyed.
```

When a writer does not follow the accepted "rules" shown in English handbooks, meaning is inexact or completely in error. In the preceding examples, the first sentence in each pair contains a restrictive dependent clause that points out *which* salesmen and *which* publications; not all salesmen have met their quotas and not all old publications originally sold for $2 or less. The same clauses in the second sentence of each pair are nonrestrictive, and are correctly set off by commas. The second sentences in each pair state that all salesmen have met their quotas and all the old publications sold for $2 or less.

A misplaced apostrophe can also cause misinterpretation. Like the comma and other marks of punctuation, the apostrophe is sometimes used to convey meaning, not merely to make the meaning expressed by words more readily understood. In the following sentence

```
The customers' orders were promptly filled
```

the meaning is not the same as in the sentence

```
The customer's orders were promptly filled
```

The first sentence indicates that there are at least two customers; the second sentence indicates that there is only one customer.

The misuse of words similar in meaning or spelling can also cause misreading and misrepresentation. Usually the words "affect" and "effect," although often confused, do not change the intended meaning. They can do so, however, as in these sentences:

```
Will the increase in total sales affect the expected salary increase?

Will the increase in total sales effect the expected salary increase?
```

Although these words are similar in spelling and pronunciation, the questions differ in meaning: the first question asks whether the increase will influence (have an effect on) the expected salary increase; the second question asks whether the increase in sales will bring about a salary increase.

We should adhere, for the most part, to established conventions because to do otherwise is distracting. For example, the reader of a report may be distracted from the intended meaning by unusual phrasing or punctuation. In addition, we need to be adept in the use of language for the pragmatic purpose of saving time. When we *know,* we do not spend time in trying to decide upon grammatical usage or trying to find exact examples or instructions in an English handbook. Although all writers should keep reference sources readily available and refer to them when it is necessary to do so, the truly efficient writer will have no need to put them to constant use.

Improving your language ability—correctness, word choice, sentence construction, conciseness, coherence, and direct, simple writing and speech—should be your first and most important step toward becoming an effective communicator, provided you do not at this time feel confident of your ability in all these areas.

English handbooks and other reference books are listed in the bibliography at the end of this book. Every writer needs a shelf of reference books, including a comprehensive dictionary. The tutorial *"Basic English Tutor,"* can be used as a handy guide to English usage.

Basic Principles of Emphasis

The report writer must understand the principles of emphasis, which contribute to readability, credibility, a psychological approach, and other attributes of effective communication. The qualities of excellent communication exist only in connection with other qualities.

Emphatic Positions

Position is one of the most important means of achieving emphasis. The beginning section of any kind of writing is the most emphatic position, provided that the writer has used this position advantageously. In most communications, this beginning position should be used to present the most important idea. This arrangement is referred to as the direct arrangement.

The first paragraph is the most emphatic section of a memorandum, a letter, or any other short written message. In a long report, the first paragraph is still an emphatic one, but because of the comparative length, the first section, often titled *Introduction*, becomes especially important because of its position, as well as for other reasons. The first sentence in a paragraph is the most emphatic one—hence the use of a topic sentence, as the first sentence, increases readability and emphasizes the principal meaning intended for that paragraph.

The first word of a sentence is in an emphatic position, except for sentences beginning with *a, an,* and *the* where the emphasis shifts to the immediately following words. Because the first position of the sentence is emphatic, do not start several sentences on the same page with *I;* the *I* becomes overemphasized and does not convey the desired you-attitude, or at least the impression of the you-attitude.

The closing word, sentence, paragraph, or section of a written message is also emphatic, next in importance to the opening word, sentence, paragraph, or section. The last word of a sentence is second in emphasis to the first word of a sentence; or, in periodic sentences, the last words are most emphatic because the preceding words build up to the conclusion. Thus, to subordinate an idea or statement, do not place it in the opening or the closing of a written work.

This principle applies throughout business writing; for example, the idea to be de-emphasized should be somewhere within the body of a letter or memorandum, not in the opening or the closing paragraph. In addition, an idea can be subordinated by sentence structure so that it is within a sentence instead of being expressed in the emphatic opening or closing position.

Emphatic Sentence and Paragraph Construction

The most emphatic way to present an idea is in a paragraph that consists of only one short, simple sentence. Because the most emphatic position is the first position, the greatest emphasis is achieved by a short, one sentence paragraph at the beginning of a letter, memorandum, or other message.

In a complex sentence, the idea to be emphasized should be placed in the main clause, with the subordinate idea in a dependent clause. A phrase can also contain an idea to be de-emphasized.

Sentences written with the verb in the active voice emphasize the "actor"; that is, the subject of the sentence is the originator of the action expressed by the verb. Sentences written with the verb in the passive voice place emphasis on the receiver of the action. Sentences should be constructed according to the desired emphasis. The active construction results in more forceful, direct, and concise statements, as discussed in more detail in Chapter 6.

For a review of sentence construction, refer to the "Basic English Tutor" computer disk.

Word Choice to Emphasize or to Subordinate

Specific, concrete language is more emphatic, as well as more descriptive and readable, than vague, abstract wording. Try to emphasize positive, pleasant ideas and to de-emphasize unpleasant ones. At times the general word, not the specific, is more diplomatic, although less emphatic and forceful.

An abstract word describes ideas or concepts that cannot be easily visualized. Examples of abstract words are *conception, democracy, abstractness, charity.* Examples of concrete words are *blackbird, plaid, crunch, dawn, rain, saxophone, automobile*—particular objects which can be seen, heard, felt, touched, smelled. These words are more vivid than abstract ones. Specific words are more emphatic than general words. An example of a general word is *music;* a more specific term is *piano solo;* a still more descriptive phrase is *Chopin's "Polonaise in A-Flat" played by Vladimir Horowitz.*

Fresh, natural words are more emphatic than stale, stereotyped expressions. Avoid trite phrases such as "spring is just around the corner" and "last but not least." These trite expressions also violate the principles of conciseness.

Attention to One Idea

Giving more space emphasizes one idea over the remaining parts of the message. Notice that this is just the opposite of the method discussed previously, in which the main idea is quickly and bluntly stated in a sentence alone. Ordinarily the writer does not think—"Well, I will just give this more space because it is important"—but writes the message giving the necessary details, which require more space. Repetition may be used with discretion in order to emphasize, but much repetition is unintentional. Repetition, even of the same words, can sometimes be effective, but the writer must be skillful and the message must be carefully planned. Repetition often is used for sales writing or advertising, especially radio and television commercials, but not always to the best advantage.

Because the main idea of a message often requires more space in order to be complete and clear, using more space is considered a method of emphasis.

Visual Display Means of Emphasis

Mechanical means are such methods as underlining or the use of all capitals, dashes, special or unusual means of letter arrangement or indenting, and lists and tabulations. Different colors of ink, especially red, are often used in sales messages. Setting off lines with plenty of white space calls attention to these lines. The visual display means of emphasis are similar to those of readability, except that at times the methods used for emphasis are more unusual and extreme.

Subheads emphasize and display the organization of material. A postscript can be used to emphasize an important idea, but the postscript should not be used for something that should have gone into the letter itself.

Mechanical means of emphasis should not be overused or they lose any emphatic value that they might otherwise possess. If many points are emphasized, then the final result is that nothing is emphasized. In addition, some persons object to a message filled with underlining, all capitals, or portions typed in red, feeling that such an approach is unbusinesslike, too emotional, or scatterbrained.

Summarizing for Emphasis

Summarizing can be used to emphasize important points, particularly in longer works. In some reports or books, each section or chapter is summarized and then the entire work is summarized, perhaps through the use of a synopsis that is attached to the report itself. Summarizing, like the other means of emphasizing, contributes to readability.

A listing of points, such as those below, makes the items stand out and imply that they are important. They are easy to read and quickly understood.

Emphasis is achieved by:

1. Position
2. Sentence and paragraph construction
3. Word choice
4. Space
5. Visual display means of emphasis
6. Summarizing

Objective Wording and Writing Style

The term *objectivity* is applied to the planning and process of research and also to writing style. As discussed in Chapter 2, material written in the impersonal tone (third-person writing style) seems more objective than material that includes first- and second-person pronouns, although true objectivity consists of far more than the use or omission of pronouns.

Word all reports specifically, objectively, and exactly. *Emphasize facts.* Support with concrete, convincing details. When preparing an analytical report, analyze the data in order to reach conclusions and recommendations. These conclusions and recommendations must be supported by *evidence* instead of being based merely on beliefs, assumptions, and desires. Although at times you must state what you believe about a situation, or what the data seem to indicate, make sure that your reader understands that such a statement is an opinion. On the other hand, avoid an appearance of hedging and timidity. The conclusions and recommendations, like all other parts of the report, should be stated in specific, concrete terms, not in general, vague, abstract wording.

Anderson, Saunders, and Weeks, authors of an early textbook in report writing, use this illustration:

> There should be no hint of bias or emotional involvement in your subject. For example, in writing a report on stream pollution in a university community, an engineer presented facts, conclusive and irrefutable, presented them impartially and objectively for seventeen pages. Then he wrote: "At the very doorstep of the university is a grossly contaminated stream visible to students and visitors from all over the world. While not necessarily pertinent to this survey, it is ironic that the fundamentals of modern sanitation are taught in buildings located on the very banks of an odoriferous creek typical of antiquated methods of waste disposal."

The newspapers quoted him; his superior reprimanded him. Yet in the whole report these were the only sentences which failed to reflect the required impartial and objective tone. Note the phrase which should have warned the writer that he was making a mistake, "While not necessarily pertinent to this survey . . ." Opinion and emotional writing are dangerous in reports.[1]

These sentences from an engineering report illustrate the fact that emotional, opinionated writing is not confined to material that includes the words *I* or *we* but can occur just as readily in the third-person writing style. Notice the emotional and nonrelevant terms: *grossly contaminated, ironic, odoriferous, antiquated,* and *visible to students and visitors from all over the world.* Although the writer should not have attempted to disguise the condition of the stream, he greatly weakened the strength of his report by the addition of the two unnecessary sentences that so clearly indicated his personal opinions of the situation. The facts alone, summarized with recommendations for cleaning the stream, would have been far more convincing and professional.

Avoid using a great number of adjectives and adverbs in report writing or, for the most part, in writing of any kind. Modifiers, or qualifiers, are less direct and forceful than well-chosen, exact, and vivid nouns and verbs. The wise choice of nouns decreases the need for adjectives; the wise choice of verbs decreases the need for adverbs. Too many adjectives and adverbs tend to slow the flow of writing. They also tend to sound effusive and exaggerated.

An objective writing style is essential to all business writing, but the approach is slightly different for effective reports than for some business letters, particularly sales material. Even in sales writing or other persuasive messages, however, conviction is built by the presentation of specific, factual material, not by a mere appeal to the reader's emotions. The direct presentation of specific, factual material is essential for reports. Other ways in which reports differ from many letters, apart from the fact that first- and second-person pronouns are more likely to be omitted, are slight differences in tone. Reports tend to be less personal and casual than many letters, although no business message should be overly casual and familiar. As mentioned in Chapter 2 and elsewhere, many letter *are* reports.

Connotative and Denotative Meanings

Words have *connotative* meanings apart from their *denotative* meanings. The denotative meaning is the relation between a word and its referent, the object to which the word refers. For example, you can point to a desk instead of saying *desk* and to your shoe instead of saying *shoe*. As you

---

1. Chester Reed Anderson, Alta Gwinn Saunders, and Francis W. Weeks, *Business Reports,* 3d ed. (New York: McGraw-Hill, 1957), p. 105.

speak or write these words, they stand for specific, tangible objects. Even these concrete words, however, or words like *post office* or *oak tree,* can be misunderstood because of the great variety of desks, shoes, post offices, and oak trees. In addition, many words that have a specific referent in one sense also have other meanings, and the same word can function as several parts of speech.

Connotative meanings are based on experiences, attitudes, beliefs, and emotions. Denotative meanings are said to be informative, while connotative meanings have affective results. To many minds, the word *home* brings thoughts of a fireside, good food, family, friends, comfort, and security; the word *house* has a more neutral meaning.

Words that usually have unpleasant connotations beyond their actual denotative meanings are *criticize, you claim,* and *cheap.* Although the word *criticize* means to evaluate, either positively or negatively, the word connotes a derogatory description, which is one dictionary meaning. *Cheap* is now considered as a cheap synonym for *inexpensive,* but far more derogatory and with an implication of poor quality. *You claim* indicates disbelief.

These words and similar ones with unpleasant general connotations should be used with caution, if at all. Other words to avoid are the negative and unpleasant words *fail, reject, turn down,* and *blame.*

We cannot know and control individual connotations based upon the personal experiences of the reader or listener. For example, if the receiver of the written or spoken message has had an automobile accident on Perkins Road, the name alone will elicit unpleasant memories and feelings. If a young man is in love with a girl named Linda, another girl with the same name may seem more attractive than a girl named Anna Lou.

Aside from their emotional effect, words have their own particular shades of meaning. Although words are described as being synonyms for other words, there are few real synonyms. Words are often similar in meaning to other words, but because of their particular connotations or the context in which they are ordinarily used, they cannot be substituted for their near-synonyms without some slight change in meaning.

A real mastery of words consists of far more than the memorization of dictionary meanings or of near-synonyms, although a good dictionary is a vital tool in learning the use of the language. You will never outgrow your need for a good dictionary regardless of how knowledgeable or professional you become. But learning the true nature of words consists of far more than looking them up in a dictionary, as is shown by the humorous misuse of words that sometimes occurs in the translation of passages from one language to another. As an example, the ''body'' of an automobile has been translated as the ''corpse.''

Words have connotations of high and low status. Garbage collectors are becoming sanitation engineers; janitors are called maintenance engineers, building engineers, or managers. Salespeople are referred to an representatives, special representatives, or registered representatives. Secretaries want to be referred to as private secretaries or administrative assistants. In our status-conscious society, perhaps titles are important. The mere change of title can be a morale booster and an asset to a person moving to another department or organization.

In department stores, what was once referred to as the complaint department became the adjustment department and then the customer service department. The credit card is now often called a courtesy card.

Words pertaining to liquor are avoided by some individuals, corporations, and government agencies. Funds for cocktail parties are referred to as ''entertainment'' or ''public relations.'' The State Department has drawn money for liquor for a ''representation fund.'' Bars are often called lounges, in which you can buy your favorite beverage and become, according to your choice of words and the amount of your favorite beverage consumed (or tippled, guzzled, swizzled, quaffed, supped, tossed down, swigged, or wet one's whistle with), tipsy, giddy, glorious, dizzy, mellow, merry, fuddled, groggy, high, lit up, tight, high as a kite, three sheets to the wind, inebriated, intoxicated, loaded, plastered, or rip-roaring drunk.

Consider the implications of the following words:

- scheme—plan—program of action
- proposition—proposal—presentation
- gamble—speculation—calculated risk
- scrawny or skinny—slim—slender
- stupid—unsound—unadvised
- favoritism—leaning—undetachment

You could make long lists of similar words. Do you recognize that words have differing and definite personalities of their own?

As much as possible, communicate with specific, concrete words with tangible referents, such as the *Mid-City Branch of First Connecticut Bank, Report Form 1281, the northeast corner of Main Street and Adams Avenue, or a bluepoint Siamese cat.* Even the most specific wording, however, will not result in exact images in the minds of the receiver and the sender of the message. For example, all bluepoint Siamese cats are not the same. Some have a crooked tail and crossed eyes, some have a straight tail and crossed eyes, some are large, some small, and on and on. Your reader or listener will think of a particular cat on the basis of individual experience—or not know the meaning of the term. Images formed on the basis of personal, individual experiences are a form of word connotations that we cannot control.

As another example, a pin oak tree may be associated with an important occurrence in the life of an individual or listener. Mention of a pin oak tree may distract from the intended written or spoken message, even though the receiver of the message may not consciously recognize the reason for the distraction.

To summarize, we should consider possible effects of our words on the minds of others. We can avoid words that have generally unpleasant connotations. We can choose words that are likely to have positive, pleasant connotations, but we can never be sure of their effect on individual readers or listeners.

Consideration for the Reader or Listener

Pleasant, positive attitudes toward ourselves, other people, and the organizations for which we work will be reflected in our writing and other communication. If we do not have positive attitudes, our writing and speech, if not blunt and unpleasant, are likely to sound strained and forced.

Although we may not agree with another's viewpoint, we should try to understand it. This ability is one of the most important factors of communication of all kinds, including report writing.

What Is Meant by the You-Attitude?

The you-attitude, or the you-approach, is a term often used in the discussion of business letters, but it also applies to memorandums and reports, even formal ones written in the third-person writing style. You consider the reader by presenting complete, accurate information; arranging the material in an easy-to-read format; organizing material for coherence and clear understanding; objectively interpreting data; and presenting conclusions and recommendations in concrete, specific words.

The you-approach, according to the preceding interpretation of the term, does not decrease or limit objectivity. Instead, it strengthens an impartial approach because emphasis is away from you, the writer, and toward the reader—or, especially, toward the information being reported. Such writing is also persuasive in that the reader is more likely to accept your ideas and recommendations than if they were presented in a jumbled arrangement and interpreted in the light of your own personal bias—an approach that is usually obvious. Although the terms *objective* and *persuasive* are often thought of as being contradictory, in this sense they are complementary and interrelated.

The you-approach is similar in meaning to the word *empathy*. Through the you-approach, we consider the receiver of our written or spoken words.

Consideration for others, although extremely important, does not guarantee proficiency in communication. Certain techniques and skills must be acquired in order to achieve all desirable qualities of effective communication, including the you-approach.

Wording that violates the you-approach is illustrated in these sentences:

1. I am pleased to announce the opening of my new office [from a letter written by a CPA to a client].
2. We are very happy that our firm is now expanding [from a letter written to customers of a marketing research organization].
3. I am very happy that my recommendations have been accepted [from a report writer to the executive who authorized the report].
4. All of us here at Planning, Inc. are delighted that you have signed a contract with us [from a letter sent from a consulting firm to a client].

Notice that each of these four sentences, when read alone, seems only to show self-confidence or pride in one's employing organization, which are worthy attitudes. But if the reader does not interpret these statements in the light of personal benefits or consideration, the passages connote writer interest, not reader interest.

You should recognize, however, that sentences such as the preceding ones are difficult to judge out of context. Provided the overall tone and content of the letters or memorandums from which the sentences were taken are considerate and positive, the passages as given could possibly be acceptable. Even so, the sentences shown above would be more effective if they were reworded:

1. You are cordially invited to the opening of my new office at 5417 Quince.
2. The addition of another specialist in marketing research will provide you with more comprehensive, up-to-date information.
3. Let me know when I can be of help in implementing the recommended changes.
4. We will soon begin the research you requested. [The original version of Sentence 4, in addition to being writer-centered, implied that Planning, Inc. did not expect the contract, with the further implications that they do not deserve the contract but need the business.]

Frequent use of the name of your organization results in an I-approach, not a you-approach. In letters or other material going outside the organization, some writers include the company name several times on each page. This is not a good practice. To do so is unnecessary, in most instances, because the company name is given in the letterhead. In addition, emphasis is away from the reader, away from the information being conveyed, and toward the writer and the organization from which the letter comes.

Another disadvantage of frequent use of a company name is that the letter, memorandum, or report sounds stuffy and formal instead of personal, natural, and friendly. The reader knows that the letter comes not from the company (companies cannot read or write) but from someone at the company. *I* and *we* should be used when to do otherwise seems awkward and unnatural.

Some writers routinely use *we* instead of *I*, even when they obviously mean *I*. Such usage is undesirable and unnecessary. If the writer means himself or herself as an individual company representative—as often occurs even though the you-attitude is used throughout—the word to use is *I*, not *we*. If the writer is speaking of a group of employees or the company as an organization of individuals, *we* is appropriate. At times *we* is appropriately used to refer to the reader and the writer.

Although almost all letters and memorandums, as well as many reports, are written in the personal tone, an abundance of *I's* and *we's* gives the impression that the message does not exemplify the you-approach. Avoid starting numerous paragraphs with *I* because the first position of the paragraph gives added emphasis to the word that is placed there.

At times the you-attitude is achieved by using neutral, impersonal wording. In addition, such wording is often more appropriate, especially in many reports, including those in which *I, we,* and *you* are acceptable. If the idea to be expressed is a disappointing one, a neutral, matter-of-fact tone may be the best choice. For example, the sentence

    Your sales have drastically decreased.

does not include the you-attitude, even though the word *your* is used. It may be necessary to convey this disappointing information to the reader. Some ideas, because of their nature, cannot be made pleasant or positive regardless of skill in word choice. In this sentence, too, the word *drastically* contributes to the overall negative effect of the sentence. Probably there is no way to make this information sound like good news, and we wouldn't want it to appear so. Merely stating the facts is preferable, as in the following sentence:

    Sales during last May were $92,300; during May of this year they were $43,250.

This sentence becomes more diplomatic by the omission of the word *you*. (The assumption is that the salesperson will know that the sales referred to are in his or her territory. If not, you have other problems.)

In summary, the you-attitude is genuine consideration for the reader or listener. Although the word *you* may appear to be more *considerate* than *I*, the entire content of the message is more important than the choice of pronouns. If the word *I* is used to an excessive and obvious extent, however, probably the emphasis is actually upon the writer, not the reader. *In disappointing or sensitive situations, the neutral approach may be more diplomatic than either the you-approach or the I-approach.*

The You-Attitude—Can It Be Real?

The interpretation of the you-attitude should not be that it is a manipulation of the readers or listeners, a way of ingratiating ourselves into their favor so that we can sell our goods or convince them to do as we wish. Even if this is the attitude of the communicator (and every person does and must determine his or her own system of values), it is difficult to simulate a concern that we do not feel. A reader or listener does not need to be completely alert to realize that the wording sounds "fishy" or that the writer or speaker is trying for a "snow job." A message that provokes these reactions is worse than one that is harshly direct, but there is no reason for either of these two extremes.

The you-attitude has been described as being nonexistent, that our concern must be for ourselves and for our own company. Much of the controversy over the application of the you-attitude stems from an inexact understanding of the meaning that the term should convey. Although using the you-approach, we must continue to be concerned with the needs of our own company and of ourselves. You as a human being are more interested in your own welfare than that of some person to whom you are writing or speaking. The recognition of these realities, however, does not preclude genuine concern for others or the desire to serve, to play fair, and to understand the reader's point of view.

Is Honesty the Best Policy?

A sound and workable system of communication is based upon openness and honesty. The old-fashioned virtues of dependability, sincerity, and loyalty still build a lasting foundation for business organizations, governments, and individuals. Without trust and confidence, there can be no real communication.

The ancient adage, "honesty is the best policy," is definitely true, overall and in the long run. But look at the meaning of this sentence, or at least the meaning that the words imply. Are we to be honest because it's the best policy—because it will bring more profit for our company and a raise for ourselves? If this motivation is our reason for being "honest," are we necessarily honest at all? Is an admirable course of action "honestly" a virtue if we are following this course of action for personal gain? Probably not. Nevertheless, honest and ethical business practices are essential for an enduring and successful business or professional organization, and for an enduring and satisfying career.

A two-year study into the problems of communication resulted in the conclusion that the approach to communication should be based on an honest "leveling" by management and employees as to their feelings, attitudes, and motivations. This approach is based on several assumptions, all of which include the precepts of sincere, nonmanipulative relationships. One assumption is quoted as follows:

> The old values of honest, sincerity, and trust, sometimes dismissed as Sunday school sentimentality, are actually Monday morning business realism in the quest for better communications. They create the climate in which communication grows. Where they do not exist, communication will be faulty, no matter how they are fertilized with methods and techniques. A man's character seems to have more influence than his personality in improving communications.[2]

No thinking, ethical person disputes the premise that messages should be sincere, honest, and truthful. Without sincerity, all the techniques of skillful writing and speech become only cleverness, a quality far less desirable than wisdom or genuine goodwill. Being honest and sincere, however, does not require bluntness and curtness, whether the communication is a factual report or a persuasive letter. Certain basic principles of effective communication—diplomacy, the you-attitude, the positive approach, and a psychological arrangement of ideas and information—are sometimes viewed with skepticism, as if all these principles should be disregarded in order to avoid hypocrisy. With this outlook, writing and speech becomes unnecessarily direct, blunt, and harsh.

An organization, as well as an individual, builds and maintains goodwill by ethical business practices and by a sincere interest in the customers or clients it serves.

A Positive, Pleasant, and Diplomatic Approach

A positive approach includes several aspects. One is the pleasant approach, which stresses the pleasant and not the unpleasant elements of a situation and states what can be done instead of what cannot be done. Another aspect of the positive approach is eliminating, as much as possi-

---

2. A. W. Lindh, "Plain Talk About Communicating in Business," in *Readings in Impersonal and Organizational Communication,* ed. Richard C. Huseman, Cal M. Logue, and Dwight L. Freshley (Boston: Holbrook Press, 1973), p. 10.

ble, grammatically negative expressions such as *no, cannot, will not,* and *can't,* as well as other negative words and phrases, including *criticize, reject, fail, turn down, must blame,* and *force.*

Success oriented is a description of another aspect of the positive approach; the opposite term is called the *doubtful tone.* Success consciousness implies acceptance or favorable action on the part of the reader or listener. Words to watch are *if, hope,* and *trust,* in addition to any other words or phrases that suggest doubt or weakness.

Notice the doubtful tone in these sentence beginnings:

```
If you want to follow these instructions . . .

If you should decide to adopt these recommendations . . .

Although you may not want to put these suggestions into effect . . .

We hope this meets your approval . . .

We trust this is a satisfactory arrangement . . .

I know this is less than you expected, but . . .

This is the best we can do because . . .

I know you will be disappointed in us, but . . .

I hope that this unfortunate occurrence will not adversely affect my
future report assignments . . .
```

All these expressions imply that the reader may not, or probably will not, agree to the suggested opinions or actions or continue to hold the writer in esteem. More persuasive wordings are shown below. *Some of the preceding statements should be omitted entirely.*

```
In order to put these instructions into effect . . .

After adoption of these recommendations . . .

I believe you will find these suggestions helpful because . . .

We are glad to make the necessary arrangements . . .
```

To achieve the positive, pleasant, diplomatic tone, we should use the techniques of emphasis and subordination. These techniques include the direct and indirect arrangements discussed in Chapter 2.

Nondiscriminatory Language

Speech or writing can be inconsiderate and undiplomatic because of words that are considered sexist by the reader or listener. Although the speaker or writer may be absolutely fair and nondiscriminatory in thought and actions, language alone can build distrust and cause communication to be ineffective.

Avoid Masculine Pronouns Except When Referring Specifically to Males

The English language has no singular pronoun to represent either sex, except for the inappropriate *it*. Because of this lack, for centuries masculine pronouns *(he, him, his, himself)* were used with the understanding that they represented either sex.

Although masculine pronouns are still widely used as a generic word to indicate either sex, by both men and women, you are wiser to avoid such usage. It is offensive to many people. Regardless of the you-approach from other standpoints, language that is considered sexist can destroy goodwill. Another reason for avoiding such usage, although less important, is that it is a bit old-fashioned. Knowledgeable writers and speakers are aware of the disadvantages of the older, discriminatory language and make every effort to avoid it.

In past years, use of masculine pronouns occurred in such sentences as

```
An engineer must know how to use his slide rule.
```

At that time the word *his* was more logical than it is today, but it is still likely to occur in such sentences as

```
An engineer must know how to use his computer.
```

The idea that only men can be engineers is now as outdated as the slide rule. All occupations are open to women, but language is slow to reflect this change. Apart from the consideration of the number of men or women in an occupation, neither masculine nor feminine pronouns should be used to describe a person whose sex is unknown. For example, do not refer to a secretary or a nurse as *she* unless you are referring to a particular woman who is a secretary or nurse. To do so is to imply that only women are secretaries or nurses, or that only women should be secretaries or nurses.

In the sentences used above as example, *his* is unnecessary in reference to either the slide rule or the computer. The simple word *a* is sufficient, whether or not the engineer actually owns the slide rule or the computer. A masculine pronoun is often used in sentences such as these, in which the use of a pronoun is not at all necessary. Substituting *a* or *the* or reconstructing the sentence in some other way to avoid using a pronoun is one of the most appropriate and convenient ways of avoiding *he, his,* or *him.*

Another method of attaining nondiscriminatory writing is to use plural nouns. For example, instead of

```
An accountant can update his knowledge by attending seminars.
```

change *an accountant* to *accountants* and *his* to *their.*

Another method of avoiding masculine or feminine pronouns is to repeat the noun, although this method should be used with discretion in order to avoid obvious repetition. Also avoid frequent use of *he or she—* although the term may be used occasionally when there is no other way to avoid sexist wording and make you meaning clear. Overuse of *he or she* is distracting and results in awkward writing.

Sometimes the passive voice can be used to avoid pronouns, although this method should also be used sparingly because the active voice is often more direct, concise, and forceful, as discussed in Chapter 6.

For example, instead of writing

```
Each employee should sign and return his or her approved vacation
request form.
```

say

```
Approved vacation request forms should be signed and returned.
```

In this particular illustration, the sentence with the verb in the passive voice is shorter than the previous one. Apart from the elimination of *his,* the second sentence is preferable because emphasis is upon *approved vacation request forms,* where the emphasis should ordinarily be placed. In sentences like the first example, *their* is often used to replace *his or her.* This usage is ungrammatical. *Each employee* is singular; *their* is plural. Pronouns should agree with their antecedents in number.

This sentence could be expressed with a plural noun, as

```
All employees should sign and return their approved vacation request
forms.
```

Still another method of avoiding masculine pronouns is to use *you.*

In the preceding example, if you are writing *to* the employees instead of *about* them, *you* should be used because it is more direct, friendly, and interesting, in addition to being a method of avoiding *his or her.* To make the preceding sentence more tactful and diplomatic, omit *should* and word the sentence this way:

```
Please sign and return the approved vacation request form.
```

Avoid Other Forms of Discriminatory Writing and Speech

In addition to masculine pronouns used to designate either sex, several other kinds of writing are viewed as sexist.

Do not use such terms as *woman attorney, male nurse, woman doctor,* or *poetess.* Use *attorney, nurse, doctor,* and *poet.*

Do not say *girl* or *my girl* when referring to an assistant. Instead, call her your assistant or, preferably, refer to her by name.

Do not use the term *businessman* unless you are referring to a particular man. Prefer *executive, business manager, businessperson,* or some other descriptive and accurate term. A *businesswoman* may be described by this term, but prefer *executive, business manager, vice president,* or another word that accurately and fairly describes her position.

Instead of *salesman,* when the sex is unknown, use *sales representative, sales clerk,* or *salesperson.*

Instead of *foreman,* use *supervisor.*

The word *chairman* is still used by many men and women, and some women prefer the term from the standpoint that it is the name of a position, not a sexist term. (Many others don't like it.) Unless you are sure that the woman to whom you are referring chooses to be addressed as *chairman,* use some other word, such as *chairperson, chairwoman, presiding officer, coordinator,* or *department head.* In all instances, follow known preferences. If, for example, the head of a college department refers to herself as chairman of the department and shows her title on letters in this way, you are being discourteous if you address her as *Chairperson* or *Chairwoman.* You may say chair of the department.

From the same standpoint, address women as *Ms., Mrs.,* or *Miss* according to their preferences, if you know these preferences. If you do not know, use *Ms.* (In examples of letters in this textbook, the use of a title other than *Ms.* is based on the assumption that the writer of the letter knew that the woman to whom the letter was addressed prefers *Mrs.* or *Miss.*) Women have the right to use the title they prefer, just as they have the right to spell or pronounce their names any way they wish. Writers are being discourteous when they do not accede to these wishes, regardless of their own opinions about language that they consider sexist. *Ms.,* however, is frequently used to refer to a woman.

       Effective communication must be based on sound knowledge and un-
derstanding of the material being communicated, as well as upon proficiency in language. Writers and speakers should adhere, for the most part,
to established conventions of language usage. To do otherwise is distracting and may lead to misunderstanding or lack of confidence in the writer's
ability.

       Emphasis is achieved by position, overall arrangement, sentence and
paragraph construction, word choice, the use of space, mechanical methods, and summarizing.

       An objective writing style is desirable in all business and professional
writing, but it is essential in reports. Conviction is built by the presentation
of specific, factual material, not by a statement of the writer's opinions or
by an appeal to the reader's emotions.

       Connotative meanings are based on experiences, attitudes, beliefs,
and emotions. Denotative meanings are dictionary or dictionary-like definitions. Denotative meanings are said to be informative, while connotative
meanings have affective results.

       The you-approach is genuine consideration for the reader or listener.
Pleasant, positive attitudes toward ourselves, other people, and the organizations for which we work will be reflected in our writing and speech.

       A positive approach stresses the pleasant and not the unpleasant ele-
ments of a situation and states what can be done instead of what cannot
be done. Negative expressions such as *fail, reject, blame,* and *turn down,* in
addition to grammatical negatives, are decreased in number, or, preferably,
omitted entirely. Wording should imply expected success; it should not
indicate doubt. The positive approach is achieved by the wise use of methods of emphasis and subordination.

Summary

Questions and Problems

1. Have you observed examples of reports, advertising material, speeches,
   or other forms of communication in which the truth was definitely and
   intentionally distorted—according to your sincere observation? (In analyzing this question, you are faced with another question: What is truth? To
   most of us, other communicators distort the truth when they disagree with
   us.) Explain.

2. Prepare a list of words of high and low status, such as sanitation engineer
   versus garbage collector; administrator versus clerk; maintenance engineer
   versus janitor.

3. Think of a word or phrase with a more favorable connotation for each of
   the following expressions. For some of the words you can think of at least
   two more favorable expressions—one or more somewhat neutral and one
   or more so favorable that it would be considered a euphemism. For exam-

ple, *scheme* can be replaced by *plan;* even more favorable is *program of action.*
Another example is *bogus* (negative), *artificial* (more neutral), and *simulated*
(still not completely positive but more so than either of the preceding).

chore	scrawny	stupid
deal	poverty	stuffed shirt (cliché)
cheap	racket	gross (slang)
affair	blemish	drunk
liar	blunder	fired
stubborn	long-winded	a dictator
bookworm	ridiculous	cheat
smart aleck	fat	you're crazy!

*When making negative terms more pleasant, you should remember that in actual
communication often the best approach is to omit them entirely.* In addition, you will
notice that you often need more words to express negative terms in a more
positive way, although they will never be completely pleasant and positive
unless you change the meaning entirely. The words shown above are examples
of "opinion" words instead of factual words, an approach inappropriate to
business, technical, and professional writing, particularly to report writing.

4. Do certain words have particularly pleasant or unpleasant connotations to
   you because of your individual experiences? Explain.

5. Can you think of words, in addition to those mentioned in this chapter,
   that have been replaced by higher status words?

6. Improve the following passages from the standpoint of the you-attitude,
   diplomacy, and the positive approach. Assume any necessary and reasonable details. Omit details that seem unnecessary and undesirable.
   a. We are pleased to inform you that we have completed your study
      [opening sentence of letter transmitting report].
   b. It's against our policy, so we must reject your suggestions for the im-
      provements of our products. Our engineers have already considered
      everything that people think are new ideas.
   c. This packaging material is not the kind that gets holes in it at the slight-
      est touch.
   d. Your research is completely unscientific, and your writing style is at
      the third-grade level.
   e. Do not fail to finish the project by the end of the week.
   f. I have not had any experience except for summer work in a small li-
      brary in my home town, where I was hired because my mother works
      there.
   g. We cannot complete the bridge until the transportation strike is over.
   h. Your memorandum indicates that you are ignorant of policies in our
      research department.
   i. If you are interested in this plan, you might let me know sometime.
   j. We trust that you won't let this unfortunate occurrence cause you to
      disbelieve us.

> **k.** You have neglected to reply to my memorandum of August 8 and telephone call of August 9.
>
> **l.** It will be impossible to do as you request; you should know that.
>
> **m.** The applicant is not shy or timid, and he doesn't seem to be stupid.
>
> **n.** If you can manage to complete your work on time, we can move on with the project.
>
> **o.** We hope that our mistake will not adversely affect our business relationship [used as last paragraph in letter].
>
> **p.** I am pleased to announce that our company, the Success Planners, is expanding and will begin classes for executives in organizations all over town, including yours, beginning on August 1.
>
> **q.** We are sorry that we must reject your request [last paragraph of letter or memorandum].
>
> **r.** I am sorry to take up so much of your valuable time, but I really need this information [from letter sent with questionnaire].
>
> **s.** We beg to extend to you our humble apologies.
>
> **t.** The instructions are plainly stated, as you can see for yourself by turning to page 5.

7. Improve the following sentences, taken from reports, from the standpoint of objective wording. A point to remember is that objective wording (unbiased) is likely to be attained by being specific. That is, you are striving for factual information, not your judgment of the matter—denotative words instead of connotative ones. Objectivity may be reached in some sentences simply by the omission of judgmental words; for example, instead of saying that costs have increased by the enormous figure of 45.2 percent say that they have increased 45.2 percent—and be specific as to which costs and which period of time.

    a. The XYZ equipment is shamefully overpriced. In comparison, competing models sell at bargain-basement prices.

    b. The tremendous increase in paperwork in our offices proves that it is foolish to tolerate the old copier any longer.

    c. The oppressive income tax awards sluggards and incompetents and penalizes those who are competent and hardworking.

    d. I can't believe that we have fallen so disgracefully behind last year's quota.

    e. The amazing increase in profits—72 percent—is unquestionably due to the superb leadership of our outstanding management team.

    f. Enormous difficulties in production contributed to a startling increase in costs.

    g. The unbelievable increase in defects—27 percent—is undoubtedly the result of lax supervision.

8. Summarize a lecture from some other course in which you are enrolled, or summarize a lecture or discussion that you heard on radio, television, or elsewhere. You are concerned with applying the principles of emphasis to stress important points. Summarize in one short paragraph the entire lecture or discussion, then use three or four paragraphs to list other points or to expand on the topic summarized in the first paragraph. Conclude

with an appropriate ending paragraph. (See the discussion in this chapter on the methods of emphasis and subordination, including the mechanical means of emphasis.)

9. This problem is based on the discussion of emphasis in Chapter 5, the explanation of the direct and indirect order in Chapter 2, the memorandum format as described and illustrated in Chapter 3, and the you-attitude and positive approach discussed in Chapter 5.

   a. CONVEYING GOOD NEWS. You are the personnel manager. Write a memorandum to all office and plant employees conveying the following information:
      - Each employee will receive a small increase in take-home pay.
      - Employees have been paying all costs of dental insurance, although they have received a low rate of group insurance. The company has been paying one-half the cost of medical insurance, but not one-half the cost of dental insurance. Now the company is treating dental care as part of overall medical coverage and assuming one-half the cost of employees' insurance premiums.
      - The effective date of these changes is January 1; the difference will first appear in paychecks received on January 31.
      - Employees have been paying an average of $18 a month for family coverage for dental care. Thus, the average premium will now be $9, resulting in a $9 increase in take-home pay. (Make sure that employees realize this figure is an average one. Single employees and married ones with no children have been paying less than $18.)

   b. CONVEYING BAD NEWS. You are the personnel manager. Write a memorandum to all employees. Instead of the information given in the preceding case, you must report an increase in medical and dental insurance. Costs of medical insurance, other than dental, will increase by 22.2 percent a month beginning January 1. Costs of dental insurance remain the same (Employees will continue to pay the entire costs of dental insurance, and the company will continue to pay one-half the costs of medical insurance.) Reasons for the increase, as stated by officials of the insurance company, are rapidly rising hospital costs and physicians' fees.

10. Write instructions for using an electrical appliance, such as a blender, tape recorder, or clock radio. Assume that your reader has never seen the appliance. Include the purpose of the appliance in your instructions.

11. Think of some area of responsibility in your present or former job. Tell a new employee exactly how to perform this task or how to handle the responsibility. Put these instructions in memorandum form. Be prepared to present these instructions orally to the class.

Additional questions and problems suitable for use at this time are given in Appendix C.

CHAPTER **6**

A Clear and Forceful Writing Style

Chapter Outline

Clear and forceful writing is concise, simple, natural, and direct. It is unpretentious and calls attention not to itself, but to the ideas being expressed. Far more knowledge and skill are required for a forceful, simple style than for a complex, involved one.

Be Concise, Complete, Considerate, Courteous, and Clear

Conciseness is not a synonym for brevity. *Brevity,* like *short, informal,* and other nonspecific words, is relative. Although a report of one hundred pages is not usually described as brief, it is concise if it is no longer than it needs to be to accomplish its particular purpose. Conversely, a one-page report, although brief, is not concise if it contains wordy phrases or unnecessary repetition.

Conciseness is a desirable quality of business communication of all kinds. Brevity is not necessarily desirable. Many writers and speakers are overly concerned with what they consider to be conciseness to the extent that their communications lack completeness, consideration, courtesy, or clarity.

Some competent letter writers, who realize the importance of building goodwill to customers and the general public, seem to think that the tone they use in their letters must be completely changed in their written or oral reports. It is true that reports ordinarily do not, and should not, contain the kind of paragraphs described in letters as "sales promotion." Nevertheless, we must continue to be concerned with goodwill in all forms of communication, including written and oral reports.

Omission of only a few words decreases understanding if these words are needed to show relationships from one thought to another or from one part of a report to another. Hasty discussion of necessary explanations and examples can delay or prevent the acceptance of recommendations.

As an extreme example of emphasis on brevity alone, suppose that after completing a comprehensive research project, you write a report that consists only of these words:

```
We should build a factory in Brazil.
```

Such a report is indeed brief, and it is the recommendation that has resulted from your research. Nevertheless, it is far from enough. The immediate questions in the mind of the reader are these: Why? How? When? Who will be responsible for this major undertaking? How much will it cost? When will this expenditure be regained? Upon what information is the recommendation based? How do I know that the research was capably done?

The report writer must provide specific, convincing answers to all these questions, and others. To do otherwise is to ensure that readers will not immediately begin work on a factory in Brazil.

The reader or listener does not want needless or irrelevant details, but enough material must be included to make the report, or other communication, understandable, convincing, courteous, and considerate. Although a communication that is unnecessarily long is expensive and annoying, one that is so brief as to be incomplete is even more expensive and annoying.

Eliminate Business Jargon

Phrases described as business jargon are used not only in business, but by many other writers in all occupations. Such jargon consists of unnecessary, trite, wordy phrases, included because the writer has seen them in other letters, memorandums, and reports. Some of these phrases are:

- at this point in time
- enclosed herewith please find
- we beg to call your kind attention to
- kindly be advised
- in reply to your recent favor (letter) we wish to state
- thanking you for your kind attention
- the same being at hand, I wish to state
- thank you in advance
- thanking you in advance
- I remain (at the end of letter)
- do not hesitate (when used routinely, unnecessarily, or insincerely)
- this is to inform you

Yes, these phrases are still used occasionally, but, fortunately, their use is decreasing. Cliches and other stereotyped, stale expressions creep into our writing or speech because we do not take the time to think of our own words instead of using worn-out ones.

Almost always, the wordy phrases and trite business jargon listed below should be omitted or simplified. Those marked with a star can safely be put into a "never" category for use in business writing, but all should ordinarily be avoided, for they are slow, wordy, and old-fashioned.

- it has come to my attention
- in the amount of (for)
- to the amount of (for)
- for the amount of (for)
- amounting to (for)
- totalling the sum of (for)
- be assured, rest assured
- *be advised, *be informed, *consider yourself informed, *this is to inform you, *this is for your information
- herewith, herein, attached herewith, attached hereto, enclosed herewith, *enclosed please find
- *beg to state, wish to state, regret to state
- *reference to same, *compliance with same, *consideration of same
- *we beg to call your attention to the fact that
- *thank you in advance, *thanking you in advance, *thanking you for your kind attention, *thanking you for your time, *thanking you for your consideration
- *we wish to remain, yours truly
- as of this date, as of this writing, as of the present time
- be kind enough
- due to the fact that, in view of the fact that
- *thank you kindly, *kindly, *we kindly thank you for
- at an early date
- along this line
- *we beg to remain
- *pursuant to your request
- *the undersigned (except in legal papers)
- pending receipt of
- for the purpose of, for the reason that, due to the fact that (for, to, because)
- in spite of the fact that (because)
- evident and apparent
- take the liberty of
- regret to advise, regret to inform, regret to state
- *your esteemed favor
- AND MANY, MANY MORE

Choose Short, Familiar, Exact Words

A simple writing style consisting of short, everyday words and fairly short sentences is far from being juvenile; the opposite is true. The Gettysburg Address and the Lord's Prayer are two examples of great works that are in simple, direct language. Simple writing does not limit the wise use of the infinite variety of language. Instead, it requires careful phrasing for the most exact expression of specific ideas, with language and approach especially adapted to the particular readers of the message.

Short words, if they are the exact words to express the desired meaning, should be preferred to long words. Business or professional writing is no medium for showing off a vocabulary of unusual or "intellectual" words. This statement does not mean that a capable writer in any field should be unconcerned about the development of an extensive vocabulary. We must know a great many words in order to write well—to know which simple words to choose and, in some instances, which long words are appropriate and exact.

We should consider our readers, especially their background and probable knowledge of the subject about which we are writing. If material is technical and specialized, some words must be defined for the reader outside the particular area of specialization, or simple words should be substituted for technical, unusual ones. We should never, however, give the appearance of writing down to the level of our readers. Nothing is more offensive than to indicate that the writer feels superior in knowledge to the reader. The purpose of communication is to express facts and ideas, not to impress the reader with a fancy style or an extensive vocabulary.

Short words, appropriately chosen, not only increase readability but also help to form a vivid and forceful writing style. Compare the simplicity of the words in the second column to those in the first:

Instead of	Prefer
Affix a signature	sign
approbation	approval
ameliorate	improve
causative factor	cause
engrossment	attention
expectancy	hope
finalize	end
inaugurate	begin
incorporate	include
interrogate	question (or ask)
peruse	read
prior to	before
promulgate	publish
salience	importance
utilizable	useful
utilize	use

Short words are not always the ones that are most clear. An unusual short word that the reader is not likely to understand is less desirable than a more familiar, longer word. In addition, many words in ordinary, everyday use are quite long.

When we are writing to specialists in our own field, as often occurs in report writing, a technical, specialized word is likely to be more understandable than a shorter one that is substituted with the mistaken purpose of making the report clear, simple, and easy to read. To an accountant, accounting terms are easily and quickly understood; to a reader unfamiliar with accounting, specialized terms interpreted in layman's language may result in completely different meanings. The same principle is true for writers and readers in the medical field and in many other occupations and professions.

The most important consideration is the precise and appropriate choice of words according to meaning, context, and readers. Few words, long or short, have exact synonyms. Use the word that is most likely to express your exact meaning to the mind of the individual reader. This word is most often a short, familiar one. *Before you can choose words to express your exact meaning, that meaning must be clear in your mind.*

Construct Short, Readable Sentences

Sentences need not and should not be the same length. In order to avoid monotony, if for no other reason, both short and fairly long sentences should be used. Most important, sentences should be of the length and construction that best convey the ideas and information so closely related that they belong in the same sentence.

Average sentence length ordinarily should not exceed seventeen to twenty words, although an experienced, skillful writer can use longer sentences and achieve a readable style. Also remember that seventeen to twenty is an *average* number. Some sentences are longer and some are shorter. A series of short, simple sentences similar to those in a first-grade reader is monotonous and unprofessional. In addition, not all ideas and relationships can be effectively expressed in short, simple sentences. (Brevity and short sentences are not the most important elements of successful business and professional writing. At times these qualities have been given too much emphasis in the teaching of business writing.)

A thorough and automatic knowledge of sentence construction is essential to the expert writer, not only from the standpoint of readability but also from the standpoints of emphasis and correctness. The type of sentence chosen for a particular idea depends upon the idea to be expressed. Experienced writers do not consciously think of sentence construction as the material is written or dictated. As they revise, they change sentence structure. The revision most often necessary is that of cutting sentence length.

Check your work to make sure that only complete sentences are used and that they vary in form. In most business writing, simple sentences should outnumber complex sentences and compound sentences. In almost all writing, compound sentences should be the fewest of the three. Complex sentences are useful to subordinate or to emphasize ideas. An idea can be subordinated, also, by placement as a phrase within a sentence of any construction.

A review of sentence structure is included in the *Basic English Tutor* disk, included in Appendix D.

Construct Short, Readable Paragraphs

Short paragraphs are useful in achieving readability. A paragraph of many lines is hard to read and discouraging to the reader, especially when time is short—as it usually is. Paragraphs in a letter, memorandum, or short report are often broken arbitrarily to increase readability.

Some writers believe that a paragraph must have more than one sentence. The belief may have originated in a class in English composition, although in all kinds of writing one-sentence paragraphs are quite acceptable to most readers. A short, one-sentence paragraph can be used for attention, interest, and emphasis. It is particularly effective in the emphatic opening or closing position of a letter or memorandum. It can be correctly used in any position—for emphasis, attention, transition, or simply for the reason that nothing else is needed in the paragraph.

Although no exact rule can be given about maximum paragraph length, you should regard with suspicion any typewritten paragraph of more than ten or eleven lines. The average number should be fewer, particularly in short reports, letters, or memorandums. If your paragraphs tend to be unusually long, perhaps the entire organization of your report or other written material could be improved. Use topic sentences to begin paragraphs. If these topic sentences are exact, each forms a summary of the individual paragraph, and all topic sentences, read in sequence, provide a summary of the entire written message. Topic sentences, however, do not always appear at the beginning of a paragraph; for emphasis and variety, some paragraphs may end with a summarizing sentence, or the main idea may be somewhere within the paragraph. In addition, an exact topic sentence is not always apparent in short written messages. (If all paragraphs in this chapter were as long as the one you are now reading, they would be too long.)

Just as skillful, experienced writers do not consciously think of sentence construction as they compose, neither do they continuously ponder paragraph construction and the use of topic sentences. When they revise written material, their knowledge of sentence and paragraph construction enables them to achieve the desired emphasis and to increase clarity and coherence.

Notice the first paragraph in this section of this chapter. The beginning sentence, *Short paragraphs are useful in achieving readability*, serves as the topic sentence. In the second paragraph of this section, the main idea is expressed in the second clause of the second sentence: *although in all kinds of writing one-sentence paragraphs are quite acceptable.* In the third and fourth paragraphs, the first sentence expresses the main idea. In the paragraph you are now reading, the topic sentence is the closing one. Although most topic sentences are used to begin the paragraph, they can also be placed in other positions.

Paragraph construction, in relation to emphasis and approach, has been previously discussed in Chapter 5.

Design Readable Formats

A letter, memorandum, report or other bit of writing should be arranged attractively, leaving plenty of white space. A minimum of one inch at the side, top, and bottom margins should be left on all work. For short and average-length letters, wider margins are better.

Subheads are essential to readability if the written message is long, and *long* usually should be considered to apply to any communication of more than one page. Subheads can also be used in material of one page or less. They add readability in several ways.

Subheads force the writer to organize the material in meaningful units. If the subhead does not include a reference to the information under it, and only to that information, it is not well chosen. Poor subheads are worse than none at all.

Lists and tabulations make ideas stand out and present ideas in a logical order. The arrangement of each statement, question, or idea on a separate line (as illustrated in the list below) makes each of the items easier to understand than if all were crowded together into a paragraph.

To illustrate the use of a listing, as well as to summarize, the following information is repeated.

Readable formats should include:

1. Plenty of white space
2. An overall attractive appearance
3. Subheads
4. Lists and tabulations.

Use Coherent Phrasing and Organization

Coherence is the logical, easy-to-understand flow of thought from the beginning to the end of a message, and is an essential element of readability. The term comes from the word *cohesion*; it literally means a *sticking together* of ideas so that the communication is unified, without abrupt shifts in arrangement or subject matter.

To be coherent, writing must also have unity. Unity and coherence are achieved by overall organization so that the message flows naturally and smoothly according to a plan decided upon before the writing or dictation is begun. (As we proceed with writing or dictation, we often see needed changes in the original plan. These changes should be made, and then the organization should follow the revised plan.)

If the message is truly coherent, the reader's mind grasps the relationships of words, sentences, and paragraphs and recognizes the overall progression of meaning. Transitional words and phrases and the repetition of key words, used with discretion, aid in the transfer of thought from one idea to another.

After you complete a letter, memorandum, report, or other communication, proofread it for abrupt changes in subject matter. The overall meaning may be perfectly clear to you, the writer, only because you knew from the beginning what you were trying to say; your reader will not have this advantage.

Prefer the Active Voice

Verbs are the strongest and the most vivid of the parts of speech. They are stronger in the active voice than in the passive. The active voice is more direct, forceful, and concise; it should ordinarily be preferred unless, as often occurs, there is a specific reason to use the passive voice. Only transitive verbs (those that have or imply an object) can be passive.

The following sentences illustrate the difference between active and passive verbs:

```
Active:    The decorator rearranged the office furniture.
Passive:   The office furniture was (has been) rearranged by the
           decorator.
```

In the second sentence, if the phrase *by the decorator* were omitted, the verb would still be passive. Of the two illustrated sentences, the first is more direct, forceful, and concise. At times, however, the person who acts, or has acted, is irrelevant or unknown. In such cases, the best sentence is the passive construction: The office furniture has been rearranged. An additional illustration is:

Active: We should include more colors in our line of denim
            slacks.

Passive: More colors should be included in our line of denim
            slacks.

The passive voice in this illustration emphasizes *More colors* by placement in the emphatic first position of the sentence. This may be the desired emphasis. In the following sentences, however, the active voice is the better choice:

Active: Ruth asked many questions.

Passive: Many questions were asked by Ruth.

Active: The committee approved two changes in the constitution.

Passive: Two changes in the constitution were approved by the
            committee.

The following sentences do not include verbs in the passive voice, but the construction results in the same slow, weak effect.

It is desirable to include more colors in our line of denim slacks.

There should be increased production of our denim slacks.

The words *there* and *it* are function words or ''structural fillers'' that replace true subjects. They are usually referred to as *expletives*. They are weaker than tangible, specific subjects.

The passive voice is in no way incorrect; neither are sentences beginning with *there* or *it*. They are discussed here because many writers use the passive voice and *it* and *there* unnecessarily, especially when writing in the impersonal tone. Regardless of the choice of personal or impersonal tone, most sentences can be and should be written with ''real'' subjects and active verbs.

Notice the differences in emphasis in the following sentences:

Active: A woman drove the truck.

Passive: The truck was driven by a woman.

A *woman* receives the most emphasis in the last position, as shown by the second sentence.

The most important consideration as to active and passive verbs, as with all word choice and sentence construction, is to express your intended meaning exactly. The desired emphasis is an aspect of meaning.

Understand Readability and Readability Formulas

Readability, as the word implies, means the ease with which the reader can obtain the desired message. As the term issued in written communication, it means immediate clearness. When written material is planned to achieve the desired emphasis, it is likely to be readable.

Readability and emphasis are influenced by word choice, sentence length, paragraph length, length of the entire message, subheads, listings, other aspects of format, organization, unity, coherence, and an attractive physical appearance.

Several formulas, or "indexes," have been developed that supposedly measure readability. Two of these are the Flesch Reading Ease Formula and the Gunning Fog Index. Rudolf Flesch's formula is presented in his book, *The Art of Readable Writing,* published in 1949.[1] Robert Gunning's formula appears in his book, *The Technique of Clear Writing.* (This book first appeared in 1952; this reference is to a revised edition.)[2]

Both the Flesch formula and the Gunning Fog Index rely heavily on sentence and word lengths to determine reading levels. Although Gunning recognizes that factors other than sentence and word length determine readability—such as percentage of verbs expressing forceful action, proportion of familiar words, proportion of abstract words—only sentence and word length are considered in his easy-to-use plan.

The readability score obtained through the use of the Gunning formula is expressed in terms of the general educational level of the reader, which may have little relationship to the actual grade completed in school. If, for example, the readability score is 17, this indicates that the material could be read easily by someone who has completed college. A score of 16 is used to mean that a person completing the sixteenth year of schooling, a college senior, could easily read the material.

Most effective writing of all kinds, however, has a lower readability score than 16 or 17, even if the material is planned for graduate students. Material may have a readability score lower than high school level and still be suitable for adults.

An important point to remember is that formulas cannot measure the quality of writing, only its complexity, and that to a limited extent. An expert writer can use long words and sentences and make a work more interesting and

1. Rudolph Flesch, *The Art of Readable Writing* (New York: Harper & Row, 1949), pp. 213–216.
2. Robert Gunning, *The Technique of Clear Writing* (New York: McGraw-Hill, 1968), pp. 30–45.

readable than a writer with less ability, although the expert's work has a higher readability score.

The formulas make no distinction between exact, well-chosen words and vague, confusing words, or between familiar words and rare ones. They measure only word length. They also do not distinguish sentences that are constructed wisely in order to exactly express the intended ideas. Excellent writing cannot be measured by any formula, but an average reader can usually recognize its quality and understand its meaning.

These cautions about using readability formulas are not given to disparage their worth, for their admittedly limited purposes are valid ones. They measure sentence and word length and express this measurement in a score that is likely to apply to different groups of readers. The formulas can be dangerous, however, if they are misused. An appropriate readability score should not be accepted without question as an indication that the writing needs no improvement. Writing with a score higher than the expected "norms" should not be automatically classified as lacking in readability, although it should be reexamined.

The Gunning Fog Index is as follows:

1. Select a sample of writing of at least 100 words. Divide the total number of words by the number of sentences. This is the average sentence length. [Using several samples will result in a more reliable score. The independent clauses of a compound sentence are counted as separate sentences.]
2. Count the number of words of three syllables or more. Don't count proper names; combinations of short, easy words, such as bookkeeper or teenager; or verb forms made into three syllables by adding *ed* or *es*. This figure is the number of "hard" words in the passage. Divide this figure by the total number of words to find the percentage of "hard" words.
3. Add the average sentence length to the percentage of hard words and multiply by 4. The figure obtained through these calculations is the Gunning Fog Index, or readability score, expressed in grade-reading level.[3]

This readability formula is not the method used by writers of material for use in many textbooks, especially those for use at the elementary school level, for in these books the vocabulary, or the actual words to be included, must be considered. In readability formulas for adult use, only the length of words is considered, along with sentence length, although some methods include the consideration of "personal interest" words.

Let's find the readability score for the following paragraph from *The*

---

3. Gunning, *The Technique of Clear Writing*, p. 39.

Mature Mind by H. A. Overstreet, written in 1949. This book is much more readable than many other books on psychological subjects, but the 12.2 score is higher than an ideal score for short, nontechnical business communications. The example paragraph is well written; even with a higher percentage of long words, provided they were no more unusual than those actually used, the passage would be easily understandable. Another passage with a similar score could be much less understandable, according to the skill in sentence construction and word choice. (Overstreet does not mention television because in the year in which this paragraph was written, television was in its infancy.)

> Newspapers, radio, movies, and advertising—these might be called the "big four" of communication. These are the four great money-making enterprises of mind-making. It would be pleasant to report that they all make for the fine maturing of human character. But the report must be otherwise. In spite of what each has contributed to our growth, each has, through its own formula, found it profitable to keep us from full psychological maturing. Or, to put the best possible face upon the matter, each has found in us some immaturity that waited to be tapped. Engaged in the tapping process, each of these powerful forces has been too busy to think about the long-range consequences of its formula.[4]

The paragraph contains 120 words and 7 sentences. The words of three or more syllables (those not excluded by the formula) total 16. "Newspapers" and "otherwise" are excluded because they are combinations of short, easy words, like "bookkeeper," mentioned in the formula.

To find the sentence length, divide 120 by 7, which gives an average sentence length of 17.1. To find the percentage of hard words, divide 16 by 120; the percentage is 13.3. Add 17.1 to 13.3; the result is 30.4. Multiply by .4 to obtain the readability score of 12.16 or 12.2.

This reading-level score means that the material should be easily read by someone in the twelfth grade, or approximately so. This is similar to the reading level of such magazines as *The Atlantic* and *Harper's,* although articles by different authors vary somewhat in difficulty. Other popular magazines, especially *Reader's Digest,* are written at a level two or three grades below this twelfth-grade score. To obtain an accurate average score of writing of considerable length, we should use far more material than the paragraph we have considered here.

Although you should check passages of your own writing occasionally, most college students do not write in an extremely complex style—unless they are trying to impress their professor. Twenty or thirty years from now, when you are a business executive, a politician, or a high-rank-

4. H. A. Overstreet, *The Mature Mind* (New York: W. W. Norton, 1949), pp. 225–226.

ing government official, check your writing by the use of the Gunning Fog Index or a similar formula. If you resemble your present-day counterparts, you will need to simplify.

Robert Gunning and his associates have used the Fog Index in an attempt to simplify writing coming from the Army, Navy, Air Force, and the Department of Agriculture. It has also been used in many industries and with writers for newspapers and magazines. For Gunning's description of the use of this formula, its advantages and disadvantages, see his article, ''The Fog Index After Twenty Years,'' which he wrote in 1968. In it he states:

> My feelings are mixed about this readability yardstick that I developed back in the 1940's; but they are much more positive than negative. The wide use the Fog Index has received is gratifying. On the other hand, occasional misunderstanding and misuse of it have been disturbing.[5]

Revise for Professional Quality

Good writing is achieved by rewriting and then perhaps rewriting again and again. Even skillful professional writers revise their work, one reason why they are skillful professional writers.

In a busy office, however, there is little time or opportunity for extensive rewriting of routine letters, memorandums, or reports. Because of pressure to meet deadlines, which seems to be common to almost every occupation, you must be able to produce acceptable work without revising extensively. Whatever your knowledge and skill, however, and regardless of the lack of time, some revision is often necessary.

When revising a communication:

1. Check organization and the flow of thought.
2. Notice the length of sentences and paragraphs. Often they could be shortened.
3. Watch for unnecessary repetition of words or ideas.
4. Make sure that no essential material is omitted.
5. Check for subject-verb agreement and pronoun-antecedent agreement.
6. Watch for misplaced or dangling modifiers.
7. Make sure that necessary transitional phrases or words have been included. Make sure that there is no abrupt change in the flow of thought.

5. Robert Gunning, ''The Fog Index after Twenty Years,'' *Journal of Business Communication* 6 (Winter 1968), p. 3.

8. Decide whether the entire message can be made more concise without making it less understandable or convincing.

Summary

1. Write simply. Don't try to impress your readers with an extensive vocabulary of five-syllable words, but don't give the impression of over-simplification or ''writing down.'' Prefer short words to longer words, provided they are the *exact* ones to express your intended meaning. Consider the connotative meanings of words as well as dictionary definitions.

2. Express your ideas exactly. To do so you must have an extensive vocabulary. Be specific. Do not state vague generalities.

3. Write clearly, concisely, coherently, and correctly. Give all necessary information convincingly.

4. Write objectively. Base your interpretations and decisions upon facts, not upon your personal desires or unsupported beliefs. Although at times you must state what you believe about a situation or what the data seem to indicate, make sure that the reader understands that this statement is an opinion. Give concrete details to support your opinion. On the other hand, avoid an appearance of hedging and timidity. Nobody expects you to have positive and definite answers to everything. If you pretend to do so, nobody will believe you.

5. Avoid using an unnecessary number of *I's*, even when you are writing in the personal tone.

6. Write in an interesting and vivid style. Keep sentences fairly short, but vary sentence length. Avoid using many sentences that begin with slow expletive openings, such as *there are* and *it is*.

7. Use the active voice to emphasize the actor, the passive voice to emphasize the receiver of the action. Do not use the passive voice when the active voice will exactly express your idea in more vivid terms, as it often will.

8. Remember techniques of achieving readability through arrangement and format. Use an attractive arrangement with plenty of white space, listings, headings, and summaries. Use special arrangements, underlining, or other special methods of mechanical emphasis, but do not use them to excess.

Questions and Problems

1. Rewrite the following passages for conciseness. Retain the complete meaning.
   a. We are in receipt of your communication of recent date and in reply wish to inform you that we thank you for your communication and the prompt submission of your report which we had assigned to you and for your kind letter that was attached thereto.

    b. This is the machine that makes the most noise of all those in the room.

    c. Graduates who are the ones with the highest grade-point average will be the ones who will be interviewed.

    d. This memorandum is in reply to your telephone call of October. In reply to this memorandum I wish to advise that in reference to your question about specifications for the Anderson contract they have not at the present time been drawn up but they will be finished and completed sometime in the very near future.

    e. Will you let us know by any means, telephone or letter or otherwise, sometime soon, in a month or two but hopefully within a month, just what to do about the situation we conversed about and discussed pursuant to the changing of the method in which the beneficiary, that is the former beneficiary, is notifed and informed that he or she is no longer the beneficiary, and that the policyholder has named and designated a new person to become the beneficiary. Or is this method and procedure mandatory, necessary, or even desirable?

    f. Eschew polysyllabic verbosity.

2. Rewrite the following sentences in the passive voice in order to increase diplomacy.

    a. You delivered the package to the wrong office.

    b. All your past employers told me something different about you.

    c. You know the instructions that I distributed to all personnel.

    d. You did not complete the investigation.

3. Rewrite the following sentences using the active voice instead of the passive voice or sentences beginning with *there* or *it*.

    a. Students were shown by the instructor how to weld the sides of the airplane.

    b. Implementation of the proposed procedure was delayed because of Leslie Brown's decision not to move ahead at this time.

    c. There has been a brief period during which our office manager closed the word processing center.

    d. It is interesting to notice from the attached statements that the exact balance of last month's account is the same as the exact balance of this month's account.

    e. Four more houses were sold by Mr. Johns, and three more contracts were drawn up.

4. Rewrite the following letter to eliminate business jargon. Also eliminate or change words that carry unpleasant or confusing connotations. You may add an inside address and closing lines and arrange your letter in your choice of the styles shown in Chapter 3. (Of *course* you wouldn't write a letter like this. But if you can turn this one into a good one, you're on your way to professionalism.) Consider conciseness, sentence structure, and all other elements of effective communication.

    Dear Mrs. James:

        We are in receipt of your letter of recent date and in reply wish to state we shall be jubilant to submit to your claim to send cheaper merchandise than the items you previously and heretofore ordered us to send.

Attached please find a new invoice for this cheaper merchandise which you claim will sell better in your store, that anything will sell better if it sells at all, which the present merchandise isn't doing much of. Your customers must be low class and down and out but are your salesmen really trying and have you thought about advertising?

Reports from manufacturers about consumers' preference, and we contributed to information shown in these reports, reports are of the nature to suggest that consumers are trying to save money so you could possibly be right.

Thanking you in advance for your esteemed favor, although I don't suppose it really is, please send your check posthaste and immediately. I am yours truly.

5. Discuss these statements:
   a. A short word can be less readable than a long one.
   b. Readability formulas can be misleading if used in the wrong way.
   c. Specific words are more emphatic and more forceful than general words, but at times the general word is the better choice.
   d. The writer may find it easier to write a long letter, memorandum, or report than to write a short one.
   e. A thorough and automatic knowledge of sentence structure is essential or helpful to the expert writer, although it is true that some writers seem to write well without knowing what they are doing.
   f. It is impossible to be completely objective.
   g. Prefer not to start several paragraphs on the same page with *I.*
   h. The use of business jargon can possibly save time, at least for the experienced writer, but the writer should work for a more original approach.
   i. The salutation and complimentary close used on most business letters (are, are not) forms of stereotyped business jargon.
   j. We can never be ''completely complete,'' as it is impossible to say everything about anything. Thus, all communication is a form of abstracting—choosing exactly what to communicate and what to omit.

6. Write specific, complete, and detailed instruction for one or more of the following procedures:
   a. How to change the ribbon on your typewriter or computer printer.
   b. How to change a tire on your automobile.
   c. How to put film into your camera.
   d. How to tie your shoe.
   e. How to draw a paper clip.
   f. How to operate a can opener.
   g. How to calculate the number of rolls of wallpaper needed to paper a room.
   h. How to brush your teeth.

    i. How to check out a book in your school library.
    j. How to check out a book in your public library.
    k. How to make a peanut butter and jelly sandwich.

7. Explaining Readability Formulas

You are the vice-president of Strong, Incorporated. Your company recently hired a communications supervisor because another vice-president learned that a competing company had done so. (Communications supervisors are becoming fashionable.)

The new communications supervisor, Noah Little, studied readability formulas in college. One of his first memorandums, addressed to all writers in the organization, contained the following instructions:

1. No written message going from the organization or used within the organization should score less than 10 or more than 12 when measured by the Gunning Fog Index, with the exception of material going to a group of college professors. These professors work with Strong, Incorporated, as consultants and with certain officials of Strong, Incorporated, on an advisory board set up to solve community problems.

    Because these people have doctoral degrees, indicating at least 19 years of formal education, letters directed to them should score at least 19 and preferably 20 on the Gunning Fog Index, or they will feel insulted. (When you asked Mr. Little why he included the figure 20, he replied that this group of professors seems to be unusually intelligent.)

2. Every writer is to check the readability score of every letter and memorandum during the next three months and prepare a report on his findings. If all written material scores within the recommended limitations, Mr. Little will assume that writers are doing a good job. He will also assume that writers who often exceed the recommended score of 12 are doing a poor job and will ask for their dismissal.

    The president of the organization, Sam Strong, describes himself as a ''self-made man.'' Although he did not finish high school, within the last 30 years he has built a multinational organization with thousands of employees. He started the business with $10,000 inherited from his grandfather.

    Mr. Strong, who received a copy of Mr. Little's memorandum, has never heard of readability formulas. He asked you to explain the whole situation to him. You go into his office to do so, but you are interrupted by Mr. Strong's secretary, who tells him about an important telephone call. He is to leave immediately for London. Because you plan to be on vacation when he returns, he asks you to put your explanation of Noah Little's memorandum in your own memorandum to him. He seems unsure of Mr. Little's policies.

    Prepare the memorandum to Mr. Strong. He has asked you to explain the meaning of the Gunning Fog Index and to include your evaluation of Mr. Little's policies. Is there other information that you should include? How should you go about writing the memorandum? Write it.

CHAPTER **7**

Planning the Report

Chapter Outline

The basis for a report is a problem. The research process, which ends with a written or oral presentation of research results, is the application of the scientific method of inquiry, or the scientific approach, to the solution of a problem.

The Scientific Method of Inquiry

The scientific method of inquiry, as it applies to the preparation of reports, consists of the following steps:

1. Determine the problem and define it in specific terms.
2. Collect essential facts pertaining to the problem.
3. Classify and organize data, with emphasis on processes, causes, and results.
4. Evaluate and interpret data in order to form generalizations toward the solution of the problem.
5. Select the most likely solution to the problem as indicated by factual evidence.

After completing the five general stages of the research process, present the solution, with reasons, explanations, and recommendations, in appropriate report form.

Plan the Research Study

The five steps given above are appropriate, valid, and necessary for research of any length and scope, resulting in a short memorandum report or a formal one of book length. For a comprehensive research study that is to result in a report of considerable length and importance, each of these steps should be thoroughly planned at the beginning of the research process and stated in a detailed written proposal, which is also described as the report plan or the research design.

Although a proposal, or a report plan, is of necessity only tentative, it serves as a guide from the beginning to the end of the report process. In addition, it is essential to the person or persons who authorize the report to keep track of the researcher's progress, often from short periodic reports during the completion of the major project. Proposals frequently are guides to funding requests, equipment and space estimates, and time or schedule allocations.

116

A written plan of procedure can be helpful when planning a short, informal study, even one that will result in a one- or two-page memorandum report. Although a preliminary written plan is not routinely required or expected for short reports, you save time and decrease errors by having a guide to the steps of the overall report process as they apply to the particular situation and the problem being investigated. A great deal of time can be saved by thinking through the process before beginning the study.

Be Objective and Decisive

In all situations, regardless of the complexity of the report, strive for objective analysis and interpretation of information. You should in no way be guided by the proposal or report plan to the extent that you interpret data in the light of expected findings and conclusions, a weakness that is all too common in research of any kind. Even if the problem statement is in the form of a hypothesis (to be discussed later in this chapter), do not set out to find facts to prove or disprove the hypothesis. Although this type of research occurs more often than it should, it by no means meets the standards of the scientific method of inquiry. The competent researcher finds all available facts, within the scope of the definition of the report problem, and interprets these facts without regard to expected or desired outcomes.

The solutions, wise or unwise, to many of the problems we face in our personal and business lives are reached without formal research resulting in a report. At times, we think about a problem without making a decision; that is, we stop somewhere in our scientific approach before reaching a solution. Refusing to make a decision is in effect making one—that the decision is to be postponed. This may be the best solution at the particular time. Like all other decisions, it should be preceded by adequate and objective investigation and analysis. More often, an inability to reach a reasonable conclusion and solution is due to weaknesses somewhere in the preceding phases of research.

Be Specific

The first step, determining and defining the problem in specific terms, is essential to the success of the remaining steps of the research process. If the problem cannot be stated in descriptive, specific, written words, it is not yet clearly in mind.

A Problem-Solving Situation

The word *research*, like the even broader term *communication*, applies to almost everything we do. As we attempt to solve ever-occurring problems, large and small, we engage in a form of research, although much of it is far from objective and scientific.

Suppose, for example, that you are driving to work and find that there is a severe traffic jam on the street you usually travel. Under ordinary conditions this street is the most direct route to your office. You have an important appointment at 9:15, and it is now 8:15. If normal traffic conditions prevailed, you could reach your office in half an hour.

Your problem is—what to do? Should you wait here and hope that the stalled automobiles will move on, or should you detour, provided you can work yourself onto a side street? (A comparable business problem would be to decide whether an organization should continue with a successful method of operation or, because of unexpected difficulties, change the method of operation.) Will the more indirect route, which is ordinarily slower because of school zones, residential areas, and stop lights, provide a quicker method of reaching the office?

You do not put this statement into written form, but, on a simple level, this situation compares to a problem you face when you undertake a business research project: You state the problem, choose a method of solution, collect and organize data, evaluate and interpret its meaning, and arrive at a solution to the problem, whether or not this solution is the best one.

Using this example, however, you usually undertake the action and find the data at the same time—that is, you embark on the assumed solution and collect and organize the data in your mind as you move along. Then your report is presented orally to your employer or associates when you arrive at the office. As you meander through the side streets or wait in your automobile in the traffic jam, you are collecting data as you keep track of the time. This may be unfavorable data, but you made your choice when you turned off the main thoroughfare or decided to wait.

Some business, professional, and government organizations seem to make their decisions in just this way; they go ahead and turn, or remain immobile on a jammed street, and figure out as time passes whether or not they made the right decision.

When you have more time and a serious problem, you cannot afford to operate in this way. Assuming you do have the time, what kind of research could you do? You could study the maps and determine the mileage by both routes. You could turn your automobile radio to the station that reports traffic conditions; perhaps you can learn the extent of the traffic blockage and when the street can be expected to be back to normal. Perhaps the radio voice could tell you something of the traffic conditions on the side streets you are considering. If you have telephone or radio contact with your office, you could find out how important it is that you arrive at the regular time, for perhaps the important appointment you are hurrying to has been cancelled for some reason, or perhaps it could be delayed.

This question, however, is not relevant to your subquestion of which route will provide the quickest trip to the office; it does apply to the question that you started with—what to do. These questions should not be analyzed together, but ones such as these tend to become jumbled as we find ourselves entangled in a problem or, especially, when putting the report into written form.

In the problem-solving situation, you would collect all this information, analyze it for its validity and applicability, and arrive at a conclusion upon which you would make your recommendation of the better choice of the two courses of action.

Your conclusion has been based partly upon inferences. If the radio voice has told you of a three-car accident that is blocking all lanes of traffic, you infer that it will be some time before your regular route is ready for travel. Your calculations of the mileage by both routes can be considered a fact if you are sure that the mapmakers were accurate—but then this assumption is also an inference. (Even though we can never be completely sure of most things, we must treat some inferences as if they were facts, at least until we have time to investigate them further.)

Reasonable inferences supported by sufficient facts may serve as a basis for recommendations, although at times these recommendations will be incorrect. Your value judgments, unsupported by facts, should not be used as a basis for recommendations. From a practical business standpoint, the fact that the side streets that make up the indirect route are more picturesque is not relevant to your question of which way to drive to the office. Your appreciation of flowering trees and clumps of daffodils is a value judgment, although many people would agree with you.

A form of secondary research would be for you to call to a person in the next car: "Sir, have you ever driven down Flamingo Street to Cherry, then to Rhodes and Barron, and then on Lamar to downtown?" If he has driven this route recently, his advice would be similar to that you might find in a business journal, located through *Business Periodicals Index*, of how another business organization solved a problem similar to the one you are now trying to solve. In all instances, you should use secondary research sources if they are available in order to take advantage of the experiences of other persons. To do otherwise is the same as reinventing the wheel each time we need a new wheelbarrow.

As you may have realized, much of successful business research and report writing is the application of mere common sense. But then common sense should not be qualified as "mere."

Determining and Defining the Problem

A problem exactly stated is a problem well on the way to being solved. Determining that a problem exists is not difficult from the standpoint of knowing that something is wrong or needs improvement. Stating in specific terms exactly what you wish to determine in a particular research study, as an aid to the solution of the problem, is more difficult.

Perhaps several studies of a problem within an organization will be necessary before a major issue is resolved, and perhaps your particular report is planned to cover only one factor of a major question. Or your study may be a comprehensive one with several contributing factors: if this is the case, you are in effect investigating a number of questions and combining the answers into a solution of the larger problem.

If the research project has been assigned to you, as ordinarily it will be, make sure that you and the person who authorized the report are in complete agreement about the purpose of the report, including limitations and boundaries of the study—exactly what you are and are not attempting to find out. You will also need to discuss cost considerations.

Other items of information that you must have before proceeding with the research process are these:

- What has been done in the past on this problem? Have previous reports been prepared? If so, where are they? Were recommendations, if any, put into effect? If so, were they successful? If they were not put into effect, why not?
- In addition to previous reports, if any, what other internal data are available?
- Who is likely to have more information on this particular subject?
- What use is to be made of this report? How the report will be used is not the same as your stated purpose; the purpose, or problem, is the question you are trying to solve by finding relevant information and interpreting that information. The report may be filed away, or it may be presented to a committee for further consideration, or recommended changes may be put into effect.
- When is the report needed?
- What limitations apply as to time, money, and facilities?
- What are the exact terms of the contract or assignment? If the study is a part of your regular employment responsibilities, the agreement is not likely to be referred to as a contract. A letter of authorization, followed by the researcher's letter of acceptance, serves as a written agreement as to what is to be done. If you are working as a consultant for a firm other than your own, you should have a written contract. Written specifications should be complete and exact.

Problem Statements: Informational Reports

Statements of purpose, described in preceding sections of this chapter, apply to analytical reports; they are planned to solve problems by analyzing information provided by research.

Definitely worded statements of purpose are also necessary for comprehensive reports that are merely informational; for example:

```
Problem Statement: To present a summary of outside employment
activities of teachers in the College of Business Administration,
Washington University, during the school year 1990-91.
```

The wording of the statement of purpose for any report can be presented in slightly different forms, as:

```
The purpose of this report is to present a summary of outside . . .
```

or

```
This report will summarize outside employment activities of
teachers . . .
```

Notice that *This report will summarize . . .* is appropriate for a proposal, or report plan, prepared at the beginning of the report process. In the final report, the sentence should read: *This report summarizes . . .*

As for analytical reports, subtopics are necessary for comprehensive informational reports. For example, a breakdown into factors of the preceding statement of purpose might include:

Teaching in other institutions
Seminars and conferences
Speaking engagements
Consulting
Writing
Other self-employment
Other paid activities

Other statements of purpose for informational reports will include those that are used for presenting results of historical research and descriptive research. *Historical research,* as the term indicates, presents information about the past; *descriptive research* ordinarily depicts present conditions, situations, activities, facilities, or circumstances.

Hypotheses: Analytical Reports

A hypothesis is a statement to be proved or disproved as a result of research; for example:

```
Employee morale will be strengthened and absenteeism decreased by
providing career apparel at company expense.
```

A null hypothesis would be worded in this way:

```
No significant difference in employee morale or absenteeism will
occur by providing career apparel at company expense.
```

The use of a null hypothesis is sometimes considered more scientific than the positive because a positive statement supposedly indicates that the researcher has already decided upon what the results will be. Nevertheless, bias can occur regardless of the wording of a hypothesis.

The declarative hypothesis states that a relationship exists between stated variables. A null hypothesis states that no relationship exists between stated variables. By stating a hypothesis, a researcher makes an assumption about the final answer, or solution, to the problem statement. Through the research process of gathering and analyzing data, the assumption stated in the hypothesis may be proved correct or incorrect, or the data may be inconclusive so that the hypothesis must be rejected.

Not all research is of the type that can be exactly formulated in terms of hypotheses. Notice that in the illustration given above, judging employee morale is a task difficult to prove or disprove to the extent that a hypothesis can be definitely tested. This business problem can be "solved," however, to the extent that the person or persons responsible for putting the research results into effect are reasonably sure that the recommended course of action is advisable. Other kinds of problems, particularly those that can be tested for a statistical significant difference, are suitable for statements of purpose in the form of a hypothesis.

Other Problem Statements: Analytical Reports

If the report is assigned, as it ordinarily will be, the report writer must know exactly what is wanted.

The questions that newspaper reporters are taught to ask—*who, what, where, when, why, and how*—apply to business report writing. Why is the report requested? Who will read it? When is this information needed? How will this information be used? Where can this information be obtained? And, most important of all, exactly what am I trying to find out?

Your answer to this last problem is your starting point, the statement of the problem. This statement of the problem may be broken into subquestions to include the answers to who, what, why, when, where, or how. All these questions must be considered together when determining and putting into an exactly written statement the problem you are trying to solve.

We face major and minor problems in all phases of our work and personal life; the difficulty arises in knowing what to include in the particular research study, for problems tend to overlap. If the statement of the problem cannot be put into definite words and stated in question form, it is not yet clearly defined. If the problem remains vague, general, and undetermined, planning helpful research, finding a solution, and reporting the solution will be difficult indeed.

This initial step of defining the problem should be discussed with whoever assigns the report. The exact purpose must be agreed upon by the person or persons who authorize the report and the person who undertakes the completion of the report.

Often the statement of the problem is used as the first sentence of the introductory section of the report itself. Notice the specific wording of the following problem statements:

> The purpose of this report is to examine all costs and revenues in the movement of sugar from the South Coast Sugar Mill in Matthews, Louisiana, and to determine whether it is profitable for the J&K Distributors to transport it with its own equipment.[1]

Although this statement is not now worded in question form, notice that it could be: "Is it profitable for the J&K Distributors to initiate a self-haul program for sugar from. . . ."

Should Countrywide Insurance Company purchase career apparel for its women employees?

Should Marketing Consultants, Inc. move from their present location in Commerce Square to the office building in Dillard Square?

Should Countrywide Insurance Company replace presently owned computers, on the established three-year trade-in basis, for computers using advanced operating systems?

Should the Seligman Realty Company continue the present method of door-to-door rent collection or establish a system of collection by mail?

Are the services and purposes of the local Chamber of Commerce well known to the citizens of the city?

Which kinds of books (recent fiction, older fiction, classics, general nonfiction, textbooks) are most widely circulated in the Whitehaven Branch Library?

Should the Advance Business School offer a course to prepare presently employed secretaries to work in the legal profession?

1. Ralph P. Smith, "Costs Involved in Buying and Maintaining 15 Semi Trucks and Tank Rigs," unpublished management report, 1990.

```
Why are the sales of the Xtra-Ezy lawnmowers 56 percent less in
District I, on the average, than in District II?
```

All the questions given above are overall statements of the problem, which should be broken down into subcategories near the beginning of the report process. For example, the question about career apparel could be detailed in this way. (We know from the wording of the title that the report is limited to women employees. Perhaps male employees are already in uniform or they have voted not to wear uniforms—or perhaps this study is to be left until later.)

```
Should Countrywide Insurance Company purchase career apparel for its
women employees?
```

- What are the benefits
  to the employer?
  to the employees?
  to the customer?
- What are the disadvantages?
- What is the approximate cost?
- Do the benefits to be derived outweigh the cost consideration and
  any other disadvantages?
- Where can this apparel be purchased?
- If this change in procedure is put into effect, how should it be
  administered?

As much as possible, think through the complete problem-solving process before you begin. Although the outline you draw up will be a tentative one, it is far better than none at all.

Limiting the Problem

The boundaries of a research problem are referred to as the *scope. Delimitations,* another term used instead of scope, describes specifically excluded factors which might have been expected in the report.

The term *limitations* is used to refer to situations or handicaps, such as the lack of time or money, that prevented a complete research study or a thorough presentation.

These considerations, especially as they are presented in the introductory section of a formal report, are discussed further in Chapter 15. In this book, the term *scope* is used to indicate boundaries; *limitations,* at least as the word is used as a description of a part of the final report, indicates limiting or detrimental factors.

However these terms are used as headings of a report, the scope of a report problem must be limited by exact and definite boundaries. We consider the scope in order to state the problem in definite and specific wording, as well as to plan research procedures.

Look back at some of the preceding problem statements. Notice that these statements also include boundaries. For example, the problem statement about Xtra-Ezy lawnmowers indicates that the study will be concerned only with District I and District II, not with other districts. We are concerned only with sales, not with other aspects of the two districts, unless these other aspects influence sales in some way, as they may. Only the one product is to be considered.

This problem statement would be improved if it also included an indication of the time span; for example, why have sales for the last year been 56 percent less? If this time element is not specified in the general problem statement, it must be included early in the report along with such information as the description of methods and sources of information.

In this report situation, you are trying to find the *why;* you are also looking for the *how,* or how the sales can be increased in the slow district. You have the *what* and the *where:* the product and the two districts. The *who* consists of the personnel in the two districts, or perhaps in the general management or in the home office. The *when* is the span of time being studied. The problem is not clearly stated until the scope is definitely and specifically defined.

A Tentative Report Plan

Before beginning research to find the answer to a predetermined business problem, consider preparing a report plan, even though it must be a tentative one. Such an outline of procedure, although it will perhaps be changed during the research process, provides a far more efficient method of approach than having no plan at all. This preliminary plan, which should be specifically worded and prepared in written form, is often referred to as a proposal if it is to be presented to another person or persons for approval. A similar report plan is useful for informational reports, as well as for analytical ones.

This preliminary step to the research and reporting process is referred to here as a report plan, not a proposal, for you will need such a plan whether or not it is presented for the approval of others. When preparing proposals, which may be for business, government, professional, or educational research, you may find that a specified format and arrangement are required, including an estimate of cost.

When a specified format is expected, it is most important that you follow it exactly, just as you adhere to a particular and specified format for the reporting itself. Basically, though, a report plan or proposal is likely to consist of the types of information discussed here, which are in turn based on the steps to a solution of a research problem.

The report plan should include the following sections:

1. A specific statement of the purpose of the report, including, if necessary, subcategories. (See the report problem used earlier: Should Countrywide Insurance Company provide career apparel for its women employees?) Try to word the statement of purpose so that the scope (or boundary) of your research is apparent. If you cannot do so, include a separate statement—or paragraphs, as needed—to make clear exactly what you intend to do.

2. Methods of finding information to lead to a solution to the problem. A tentative bibliography may be included in this section.

3. Methods of organizing, evaluating, and interpreting the data in order to reach a solution. Although this step will not be necessary for all report plans and proposals, it is essential in some situations. If the methods consist only of looking at the data, determining what they mean, and putting them into report form, then these duties can logically be assumed without a definite statement in the report plan. If the data are to be analyzed statistically, or in any special or unusual manner, these methods should be stated.

4. A tentative presentation of the report. This step, like the one preceding, will not be required of many proposals or report plans, but it is helpful to you for your own planning and is also useful in class assignments. Although you cannot determine the exact outline until you have completed the research or even later, a beginning outline keeps you from going too far astray in your thinking or in working toward a solution.

This tentative outline is also a tentative table of contents, with the headings of the main divisions of the report based upon the subdivisions of the problem statement. In the report about Countrywide Insurance and career apparel, the divisions of the problem statement (benefits, disadvantages, cost, etc.) are logical divisions of the final report.

In addition to the preceding items to be included in the report plan, state specifically in written form, if only for your own use, the answer to these questions:

- Is this report to be analytical or merely informational?
- Is it to be formal or informal, considering both the format and the writing style?
- Is it to be written in the personal or the impersonal tone?

The example shown in Figure 7–1 should not be considered as the only possible report plan or proposal. In some instances certain of the

```
PLAN OF PROPOSED REPORT

Tentative title:   SHOULD THE CHICKASAW BRANCH OF
                   COUNTRYWIDE INSURANCE COMPANY
                   CONVERT FROM GENERALIST SECRETARIES
                   TO AN INFORMATION AND WORD PROCESSING AND
                   ADMINISTRATIVE SUPPORT CENTER?

Author: Herbert L. Collins, Director of Personnel and Training

Statement of Purpose: The purpose of this report is to explore the possibilities
of information and word processing and administrative support operations for the
Chickasaw Branch of Countrywide Insurance Company and to determine the feasibility
of converting to a word processing system. The study is necessary because of
rapidly increasing costs in administrative operations and an increased volume of
typewriting and related printing.

Scope: This study deals primarily with the potential for an information and word
processing system to cut secretarial administrative costs by increasing the
productivity of each secretary through specialization. Not included in this
research is a complete analysis of the most desirable equipment, as presently
owned equipment will be adequate at the beginning of the operation and possibly
for some time to come. Another aspect of the problem not considered is the exact
nature of the training to be provided to secretaries and executives. Also excluded
is consideration of the increase or decrease in morale because of the conversion
to word processing. A basic premise that cannot be considered in this research
study is that efficiency and economy are achieved, more so than by any other
element, through capable, efficient, and dedicated personnel.

Limitations: Professional consultation on information and word processing needs is
not available in this city except from vendors of equipment. The cost of
consultation with professionals from outside the city would exceed the amount
considered reasonable for this preliminary study.

Readers: Anna Rose Tatum, President of Countrywide Insurance Company, and Lynn G.
Bertagna, Manager of Chickasaw Branch.

Sources and Methods of Collecting Data: Secondary sources will be used to provide
information about information and word processing systems used in other firms,
types of equipment available as compared to present equipment at Chickasaw Branch,
and costs of typewriting by present and proposed systems. A tentative bibliography
is attached to this report plan.

Interviews with management and secretarial personnel will be conducted in order to
learn the general functions now being performed and the percentage of time spent
in each function.
```

Figure 7–1. *Example of a tentative report plan.*

```
Sales representatives from IBM, Wang, Xerox, and AT&T will be consulted as to the
advisability of establishing an information and word processing center, although
no further equipment is to be purchased immediately. Telephone or on-site
interviews will be conducted with office managers and supervisors in local
companies that now use information and word processing systems similar to the
proposed one.

Tentative Table of Contents of Report: (see attached outline)
```

Figure 7–1. *continued*

items shown here may be omitted, and others not shown here may be needed. In all instances, include purpose, methods, and sources of data.

An introduction to a formal report, containing similar information to that shown in Figure 7–1, is included in Chapter 15 with the discussion of the arrangement and content of a completed report.

A Tentative Table of Contents

A tentative table of contents is shown in Figure 7–2. If you prefer, refer to such an outline *as* an outline, as you have done when planning papers for other purposes. Regardless of how you describe it, such a written plan for the material to be included and the order of presentation will aid throughout the research, interpretation, and writing processes.

A complete report plan, including a tentative table of contents, facilitates the preparation of the introduction (often described by another title) of a formal report arranged in the inductive (or indirect) order. A complete report plan *becomes* the introductory section of the report itself, after appropriate modifications in wording and changes to reflect any final deviations from the original plan.

Read the headings of the tentative table of contents shown in Figure 7–2. Notice that the researcher has, in effect, stated a hypothesis, a prediction of the results of the study. The competent and conscientious researcher will not be influenced by these statements, just as stating a hypothesis, or a null hypothesis, has no bearing on thorough and objective research and analysis. Some readers of such preliminary statements, however, would interpret them to mean that the researcher's mind is already made up, regardless of findings, and that the results of the research are likely to reflect this nonobjective attitude. Headings as shown could be easily changed so that they would not predict the outcome; for example,

```
                    TENTATIVE TABLE OF CONTENTS

           (An Outline of Possible Divisions of Completed Report)

PURPOSE, SOURCES, AND METHODS OF RESEARCH
   Purpose
   Scope
   Limitations
   Sources and Methods of Collecting Data
   Basic Plan of Presentation

WHY INFORMATION AND WORD PROCESSING SHOULD BE CONSIDERED
   What Is Information Processing?
   What Has Word Processing Done for Other Firms?

PROPOSED PERSONNEL CHANGES WITH INFORMATION AND WORD PROCESSING
   Secretarial Staff Can Be Reduced from Ten to Eight
   Career Patterns Can Be Established for Secretaries

ECONOMY AND EFFICIENCY THROUGH INFORMATION AND WORD PROCESSING
   Functions and Costs Prior to Word Processing
   Functions and Costs with Word Processing

WHY COUNTRYWIDE INSURANCE COMPANY SHOULD INSTALL AN INFORMATION AND WORD
   PROCESSING CENTER
```

Figure 7–2. *Sample tentative table of contents.*

in the third major section the heading ''Secretarial Staff Can Be Reduced from Ten to Eight'' could be changed to ''Can the Secretarial Staff Be Reduced?''

If you are preparing a tentative table of contents as a class assignment preliminary to a research project, ask for your instructor's advice as to whether wordings of headings should reflect outcomes. In any event, it is not necessary that headings do so, even in the finished report, although they are an aid to readability and serve as a summary of the entire report. Your instructor may also ask that you prepare a tentative introduction at this time, although, for the most part, it is merely a repetition of the report plan. As you complete the introduction of the final report, remember to make appropriate changes in wording from the report plan or introduction prepared early in the research process.

A Proposal

A report plan, such as the one illustrated in Figure 7–1, is a proposal for a research project. The terms *proposal, research proposal,* and *proposal report,* however, are ordinarily used to denote a longer and more formal written presentation than what is ordinarily described as a *report plan,* particularly a plan for a class report or a short, informal business report.

The parts of a report plan discussed and illustrated earlier in this chapter are also parts of a research proposal (using the term in its more formal sense), but the proposal usually requires further information in addition to that shown in Figure 7–1. The word *proposal* is used not only as an offer to supply services as a researcher, but also as an offer of other services, such as consultation, or as a bid on a contract.

A statement of purpose and a description of proposed methodology are essential in the written presentation of any report project. Other categories of information that are likely to be necessary for complete research proposals include an estimate of costs, perhaps with a long, detailed budget; qualifications of researchers and other personnel involved in the work; necessary equipment and facilities; a summary of previous research in the area to be studied, including a bibliography and perhaps a summary of all previous investigation; a detailed work schedule, including a date when the project is to be finished; provision for evaluation of the entire project; and suggestions for continuing research.

The physical appearance of many proposals is somewhere between the simple report plan illustrated in Figure 7–1 and a complete formal report illustrated in Chapter 15. Proposals may be presented in letter, memorandum, or manuscript format, as illustrated by the short reports shown in Chapters 3 and 4. A long proposal should begin with an abstract, which is similar to the synopsis discussed in Chapter 15 and shown with a formal report. Like a synopsis (sometimes the terms are used interchangeably), an abstract summarizes the main idea of the report or proposal, with emphasis on the overall purpose and expected results. An abstract provides an immediate answer as to what the longer proposal is about and thus increases readability.

Solicited and Unsolicited Proposals

Proposals are *solicited* or *unsolicited.* Solicited proposals are submitted in response to requests for such proposals, which are often in the form of printed announcements. Unsolicited proposals are originated by the person or persons who submit them.

Requests for proposals come from government agencies, educational institutions, foundations, business and professional organizations, many other groups, and from individuals. Announcements that request proposals may include detailed, specific instructions on how the proposals are to be submitted, arranged, and written. These instructions should be followed exactly.

Unsolicited proposals differ little from solicited ones, although they may be more difficult to prepare because of the lack of guidelines. If no information is provided, the proposal should be prepared in the most easily read format and in the arrangement that seems most likely to obtain the desired results because of the proper use of emphasis.

All the attributes of effective writing apply to the preparation of proposals of any kind. Organization, conciseness, and readability are of particular importance. As in all communication, your ideas are most likely to be accepted if your readers are convinced that what you propose will meet their needs and desires.

Suggested Content of a Proposal

The sequence of information shown in Figure 7–1 can be adapted and expanded to serve as a research proposal. Such a proposal might contain the following areas of content:

1. A *cover sheet* that shows the following items:
   a. title of the proposal;
   b. name of the person, with position and organization, to whom the proposal is submitted;
   c. any necessary identifying numbers or phrasing to show that the proposal is in response to a particular announcement or set of specifications;
   d. person or persons submitting the proposal, with name, position, employing organization, address, and telephone number;
   e. date the report is submitted.
2. An *abstract* that summarizes the entire proposal.
3. A *table of contents* if one would be helpful.
4. An *introductory or background section,* provided that such information is necessary before going directly to the statement of purpose.
5. A specifically worded *statement of purpose* with necessary subcategories.
6. A *summary of related research.*
7. *Procedures,* which may also be described as *Methodology, Methods and Sources,* or *Sources of Data.*
8. *Personnel* to be involved in the project, with a summary of their background and qualifications.
9. *Facilities* and *equipment* to be used in the project.

10. *Cost estimate,* which may necessitate a long, detailed budget and a firm contractual maximum.
11. *Provision for reporting results.*
12. *Provision for evaluation of research.*
13. Provision for putting results into effect.
14. *Suggestions* for probable further research.

The suggested sections of a proposal can be modified in various ways according to the purpose of the research, readers, overall length, and specified format.

Summary

The scientific method of inquiry, or the scientific approach, as it applies to the preparation of reports, consists of the following steps: (1) determining the problem and stating it in specific terms; (2) collecting data; (3) classifying and organizing data; (4) evaluating and interpreting data; and (5) determining the most likely solution to the stated problem as indicated by factual evidence.

After completing the five general stages of the research process, the researcher presents the solution, with reasons, explanations, and recommendations, in appropriate report form.

The basis of a report is a problem. The first and most important step in the report process is determining what the problem is and stating it exactly, with necessary and helpful subcategories.

The report writer should think through the complete problem-solving process before beginning the research project, even though the plans will be somewhat tentative. As a guide to further steps, a written report plan saves time and keeps the researcher on track. A report plan, or proposal, is often submitted to another person, or to a group, for approval.

Questions and Problems

1. For each of the following problem situations, state the problem (purpose), either in the form of a question or as an infinitive phrase. For example, a report planned to study the advisability of providing career apparel can be stated as:

Should the Countrywide Insurance Company provide career apparel for its women employees? *(Question)*

Purpose: To determine whether the Countrywide Insurance Company should provide career apparel for its women employees. *(Infinitive phrase)*

Be specific, but omit subcategories of the problem. Assume necessary and reasonable details, including names.

    a. A restaurant manager wants to know how to improve crowded conditions at the midday meal.

    b. A restaurant manager wants to know how to increase profits on the midday meal.

    c. A restaurant manager wants to know the choices most often made from the luncheon menu.

    d. College professors are trying to decide whether to authorize monthly deductions from their paychecks for deposit in a tax-sheltered annuity fund.

    e. The professors have decided to invest in a tax-sheltered annuity fund, but they do not know which one to choose.

    f. An officer manager must choose a copying machine.

    g. Study what hardware and software facilities are necessary to install the "HyperCard" and/or "HyperVision" developments in our headquarter's office systems.

    h. A Chamber of Commerce wants to know what local citizens think of the Chamber's services and purposes.

    i. A dean of a college of business administration wants to determine the business course or courses that alumni believe to have been the most beneficial.

    j. A discount department store wants to know something of its "image."

    k. A large construction company is considering adopting a pension plan.

    l. The Park Commission is thinking of piping in music to all offices.

    m. A manufacturer needs to know how to market a new product, a compact refrigerator-icemaker.

2. For one or more of the problem situations listed in Question 1, state the problem in the form of a null hypothesis.

3. Choose a question that you wish to investigate in order to report the results in the formal business report. Prepare a tentative report plan, as shown in this chapter. Include a tentative title, statement of purpose, scope (or scope and limitations), readers, and sources and methods of collecting data.

4. Prepare a tentative table of contents for the research you planned in Question 3.

5. Assign a committee to investigate the air quality conditions in the information systems room. Outline the problems and conditions in the facilities and assess the "No Smoking" rules.

CHAPTER **8**

Gathering Information from Secondary Sources

Chapter Outline

In the preceding chapter, emphasis was upon the first steps of the report process: determining the problem, defining it in specific terms, and deciding upon the methods of finding a solution to the problem. This chapter moves to what is ordinarily the next step in the report process: gathering information from secondary sources.

The Importance of Secondary Research

Sources of data are described as being *secondary* or *primary*. The word *secondary* is used to mean that data have already been gathered and recorded by someone else. Because much of this information is in published form and available in libraries, secondary research is often referred to as library research. Secondary data, however, include unpublished material and can be found in places other than a library, often in the files of your own company. Unpublished sources include reports of various kinds, dissertations, brochures, booklets, operating and procedures manuals, and texts of public speeches.

Primary is the term used to describe data that have not already been gathered and recorded by someone else. Primary data are obtained through observation, experimentation, and surveys. Surveys employ the use of questionnaires and formal or informal interviews done in person or by telephone.

Distinguish Between Primary and Secondary Data

Distinguishing between primary and secondary data is far more important than merely knowing the meaning of the terms. Whenever you use another's material in any way, you are professionally and ethically obligated to give credit to the originator of that material. Customary methods of documentation, along with a brief discussion of copyright laws with their "fair use" provisions, are given in Chapter 12. No other consideration in research and report writing is more vital than the precept of giving credit where credit is due.

Begin with Secondary Research

Secondary research should ordinarily be the starting point in the data-gathering process. Regardless of the problem you are trying to solve, similar ones are likely to have occurred in other organizations or with other individuals. The solutions to these problems may be reported in business periodicals or elsewhere. Although these problems will be at least slightly different from your own, your knowledge of what other individuals and organizations have concluded in similar situations can help to answer your own questions.

We must build on the experience of others because there is no time to do otherwise. You should not spend time in completing a research project that has already been done unless you want to check the validity and reliability of the previous research study, expand upon it in some way, or update it.

For example, if a construction company needs to know the rate of increase or decrease in housing starts or in the price of an average new house in a given city, the researcher will find that recent studies have already been made of these questions, as well as of many others that often arise when a company plans its operations. Chambers of Commerce, government agencies, colleges and universities, and professional organizations are engaged continuously in such research and in reporting their findings for the benefit of business organizations and the public in general.

Library research should not be thought of as only supplemental, even for reports to be based mostly on primary data of one kind or another. In addition to finding specific information that applies directly to your problem, you may be able to obtain a general overview of the entire question you are investigating. Secondary research at the beginning of the report-writing process provides ideas for other methods of investigation. In addition, as you examine what seem to be the most relevant library sources, you are likely to be referred to other references, often better ones.

Finding Specialized Information

A large library can be confusing and frustrating even to experienced researchers. You may feel that you are surrounded by billions of words, all of which have absolutely nothing to do with the problem you are investigating. Although it is quite possible that the exact information for which you are searching is unavailable, it is more likely that helpful information is somewhere in the library—if you can only find it. Because of the rapidly increasing numbers of books, periodicals, and other reference and reading sources, developing skills in locating information is absolutely essential.

Numerous data search computer packages exist now and many company and university libraries are becoming computerized. Some of the more common services include card catalog search programs, references available search programs (ERIC, InfoTrac, Wilsonline, BYLINE), and specific search and retrieval databases.

Do you know how to find specialized information? Suppose, for example, that you want to read recent articles on communication as it applies to management, especially communication from employees to management. Or, more specifically, suppose that you are investigating the question of whether to have fifteen-minute meetings of all employees at the beginning of each work day. Where would you go to find out what benefits other organizations have derived from such meetings? Do you know the names of government publications that supply data about retail and wholesale trade, construction, agriculture, employment, and many other kinds of business information?

Can you find a list of all books on report writing that have been published during the past two years? Can you quickly determine the names of books written by any particular writer and whether or not these books are still available for purchase? Can you find out whether your particular library owns these books? Do you know how to locate articles that have appeared in business journals about the organization to which you are submitting an employment application? Can you find the names of articles that have appeared in *Reader's Digest* in 1986 on the subject of inflation, without having the 1986 magazines available?

Do you know the leading business periodicals in your particular field of study? Does your school library subscribe to these periodicals? Where are past issues stored, and have they been bound or reproduced on microfilm? Which method of classification does your library use, the Library of Congress system or the Dewey decimal system? Where is the reference room? Does the library have open stacks? In addition to printed material, what other library sources are available, such as sound cassettes, films, film strips, transparancies, videocassettes, sound on page, disk data or "Hyper" data? Does your library provide databases, including *ABI/Inform*, on compact laser disks?

What is the *Business Periodicals Index?* What information will you find in *Moody's Manuals?* In addition to your school library, how many other libraries are available in your city or community for your use? Does your own company have a library? What information is made available by your local Chamber of Commerce?

Answers to some of the preceding questions are given below.

Basic Reference Sources

Only a few of the thousands of reference sources available can be listed in this book, but the following ones are likely to be most beneficial to you.

Bibliographies

The term *bibliography,* as used here to describe a reference source, means a complete or selective list of readings on a particular subject. Bibliographies have been prepared in many subject fields. They will be useful if they are specific enough for your particular purpose and are up to date. Bibliographies frequently accompany articles, books, master's theses and doctoral dissertations, research reports, and publications from trade and professional organizations.

One general source of bibliographies is:

> *Bibliographic Index: A Cumulative Bibliography of Bibliographies.* New York: H. W. Wilson Company, 1937 to date.

This index is organized by subject. It is a guide to books, articles, and other published sources that include a bibliography.

Investment Information Sources, Public Finance Information Sources, Real Estate Information Sources, and *Textile Industry Information Sources* are publications of Gale Research Company, which provides various other services to business.

General Guides to Business Research and Reference Materials

The following guides to business research and reference materials are helpful in finding or constructing bibliographies on business topics. They provide an overview of the process of finding secondary information and basic reference sources.

> *Encyclopedia of Business Information Sources,* 6th ed. James Woy, ed. Detroit: Gale Research Company, 7th ed. 1988.
>
> *How to Use the Business Library,* 5th ed. Herbert Webster Johnson. Cincinnati: South-Western Publishing Company, 1984.
>
> *Where to Find Business Information: A Worldwide Guide for Everyone Who Needs Answers to Business Questions,* 2d ed. David M. Brownstone and Gordon Carruth. New York: John Wiley and Sons, 1982.
>
> *Canadian Business and Economics: A Guide to Sources of Information.* Barbara Brown, ed. Ottawa: Canadian Library Association, 1984.
>
> *A Business Information Guidebook.* Oscar Figueroa and Charles Winkler. New York: AMACOM, 1980.
>
> *Directory of Business and Finance Services,* 7th ed. New York: Special Libraries Association, 1976.
>
> *Materials and Methods for Business Research.* Linda J. Piele, John C. Tyson, and Michael B. Sheffey. New York: Neal-Schuman, 1980.

In addition to the general guides to information listed above, many other reference sources are helpful to the researcher. *Libraries issue brochures or other printed guides to material on their own shelves and in other libraries.*

The Card Catalog and the On-Line Catalog

The card catalog (also referred to as the public catalog) of a library lists the material available at that particular library. Most libraries use divided catalogs where authors, titles, and subjects are alphabetized in two or three separate catalogs.

Catalogs in libraries may not be in card form at all. Most libraries now have fully automated systems with computer terminals for users to access the cataloging records. The on-line catalogs provide numerous advantages over the older card catalogs. Computer terminals are capable of displaying information about the thousands of books in a large library. They give more data about each book, including a description of its contents and whether it is available for immediate use.

Libraries usually classify books by either the Dewey decimal system or the Library of Congress system. The Library of Congress system provides for a larger number of divisions and is more suitable for large libraries than is the Dewey system.

The major classifications of the Dewey system are:

000—General Works
100—Philosophy
200—Religion
300—Social Sciences—Sociology
400—Philology
500—Pure Science
600—Useful Arts—Applied Science
700—Fine Arts—Recreation
800—Literature
900—History

The major classifications of the Library of Congress system are:

A—General Works
B—Philosophy and Religion
C—History—Auxiliary Sciences
D—Universal and Old World History
E,F—America
G—Geography, Anthropology, Folklore, Manners and Customs, Sports and Games
H—Social Sciences
J—Political Science
K—Law
L—Education
M—Music
N—Fine Arts

P—Language and Literature
Q—Science
R—Medicine
S—Agriculture
T—Technology
U—Military Science
V—Naval Science
Z—Bibliography and Library Science

Within the categories of both the Library of Congress system and the Dewey system, further divisions allow for more specific classifications. For example, books on business subjects are numbered 650–659 in the Dewey system and classified under HF (Commerce, General) in the Library of Congress system.

Knowing the subject classification of a topic you are investigating helps you find useful books simply by browsing the shelves of a library with open stacks. Although this method is admittedly casual and disorganized, it may provide information that you would not find otherwise. In addition, the books you discover, through their own bibliographies, indicate other relevant books.

Books shown in a card catalog in any one library obviously do not make up the same list of books as those shown in the *Cumulative* (International) *Book Index, Books in Print*, or similar indexes. Even the largest library is not likely to own all published books in any area or all that are currently available from publishers. In addition, the card catalog may show books, particularly old ones, that are not listed in the indexes. (These indexes and other sources are discussed in a following section of this chapter.)

If you are unsure of the most applicable subject heading, you may wish to refer to

> *Library of Congress Subject Headings,* 10th ed. Washington: Library of Congress, 1986.

The typical catalog card lists the classification number, author's name, title of publication, place of publication, date of publication, pagination, notes on special features such as bibliographies, and sometimes comments on contents of the book. The card also shows the other subject headings under which the book is filed; these headings serve as a guide to the most important content areas of the book.

Guides to Books

A major guide to books, whether or not they are in your particular library, is

> *Cumulative Book Index: A World List of Books in the English Language.*
> New York: H. W. Wilson, 1928–present.

Before 1928, this index was referred to as the *United States Catalog.* The *Cumulative Book Index* includes books published in the English language all over the world, recorded by author, title, and subject. Monthly indexes are bound into annual indexes.

Two guides to books on a particular topic are

> *Subject Guide to Books in Print.* New York: R. R. Bowker, 1957–present. This index, which also classifies books according to author and title, includes books currently available for purchase in the United States.
> *Canadian Books in Print.* Toronto: University of Toronto Press, 1975–present.

Encyclopedias

Although the scope of your research must include much more than information given in encyclopedias, they are a good place to begin because they give an overall view of a particular field or of supplementary aspects of a report project. Encyclopedias are useful for general background information. They may also include a list of supplementary reading materials for your particular topic.

In addition to general encyclopedias, a number of specialized ones are available for coverage of specialized areas of knowledge. Some of these are the *Encyclopedia of Social Science, Exporter's Encyclopedia, Accountant's Encyclopedia,* and *Encyclopedia of Banking and Finance.*

Dictionaries

Dictionaries remain an important library source. In addition to general dictionaries, there are many specialized ones, just as there are specialized encyclopedias. In fact, the terms are overlapping; one book described as an encyclopedia may be similar to another described as a specialized dictionary. Some books use *both dictionary and encyclopedia* in their titles.

Specialized business dictionaries are especially good for definitions of business terms. Two such books are listed below:

> *Concise Dictionary of Business Terminology.* Albert Giordana. Englewood Cliffs, N.J.: Prentice-Hall, 1981
> *Dictionary of Business and Management.* Jerry Rosenberg. New York: John Wiley and Sons, 1983.

Handbooks and Manuals

Handbooks are similar to specialized encyclopedias and dictionaries, although they tend to be more complete than dictionaries. A business handbook presents a condensed picture of an entire field of business.

These handbooks, which are frequently revised in order to retain only accurate information, include the *Handbook of Auditing Methods, Industrial Accountant's Handbook, Handbook of Business Administration, Handbook of Insurance, Management Handbook, Marketing Handbook, Sales Executives' Handbook,* and *Real Estate Handbook.* Many other manuals and handbooks are also available, such as the *United States Postal Manual* and the *United States Government Organizations Manual.*

Yearbooks and Almanacs

Yearbooks, in addition to those that supplement encyclopedias, are published by various countries, trades, and professions. One important one is the *Statistical Abstract of the United States.*

Almanacs, such as the widely available *World Almanac and Book of Facts,* contain a wealth of information on many subjects.

Canada Year Book, published by Statistics, Canada, provides economic data about many facets of Canadian business and government, as does *The Corpus Almanac of Canada.*

Biographical Directories

Biographical directories provide information about leaders or well-known persons, living or dead. The best known is *Who's Who in America,* which summarizes the lives of living Americans who have achieved prominence in any field. A similar reference source is *Canadian Who's Who.* Specialized directories include *Who's Who in Insurance, Who's Who in Education,* and *American Men and Women of Science,* as well as many other occupational fields. In addition to those that are specialized according to profession, directories are also specialized according to sections of the U.S.; for example, *Who's Who in the South and Southwest.*

Who's Who in Finance and Industry is a directory of prominent business people. Another directory is *Who's Who in Finance and Industry (Canada).* *Poor's Register of Corporations, Directors and Executives* is a similar publication but more exclusive. *The Biography Index,* published quarterly, is a guide to biographical material in books and magazines.

Business Services

Business services provide business information of many kinds. Some of these publications and service organizations are listed and described below.

Moody's Manuals summarize data for all major companies. These manuals include five divisions: Industrials, Banks and Finance, Public Utilities, Transportation, and Municipals and Government. Although much of the information is planned for the investor or for investors' advisors, much is meaningful to the business researcher in areas other than investments.

Information is provided about the history of each company, a description of products or services, locations of home office and most important plants, a list of officers and directors, and financial data.

Corporation Records, a loose-leaf publication of financial information and other facts about the corporations described, is published by Standard and Poor's Corporation.

Federal Taxes, published by Prentice-Hall, Inc., reprints U.S. government tax laws, rulings, and decisions, along with editorial comments.

Another well-known service organization is Predicasts, Inc., which provides various services in addition to forecasts and market data, classified by company, product, and service.

Many, if not all, of these business services are available through the use of databases as well as in printed form.

Guides to Periodicals and Pamphlets

Periodicals are often more helpful than books for use in business research. Thousands of publications in all fields cover every subject imaginable. Like information from books, data found in periodicals must be evaluated for appropriateness, reliability, and current value. Various indexes serve as a guide to the contents of general and specialized periodicals. Some of these indexes are listed and described below.

The *Reader's Guide to Periodical Literature* is a guide to articles in approximately 160 general-interest magazines such as *Reader's Digest, Good Housekeeping, Time, Newsweek, Business Week, Fortune, Atlantic,* and *Harper's.*

The *Business Periodicals Index* is a guide to articles in business, industrial, and trade magazines, including English language periodicals printed in Canada and elsewhere outside the United States. This index is one of the most useful in business research, particularly for the practical phases of business operations and for solutions to problems in specific industries. The *Business Periodicals Index* dates from 1958; its predecessor, the *Industrial Arts Index,* began publication in 1913. About 165 titles are indexed, including periodicals in accounting, advertising, banking, and all other major business and economic fields. The *Canadian Business Periodicals Index* has been published since 1975.

The *Applied Science and Technology Index* is a guide to articles in about 200 English language publications on scientific and technological subjects.

The *Public Affairs Information Service Bulletin,* referred to as PAIS, is an index, classified by subject, of periodicals, government publications, and pamphlets, especially in the area of economics and social conditions, public administration, and international affairs.

The F & S Index of Corporations and Industries (Predicasts, 1962 to date) covers company, product, and industry information from more than 750 financial publications, business-oriented newspapers, trade magazines, and special reports. The European edition and the International edition provide similar information about countries outside the United States, including U.S. company operations abroad. This index is a valuable reference source.

Other indexes of interest are the *Engineering Index, Education Index, Business Education Index, Biological and Agriculture Index, New York Times Index, Wall Street Journal Index,* and the index to *Fortune.* In addition, most large newspapers are indexed in guides available in local and regional libraries.

Even with the numerous indexes to periodicals, including others not listed here, some periodicals are not indexed, particularly regional and highly specialized ones. To find lists of publications in all fields, consult the *Ayer Directory of Publications, Standard Periodical Directory, Union List of Serials in Libraries of the United States and Canada, Ulrich's International Periodical Directory,* and other directories of publications.

These indexes are available through the use of databases.

Trade Directories

Thomas' Register of American Manufacturers and *Thomas' Register Catalog File* list thousands of products, with the names of companies that manufacture each product. *Encyclopedia of Associations,* the *Million Dollar Directory,* and *Middle Market Directory* are other publications that include specific information about various companies and associations.

Government Publications

Information of many kinds, especially statistical information, is collected and published by the federal government. Some of the sources already described, including PAIS, serve as guides to government publications.

United States Government Publications: Monthly Catalog lists publications issued by all branches of the federal government. This catalog serves as a guide to government publications in the same way that the public catalog (card catalog) serves as a guide to other publications.

Other sources that serve as guides to locating government publications are *American Statistics Index* (Congressional Service); *Guide to U.S.*

Government Publications by John L. Androit; *Statistical Services of the United States Government* (U.S. Bureau of the Budget); and *Statistics Sources,* published by Gale Research Company, which also includes sources of statistics other than government publications.

Sources mentioned in the preceding paragraph serve as *guides* to statistical information, not compilations of statistical information. Other government publications serve as direct sources of statistical information, particularly data gathered by the Bureau of the Census. One of the best known is *Statistical Abstract of the United States,* which is issued annually. Supplements to the *Statistical Abstract* include the *County and City Data Book, Historical Statistics of the United States,* and the *Congressional District Data Book.*

Other information provided by the Bureau of the Census is derived from the periodic censuses that have been taken by the United States government. The first Census of Population was taken in 1790, and it has been repeated at ten-year intervals since that time. The Bureau of the Census also conducts special censuses other than at the ten-year intervals and publishes the data collected. These include censuses of housing, agriculture, manufacturers, transportation, mineral industries, governments, retail trade, wholesale trade, and selected services.

Some governmental periodicals are issued monthly. These include *Survey of Current Business,* which provides data on income, expenditures, production, prices, and many other economic elements; the *Federal Reserve Bulletin,* which emphasizes financial data; *Monthly Labor Review,* with data on employment, wages, consumer price indexes, and other similar areas; and *Business Conditions Digest,* an aid to forecasters and business analysts.

Many other government periodicals include various other types of information. Regularly released statistical information is also available from state and local governments.

Miscellaneous Reference Sources

"A Survey of Consumer Buying Power" is published annually by *Sales Management* magazine. This survey reports estimates of figures on population, income, sales, and buying power of cities, counties, and standard metropolitan statistical areas. The *Editor and Publisher Market Guide* provides similar statistics.

Doctoral dissertations can be located through *American Doctoral Dissertations,* 1955/56 to present, and *Dissertation Abstracts International,* 1938 to present. *American Doctoral Dissertations* intends to provide a complete listing of all doctoral dissertations accepted by American and Canadian universities. Abstracts of the dissertations describe the dissertations and provide an overview of each, in addition to providing information on how to obtain a copy of the dissertation. Both of these guides are published by University Microfilms International, Ann Arbor, Michigan.

Another guide to business and economic research is *Index of Publications of Bureaus of Business and Economic Research,* 1957 to present, which is published by the Associated University Bureaus of Business and Economic Research.

Commercial Computerized Databases

Databases now provide valuable information for various research purposes. Many of the printed sources mentioned previously in this chapter also are available as databases to be accessed by computers, including microcomputers. These databases, along with other computer functions and capabilities, are discussed in Chapters 13 and 14. The following list is shown here because databases provide an important source of secondary information, with additional advantages of speed and ease of access.

The list of databases is far from complete, but it provides an illustration of the many and various kinds of information that are available as commercial computerized databases.

BCN (Business Computer Network, P.O. Box 36, 1000 College View Drive, Riverton, Wyoming 82510.)

BCN is a subscription service that provides access to a large number of different databases. The user is saved the time and trouble of signing up for each individual system. Among the databases that can be accessed through BCN are the following:

• BRS (Bibliographical Retrieval Service): Contains 70 separate databases covering education, engineering, medicine, behavioral sciences, and business-related subjects.

• DIALOG: Contains over 300 databases covering corporations, engineering and technology, law, medicine, agriculture, education, and physical sciences.

• INFOMAGIC: Contains statistical information relating to securities, economics, banking, finance, aviation and energy.

• DC (System Development Corporation): Contains 80 databases of bibliographic information on energy, chemistry, environmental concerns, law, patents, and political science.

• Securities Data Company: Contains reports on bonds, common and preferred stocks, and future issues.

COMPUSERVE (Computer Information Service, 5000 Arlington Centre Blvd., P.O. Box 20212, Columbus, Ohio 43220)

This service contains a wide variety of features for all users. There are on-line editions of some newspapers, a database (Business Information Wire) surveying 111 daily Canadian newspapers, CIS Business Wire—containing 40–50 news releases from major companies—and Standard & Poor's General Information File—containing data on 3000 major publicly held companies.

ITT DIALCOM (1109 Spring St., Silver Spring, Maryland 20910)

ITT DIALCOM is primarily an electronic mail system for sending and receiving letters, memorandums, and other documents. However, users can also access databases, including:

- UPI News: Contains news wire information and other governmental and broadcast information.
- BNA: Contains databases on business accounting and tax news and the text of the *Security and Exchange Commission News Digest.*

NEWSNET (945 Haverford Rd., Bryn Mawr, Pennsylvania 19010)

NEWSNET involves a business-oriented newsletter covering a variety of fields like advertising, gas and oil, government, and technology. It can be searched and read on-line.

DOW JONES NEWS/RETRIEVAL (P.O. Box 300, Princeton, New Jersey 08540)

This is a collection of databases that covers securities and economic news. Users can access current news, current stock prices, historical stock performance, corporate earnings estimations, economic surveys, and excerpts from the *Wall Street Journal* and *Wall Street Week,* among others.

THE SOURCE (1616 Anderson Rd., McLean, Virginia 22102)

THE SOURCE contains a large number of personal, recreational, and business databases, as well as other computer functions. It is a menu-driven system by which the user can progressively narrow the search for desired information. Some of the relevant databases include Commodity News Service, and on-line abstracts from *Forbes, Futurist, Venture, Harvard Business Review.*

INFOTRAC (Information Access Company, 11 Davis Drive, Belmont, California 94002)

Computerized database, disk-based, includes current references for 550 business journals, multisubject search and key word use; is userfriendly. Free.

NIKKE: TELECOM (Nihon Keizai Shimbun, Inc., 1–9–5 Otemachi, Chiyodq-Ku, Tokyo 100, Japan)

English edition of Japanese business and published sources. Includes 12 business databases and daily international market reports.)

NATIONAL NEWSPAPER INDEX (Information Access Company, 11 Davis Drive, Belmont, California 94002)

Latest three months of newspaper reports and articles.

WILSON LINE INDEXES (H. W. Wilson Company, 950 University Avenue, Bronx, New York 10452)

Includes 450 general and business periodicals—30 percent overlap with INFOTRAC; includes 150 references in social sciences.

U.S. GOVERNMENT DOCUMENTS (Superintendent of Documents, U.S. Government Printing Office, Washington, D.C. 20402)

Monthly update of all U.S. Government publications.

A particularly valuable database for business research is ABI/Inform, which indexes more than 800 periodicals. It is likely to be available in libraries, stored on read-only compact laser disks and displayed on the screens of computer terminals. It provides information similar to that in *Business Periodicals Index,* but it is far more comprehensive. In addition, it includes abstracts of journal articles, not mere listings. Terms may be combined in order to narrow research topics.

A Library Search Procedure

Suppose that you are authorized to complete the research and to prepare the report for the question presented in Chapter 7, "Should Countrywide Insurance Company provide career apparel for women employees?" Subcategories for this problem are given in Chapter 7, with details for the scope of the problem.

You realize that you cannot depend upon library research alone if the study is to be beneficial for a special purpose and for the particular company for which the research is planned. The researcher obtained the opinions of workers, who would wear the career apparel, by the use of interviews and a questionnaire. She obtained further information by studying professional and sales literature of companies that could supply the apparel and by talking with sales representatives.

Before she took these steps, however, she looked at library sources. Why? No book or magazine article will completely answer her question. She looked at library sources first—as you should do in a project of this type—in order to determine the experience of other companies with career apparel and to learn, if possible, decisions other persons had made in answer to the following questions:

Has this policy been conducive to better employee morale? Have employees objected to this policy or refused to wear the apparel? Does the employing company ordinarily furnish this clothing without charge, or at a reduced charge, or is the employee expected to pay the entire cost? Do policies differ from organization to organization?

Because employees now pay for their clothes, is it reasonable that they should pay at least part of the cost? Can apparel be planned so that the appearance of each employee can be varied from day to day by the use of a change of blouse or accessories? How can each employee be prevented from being identical in appearance to every other employee? Can apparel be purchased that will be flattering to workers of all ages and sizes?

The steps that follow are not necessarily in the order that you should take them. Much could depend upon the arrangement of your particular library, the availability of other libraries in your city, and information given with library sources that lead to additional reference sources.

You realize that it is unlikely that a book will be written on career apparel and that your most likely source of information is in magazines, especially business journals. You are not completely sure, however, that there are no books on career apparel; as you know, books are written on many thousands of subjects. You look in the card catalog or the on-line catalog and find nothing. You realize, though, that such a book may be in print but not available at this particular library.

A specialized business library, part of the public library system, is located in the downtown area of your city. The main city library contains thousands of books, and many are shelved in the several branches. Several other college and business libraries are within easy driving distance.

You decide to look in *Books in Print* or the *Cumulative Book Index* to determine whether a book has been written about career apparel. You look in one or both of these indexes and find nothing, as you expected. Now what? You consider that your problem is a business area that is a facet of office management, personnel management, and general business management.

You look in *Books in Print* or the *Cumulative Book Index* to find the name of the most recent books in these areas. Then you check the card catalog or the on-line catalog and find that your library owns these books. You write down the call number. If you have access to shelved books, that is, if your library has open stacks, you may find not only the books that you have noted but others on the same or similar subjects, shelved in the same general location. By checking the indexes of these books you find references to your particular subject.

Your next step is to go to the *Business Periodicals Index* and to the *ABI/ Inform* database to find articles that apply. You check the *Public Affairs Information Service* to find any other relevant articles. You check local newspaper indexes and the *New York Times Index* and the *Wall Street Journal Index* as guides to newspaper articles.

Because you wish to be completely thorough in your approach, you also look in the *Reader's Guide to Periodical Literature*, although you realize that your subject is a specialized business one and not likely to be reported in magazines of general interest. Some business articles, however, do appear in general magazines that are not listed in the *Business Periodicals Index*. Then you ask the reference librarian to suggest additional sources that you may have overlooked.

You read all of the material you find, even though very little may go into the final report. You will have a better overview of the problem after a general reading in the field, even though none of the material seems to describe your own particular problem. Your report, however, will be more convincing if you include a section on how career apparel has worked for other companies.

Evaluating Library Materials

Evaluating secondary sources, as well as primary ones, is one of the most important but most difficult phases of the report process.

Evaluation of data is discussed in more detail in Chapter 10, where emphasis is upon the analysis of data you have previously collected. Some evaluation must be done, however, as you proceed with library research. If you do not evaluate during the collection process, you will gather much information that is irrelevant or redundant, perhaps some that is misleading.

Wide research is probably the most dependable method of determining that information gathered through library research is valid and reliable. If, for example, you rely only upon one or a few sources, you do not have complete assurance that you have not by chance picked writers who, for one reason or another, give incomplete or inaccurate information.

Be careful to use only recent sources, except for general, mostly unchanging principles, or for historical research. If you believe that the information that you are seeking fits into the category for which you can use standard, older works (sometimes referred to as classics), be sure to compare these sources with later ones to make certain that the included information is still current.

Books, magazine articles, or any other form of written or spoken communication may be reliable or unreliable, truthful or untruthful. The quality of secondary data depends, to a great extent, upon the author and the publisher, although incorrect information can and does come from the best-known authorities and publishing houses. Reference librarians can be most helpful in your search for data, as well as in giving advice about the probable accuracy of various sources.

Observing the date, edition, and publisher of a book is helpful, but far from being completely descriptive. Learning the identity of the author, as far as his or her position or experience relates to the subject of the book, helps somewhat in judging approach and reliability.

Book reviews, which are usually published within a year after the book appears, aid in overall evaluation of the publication. They also provide information about areas of content. Reviewers often disagree; as in every other instance, the researcher must take final responsibility for judging the value of secondary information.

Book Review Digest is a general index that locates and gives excerpts from book reviews found in popular American, Canadian, and British periodicals.

Business Periodicals Index, beginning with 1972, locates book reviews found in English language periodicals in accounting, banking, communications, and various other business subjects. To locate reviews in the annual volumes from 1972 to 1974, look under the heading "Book Reviews—Single Books." Beginning in 1975, a separate listing of book reviews is found at the back of each volume.

Technical Book Review Index, beginning in 1941, locates and gives excerpts from book reviews published in journals in all fields of science and technology. Other indexes help to locate book reviews of publications in various fields; these indexes include *Education Index, New York Times Book Review,* and *Social Science Index.*

Gathering and Recording Notes

If you know exactly the information you are looking for, such as a figure on housing or income as reported by the Bureau of the Census, note-taking consists only of writing down the desired information and the complete bibliographical reference, including page numbers. A similar situation exists when you set out to find what one well-known person has written in a particular book or journal article about a particular topic.

Most library research is more complicated and comprehensive than that described above, even if the major portion of your data will come from primary sources. If much or all of the data will come from secondary sources, as can occur in many kinds of business and professional reports, the research procedure requires planning and organization in order to be effective and efficient. Notes must be classified in some usable, accurate, and time-saving arrangement before they are analyzed and presented in final report form.

Perhaps you think that you need no further instruction in the simple matter of taking notes. Nevertheless, time spent in organization during the library search process can save much more time in the final organizing, evaluating, and writing process.

First, decide which information is to be recorded. This decision will be guided by the specific purpose of your research project. As discussed in Chapter 7, a specifically worded, exactly limited statement of purpose serves as a guide to all steps of the research and reporting procedure.

The statement of purpose may be separated into categories, also illustrated in Chapter 7. The outline of the overall report may be based on such a subdivided statement of purpose. Although the overall organization of the final report may differ from the tentative plan, preparing a tentative outline helps in the data-gathering process by preventing the collection of irrelevant or repetitive information.

Another question is how to record passages from published material. Should it be recorded verbatim, paraphrased, or outlined? Verbatim passages must be clearly distinguished as such. Although you think you will remember exact quotes, when compiling and presenting information it is only too easy to show such passages as paraphrased wording or to omit credit when you consider information to be general knowledge.

A well-known system of gathering and recording information utilizes note cards. Photocopying pages from sources to be used decreases the amount of material to be copied on note cards. This method is especially advantageous if much material is to be quoted verbatim. Screen prints or ''Hyper-Window'' printouts are extensions of computerized library sources.

Note cards showing the source of information, arranged according to the method shown in the style manual you are using as a guide, are an aid when typewriting the final copy. Small cards (3- by 5-inch) are large enough for this purpose. Larger cards are more convenient for recording excerpts from library sources. The smaller cards that contain bibliographical references can be numbered, with the corresponding number shown on the larger card or cards that contain data taken from the particular reference source. Or, instead of a numbering system, a short form of the reference can be used; for example, ''Brown, p. 17.'' Make sure that page numbers are recorded for all information, whether or not the passage is to be exactly quoted.

These information cards should also be keyed to the portion of the report, or the chapter of the book or other work, to which the passage most specifically applies. Such a system aids in sorting the data and in planning the final organization of the report.

Do not look for authors to support your point of view, and do not ignore those who disagree with the majority of other writers. You as a researcher have set out to find the truth, as much as you can possibly do so. At times it is ''neater'' to include only the authorities who build your case, but to do so is far from being objective.

Summary

Methods of obtaining information include primary and secondary research. The word *secondary* means that the information has already been gathered and recorded by someone else. Much secondary data can be obtained from published sources, but some sources are unpublished. Secondary information can also be found by a search of organizational records. Primary research has *not* been found and recorded by someone else.

Library research should usually be the starting point in the data-gathering process, even if most of the data is to come from primary sources. The competent researcher is familiar with basic reference sources and can find needed information.

Previously prepared bibliographies and basic guides to reference materials should be consulted early in the research process.

Business services publications provide valuable information of many kinds. These publications are available in most large libraries.

The *Business Periodicals Index* is a basic guide to articles that have appeared in specialized business magazines. The *ABI/Inform* database is a valuable computerized guide to business publications. Various other indexes serve as guides to other specialized groups of periodicals.

U.S. government publications, particularly those released by the Bureau of the Census, are valuable sources of statistical information.

Library materials must be evaluated for current usefulness, appropriateness for the particular purpose, reliability, and objectivity. Book reviews, which can be located through various guides and indexes, help somewhat in judging the value of books.

An orderly system of extracting and recording notes helps in all future steps of the report-writing process and increases accuracy, efficiency, and objectivity.

Questions and Problems

1. Prepare a tentative bibliography of at least five recent sources that seem to apply to the problem for which you prepared a report plan. Use the form shown in Chapter 12.

2. Prepare an annotated bibliography (see Chapter 12) of five or more recent journal articles on (a) the topic of communication as applied to one of these fields; and (b) recent developments in these fields:
   • accounting
   • communication
   • management of a small business
   • personnel management
   • marketing
   • office management
   • your major field of study, if not listed above
   • word processing
   • computers
   • robots

3. Prepare a list of periodicals that apply especially to your major field of study.

4. Does your school library classify books according to the Dewey decimal system, the Library of Congress system, or both? How does the public library system in your city or town classify books? Write a short memorandum report to your instructor in which you describe the methods of classification in these libraries.

5. Use *Moody's Manuals* or Standard and Poor's *Corporation Records* to find information about a large national corporation. Write a short memorandum to your instructor in which you describe the kinds of information available in the reference source.

6. Examine a recent copy of the *Statistical Abstract*. Determine three topics (from the many) that are included in this reference source. Write a short memo to your instructor listing these topics and including one short bit of information about each, as given in the *Statistical Abstract*. Also specify the library and the location within the library where this reference source is kept.

7. Complete the secondary research of the report you proposed in the report plan assigned in Chapter 7. Write a progress report to your instructor, summarizing your secondary research efforts, problems, and work yet left to do. Ask for your instructor's suggestions.

8. Secure a computer printout from your library's electronic or computerized search systems. Learn how to use the "key word" concept in source search. See Problems in Appendix C that are based primarily on secondary research.

CHAPTER **9**

Collecting Information
Through Primary Research

Chapter Outline

The term *primary* research, as distinguished from *secondary*, includes collection of data by all methods except reading the words of other writers. Usual methods are through observation, experimentation, and surveys of various kinds.

Observation

Observation, as the term describes a method of research, means the examination of phenomena under real, presently existing conditions. Observation under controlled or manipulated conditions is referred to as *experimentation*. Observation includes both casual and informal observation and planned, carefully recorded and tabulated instances of observed actions or occurrences. The term may also be used to describe a search through company records. Many accounting reports and auditing reports are based on an examination and analysis of financial records. Hence, the method of data collection is observation, although such reports are not usually described as such.

In the research proposed in the report plan illustrated in Chapter 7, the researcher observed present work activities of secretaries at Countrywide Insurance as one of several methods of research used in the study. In another report done for Countrywide Insurance Company, the researcher who studied the advisability of career apparel used casual observation of the present dress of the women employees. The researcher could possibly have used a planned, structured form of observation.

For example, detailed, daily records of the dress of all employees could be used to determine something of their choice of color and style as well as to consider whether career apparel was needed to improve the overall appearance of the employees. This subject would have been a sensitive one if the study had been kept secret from the people being studied. The information to be gained would probably not have been worth the risk of discovery with its subsequent mistrust. If the employees had been informed of the study while it was being done, no doubt their appearance would not have been typical of their usual dress.

The results of information obtained through observation, like that obtained in any other way, can be trustworthy or not, depending upon the care and judgment of the researcher as well as upon many other contributing factors. Comprehensive, carefully planned observational research is more likely to provide dependable results than is the casual and informal

158

notice of conditions and occurrences, although this form of observation should not be overlooked. As in all other forms of research, accurate and complete records should be kept as data are collected. Then the data must be carefully and accurately organized, analyzed, and interpreted.

Uses of Observation as a Method of Research

Observation consists of more than "watching." It also includes listening and reading. In addition, the term *unobtrusive measures* is used to refer to indirect methods of observational research. An example of such research is noting the frequency of replacement of vinyl tile in front of various museum exhibits in order to measure their popularity. Another example is studying the wear and tear of pages of library books in order to measure their use. Another type of such research is analyzing contents of garbage cans and trash barrels in order to estimate such factors as choice of magazines and amount of liquor consumption.

Analyses of nonverbal behavior, as illustrated by C. William Emory, include study of body movements of workers assembling a product, exchanged glances during a discussion, and eyeblink rates as indicators of interest in advertising messages.[1] Such research also includes noticing pupils of the eyes, which expand to indicate interest or acceptance and contract to indicate dislike or displeasure.

An analysis of linguistic behavior includes counting the *ah's, oh's, you know's,* and other interrupting or annoying sounds or words that often accompany speech. Extra-linguistic behavior includes other speech characteristics, such as pitch of voice; interaction, such as a tendency to dominate a conversation; speaking rate; and vocabulary and pronunciation peculiarities. The observation of spatial relationships includes aspects such as the study of the arrangement of furniture, crowding in shops or offices, and the personal space maintained between sales representatives and customers.

Advantages and Disadvantages of Observation as a Method of Research

Observation is the only method of obtaining some kinds of information; for example, the study of records, mechanical processes, or actions of animals or young children. Data obtained from the study of group processes are more accurate when observed and recorded by an objective and perceptive researcher than when reported by members of the group itself, as individuals are likely to report group actions based on their own perceptions of the event and upon varying personal relationships. Research

1. C. William Emory, *Business Research Methods,* Rev ed. (Homewood, Ill.: Richard D. Irwin, 1980), p. 289.

through observation, provided that the method is wisely used, is more likely to provide accurate data than personal, mail, or telephone surveys, although information obtained is of a different kind. Observation measures only overt acts; it cannot determine reasons for these acts.

Disadvantages of observation as a method of research are that it is often complicated, time-consuming, and expensive. In order to make sure that observed incidents are not isolated events, the researcher must use extreme care in selecting times and sites for research.

For example, suppose a manufacturer of inexpensive toys, displayed on racks in supermarkets, wants to know which family member is most likely to choose the toys—mother, father, or child. Such knowledge could influence advertising, packaging, location of racks, placement on racks, and other decisions. Additional information that could be helpful is the number and kinds of toys chosen. The researcher must consider the time of day, week, month, and year for the study. If, for example, one researcher observed toy racks late at night, results might be quite different from those of another researcher who observed the racks on Saturday afternoons. One more consideration that might affect the results is the location in the city of each supermarket.

Another disadvantage of observation is that the *observer* may influence behavior, especially if the persons being observed are aware of the procedure. Observed behavior, when subjects are aware that they are being studied, is likely to be different from their typical behavior, as illustrated by the well-known Hawthorne effect.[2]

Experimentation

Experimentation, scientifically done, is reliable and accurate—more so than any other research method. But even experimentation is subject to error. In addition, many business problems are not of the type that lend themselves to the experimental type of research.

In business, as in other areas, the purpose of experimental research is to determine the effect of change under a given set of conditions. The conditions must be carefully constructed so that only one variable is tested at a time. For example, an experiment to determine the effect of career apparel upon employee morale would be difficult to conduct in a completely scientific manner because of the element of human behavior.

2. The Hawthorne effect was discovered as the result of an experiment that was intended to measure the effect of lighting conditions on the output of factory workers. Regardless of what changes were made in lighting, factory output increased. The experimental results seem to illustrate that the increase occurred not because of the lighting changes, but because employees worked harder, knowing they were the object of concerned observation. This study illustrates an important principle of management: *Employees want somebody to pay attention to them.*

Suppose that you want to test the effectiveness of two different sales letters. One is mailed to homeowners in one state, and one is mailed to the homeowners in another state. Depending upon the product, the observed difference in effectiveness of the letters could have a great deal more to do with the choice of states than with the wording of the letter. If you try to sell wind-turned attic ventilators through a letter sent to homeowners in Maine and through another letter sent to homeowners in Alabama, you are adding variables to the one you set out to test—the effectiveness of the differing letters.

If you sell more ventilators to those people in Alabama, you may consider the warmer climate to be a factor—but then you realize that people in Maine really should buy more because they are not so likely to have central air conditioners—and then you consider that people in Alabama need ventilators in order to decrease the cost of electricity. With all these unanswered questions, you cannot be sure that differences in the letter had any effect.

This illustration is perhaps a rather extreme example of uncontrolled experimentation. Competent researchers would not attempt an experiment without attempting to control all contributing factors except the one being tested. But, except in scientific laboratories, it is often difficult to control all factors entirely.

The law of the single variable must be followed in every experimental situation: *Vary only one circumstance at a time, and maintain all other circumstances completely unchanged.*

Determine Experimental Design

As with all other forms of research, an experimental study must be carefully planned. Experimentation includes the control and manipulation of the research setting, conditions, and processes in order to obtain the desired information.

Before-After Design Using a Control Group. An experimental research study often involves two or more groups, one of which is the control group. Both groups are measured according to predetermined, specific criteria at the beginning of the experiment; that is, the variable being tested is measured in both groups. Then researchers inject an experimental factor into the experimental group, but not into the control group, and both groups are measured to determine any change that has taken place.

An example of a simple experiment using a control group could be one conducted by a national chain of inns. Suppose, for example, that reservation clerks have not been suggesting to departing guests that they make reservations in another inn in the chain for the following night, although computer reservations are available. In the experiment, inns are randomly assigned to either the experimental group or the control group. Clerks in the experimental group are instructed always to offer to make reservations in another inn, with suggestions to be given in similar ways by all clerks. If reservations greatly increase in the experimental group but not in the control group, a reasonable assumption is that routine suggestions according to a specified procedure have increased subsequent reservations.

Perhaps in this particular situation such an assumption could be made without research, but many experiments are conducted to "prove" less obvious conclusions. In addition, clerks are more likely to be convinced to follow the suggested procedure after learning of the experiment. Another consideration is that routine suggestions may *not* increase reservations, an indication that something is wrong with the procedure or, perhaps, the whole idea.

Before-After Design with No Control Group.   An experiment can be conducted without a control group, although such a method is less accurate because there is more likelihood that factors other than the variable being tested have influenced results. In this type of experiment, the chain of inns would simply determine the number of subsequent reservations for a preceding month or other time period, begin the procedure of suggestions from the clerk, and determine the number of subsequent reservations in the following month or comparable time period. By doing so, however, no consideration is given to other factors that may have influenced the outcome. For example, perhaps guests are more susceptible to suggestion in a sunny June than in a dreary March.

Computer Simulation.   A computer can be used to create a simulated environment in which variables are manipulated and analyzed. A researcher can test many more variables than would be feasible in actual research situations. The disadvantage of this method of "research" is that it *is* simulation, not a real-life situation. As techniques improve, research projects now thought unlikely or impossible are likely to be completed by the use of computers. (Computers are used in various other problems of research, as in counting, organizing, comparing, analyzing, and interpreting data.)

Make Sure That an Experiment Is Suitable for Your Particular Research

Although experimental research is highly regarded as the most reliable method of scientific research, it is not suitable for the solution of many problems in business and other social sciences. It is an orderly method of testing, limited to the effects of a single variable on a given set of conditions. If conditions cannot be controlled, results of a research study cannot be accepted as conclusive.

Evaluation of Surveys Used as a Method of Research

Surveys are widely used in obtaining information. They are conducted through personal and telephone interviews and through the use of questionnaires, often sent through the mails.

The survey is open to criticism because it depends completely on verbal responses, and words are inexact. (All other methods of research also have weaknesses.) The respondent, when filling out a questionnaire or talking with a researcher in a personal interview or on the telephone, is likely to provide untrue, incomplete, or inaccurate and misleading information. Even if respondents wish to provide complete and accurate answers, they often do not do so because of inaccurate memories, lack of knowledge and detailed information, tendency to give the expected response, and any number of other reasons.

Influences of all kinds enter into results of interviews and questionnaires, as into all other areas of oral and written communication. People who answer an interviewer's questions are affected by their perceptions of the interviewer, of the situation, and of themselves. Their mood of the moment influences their responses and whether a questionnaire sent through the mail is returned.

Regardless of the interviewer, questionnaire, or topic being investigated, respondents tend to exaggerate incomes, education, social status, and other favorable aspects of their experiences. They tend to minimize unfavorable aspects. These inaccuracies occur even when there is absolutely no possibility that their questionnaires can be identified.

Another weakness of the survey method is that questionnaire design, extremely important in achieving accurate information, is often approached casually and haphazardly. A poor questionnaire or poorly structured interview is almost certain to result in incomplete or incorrect data. Questionnaire construction requires much thought and time. Ideally, a questionnaire is tested with a small group before it is used on a large scale.

Questionnaires and interviews are so widely used, often with poorly designed survey instruments, their respondents do not consider their answers important or do not answer at all. Another factor is that the researcher has no way of being sure that respondents who return questionnaires are representative of the entire population being surveyed. For example, if a member of Congress asks whether or not to introduce a bill, respondents are most likely to be those who will benefit from the proposed law or those who have some special reason for not wanting it. Many people without special interests, who are more likely to make a wise decision, do not take the time to return questionnaires.

If you survey alumni of a school and ask questions about jobs and salaries, those who feel successful are much more likely to return questionnaires, even if their names are not used, than those who feel otherwise. The researcher who attempts to obtain the mean or median salary of such a group would report an average salary higher than the typical salary of all class members.

Even with its many weaknesses and disadvantages, the survey is the only practical way to obtain many kinds of information. It is difficult to determine what people think, know, or believe without asking them. We cannot know their likes and dislikes, their desires, or their intended actions. We cannot gain the benefit of their recommendations without asking for them. In addition, events that have already occurred evidently cannot be observed. They must be described by others in written or spoken words.

Much business research is of necessity done by the use of surveys. Although researchers know that such information will be less than perfectly accurate, a survey wisely planned and conducted can supply information sufficient for effective and efficient management decisions.

Obtaining a Representative Sample

Unless all members of the entire group are to be surveyed, the assumption must be that those who have been picked to be the respondents are representative of the entire group. Reliability can result only from a representative sample. In research terms, *reliability* is understood to be the assurance that the data are truthful.

To arrive at this truthfulness, surveys must be scientifically administered. In addition, the survey instrument must be *valid*. This word, in research terminology, means that the research instrument measures what it is intended to measure. For example, you cannot find the weight of an object by using a yardstick, nor can you find its length by using a bathroom scale, because a yardstick is not a valid instrument for measuring weight and a scale is not a valid instrument for measuring length. The yardstick is not *reliable* even for measuring length if it expands or shrinks, nor is the scale reliable for measuring weight if it gives varying readings each time an unchanging object is weighed.

An example of data that are not reliable, even though you used a yardstick, are measurements to determine the average height of a group of employees. If you measure three women and find that their average height is 61 inches, this conclusion seems to indicate that by chance you have chosen a nonrepresentative sample of the total group. (The total group to be studied is known as the population.) What has gone wrong here is that too few employees have been chosen. If the total number of women employees in this organization is 100, certainly you should sample more than three.

If you had measured the height of 25 or 30 women, the obtained average would ordinarily have been fairly close to the average that you would have obtained if you had measured all 100, provided you had used a method of random sampling. However, your average would not be correct, if, for example, you had measured the twenty players on the company basketball teams and had included them in the sample.

When beginning the sampling procedure, the researcher must consider the persons who are to be surveyed, the number, and how to be reasonably assured that those surveyed are representative of the whole group.

A general law of sampling is that a sufficiently large number of items (or opinions, etc.) taken at random from a large group will have the characteristics of the larger group. If the group is small, each item should be examined or each person should be asked for an opinion.

A researcher seeking to improve the sound equipment in a theater asked for the opinion of all persons who work or have worked with this equipment. In another study about career apparel, each employee was asked for her opinion. Because of the time and expense required for a large-scale survey, however, we cannot economically question each person in a large group. We must limit our questioning to a number that we believe will give reliable results and that will not be extravagant in the use of time and money. Anyway, according to experts in statistics, a well-chosen and adequately large sample is likely to be as reliable as examining the entire group.

Random Sampling

Random sampling is defined as the sampling method by which every item in the population has an equal chance of being chosen. In order to ensure that every individual has the same opportunity to be chosen, the researcher must have a complete list of all items (persons, etc.) in the population.

The old "putting names in a barrel" is a true random sample if you can be sure that the names are thoroughly mixed and that no element other than chance enters into the selection. Remember that random sampling, as it is used in statistics, does not mean *hit or miss* as the word *random* does when used in other instances.

Randomness is most often achieved by the use of a table of random numbers. These tables ordinarily consist of many groups of five-digit numbers. Random numbers can be employed by a systematic method since each of the digits has been selected at random, most likely by a computer. To use these tables, the researcher matches the numbers with previously numbered names or items, taken from a list of the complete group.

Stratified Random Sampling

Stratified random sampling is done by conducting a random sample of subgroups within the universe. To sample the opinions of students in your university, you can use subgroups of classes (freshmen, sophomore, etc.), sex, major fields of interest, age, or many other divisions.

Usually the desired number in each division should be the same as the portion of the universe that the group comprises. For example, if you try to find data that apply to the entire student body, and in your school there are twice as many freshmen as there are seniors, include in your sample twice as many freshmen as you do seniors.

Quota Sampling

Quota sampling is similar to stratified random sampling in that sampling is done from subgroups of the entire population. The sample, however, is based on a quota, not on a random selection. For example, if within a student body the freshman class consists of 4,000, the sophomore class of 3,000, the junior class of 2,000, and the senior class of 1,000, the number of students questioned, from a total sample of 100, might be 40, 30, 20, and 10, respectively.

Although this method of sampling is easier to administer, in many cases, results are less likely to be truly representative than in stratified random sampling. As in all sampling, the likelihood of reliability increases as the sample size increases. If quota sampling is used, an attempt should be made to obtain samples from all groups within the subgroups. For example, if you were attempting to obtain a quota of 100 from your senior class of 1,000, results would not be representative if you limited the number in your sample to engineering students.

Systematic Sampling

Systematic sampling is the technique of taking selections at definite and unchanging intervals from a list of the members of the population. If you have a list of all the students in your college, you would do systematic sampling by taking, for example, each fifteenth name on the list.

Although this method is not strictly random sampling, ordinarily the effect will be the same if the sample size is large enough. To ensure an even greater degree of randomness, the researcher could take the first number entirely by chance and proceed through the list using the same number.

Various other sampling methods are described in textbooks and handbooks in statistics. If you have not studied statistics, you should read further into the field of sampling theory before undertaking a research project which makes use of this method of investigation.

Determining Sample Size

Ordinarily, 25 to 30 percent of a large group, based on numbers alone, should provide representative data. At times you will not be able to sample this many because of the time and expense involved. In this case you will need to use some method of determining adequate sample size. A simple method is to split the sample into two or more parts and to compare the results from the various parts. A similarity of results from these parts of the total sample indicates that overall results are likely to be acceptable.

Formulas can be used for checking the adequacy of sample size. These formulas can be applied when you have enough returns to estimate the apparent division of answers. These formulas are given in books on statistics and in books devoted entirely to research.

Constructing the Questionnaire

When you plan a questionnaire, your goals are to secure a satisfactory rate of return and complete, objective answers. Another consideration is the ease and accuracy with which results can be tabulated and analyzed.

With the questionnaire, include a convincing explanatory letter, which is usually on a separate sheet but sometimes shown at the top of the printed questionnaire. The most effective way to convince readers to respond is to show them benefits to themselves. Even if there is no immediate benefit, many people will cooperate if you carefully and convincingly explain the purpose of the study and why you need their opinions. To increase returns, do everything possible to make response easy; for example, keep the questionnaire as short as possible, ask for check marks instead of long written replies, and enclose a stamped, addressed envelope.

Write and Arrange Questions Carefully

The construction of the questionnaire, including its physical appearance, will influence the percentage of returns and the value of the answers. Specific principles of questionnaire construction are listed below. In addition, principles of communication you have studied throughout this course are most important as you plan the survey instruments and the cover letter. Clearness, conciseness, the you-attitude, and all the other attributes of effective communication apply to obtaining business information through the use of questionnaires.

1. Make the questions easy to understand and concerned with one topic only. Avoid ambiguous wording. For example, the question "Why did you buy your last car?" could lead to the response that the respondent liked the color, the price, or the design. Another respondent might answer that he bought the car because he had wrecked his older one, or because a spouse wouldn't buy a motorcycle. Avoid broad, relative terms such as *often, a long time,* and *seldom,* unless these terms are specifically defined.

2. Make the questionnaire easy to answer. Providing blanks to be checked facilitates response as well as the researcher's tabulation of the answers.

3. Provide for all likely answers. Although some questions can be answered by a *yes* or a *no,* many are somewhere in between. Provide for categories such as *I don't know,* or *no opinion, disagree,* or *strongly disagree.* Allowing for shadings of opinions is much more descriptive and accurate than mere *agree* or *disagree* questions.

4. Ask only for information that can be easily remembered.

5. Keep the questionnaire as short as possible by asking only for needed information.

6. Avoid questions that touch on pride or personal bias, or those that give the effect of prying. Such areas include age, income, morals, and personal habits. A question about education may have a prying effect with persons of limited educational background. Information about age, income status, or education may be necessary in order to accomplish the particular purpose of the report. Even if you need this information, however, you will ordinarily not need the exact age, the exact amount of income, or the exact number of years the person has been in school.

To encourage response, as well as to facilitate evaluation of the answers, provide ranges from which the respondent may choose to show age and income. For example, you can show age brackets *under 21, 20 to 25,* and set up income brackets in the same way. Age and income brackets can be an important consideration in marketing research when planning products to manufacture or outlets for distribution.

7. Arrange questions in a logical order.

8. If the questionnaire is mailed, enclose a stamped and addressed envelope.

9. Avoid leading questions—those that by their working suggest an answer.

10. Provide for additional comments, if any, by the respondent by the use of open-ended questions in which comments can be included in the respondent's own words. Although these questions are more difficult to tabulate than answers that are shown by check mark, these comments may be more helpful than all the other answers. In addition, they may encourage respondents to speak freely.

Figure 9–1 is an illustration of a questionnaire sent to furniture manufacturers. In this survey all furniture manufacturers in a particular geographic region were questioned. Other questionnaire examples are illustrated in Chapter 15.

The questionnaire itself begins with a short transmittal message. A cover letter on company letterhead, signed by an official of the company, was included with the questionnaire. Such a method is not necessary with all questionnaires. The researcher directed the cover letter to the president or other executive within each organization. Because the researcher knew that the cover letter might not be passed on to the respondent completing the questionnaire, a note of explanation was included on the first page of the questionnaire itself.

The questionnaire shown in Figure 9–1 illustrates an effective way of handling an approach that is often confusing to respondents, as illustrated in Question 4. The researcher wanted certain bits of information from manufacturers who do not sell scrap materials to employees, based on the assumption that such materials are sold elsewhere. By instructing respondents who answer *Yes* to Question 4 to proceed to page 2, and those who answer *No* to proceed to page 3, confusion is reduced or eliminated (pages 2 and 3 are omitted from this illustration).

Arrange Questions in an Appropriate Sequence

The sequence of questions influences cooperation, interest, and final results. Use special care with opening questions. As in other forms of communication, opening statements are particularly emphatic. If personal questions even slightly threatening to the ego must be included in the survey instrument, they should not be asked first. And, as in instructional material, questions should move from the simple to the complex. (As much as possible, keep all questions simple.)

Early questions should build reader interest and provide motivation for completing the questionnaire. In some survey situations, questions should proceed from the general to the specific.

Consider the Use of Scaling Techniques

Rating scales measure intensity of feeling; for example, like—dislike, approve—disapprove—indifferent, strongly oppose—oppose—no opinion—favor—strongly favor. Scales are of different lengths. Three-, four-, and five-point scales are widely used. Some scales are even longer.

An example of a five-point scale is:

Will you help us obtain needed information?

Your answer to the following questions will help us to determine whether to authorize the sale of scrap materials to employees.

This questionnaire is being sent to eighty-six furniture manufacturing companies. Do you want a summary of the findings of this study? _____ Yes _____ No

Will you please return the completed questionnaire so that we will receive it by November 19? We plan to start compiling the data at that time. A stamped, addressed envelope is enclosed.

We shall greatly appreciate your assistance.

1. What is the size of your company measured by number of employees?
   _____ 1-50 _____ 51-200 _____ 201-500 _____ Over 500

2. Does your company sell new raw materials to employees?
   _____ Yes _____ No

3. If your answer is <u>yes,</u> how are raw materials priced?
   _____ Retail   _____ Cost
   _____ Cost Plus   _____ Percent

   _____ Other Please explain. _____
   _____

4. Does your company sell scrap to employees?
   _____ Yes _____ No
   IF ANSWER IS <u>YES,</u> GO TO PAGE 2.
   IF ANSWER IS <u>NO,</u> GO TO PAGE 3.

5. Why do you sell scrap to employees?
   _____ Sale of scrap to employees generates goodwill with employees.
   _____ Sale of scrap to employees generates more return than sales to others.
   _____ There is union pressure or contract to sell scrap to employees.
   _____ Other Explain. _____
   _____

6. What is the average dollar amount of each sale of scrap to employees?
   To $5 $5.01 to $25 $25.01 to $50   Over $50
   _____   _____   _____

7. Why do you not sell scrap to employees?
   _____ Sale of scrap to employees may increase scrap production.
   _____ Sale of scrap to employees generates less return than sales to others.
   _____ Other. Explain _____
   _____

8. What is the average dollar amount of each sale of scrap other than to employees?
   $0 $.01 to $5 $5.01 to $25 $25.01 to $50   Over $50
   __   _____   _____   _____   _____

Figure 9–1. *A questionnaire (two pages omitted) combined with a cover letter.*

What is your opinion of the following statement?

''If men are drafted, women should also be drafted.''

strongly disagree	disagree	no opinion	agree	strongly agree
−2	−1	0	+1	+2

The five-point scale shown above could be extended to a seven-point scale by inserting another category. For example, the *agree* could be broken into *slightly agree* and *moderately agree*. Such as addition, however, would add little to usable results, perhaps confuse the respondent, and complicate tabulation.

The scale illustrated here is a simple one compared to numerous others that are more complicated and sophisticated. These simpler ones are easier to use and often more practical for most research. If you spend a great deal of time with surveys, however, you should become familiar with the various types of scaling techniques that are beyond the scope of this book. Some of the many reference sources on research methodology are listed in the bibliography of this book.

Interviewing in Person and by Telephone

When surveys are conducted through face-to-face or telephone interviews, a form of questionnaire should be drawn up as a guide to the interviewer. Questions should be presented to all respondents in a uniform way, and, as in written questionnaires, wording should be objective and specific. Care should be taken to avoid leading questions or statements, or those that seem to pry. Include necessary information about why you are questioning the reader and how the answers will be used. If you can find a reasonable reader benefit, subtly point it out. And, as in other request letters, a statement of when the completed questionnaire is needed will help to prevent procrastination and a delayed or forgotten return.

Personal interviewing must be limited to a relatively small geographical area unless cost is of no consideration, an unlikely occurrence. Telephone interviewing, although it has other disadvantages, is less expensive and time-consuming. All types of interviewing must be carefully planned and conducted, and responses must be recorded carefully and completely.

Personal Interviews

As compared with questionnaires sent through the mail, personal interviewing provides some of the advantages of oral communication over written communication: immediate feedback, messages sent through the various means of nonverbal communication, and the ability of the communicator to explain further when the respondent doesn't understand the question. Human errors enter into the interview process, however, through all the many ways that communication goes astray. In addition, the respondent may consider the questions an invasion of privacy. The reaction of the respondent to the interviewer is reflected in the information being supplied. Also, because the interviewer interprets responses, these interpretations may be less than completely exact.

Interviews, especially when they are given to many respondents, are ordinarily limited to specific, factual data that the respondent is likely to remember. All interviews should be given according to the same plan of procedure. Questions should be asked in the same sequence and in exactly the same words, explanations should be given in the same way, and the other details of all the interviews should be the same. Because of the varying reactions of the persons being interviewed, procedures cannot be exactly planned in advance, but an effort should be made for all interviewers to proceed in the same way.

In addition to interviews limited to factual information, *depth* interviews are unstructured and informal conversations. These interviews must be done by competent, highly skilled researchers. Psychologists often use this type of approach.

Telephone Interviews

Interviewing by telephone is quicker and less expensive than personal interviews. Random sampling can be used in selecting respondents to be called, provided the population is limited to individuals with listed telephone numbers. Because of the number of people with no available numbers and because some persons whose numbers are listed are never reached, the selection is not truly random.

Many people object to answering questions during telephone interviewing. The telephone is frequently used for sales promotion, often after remarks such as "If you can answer this question . . ." Because of this approach, listeners are often in no mood to respond to serious efforts to obtain information. Some people consider all telephone calls, except for reasons that are of some benefit to themselves, as an intrusion on their time and an invasion of their privacy. Because of these attitudes, they refuse to cooperate, or, if they do so, are likely to give inaccurate or incomplete answers.

Telephone interviewing, in spite of its weaknesses, may be desirable in many instances. If so, the interviewer should use the same care and courtesy as in personal interviews. As in all surveys, explanation of the purpose and benefits of the survey will help to obtain respondent cooperation.

Summary

Methods of primary research are observation, experimentation, and surveys. Surveys employ the use of mail questionnaires and formal and informal interviews; some interviews are conducted by the use of questionnaires or a pre-planned series of questions asked by the researcher. Surveys are conducted by telephone and person-to-person.

Although observation as a method of research is often complicated, time-consuming, and expensive, it is the only method of obtaining some kinds of information.

Experimentation, scientifically and objectively done, is reliable and accurate, but even experimentation is subject to human error.

Surveys are widely used in research of many kinds. Their frequent use results in a disadvantage because many respondents are tired of completing questionnaires or do not believe that they are important.

Reliability in sampling can result only with a representative sample. A general rule of sampling is that a sufficiently large number of items or opinions taken at random from a large group will have the characteristics of the entire group.

Random sampling is defined as a sampling method by which every item in the population has an equal chance of being chosen. Stratified random sampling is done by conducting a random sampling of subgroups within the population.

Questionnaires must be constructed with care in order to encourage response, to obtain the needed information, and to facilitate tabulation of results.

All methods of research are subject to the many kinds of human error that result in miscommunication.

Questions and Problems

1. Explain the difference between observation and experimentation as methods of research.

2. Describe the difference between the before-after design using a control group and the before-after design with no control group.

3. Can you think of a question that should be answered in your employing organization or in your school or university? Which method or methods of research should be used in finding the answer to this question? Explain.

4. Explain how the following questions (not from the same questionnaire) violate the principles of effective questionnaire construction.
   a. Don't you feel that you earn more interest at United Bank?
   b. Do you bathe daily?
   c. How much do you earn each month?
   d. How much have your grocery bills increased since 1988?
   e. How do you manage when your weekly check won't cover your expenses?

    f. Do you approve of Bill Number 213 now being considered in the Senate? Yes _____ No _____

    g. Do you leave work early? Always _____ Occasionally _____ Sometimes _____ Never _____

5. Find a questionnaire that was sent through the mail or administered during an interview. Analyze this questionnaire according to the ten suggestions included in the section of this chapter entitled "Write and Arrange Questions Carefully." As your instructor directs, present your analysis in a memorandum addressed to your instructor, or be prepared to show the questionnaire to the class and to comment on its construction.

6. Prepare a questionnaire to use in the research project for which you prepared a report plan (Chapter 7). If an appropriate projector is available for your use, show your questionnaire to the class. Ask for comments and suggestions for improvement. You may also wish to provide copies and ask students to complete the questionnaire.

7. Write a cover letter to accompany the questionnaire prepared in answer to Question 6.

8. Prepare a questionnaire to use in solving one of the research problems suggested in Chapter 7 or for a similar problem. Assume the type of respondents and any other necessary or helpful details. Show your questionnaire to the class (or ask students to fill it out) and ask for suggestions for improvement.

9. Pilot your questionnaire with a selected sample of your population. Watch for confusing responses and complete preliminary statistical analyses if possible.

10. Rough out tables, graphs, or charts that complement your data. See Chapter 11 for instructions. Or, use an appropriate computer graphic package (Microsoft CHART, DrawPerfect, or Harvard Presentation Graphics) as a preliminary organizing experience to see if your data are adequate.

CHAPTER 10

Interpreting and Organizing the Data

Chapter Outline

After the data have been collected, they must be evaluated and organized for presentation in the most appropriate form. A systematic method of collecting and recording information greatly simplifies the remaining steps of the research process.

These processes of evaluating and organizing, as well as preceding and following steps in research and report writing, do not fall into discrete divisions. We do not abruptly begin evaluating material only after the collection process is completed. Ideally, data are evaluated and organized as much as possible as they are collected. We must use judgment in the collection process or we will find that we have gathered great quantities of material, much of it meaningless or irrelevant.

At some point we must stop formally adding to the collection of data and begin the finishing steps of the research process. If additional information or opinions come to light, however, we cannot afford to ignore them merely to end the search, although at times we may be tempted to do so.

Determining the Meaning of Data

In report preparation and presentation, we must be extremely careful to be completely and thoroughly objective. Objectivity from the standpoint of phrasing and word choice is discussed in Chapter 5. But true objectivity consists of far more than nonemotional writing: it is an attitude that must be kept constantly in mind throughout the entire report process. Objectivity, or the lack of it, influences the complete and nonbiased search for information and the organizing, evaluating, and reporting portions of the overall project.

Because we are human, predetermined beliefs or desires tend to affect everything we do, including research and reporting duties. With awareness of this natural tendency, however, we can work toward honest and objective interpretations.

Causes of Error in Interpretation

In order to interpret data correctly and impartially and to evaluate it for accuracy, the researcher must keep in mind the several ways in which

176

communication errors can occur. These errors of evaluation and interpretation are similar to those that occur in the overall process of communication.

Varying Perceptions

A major source of miscommunication of all kinds is differing perceptions in the minds of the sender and receiver of a message. This barrier to communication occurs in research and report writing in various ways. Researchers tend to discount secondary and primary sources that disagree with their outlook about the subject. In turn, readers of reports are influenced by their attitudes and previously formed opinions (their perception) to the extent that they do not understand or believe reported results.

Our emotions affect the perception of words and situations and thus the ensuing words and actions. Even if we could be in perfect control of all emotions, perception would be limited because we cannot perfectly see, hear, taste, feel, or smell. As you look out your window, you cannot see and your mind cannot recognize all the minute details of what is before your eyes. You cannot listen to several conversations at the same time, although all are within hearing distance. You do not see everything that happens in a football game, a play, or an automobile accident.

Your perception and remembrance of a happening or a situation will differ from that of other people around you. This difference has been illustrated many times by varying descriptions of an accident, an individual involved in a crime, or even of a television program. We have all seen pictures that can be interpreted in two completely different ways depending upon how we perceive them.

We always perceive a portion of reality, not the whole. Our perceptions differ because of individual experiences. In addition, we generalize and assume that the whole truth is the part of the situation we recognize and understand.

Another cause of inaccurate perception is that we tend to see what we expect to see, or what we want to see. Research studies in education have indicated that teachers tend to perceive students as they expect them to be, based on information shown by school records of intelligence test scores and behavior patterns. Because the teacher expects certain children to be slow, or to have problems with the expected classroom behavior, they are treated as such; and they will often live up to the teacher's expectations, even if their school records are incorrect.

Perception influences understanding and interpretation. Being subject to all the fallacies of human intelligence, the researcher often foresees results before beginning a research study, although these anticipated findings may be incorrect. Although no researcher is absolutely and completely objective, by being forewarned of the likelihood of incorrect interpretation, we are likely to be less biased and more impartial.

Misinterpretation Through Inferences and Value Judgments

Facts are verifiable by direct observation. An inference is an assumption, or "an educated guess," based on known facts. A value judgment is a subjective evaluation based on an individual's particular way of looking at the world.

One illustration of facts, inferences, and value judgments, attributed to Irving Lee when he was a professor at Northwestern University, is based on the statement, "There are seeds in this apple." Is this statement a factual one, or is it an inference? Or perhaps a statement of judgment? You will be making a logical assumption, or inference, when you say that there are seeds in the apple until you cut the apple open and see the seeds. Your value judgment about the apple could be one or all of these: "This is a good apple." "This apple is sour." "I don't like apples." "This apple is pretty." "This is an inferior apple."

For a discussion of inferences and value judgments (longer than can be included in this textbook), see Chapter 3, "The Language of Reports," in *Language in Thought and Action,* by S. I. Hayakawa. Hayakawa uses the term *reports* instead of the word *facts.* He states:

> Reports adhere to the following rules: first, they are *capable of verification;* second, they *exclude,* as far as possible, *inferences and judgments.*

> An inference, as we shall use the term, is *a statement about the unknown made on the basis of the known.*

> By judgments, we shall mean *all expressions of the writer's approval or disapproval of the occurrences, persons, or objects he is describing.*[1]

Now let's apply Hayakawa's definitions to illustrations of our own. Suppose you say, "A magnolia tree is in bloom in Overton Park—I saw it on the way to work." Is this a report or an inference? If you are not sure that it is a magnolia tree, it is an inference. Suppose you say, "I saw a tree covered with white blossoms, as I drove by Overton Park on my way to work." Perhaps the tree is really a magnolia; inferences can be correct as well as incorrect. Suppose you say, "The blossoms have a sickening sweet smell." This statement is a value judgment.

Inferences are based upon matters that seem to be correct, based upon what one has observed. For example, a person who has never seen a magnolia tree looks at a tree blooming in Overton Park in Memphis and reaches the conclusion that it is a magnolia tree based upon these known facts: Overton Park is in Memphis, Tennessee, but only a few miles from

---

1. S. I. Hayakawa, *Language in Thought and Action,* 4th ed. (New York: Harcourt, Brace & World, 1978), pp. 38, 41, 42.

the state of Mississippi. Mississippi is known as the Magnolia State. One variety of magnolia has white blossoms and blooms in late spring and early summer. It is now May; the tree has white blossoms. The assumption that the observed tree is a magnolia is a reasonable inference, but it may be absolutely incorrect. Several other kinds of trees having white blossoms bloom in Memphis and in Mississippi in spring and early summer.

Suppose that you are tailgating and run into the back of a truck ahead of you. This occurrence, unfortunately, is a fact; when you tell others about it, it is a report—as long as you do not embellish it. The driver stops and comes toward you. His face is red, he is frowning, and his fists are clenched. You infer that he is angry, but you can't really be sure—maybe he looks like that all the time! You say (to yourself), "Truckers are nasty, mean people." This is a value judgment.

We cannot live or work without making inferences. Value judgments also will continue to be part of our lives—if we have a system of values, to say nothing of attitudes and opinions of our own. We should not try to eliminate inferences and value judgments, only to recognize them in our own minds and in the communication of others. We cannot limit our conversation to our actual observed experiences; we must make inferences in order to survive. Inferences and value judgments, however, are a source of human miscommunication because we confuse them. We interpret facts in the light of our limited experiences or nonobjective mind and arrive at inferences that are far from accurate. Then we accept these inferences as facts and communicate them as if they were facts.

Report conclusions and recommendations are often, if not usually, based on inferences. They must be. But the inferences must be based on facts.

Because evaluation and interpretation are mental processes, the ability to evaluate and interpret is closely related to mental capacity. This ability is improved by knowledge gained through experience and by specific and accurate information about the problem being studied. Most of all, critical ability is strengthened by the recognition that we are likely to think and act on the basis of what we believe and feel—that is, upon our emotions, instead of upon verifiable facts or upon reasonable inferences based upon verifiable and observable facts.

A basic cause of error is that of twisting the facts to obtain definite and specific conclusions, especially preconceived ones. Although we should not hedge with an abundance of indefinite terms such as *it seems, possibly,* and *perhaps* when conclusions or recommendations are based on inferences, these inferences should be clearly understood.

Most decisions of all kinds must be based at least partly upon inferences. And, being human, we will continue to make decisions based only on value judgments—as perhaps we should. The greatest danger lies in letting our value judgments, which can easily become prejudice and bias, close our minds to the truth, or at least to the search for truth. The gag saying "Don't bother me with facts; my mind is already made up" is a wise commentary, unfortunately, on the usual problem-solving approach.

In summary, errors in communication occur because our attitudes, opinions, and emotions influence our interpretation of events, as well as the interpretation of words and other symbols. Poor communication also occurs because of our lack of ability to handle words sanely and skillfully. Many of these errors are basically due to faulty perception.

Failure to Discriminate

We tend to interpret two events as if they were identical or to think in terms of stereotypes. The job we are now doing is not exactly the same as the one we did last year or even last week. Our co-workers are not the same as those we worked with in another organization. The employees we supervise are different from one another and will no doubt require different types of instruction and motivation. An application letter sent to one corporation should not be exactly like one sent to a differing organization. You are not the same person that you were ten years ago, last year, or even last week. The report you submit cannot tell everything you know about the subject; how can you be sure that you have chosen wisely the material to abstract?

We tend to see similarities instead of differences. We may communicate and react in terms of categories, generalizations, and stereotypes, when we should be looking for uniqueness. Although we do and should see similarities and use them for generalizing, categorizing, and arriving at conclusions, we should keep in mind that events are not truly identical and that events have unlimited characteristics.

The statement that an event has unlimited characteristics could be restated as "The statement is never the whole story." Can you tell everything about anything? Could you describe yesterday in complete detail, including all the elements of your environment? Could you completely describe the past hour or the past minute? Could you tell all there is to know about the pencil you hold in your hand or the view from your window?

We fail to discriminate when we do not choose the most fitting things to communicate about a particular event or situation, or when we do not adequately judge the most important points of the communication of others. The missing elements are perhaps the most important ones.

From a practical standpoint, we must classify and generalize, for to do otherwise would result only in chaos. We should realize, however, that all classifications will not be completely and perfectly accurate in every respect.

This lack of complete certainty even under the best of conditions is no justification for accepting hasty conclusions. That this lack of perfect classification and judgment is inevitable is only the more reason that we use extreme care in our limited observation so as to present the "true facts" as much as is humanly possible.

We fail to discriminate in our judgment of events as we analyze research findings, as well as in other situations. We tend to think in stereotypes and make false analogies, although in order to reach conclusions of any kind we must generalize. We should avoid making hurried and incomplete generalizations based on insufficient evidence.

For example, a researcher studying the question of career apparel found an article in a business periodical in which the author wrote that the career apparel had been enthusiastically accepted by an organization in New York. If this researcher had assumed that because of this acceptance the apparel was sure to be welcome in her own company, this assumption would not necessarily be correct. The researcher would have failed to discriminate between conditions from one organization to the next as well as from one part of the country to another. If she had justified the cost savings from the fact that the employees invest in a credit union, hence they must have a desire to spend little money on clothing, then the comparison would be even more unconvincing.

Interpreting events as to cause-and-effect relationships may lead to erroneous interpretation. The observed effect may not be a result of a previous event; it may be that another event occurred previously and, by chance, the observed effect followed. Or, as often happens, a result can be attributable to more than one cause, perhaps to many.

Trying to Validate a Point of View

A true report does not present evidence to support a particular point of view, but presents all relevant and obtainable evidence on both sides of a question and interprets the meaning of these findings. Although some so-called reports are planned to present "a case" for a decision or an emotional appeal to action, this kind of writing is not a real report as discussed here.

As you arrange information into report form, remember that most courses of action have disadvantages as well as advantages. Your work will be unconvincing if it lists only advantages—unless you have encountered a rare situation in which disadvantages are so minor that they are not worth mentioning.

Believing That Definite Conclusions Are Essential

You cannot expect to reach definite conclusions at the end of all research studies. (If you *never* come to reasonable conclusions, perhaps you will be reassigned to other work.)

It is far better to say "we still don't know . . ." than to guess at conclusions. In some instances, explanations are necessary, and sometimes the reader may be told that two or more courses of action are likely to be beneficial—or that maybe it does not make any difference, after all.

Cause-Effect Confusion

When one event precedes another in time, the first is assumed to be the cause of the second. Because a rooster crows each morning before sunrise, perhaps he thinks that his crowing causes the sun to rise. After you have had a rather nasty day, you read your horoscope in the newspaper, and find that you were supposed to have a nasty day, and assume that your destiny was already fixed. (If you had read your horoscope in the morning, your bad day could have resulted from a self-fulfilling prophecy.) You walk under a ladder and, on that morning, miss your bus. The superstition itself probably resulted from just such an occurrence, but walking under the ladder did not cause you to miss the bus unless you took a long time in doing it. Yet causes and effects are presented in reports in just this way.

We cannot always determine whether a noted cause brings about an observed effect. Such a question might be the topic of another research study.

Arguing in Circles

An example of arguing in circles is:

> *Fortunate teller to client:* "You'll be famous if you live long enough."
> *Client:* "What will I be famous for?"
> *Fortune teller:* "For having lived so long."[2]

In this type of reasoning, what is stated as a conclusion is only a restatement of the original assumption.

Monroe C. Beardsley, in the book *Thinking Straight*, uses this illustration.

> I am sure that none of our really responsible citizens are opposed to the City Council's plan to build a gigantic new municipal sports stadium over the Pennsylvania railroad tracks. Obviously the health of our citizens is a prime consideration, which any responsible citizen supports, and sports mean health. If we attract a major franchise, it will also bring money to the city. I realize that some will question my argument, and cite the names of various

---

2. Stuart Chase, *Guides to Straight Thinking* (New York: Harper and Row, 1956), pp. 37–38.

people who have expressed disagreement with the City Council's position, but that does not refute my claim. For if they are opposed to so excellent a plan, then by the same token they must be lacking in responsibility.[3]

Beardsley comments on this passage:

> One way of exposing the circularity is to take the first statement, "no responsible citizens are opposed to the plan," as the conclusion. This is supported by a rather shaky syllogism, but let that pass. The speaker seems to be aware that further support would not be amiss, and so he tries a second approach: suppose, he says, that someone is cited as opposed to the plan, since they are opposed, it follows that they are not responsible.
>
> The word "really" in the very first sentence should put us on guard. Not that it is always a sign that a question is being begged, but when a writer or speaker qualifies a general statement with "essentially," or "genuinely," or "truly," or "at heart," there is a strong possibility that something odd is taking place.[4]

Circular arguments, like many of the arguments used in reports, as well as tenets we live by, just don't make sense.

Self-Evident Truths

If the truths were self-evident, you wouldn't need to write a report. Arguing through a self-evident truth is similar to arguing in circles except that the writer or speaker doesn't bother even to reach the conclusion that was originally the assumption. Arguing through self-evident truths is taking for granted that there is no disagreement or using intimidation to keep people from disagreeing (it doesn't work), as in "All thinking people agree . . ."

Other phrases that indicate the use of self-evident truths are these:

It is common knowledge . . .
As everybody knows . . .
You can't deny that . . .
It goes without saying . . .
Any child knows . . .
As known to every schoolboy . . .
As every intelligent person knows . . .

---

3. Monroe C. Beardsley, *Thinking Straight*, 3d ed. (Englewood Cliffs, N.J.: Prentice-Hall, 1966), p. 86.
4. Beardsley, pp. 86–87.

Black-or-White Thinking

We tend to try to fit all answers into definite categories of black or white, yes or no, right or wrong. Such arrangements simplify thought processes (or dispense with them entirely), but they are not always accurate. Not all situations or ideas can be neatly categorized into such opposing divisions. Some areas must remain in varying shades of gray.

Basing Conclusions on Insufficient Data

Basing conclusions on insufficient evidence is an example of overgeneralization. Although we will never be able to find absolutely complete information about anything, the cliché "jumping to conclusions" applies to errors in judgment and communication of all kinds.

Basing Conclusions on Noncomparable Data

If the present salaries of Viet Nam veterans should be compared to those of other veterans, the conclusion would be meaningless if it is based on the belief that veterans of a "real" war or a "patriotic" war are more dependable and able to earn a higher salary. Various factors have been left out of consideration. For example, veterans of the Korean War or World War II are far older; they have had more time to reach their peak earning power. Or, if the same comparison is made later, it would be meaningless to state that Viet Nam veterans are increasing their earning power and Korean veterans are now earning less. The reason for the declining "average" salaries of the older veterans is that many have retired or died.

Basing Decisions on Personalities Instead of on Facts

Even nationally known "authorities" in a field can be wrong, although they are more likely to be correct than people outside the field. Communication error that results from an unquestioning belief in the opinions of other people, especially of well-known people, is described as "wise men can't be wrong." (Wise men and women know that they *can* be wrong.)

Although we should respect authoritative opinions, we should prefer facts if they are available. (We still have the problem of determining exactly what are the facts.) Another guide to valid reasoning is this: "If ten thousand persons say a foolish thing, it is still a foolish thing." If an opinion poll had been taken a number of centuries ago as to whether or not the world is round, overwhelming votes for flatness would have been considered conclusive. At that time, the idea that the world could be other than flat was contrary to ordinary common sense. (It is sad to accept the fact that common sense is sometimes misleading.)

Another self-evident truth and an example of basing conclusions on opinions is this: ''Fifty million Frenchmen can't be wrong.'' They can, as can fifty million Americans. If we are conductng a survey, however, of ten thousand or fifty million respondents, their opinions must be carefully recorded, analyzed, and reported. If the purpose of the research is to report opinions, that purpose has been accomplished even if those opinions are wrong. (You are not required to agree with the opinions.)

Conclusions, Based on Findings; Recommendations, Based on Conclusions

The statement that *conclusions are based on findings* may seem obvious to you, but the principle is often violated. If you make recommendations ''off-the-top-of-your-head,'' why should you gather and interpret data?

Valid conclusions are based on complete and relevant data interpreted objectively in the light of the problem to be solved. Recommendations, or ''what to do about it,'' are based on conclusions about what the data mean.

Ordinarily, the conclusions and recommendation section is the last section of a formal, analytical report arranged in the inductive order, as described in Chapter 2, or the conclusions and recommendations may be presented in two separate sections. In some long and comprehensive reports, each major section is treated as a separate report in that the writer arrives at conclusions based on findings presented in each section. In this arrangement, the effect is of several short reports combined into one. This arrangement is especially appropriate when a major research study is completed by several researchers, as often happens, but it can also be used in a long report prepared by one person. The entire report concludes with a summarizing section.

To repeat and emphasize: *Report evidence, interpret this evidence, and make recommendations. Be sure your conclusions, usually in a report section with recommendations, are based on clearly stated evidence.*

Interpreting with Statistics

Simple statistical terms include the following:

- *Mean.* The arithmetic average obtained by totaling the figures and dividing by the number of cases.

- *Median.* The midpoint, or middle value, in a series of values arranged in the order of magnitude.
- *Mode.* The most frequently occurring value. (The mean, median, and mode are all measures of central tendency.)
- *Range.* The spread between the lowest and the highest values in a series.
- *Standard deviation.* A measure of dispersion in a frequency distribution—a measure of the spread of the normal distribution.

This book cannot cover the study of statistics in a great deal of detail. A basic knowledge of statistics, however, is essential to the analysis of research findings and to their interpretation.

For an interesting and enlightening discussion of how figures can mislead, either intentionally or otherwise, read the book that has now become a classic in its field, *How to Lie with Statistics,* by Darrell Huff.[5] He illustrates how the term *average* can mean almost anything to nothing, depending on how it is used. In other words, the *mean* may be meaningless.

For example, a statement can be literally true that the average income of a college graduating class of a particular year is $97,000 a year, but it is very unlikely that this figure is the typical income. A few extremely high figures distort the mean. Suppose that the graduating class consisted of only ten members. Each of nine of these persons is now earning about $15,000 annually, and the tenth one earns $835,000—thus the arithmetic mean is $97,000. But if the figure is used to mean that each of the members is a potential customer for a yacht, you have misinterpreted the data.

Organizing the Data

Organization of the data, like evaluation, should not be left for a certain time period in the research and reporting process. Throughout the study, organization should be kept in mind as you decide what to present where. In addition, the tentative table of contents or outline prepared at the beginning of the study helps the final process of arranging ideas and prevents the investigation from going astray. During your final process of putting the report into written form, you are likely to see needed changes in the preliminary plan. After the first draft of the manuscript, you are likely to make further changes.

A well-known method of organizing material is the card method. Write on separate cards or slips of paper the headings of the report that seem to describe major divisions. Include those shown on the tentative

5. Darrell Huff, *How to Lie with Statistics* (New York: W. W. Norton & Co., 1954).

table of contents, as well as additional ones that now occur to you. Be careful not to express the same idea in different words.

After you have noted on the cards the possible divisions, arrange them in the order that seems to be natural, whether or not this sequence agrees with the original outline. As you study and sort the cards, you often find a new arrangement that will best express your ideas.

This method of organization also helps you to see weaknesses and omissions in the presentation, as well as redundancy. A logical sequence of topics of the complete report is essential whether the plan of arrangement is to be the direct (deductive) or indirect (inductive) order, as discussed in Chapter 2. If you are using the traditional and formal report arrangement in the inductive order, you already know you will begin with the introduction, whatever you choose to call it, follow with findings and analyses, and end with conclusions and recommendations, as discussed in Chapters 2 and 7.

Even though you already have this arrangement in mind, you must decide upon the arrangement of topics in the middle section of the report, as well as the arrangement of information in the introductory and concluding sections. The contents of the various preliminary and supplementary portions of the formal report, such as the synopsis, offer few problems in organization. You can safely leave their exact planning until the report itself is completed.

The organization process, when planning reports to be arranged in the direct order, requires the same careful attention to an orderly sequence of ideas. In the direct order, as you remember, you place recommendations at the beginning of the report, as well as any necessary explanatory conclusions, and follow with supporting information. Several report organizers or "windows" are available to aid you when you organize your report on your computer.

Choose Appropriate Report Divisions

When the report consists of comparisons, consider the use of the criteria of the comparisons as major divisions instead of the items to be compared. For example, if you are examining three possible locations according to cost of land, labor availability, and access to market, these criteria, instead of the locations, are likely to make for a more easily comprehensible format.

You may find instances in which, for one reason or another, such reports are best arranged by possible locations, not by the criteria for these choices. Like other problems in communication, use your own judgment based on an individual approach.

The choice of divisions of a report is extremely important to the logical progression of thought and to readability. Spend all the time necessary to achieve the best possible arrangement.

Word Headings Carefully

Each heading describes the contents of the subdivisions that come under it. "A," "B," "C," and "D" headings combine to equal the heading above them. Phrase headings carefully, not only from the standpoint of readability and clarity but also to check the flow of thought. Even when the actual text of a report is arranged in a logical sequence, inexact headings are confusing and misleading.

A discussion of headings is presented in Chapter 4, where emphasis is given to the format of various methods of arranging headings. Perhaps you will wish to reread this particular section as you prepare a longer report than those discussed earlier. Because the precise use of headings is helpful in reports of all lengths and levels of formality, they were discussed early in the text along with the discussion of short, informal reports.

Headings in the text of the report must agree exactly with headings shown in the table of contents.

Summary

In the evaluation of data, as well as in report presentation, we must do everything possible to be completely and thoroughly objective. We must use unbiased evaluation and interpretation in order to present findings in a matter-of-fact way and to show how these findings lead to the stated conclusions and recommendations.

Errors in data interpretation are the same as those that occur in all forms of communication, including inaccurate perception, confusing facts with inferences and value judgments, hasty generalizations, and basing decisions on predetermined beliefs.

Statistical measures are useful in the interpretation of data, although statistics can be used in confusing and misleading ways.

The report writer should carefully consider the organization of the report into appropriate divisions. Headings should describe the material that comes under them. Headings in the text of the report should agree exactly with those in the table of contents.

Questions and Problems

1. More than one overall plan of organization is possible and acceptable for most reports. As discussed in this chapter, a study of three possible sites for a new factory could be presented with major report divisions about each site, or by the arrangement, often preferable, of major criteria by which the

sites are judged. As you consider the following report situations, because of limited information you have no way of knowing the best possible arrangement. By assuming reasonable details, however, you can list major categories into which findings could be organized. Describe these categories in the form of major headings of the report.

   a. You have interviewed a representative group of citizens about their opinions of the overall quality of your city government.

   b. You have obtained personnel managers' opinions about the preparation of effective employment resumes.

   c. You have interviewed office managers about the importance of attractively arranged and laser printed business letters and how these letters can be prepared.

   d. You have compared two possible employers in order to determine where you want to apply for a job.

   e. You compare two competing brands of equipment with which you are familiar.

   f. You report on the fringe benefits offered by your employing organization or another organization with which you are familiar.

   g. You question recent graduates of the educational institution that you attended in order to find their opinions of improvements that should be made in the educational program. Assume that this study is limited to students in your major field.

   h. You try to determine how a small real estate company can increase profits.

2. As you did in problem 1, above, determine major report divisions of problems listed in question 1, Chapter 7.

3. If you prepared a tentative table of contents for a major report, as directed in problem 4, Chapter 7, recheck your table of contents at this time. Do you now see ways in which its organization can be improved? Make necessary changes. Also recheck the wording of your headings according to instructions in this chapter and in Chapter 4.

4. You learn that the average family income of your home town, which has a population of 1,500 is $62,000. You know that many of the residents are eligible for food stamps. If you accept both these descriptions as being correct, explain the apparent discrepancy.

5. Discuss possible errors in interpretation in the following situations:

   a. A researcher finds that engineering graduates of a particular university start at higher salaries than liberal arts graduates and concludes that the engineering school is more efficient than liberal arts departments.

   b. A textbook is described as being superior to a book of poetry because of a far greater number of sales.

   c. A senator reports that the majority of letters received supports a bill to increase the salary of postal workers.

   d. You survey alumni of your university to find their present earnings. You receive a 30 percent response to your questionnaire. You find the mean and median earnings of the respondents and report that graduates of your university far exceed the national average of college graduates in earning ability.

e. A newly appointed executive does a miserable job and is replaced. You conclude that inexperienced executives cannot bear the stress of executive responsibility.

f. A university liberalizes its drop policy so that students can now drop a course at any time before final examinations. The grade-point average increases. You reason that because students now have a less stressful semester, they are able to relax and make better grades.

g. Magazines sometimes use mailing lists of other magazines to solicit subscriptions. *True Confessions* purchased a mailing list from *Atlantic*. No subscriptions were sold. Sales personnel concluded that direct mail doesn't work.

h. You learn that more freshmen than seniors drop out of college. You conclude that freshman courses are more difficult than senior courses.

i. You find that early-stage collection letters bring in more payments, on the average, than late-stage letters. You reason that people who have already received three or four collection letters are tired of them and that you should wait at least three months before sending any letters at all. (Besides, it would save a lot of trouble.)

j. You report that a statement is unquestionably true because Dr. Brown, who is an M.D. and a Ph.D., agrees with you.

k. You conclude that the cost of a proposed office building is outrageous; it is smaller than the old building, constructed in 1960, and costs four times as much.

l. A newspaper reports that younger married women who have full-time employment are more affluent than older married women who are employed full-time. The evidence is that 45 percent of women within the age bracket of 25–39 have household help, while only 20 percent of the women within the age bracket of 40–55 have household help.

CHAPTER **11**

Interpreting with Graphic Aids

Chapter Outline

Graphic aids are used in both written and oral reports to emphasize important factors and to show trends and relationships. The terms *chart* and *graph* often are used interchangeably. In this chapter, *chart* refers to any form of graphic illustration other than a table.

Purposes and Advantages of Graphic Aids

Graphic aids, is wisely planned and attractively presented, bring out relationships that could be easily overlooked by the reader. A well-planned chart can present and analyze important points that would require many pages to explain and discuss. In addition, attractive graphic aids increase readability of a report merely from the standpoint of format and appearance. As discussed in previous chapters, mechanical aids to readability—white space, listings, subheadings, tables of content, and fairly short paragraphs—help the reader to understand important meanings and to obtain a summary of the overall report, even when it is read hastily. Well-planned graphic aids accomplish the same purposes.

Some reports consist mostly of tables, charts, and other graphic aids, with supporting text to explain and comment on the graphics. These simplified reports may be useful for information material prepared for the general public. They also serve as executive summaries for readers who do not want or need supporting details. For business reports prepared to serve as a basis for decision making, a complete form is preferred, with supporting evidence to justify conclusions and recommendations. In some situations, the same report may be prepared in summary form and in complete form.

Tables present numerical data in tabular form. Charts are used to show relationships, trends, and approximate values.

Tables, not charts, should be chosen for the presentation of numerous figures, particularly if the reader is interested in exact amounts. *Approximations, trends,* and *relationships are best shown on a chart of some kind.* A chart can be considered a pictorial representation of data.

Some kinds of information should be shown in more than one way in the same report. For example, the reader may need exact numbers shown in a table in addition to approximate figures used to show trends on accompanying charts. A detailed table can serve as the basis for many charts, which are used to illustrate, interpret, and emphasize various aspects of information shown in the table.

Placement of Graphic Aids

Ordinarily, a chart, table, or other graphic aid should be placed within the text of a report as near as possible to the portion of text that it is used to illustrate or explain. If the graphic is not closely related to the material being discussed, it should be placed in an appendix. Tables and charts, like other supplementary material, should also be placed in an appendix if they cannot be considered as an essential part of the report itself.

Extremely long tables or other kinds of material should be placed as appendices even if they cannot be considered supplemental. The reader is referred to these appendices as relevant material is discussed.

The most desirable placement of graphic aids is sometimes difficult to achieve either in typewritten or printed material. At times a table is too long to fit on the page where it is discussed. Dividing the table would be worse than placing it on a following page. If you are using both sides of the paper, as in a printed book, an illustration can often be placed on a page facing the page on which it is discussed. In addition, sometimes the size of a chart or other illustration can be reduced photographically so that it will fit on a page, but it should remain easily readable. This process, however, could consume more time than the ideal placement would be worth.

Long tables placed in appendices may have short summary tables placed in the text of the report. These short summary tables are known as *spot* or *spotlight* tables. Other short tables, not based on a longer one, can also be placed in this way. They are woven into the discussion, as illustrated below:

```
Sales in August, 1989 .........................................$117,267
Sales in August, 1990 ......................................... 121,219
Sales in August, 1991 ......................................... 192,719
```

This simple arrangement, like a listing of other kinds of information or questions, adds emphasis and aids immediate comprehension of the displayed data. This table is in effect part of the discussion. Tables are short and simple as the one shown need not be labeled and numbered unless the omission would result in confusion or inconsistency with other illustrations throughout the report.

All graphic aids, although often longer and more formal than the preceding table, should be part of the discussion in that they directly relate to the point being discussed. Anything that stops the reader's flow of thought, such as an unrelated illustration or inconvenient placement, is distracting and undesirable.

At times the discussion of a chart or other graphic aid may extend through several pages. When this occurs, the illustration should be near the beginning of the discussion.

Discussion of Graphic Aids within Text of Report

Introduce a graphic aid before presenting it, and, preferably, follow it with a few lines of discussion. It is important to remember that the complete report should be related through discussion, with illustrations used to emphasize and interpret. Minor details may be shown in illustrations without related discussion.

In introductory remarks to the graphic aid, point out highlights of the information it shows. By identifying items of major importance, as shown on the table or chart, you are able to refer subordinately to the illustration:

```
The greatest increase in sales occurred in District I (72 percent)
and the smallest in District 7 (17 percent), as shown in Table III.
```

Although the table should be referred to, do not build introductory sentences around the fact that certain tables or charts follow, and that the reader should look at them. Instead, emphasize important elements of information that are shown in following tables or graphs, which are referred to subordinately.

Identification of Graphic Aids within Text of Report

Use identifying titles and numbers on all illustrations throughout the report with the exception of minor tables or listings that can be considered a part of the text itself, as discussed previously.

Labeling and Numbering

Traditionally, tables are not grouped with other forms of illustrations but are numbered separately throughout the report with Roman numerals: Table I, Table II, and so on. Charts are shown with Arabic numerals: Chart 1, Chart 2, and so on. This traditional method of numbering is being replaced by some writers and organizations with the word *Figure*, which may be used to refer to *all* kinds of illustrations, and with consecutive numbering throughout. Another variation is to use the word *Table* for tables, numbered consecutively throughout the report with Roman numerals, and to use the word *Figure*, numbered consecutively throughout the report with Arabic numerals, for all illustrations except tables.

Writing Appropriate Titles

Like subheadings in a report and titles of all works, titles of tables and other graphic aids should concisely but accurately describe the data presented in the illustration. Titles of tables are usually placed above the table, shown in larger type than material in the table itself. In typewritten work, use solid capitals with no underscore. Titles of charts or figures are usually placed at the bottom of the illustration, shown in regular type. Titles of charts and other illustrations can also be placed at the top.

Citing the Source

If tables, charts, or other illustrations are prepared by the report writer, they are considered primary. This fact may be shown thus: *Source: Primary.* It is also acceptable, and more usual, merely to omit the source note for primary data. Credit must be given for material taken from another source; for example, "Source: *U. S. News and World Report*, December 28, 1990, p. 79." These source notes are usually placed one *double-space* below a chart or table, but at times they may be placed underneath the title.

Format of Tables

Tables are necessary for the presentation of exact, detailed information. They often serve as a basis for additional graphic aids, in the form of charts of various kinds used to illustrate specific groups of figures shown as part of the total data displayed in the table.

The format of a simple table is shown in Figure 11–1.

Figure 11–2 shows an example of a ruled table.

Format of Charts

A basic consideration in the construction of charts of all kinds is that they be kept simple. Charts that are complexly designed in an attempt to convey many kinds of information are counterproductive because they are harder to understand than carefully chosen words. Several simple charts that clearly show limited quantities of data are preferable to one complicated, hard-to-read illustration.

The types of charts (graphs) most frequently used are the *bar, line,* and *pie,* with numerous variations of the bar and line. Vertical bar charts are also referred to as *column charts,* or *column graphs,* and pie charts are also referred to as *circle,* or *segment,* charts or graphs. In addition, types of

Table 1
States with the biggest and smallest percentage
change in population, 1980–87:

State	% Change	State	% Change
Alaska	+31%	Iowa	−2.7%
Nevada	+26%	West Virginia	−2.7%
Arizona	+25%	Michigan	−0.7%
Florida	+23%	Ohio	−0.1%
Texas	+18%	Pennsylvania	+0.6%

* *Source: U.S. Census Bureau.*

charts can be combined; for example, a line chart is often imposed on a vertical bar chart, as shown in Figure 11–28.

Simple Bar Charts

Simple bar charts, both horizontal and vertical, compare quantities. The length or height of the bars indicates quantity. All bars should be the

Table 25
Employment Responsibilities of Total Group of 565
Certified Professional Secretaries for Editing
and Revising Writing of Other Persons

Frequency	Number	Percent
Regularly or Often	391	69.2
Occasionally	128	22.7
Never	46	8.1

* *Source:* Primary

same width. As discussed later in the chapter, varying the width of the bars results in distortion of data, at least to the hasty or casual observer. Spaces between the bars should also be equal. (A vertical bar graph with no spaces between the columns is referred to as a *histogram*). A horizontal bar chart is shown in Figure 11–3.

The quantitative axis should begin at zero unless to do so would make the chart too large. "Cutting off the bottom" is an error that sometimes occurs in chart making. When the amounts to be shown are relatively large in value, you may find it necessary to break the scale somewhere between

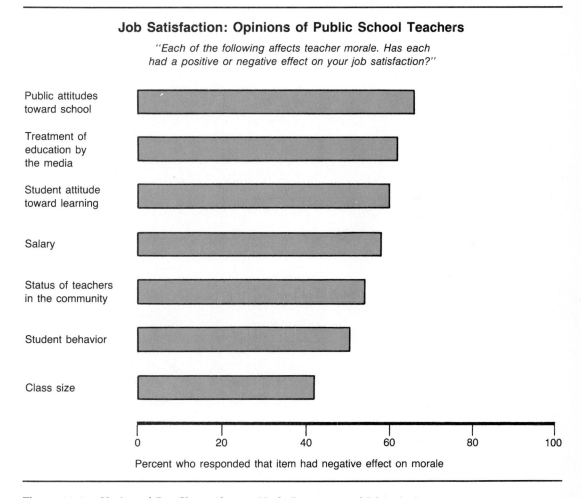

Figure 11–3. *Horizontal Bar Chart. (Source: U. S. Department of Education)*

zero and the lowest value. This break should be indicated to the reader by broken lines between zero and the first value shown.

A bar chart with vertical columns is shown in Figure 11–4. This chart is also referred to as a column chart.

Bilateral Bar Charts

A bilateral bar chart shows increases and decreases from a central point of reference. Bilateral bar charts are especially useful to show

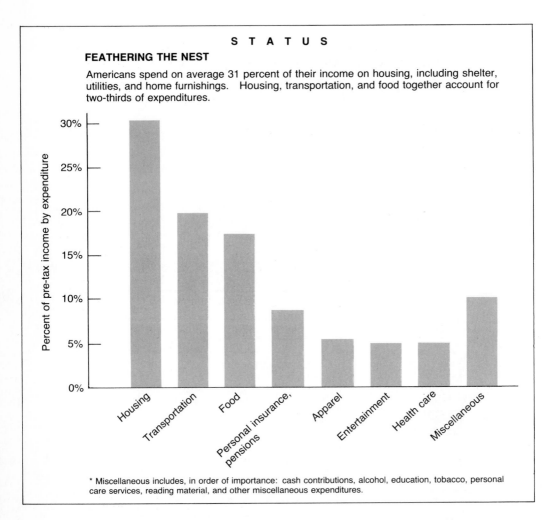

Figure 11–4. *Vertical bar chart. (Source: American Demographics,* February 1986, p. 12. Reprinted with permission.)

changes in percentages, but they may also be used for any series of data that contains negative quantities. Figure 11-5 shows the fluctuation of trade and service balances in West Germany for two years. Bilateral charts usually illustrate ''highs'' and ''lows'' and assist immediate understanding.

Bilateral bar charts may be designed with horizontal bars as well as vertical bars, as illustrated in Figure 11-6. This chart shows the relative changes in employment in the mining, manufacturing, and other major industries.

Multiple Bar and Subdivided Bar Charts

Variations of the simple bar chart, in addition to bilateral bar charts, include multiple bars and subdivided bars, with variations and combinations of each. A subdivided bar chart is shown in Figure 11-7.

A multiple bar chart is shown in Figure 11-8.

Charts of all kinds, but particularly bar charts, can be varied in numerous ways. Your main purpose in designing charts could be to choose

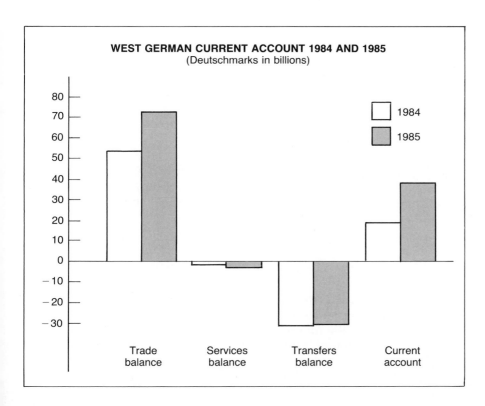

Figure 11–5.
Bilateral bar chart, vertical columns. (Source: Standard Chartered Review, July 1986, p. 44. Reprinted with permission.)

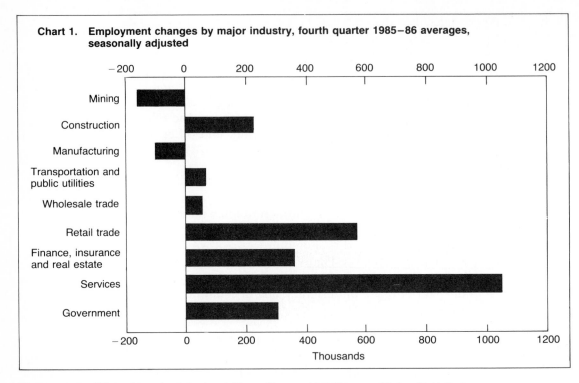

Chart 1. **Employment changes by major industry, fourth quarter 1985–86 averages, seasonally adjusted**

Figure 11–6. *Bilateral bar chart, horizontal bars. (Source: U.S. Bureau of Labor Statistics)*

the arrangement that will vividly, yet simply, compare the relationships you wish to emphasize.

A variation of a vertical bar chart is shown in Figure 11–9. This design is similar to the usual bilateral bar chart in that bars extend right or left from a central point of reference. The values shown, however, are not truly plus or minus values, but "Professional, managerial, and nonretail sales" and "Other."

Another kind of bar chart is the subdivided 100-percent bar. These charts may consist of either vertical or horizonal bars. They differ from ordinary bar charts in that all bars are the same length, with each bar representing 100 percent. These 100-percent bar charts serve the same purpose as pie charts (discussed later in this chapter) because they show divisions of the whole. Using photographs or objects assists immediate comprehension in charts. Note the thermometer illustrated in Figure 11–10. The suggestions of "soundness" and "health" are communicated in addition to the illustration of funds distribution.

A subdivided 100-percent bar chart is shown in Figure 11–11.

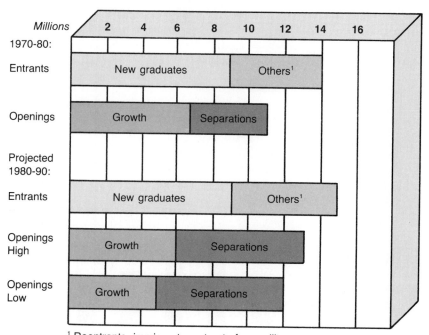

As During the 1970's, College Graduates Entering the Labor Force During the 1980's Are Expected to Exceed Openings by as Much as 3 Million

Figure 11–7. *Subdivided bar chart. (Source: U.S. Bureau of Labor Statistics)*

[1] Reentrants, immigrants, entrants from military, etc.

A chart that consists of groups of subdivided bars is shown in Figure 11–12.

Range Charts

A range chart shows minimum and maximum values, as illustrated in Figure 11–13. This particular line chart also includes minus values, showing that employment in agriculture is expected to decrease during the 1980s.

Line Charts

A line chart is used to show changes over a period of time, as illustrated in Figure 11–14. This figure is described as a multiple line chart be-

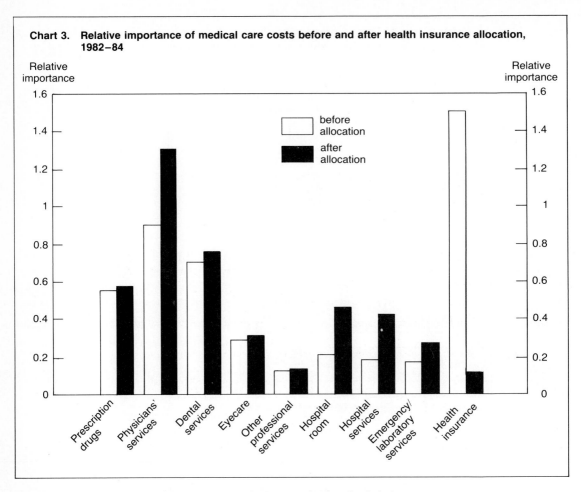

Figure 11–8. *Multiple bar chart. (Source: U.S. Bureau of Labor Statistics)*

cause it has more than one line; the three lines show increases from 1973 through 1985.

A variation of the usual multiple line chart is shown in Figure 11–15.

Index line charts, as illustrated in Figure 11–16, begin at some selected point of reference; in this instance, the year 1973.

In addition to the several variations of the line chart illustrated in this chapter, line charts may be combined with other charts, modified by special illustrations to become a pictorial chart, or presented in various other ways. For example, a line chart can be superimposed over the tops of vertical bars.

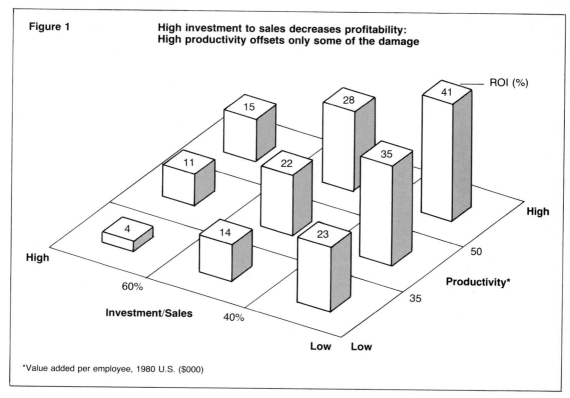

Figure 11–9. *Variation of vertical bar chart. (Source: Sloan Management Review,* Fall 1987, pp. 24, 28. Reprinted by permission of the publisher. Copyright © 1987 by the Sloan Management Review Association. All rights reserved.)

Work for simplicity. Regardless of the originality of the graphic aid, it is ineffective if overly complex.

A cumulative line chart also is referred to as a component-part line chart or as a belt chart. As shown in Figure 11–17, the top line represents the total. Color or crosshatching distinguishes the component parts.

Pie Charts

A pie chart, also described as a circle chart (or pie graph or circle graph) shows the component parts of a whole. Examples of two pie charts are shown in Figure 11–18. As in these illustrations, segments of the circle should be individually labeled, either within the segments or outside the circle. Exact amounts of percentages also should be shown. Figures in the

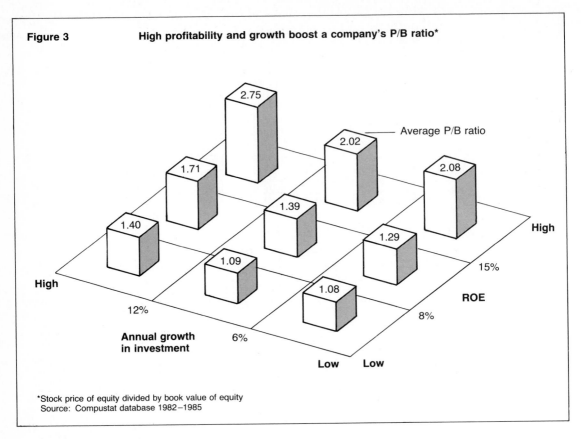

Figure 11–9. *continued*

segments of circles shown in Figure 11–18 represent industries where Master of Business Administration (MBA) graduates accepted employment. More often, segments of pie charts are marked with percentages, not numbers.

Combination Charts, Pictograms, Maps, Drawings, Flow Charts, and Other Graphic Aids

As mentioned previously, charts can be combined in various ways. The illustrations shown in Figure 11–19, however, cannot be described as a true combination chart; they ae two types of charts shown together. The second pie chart varies from the arrangement often recommended—that the largest segment start at the top, or the twelve o'clock position.

The illustrations of dollar signs in Figure 11–20 replace the usual verti-

Estimated distribution of net premium and investment dollar under California's Workers' Compensation Program 1986 (in percent)

Medical benefits 28.8

Permanent total benefits 1

Temporary benefits 9.2

Other expenses 9.4

Vocational rehabilitation benefits 10

Loss adjustment expenses 8.7

Permanent partial benefits 17.2

Death benefits 1.1

Commissions/Fees 5.8

Taxes 4.0

Profits 4.8

Benefits 67.3

Operating costs 27.9

Profits 4.8

Figure 11–10.
100-percent bar chart. (Source: Business and Health, March 1987, p. 27. Reprinted with permission.)

cal bars in a simple bar chart. The designer followed a principle of accurate construction by making all the illustrations equal in width.

Data in the pictorial chart shown in Figure 11–21 also could have been shown in pie charts or in the more usual 100-percent subdivided bar.

In the pictorial chart shown in Figure 11–22, individual drawings represent units of data. The designer correctly drew each item (hat, truck, and so on) the same size as all the others in the group. To do otherwise would result in distraction and at least momentary misrepresentation.

Population changes in each major section of the United States are shown in percentages displayed on the map, Figure 11–23.

Drawings are frequently used in many reports and other kinds of writing, particularly technical material. The description of how robots move, as illustrated in Figure 11–24, would require many additional words if the drawing were omitted. Drawings are necessary to depict mechanical processes and equipment.

An example of a flow chart is shown in Figure 11–25.

Figure 11–11.
Subdivided 100-percent bar chart.
(Source: Bureau of Industrial Economics, U.S. Department of Commerce)

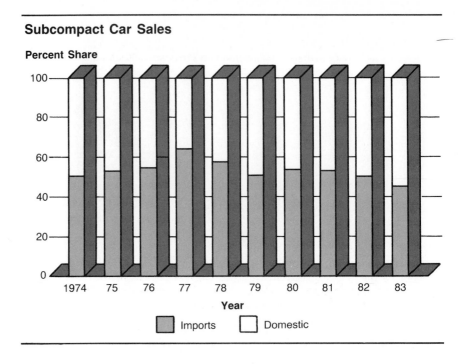

Subcompact Car Sales

Accurate and Honest Presentation of Data

The purpose of graphic aids is to show trends and relationships quickly, clearly, and accurately. Poorly constructed graphics do the opposite. Some of the ways these distortions of quantities, trends, and relationships result have already been mentioned as the various types of graphic aids were discussed. In summary, distortions are likely to be due to one or more of the following factors:

1. An inappropriately chosen grid. (A grid is the network of horizontal and vertical lines on which the chart is plotted.)

2. Inappropriate plotting on the grid; for example, not keeping the time schedule uniform.

3. Beginning the quantitative axis somewhere other than zero without making the omission immediately clear to the reader. This omission results in cutting off the bottom of a line or bar chart. Use all such charts with extreme caution. Even when readers are warned by broken lines that the scale has been broken, they are more likely to notice the overall effect of the chart than the broken lines.

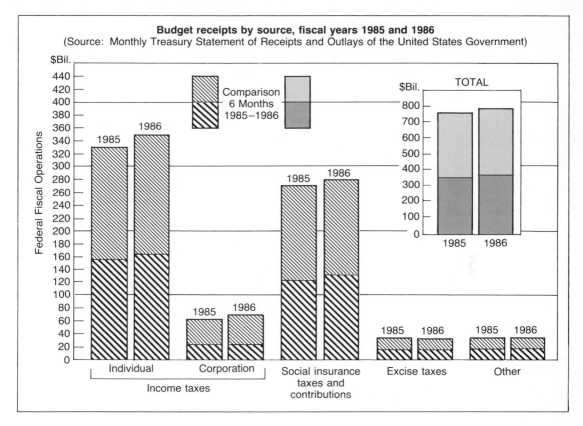

Figure 11–12. *Multiple bar chart with subdivided bars. (Source: U.S. Department of Treasury)*

Notice the effect of cutting off the bottom of the vertical bar graph shown in Figure 11–26. The differences between the amounts shown in the three columns seem to be drastically increased.

At times, because of lack of space a scale must be broken so that it does not begin at zero. In Figure 11–27, a chart planned to be shown on a projector to illustrate an oral report, the "jog" indicates to the viewer that the entire chart is not shown. If the chart had started at zero and was drawn to scale, it could not have fitted on a transparency in such readable form.

4. Varying more than one dimension in bar charts or pictograms. For example, if you are comparing hog production, use three hogs of identical size to indicate that three million were grown in 1982 as compared to 1972, when one million were grown, shown by one hog of identicial size. Do *not*

Figure 11–13.
Range chart.
(Source: U.S.
Bureau of Labor
Statistics)

Through the 1980s, Changes in Employment Will Vary Widely Among Industries

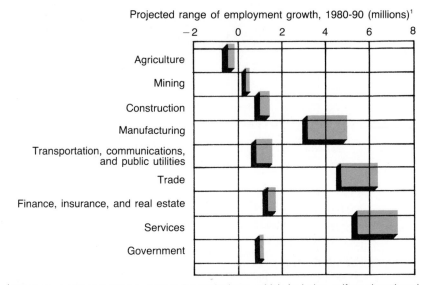

Projected range of employment growth, 1980-90 (millions)[1]

[1] Wage and salary workers, except for agriculture, which includes self-employed and unpaid family workers

attempt to make one hog three times larger to show the increase in number for 1982. (Unless you need something to do, forget about drawing hogs and use a simple bar graph or table. If your data are no more extensive than the numbers given here, forget about a chart.)

In order to prevent misinterpretation, other than that which can be caused by the design of the graphic aid, observe the following guidelines:

1. Interpret the information shown in the chart to the extent that you are sure your reader will understand its meaning. (The charts shown in this chapter are used to illustrate the different kinds of graphic aids, not to present the information itself. Thus discussion of the information presented on the charts is less than would be required if the charts were used in a business or technical report.)

2. Give credit where credit is due, as when using verbal passages other than your own.

3. Make sure that titles, legends, and explanatory notes adequately describe the purpose and content of each chart.

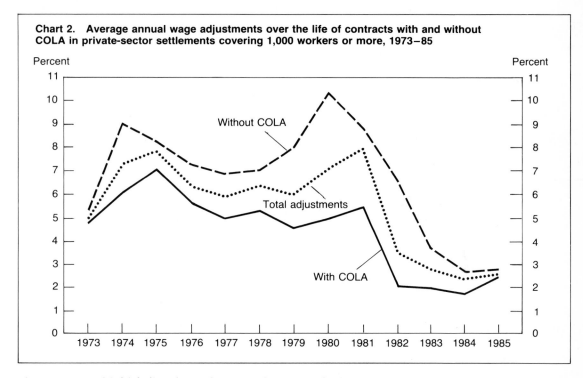

Figure 11–14. *Multiple line chart. (Source: U.S. Bureau of Labor Statistics)*

Graphic Aids Constructed by Computers

If you attempted to draw each of the graphic aids shown in this chapter, you would find that such a project requires a great deal of time and artistic ability. A few years ago, you would have constructed any necessary graphic aids by using pens, pencils, compasses, protractors, and rulers. For important material, you would perhaps have sent your suggested drawings to a professional artist, within or outside your organization.

Now almost all graphic aids can be quickly and easily constructed by computers, which can convert raw data into tables, charts, and designs of many kinds. Such presentation is possible through the use of mainframe computer terminals or microcomputers. You are likely to have a terminal or a microcomputer at your desk. Your software may include DrawPerfect, Microsoft Chart, Harvard Presentation Graphics, or some other charting software. Laser printers, plotters and other printers now permit excellent detail and colors.

Engineers' Annual Salaries Compared With Other Workers'

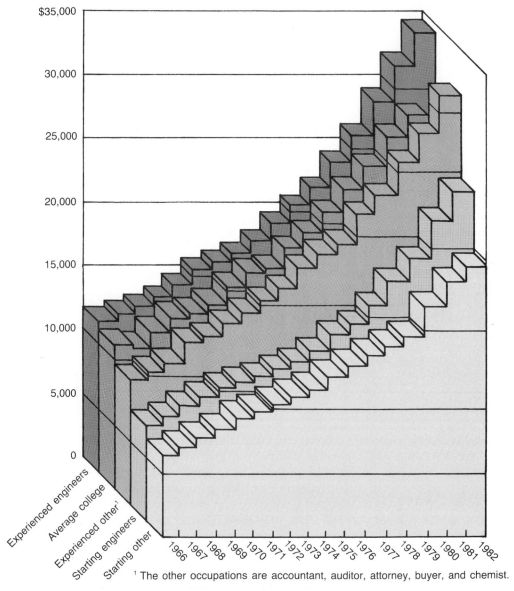

¹ The other occupations are accountant, auditor, attorney, buyer, and chemist.

Figure 11–15. *Multiple line chart. Source: Occupational Outlook Quarterly, Summer 1983, p. 4.)*

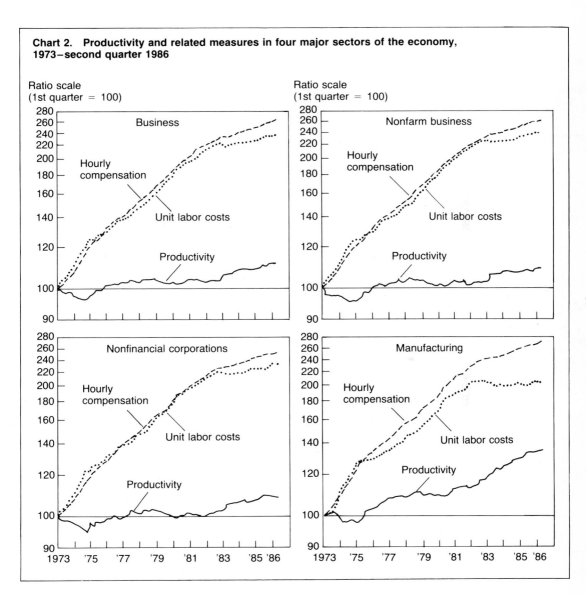

Figure 11–16. *Index line chart. (Source: U.S. Bureau of Labor Statistics)*

Outlays for Transportation

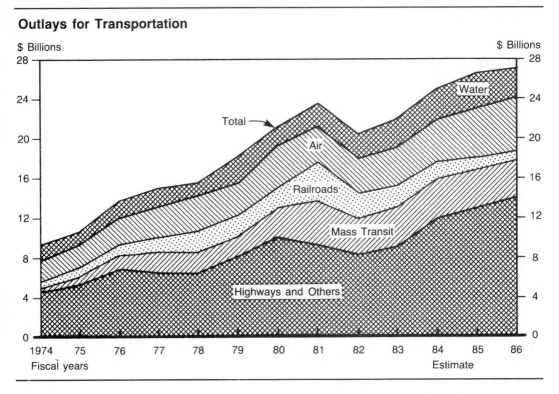

Figure 11–17. *Cumulative line chart. (Source: "The United States Budget in Brief. Fiscal Year 1984," Executive Office of the President, Office of Management and Budget.)*

If you have the proper equipment and software, you can select the kind of design you wish and, by a simple procedure, instruct the computer to show your selected display on the screen. See Lotus 1–2–3 sample in Figure 11–31. Microsoft Chart software produced the charts in Figures 11–28 and 11–29. Harvard Presentation Graphics software produced Figure 11–30. Then, when your design meets your specifications, it can be printed in various ways. Some equipment will transfer your graphic aids onto color prints, transparencies, and 35 millimeter slides.

Although the actual construction of graphic aids is far easier than it was in past years, you still have the responsibility of choosing the most appropriate chart to display your particular data. In some instances, you will need several different charts in order to present varying aspects of your data. All the principles of graphic presentation discussed in this chapter apply, whether or not they are constructed by a computer. In fact, as construction becomes easier and quicker, you will find that you increase your use of graphic aids.

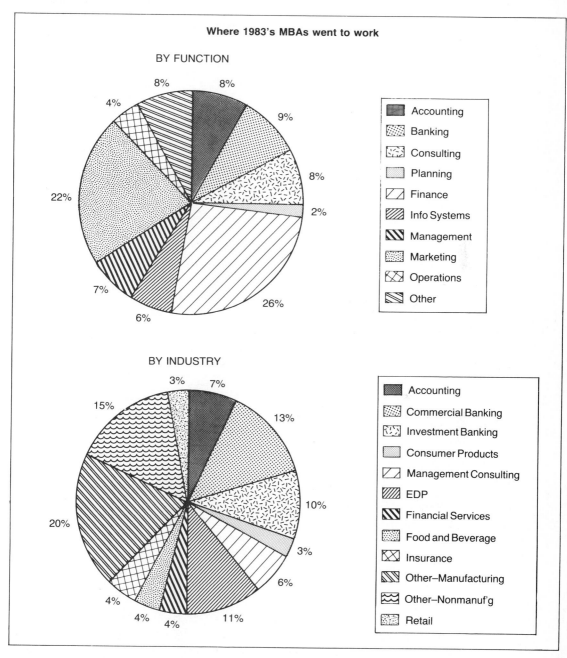

Figure 11–18. *Pie charts. (Source:* Occupational Outlook Quarterly, Winter 1985, pp. 4–5) Prepared on Microsoft Chart.

Figure 11–19.
*Horizontal bar
chart shown with
two pie charts.
(U.S. Bureau of
the Census)*

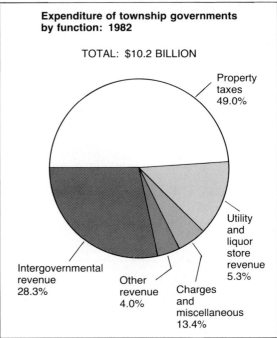

**Expenditure of township governments
by function: 1982**

TOTAL: $10.2 BILLION

Property
taxes
49.0%

Utility
and
liquor
store
revenue
5.3%

Intergovernmental
revenue
28.3%

Other
revenue
4.0%

Charges
and
miscellaneous
13.4%

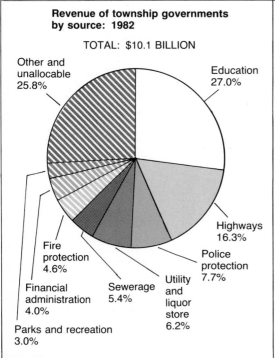

**Revenue of township governments
by source: 1982**

TOTAL: $10.1 BILLION

Other and
unallocable
25.8%

Education
27.0%

Highways
16.3%

Police
protection
7.7%

Fire
protection
4.6%

Utility
and
liquor
store
6.2%

Sewerage
5.4%

Financial
administration
4.0%

Parks and recreation
3.0%

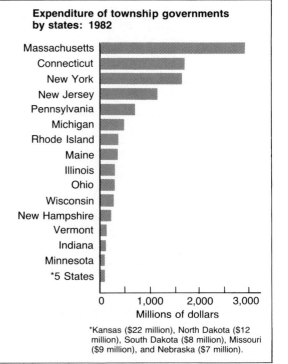

**Expenditure of township governments
by states: 1982**

Massachusetts
Connecticut
New York
New Jersey
Pennsylvania
Michigan
Rhode Island
Maine
Illinois
Ohio
Wisconsin
New Hampshire
Vermont
Indiana
Minnesota
*5 States

0   1,000   2,000   3,000
Millions of dollars

*Kansas ($22 million), North Dakota ($12
million), South Dakota ($8 million), Missouri
($9 million), and Nebraska ($7 million).

Total State/Local Dollars Spent for Each Federal Dollar Under Vocational Education Act (VEA)

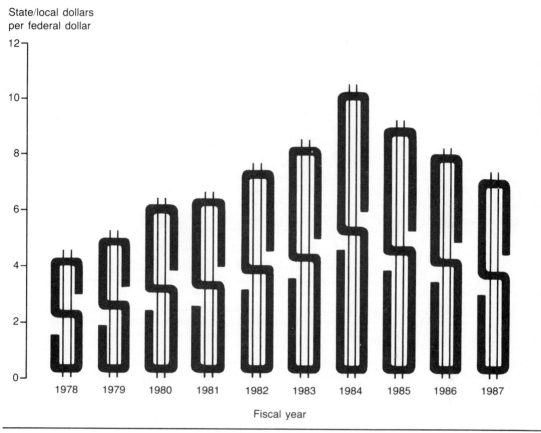

Figure 11–20. *Pictorial bar chart. (Source: U.S. Department of Education)*

As with other improvements and innovations that speed routine work, such as word processing equipment that saves typewriting time, computers do not decrease the importance of your knowledge, judgment, and careful thought. Instead, you will find it even more essential to know the basic underlying principles of communication tasks that now can be handled automatically, once you have made correct choices and given appropriate, exact instructions.

1,000 Hotels and Motels: Source and Disposition of the Industry Dollar

Rooms 60.5¢

Food 23.5¢

Beverages 8.9¢

Other operated departments 4.9¢

All other 2.2¢

Employees' wages and meals 28.1¢

Cost of goods sold 12.1¢

Operating supplies and expenses 30.7¢

Taxing authorities* 5.5¢

Income available for depreciation, rent, interest, amortization and income taxes 23.6¢

* Real Estate, Social Security and other direct taxes except Federal Income.

Figure 11–21. *Pictorial chart showing component parts of a whole. (Source: Prepared by Pannell Kerr Forster)*

Oil and Gas Exploration and Extraction Employ About Half of All Workers in the Mining and Petroleum Industries.

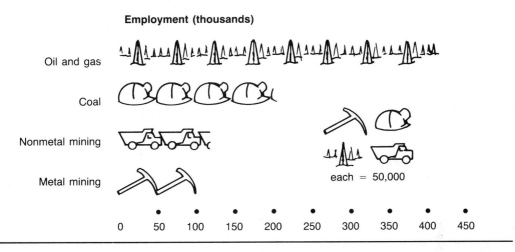

Employment (thousands)

Oil and gas

Coal

Nonmetal mining

Metal mining

each = 50,000

0   50   100   150   200   250   300   350   400   450

Figure 11–22. *A pictorial chart. (Source: U.S. Bureau of Labor Statistics)*

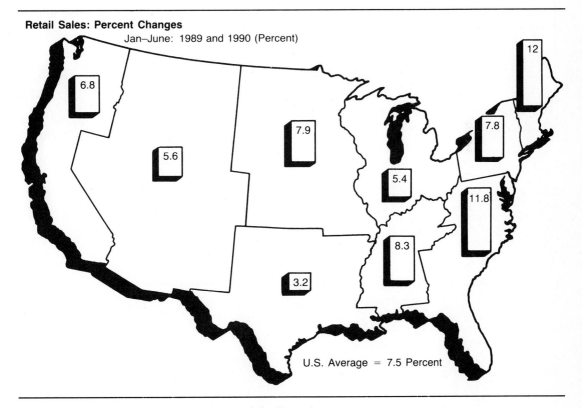

Retail Sales: Percent Changes
Jan–June: 1989 and 1990 (Percent)

6.8

12

5.6

7.9

7.8

5.4

11.8

8.3

3.2

U.S. Average = 7.5 Percent

Figure 11–23. *Map. (Source: U.S. Bureau of the Census)*

How Robots Move

Figure 11–24. *Drawing. (Source: Occupational Outlook Quarterly, Fall 1982, p. 10.)*

Student Placement System

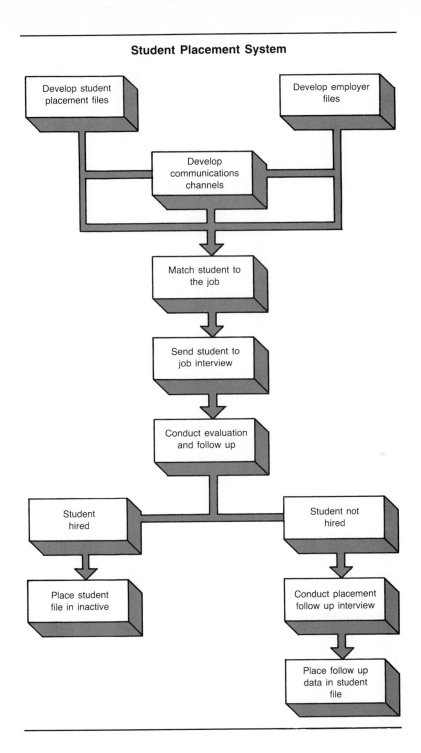

Develop student placement files

Develop employer files

Develop communications channels

Match student to the job

Send student to job interview

Conduct evaluation and follow up

Student hired

Student not hired

Place student file in inactive

Conduct placement follow up interview

Place follow up data in student file

Figure 11–25.
Flow chart.
(Source: Occupational Outlook Quarterly,
Spring 1982, p. 37)

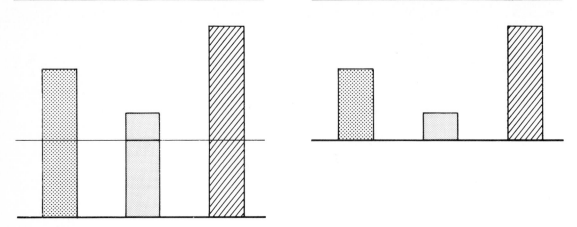

Figure 11–26. *Illustration of how a vertical bar chart can be distorted by starting at some point other than zero.*

Figure 11–27. *Illustrations of chart with a scale break.*

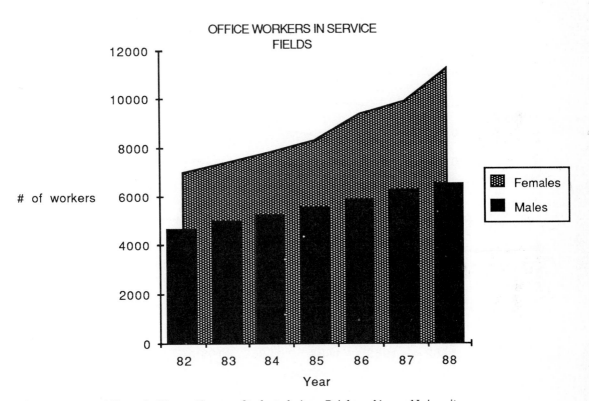

Figure 11–28. *Microsoft Chart. (Source: Student design, Brigham Young University, 1989.)*

WIDGETS UNLIMITED, INC.

Figure 11–29. *Microsoft Chart. (Source: Student design, Brigham Young University, 1989.)*

ANNUAL IMPORTS
OPEC and Non-OPEC Sources

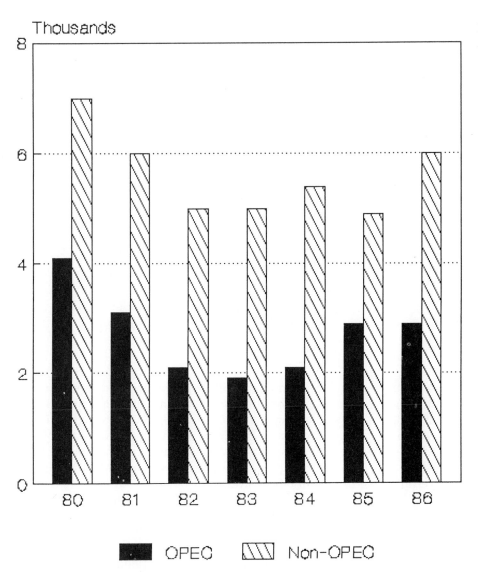

Figure 11–30.
Harvard Presentation Graphics. (Data: U.S. Department of Energy, Energy Information Administration)

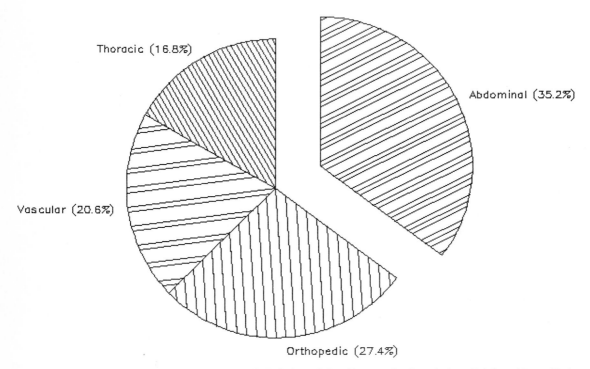

Figure 11–31. *Lotus 1–2–3, Release 2.01. (Source: Student design, Brigham Young University, 1989.)*

Summary

1. Use charts, tables, and other illustrations as needed to express meaning quickly and clearly, but do not use them merely to impress.

2. Choose the appropriate type of chart, table, or other graphic aid to best convey the desired meaning or comparison. Some information should be shown in more than one way in the same report. For example, the reader may need exact figures instead of trends and relationships; if so, present these figures in tabular form.

3. Ordinarily, a graphic aid should be placed within the text of the report, as near as possible to the portion of the text that it is used to illustrate or explain. If it is not closely related to the material being discussed, it should either be omitted or placed in the appendix of the report. Tables and charts, like other information, belong in the appendix if they can be considered supplementary to the report itself.

4. Introduce the graphic device before presenting it, and, preferably, include a few words of discussion after the device has been presented.

5. Point out the highlights of the graphic aid. By pointing out items of major importance shown by the table or chart, you are able to refer subordinately to the graphic aid, as in ''The greatest increase in sales occurred in District 1 (72%) and the smallest in District 7 (17%), as shown in Table 3.''

6. Make sure that graphic aids are constructed so that relationships are not distorted. Use reasonable proportion. Start at zero or show by broken lines that, because of space limitations, it was impractical to start at zero.

7. Carefully label each graphic device. Provide a key (also called a legend) if it will be helpful to the reader.

8. Keep all tables and charts simple. Do not try to show too much information on one chart.

1. Which form of graphic illustration would you construct to illustrate the following types of information? Support your decision. For some of the items, several choices could be used.
   a. Record of the earnings per share of The Local Corporation for the past seventeen years.
   b. Comparison of sales of The Local Corporation for three product lines for the past three years.
   c. A comparison of the change in net profit for the twenty restaurants of Bigger Burger, Inc.
   d. Comparison of white collar, blue collar, service, and farm workers in the U.S. labor force for each year ending in five or zero from 1975 to the present.
   e. Breakdown of how the federal government dollar was spent last year.
   f. Mean, maximum, and minimum temperatures in your city or town for each month of the year.
   g. Average number of days per year with hail, by geographical area of the United States.
   h. Comparison within the Morano Shoe Corporation to show which subsidiary companies account for different percentages of total sales for the product groups.
   i. Comparison of the world's ten largest cities to show population changes for the past ten-year period.
   j. Comparison of the consumer price index to the producer price index over the past twenty years.
   k. Residential buildings permits (single family, multiple family, and total) for Los Angeles County, 1978–1988.
2. Assume reasonable data and construct appropriate graphic aids to illustrate the comparisons and presentations described in question 1.

Questions and Problems

3. Bring to class a photocopy of a graphic presentation as shown in a magazine, newspaper, or recent textbook. Be prepared to show this graphic aid on the opaque projector and to comment on the illustration shown. Is the chart the most appropriate one for the particular data and the desired comparison of relationships? Is the chart correctly and accurately made?

4. Present the information requested in problem 3 in a memorandum attached to the illustrated chart or other graphic aid.

5. Write one or more introductory paragraphs to precede Figures 11–3, 11–4, 11–5, 11–6, 11–7, 11–8, 11–9, 11–10, 11–11, 11–12, 11–13, 11–14, 11–15, 11–16, 11–17, 11–18, 11–19 and 11–20. As your instructor directs, write another paragraph to follow each chart.

6. Design a chart to show the data in Figure 11–1 now shown as an example of an unruled table.

7. Design a chart you compose on your computer. Identify appropriate title and axis legends. Print out the chart or submit a disk as your instructor prefers. Eventually you will transfer the assignment to your boss's or instructor's data files and, after modification, the chart can be printed or transferred (via modem) back to your office and computer.

CHAPTER **12**

Purposes and Methods of Documentation

Chapter Outline

This chapter discusses the importance and purposes of exact documentation; describes the placement, arrangement, and content of cited material, footnotes, and bibliographies; and lists widely used style manuals. The last section of this chapter summarizes principles of documentation with illustrations from the chapter itself.

Purposes of Documentation

When you use material other than your own, whether in the direct words of the author or in paraphrased form, give credit to the originator of the material. Give complete information about the source of the borrowed words. To do otherwise is plagiarism, a form of theft. Penalties are severe.

Information considered to be general knowledge need not be footnoted unless you use the exact words or mode of expression of an individual writer or speaker. For example, if you should state that the computer has brought vast changes to the business world and has influenced our entire society, you need not quote one particular writer or speaker who has made a similar statement.

If you are not completely sure that material you find in secondary sources is considered common knowledge, give credit in the usual way. Even when an item is considered common knowledge, you may choose to footnote in order to add authority to the statement.

Meaning of the Terms "Reference Notes" and "Bibliography"

Reference notes, which may be arranged in various ways and placed in several positions, quote specific references, including page numbers of written sources. An entry in a bibliography refers to an entire source, such as a book, journal article, personal or telephone interview, or government document. A report or other paper may have footnotes but no bibliography. It is also possible that a bibliography is appropriate when no footnotes are necessary.

Reference Notes

The term *footnote* is derived from the traditional placement of the note at the bottom of a page. References to cited material also can be placed at the end of a manuscript, report, chapter, or book, where they are referred to as *notes* or *endnotes*. Placement also may be within the text of the written work. Regardless of placement, reference notes accomplish the same purpose, that of citing a particular page of a printed source or adding explanatory material.

Bibliographies

The prefix *biblio* is the Greek word that means "book." For this reason, some teachers and researchers prefer not to include nonbook sources, such as speeches or personal interviews, under the heading *Bibliography*. Instead, they use *References, Reference Sources, Sources of Data, References Consulted*, or a similar term. In general use, however, and ordinarily acceptable, the term *bibliography* includes interviews, letters, unpublished material, and secondary sources, including those that contributed to the paper without being specifically cited in footnotes. The heading *Works Cited* is more exclusive, including only those works cited specifically in footnotes.

Some confusion of meaning exists between the terms *selected bibliography* and *bibliography*. Campbell and Ballou make these distinctions:

> However, some writers insist that a bibliography should include all the works of an author or all the writings about a given topic; consequently, according to them, a proper heading in a paper or dissertation is *Selected Bibliography, Works Cited,* or something similar. Current usage and the preceding definition justify using *Bibliography* as a heading if the writer so chooses; the assumption here is that either option is acceptable.[1]

Campbell and Ballou state further:

> You may experience uncertainty about what should or may be included in a bibliography. You should list all sources quoted or referred to in the paper, and you may include useful background references in a selected bibliography, even though they are not cited in the paper. You are not obligated to quote or to list mediocre references; thus, in this sense, most bibliographies are "selected."[2]

Regardless of the title of the reference section usually referred to as a *bibliography,* it must include *all* sources used as documentation and presented in footnotes or endnotes. If sources other than those referred to by footnotes contributed to the content of the report, these sources must also be included in the bibliography.

1. William Giles Campbell, Stephen Vaughan Ballou, and Carole Slade, *Form and Style: Theses, Reports, Term Papers,* 6th ed. (Boston: Houghton Mifflin, 1982), p. 103.

2. Campbell and Ballou, p. 104.

When determining sources to be included, you should not interpret the word *consulted* to mean all secondary sources you examine in order to determine their usefulness and applicability. For example, you may think that a book listed in the card catalog contains the exact information you are seeking, only to find upon examination that the book is not suitable in any way. Book titles in themselves are often misleading.[3] A thorough examination of the description given in the card catalog, however, will usually indicate the content of the particular book.

Using Quoted and Paraphrased Passages

As you include information from secondary sources, you may choose to use it *verbatim;* that is, in the exact words of the writer you are quoting. Paraphrased material is expressed in your own words, although you have taken the information from another source.

Passages that you quote verbatim must be clearly distinguished from the rest of the text. Paraphrased passages are not set off, but your footnotes should make clear what portion of the text you are documenting. Footnote numbers follow the cited material.

According to Turabian, "... short, direct prose quotations should be incorporated into the text of the paper and enclosed in double quotation marks."[4] Quoted material of no more than three typewritten lines is typed within the text, is illustrated by the immediately preceding sentence. If the quoted material is longer than three typewritten lines, it should be set off from the text by single spacing, as explained in the words of Kate Turabian:

> Longer quotations—two or more sentences which would occupy four or more typewritten lines—should be set off from the text in single spacing and indented in their entirety four spaces from the left marginal line of text, omitting quotation marks at beginning and end. .... If paragraph indention is necessary, indent another four spaces for the beginning of a paragraph.[5]

The *ellipsis* is a series of three periods, in addition to a period at the end of a sentence, if necessary, typed with intervening spaces. The ellipsis in the quoted material displayed above indicates that some of the exact words of the original source have been omitted. Because omissions can

3. Wilma Dykeman, who in 1965 published a book entitled *The French Broad,* remarked that the book has sold much better than other books in the *River of America* series. The French Broad is a river in Appalachia.

4. Kate L. Turabian, *A Manual for Writers of Term Papers, Theses, and Dissertations,* 5th ed., rev. (Chicago: University of Chicago Press, 1987), p. 69.

5. Turabian, p. 69.

distort meaning, conventional usage is to insert an ellipsis to indicate that a portion of the original passage is not included. You are further obligated to make sure that omissions, even when so indicated, do not change the writer's overall intent and overall meaning. Omission of a paragraph or more is sometimes shown by a complete line of spaced periods.

Use care and judgment in citing secondary information. When you include a statement or opinion of someone else, you imply that you agree with the cited material unless you state otherwise. The material must be relevant to your overall approach and content. It must carry forward the flow of thought and amplify and strengthen your own discussion.

Barzun and Graff comment on occasions when you may omit footnotes:

> In citing and crediting authors, you must, as in all other phases of research and writing, use judgment. Many obvious quotations need no author's name. For instance, if you are so unadventurous that you find yourself quoting "to be or not to be," leave the author in decent obscurity. If you quote for purely decorative purpose an anecdote that is going the rounds and that you found in your local newspaper, or a trifling news item from the same source, no reference is needed to the place and date. . . . Remember, in other words, that quoting is for illustration and citing is for possible verification.[6]

Although you may omit footnotes in instances like those mentioned in the quotation above, be extremely careful not to omit needed documentation. *When in doubt, footnote.*

Even though you give proper credit to the author of the information you include, you are not free to use an unlimited amount of material from one particular source without express permission. For example, an entire chapter from *The Modern Researcher* by Barzun and Graff could not be legally or ethically included in this textbook without permission from the copyright holder. The use of the preceding passage and the following one is permitted under the "Fair Use" provision of the copyright laws. Barzun and Graff state:

> But do you ask for six words? Obviously not. Some publishers allow passages of 250 to 500 words to be quoted without permission having to be asked. This latitude is sometimes stated on the copyright page; look there for the exact wordage granted free. Remember than an aggregate of, say, 300 words quoted by you here and there requires permission as if it were one long passage.[7]

6. Jacques Barzun and Henry F. Graff, *The Modern Researcher,* 4th ed. (New York: Harcourt Brace Jovanovich, 1985), p. 344.

7. Barzun and Graff, p. 343.

A limit of 250 words is the usual guideline at this time. If you are unsure whether you are exceeding the accepted limit, check with the particular publisher.

Placement of Footnotes and Other Reference Notes

Footnotes may be placed at the bottom of a page, separated from the text by a typewritten line one and one-half inches long, beginning at the left margin. Complete notes are also placed within the text itself, as near as possible to the cited passage. Another method is to place all references at the end of a report or other written work. With this arrangement, the bibliography is often omitted. Reference notes may be placed at the end of chapters in a book or at the end of the book itself.

Placement within the text may be in one of several forms. One arrangement is to separate the footnote from the text by the use of top and bottom lines that extend the full width of the page. Another is to enclose the footnote within parentheses. As with bottom-of-page placement, footnote numbers follow cited material.

A disadvantage of the traditional bottom-of-page arrangement is that it makes manuscripts more difficult to type than when footnotes are placed together on one page at the end of the report. Word processing software assists spacing and typing footnotes on each page, but for text that is not technical, readers do not mind using end of chapter or end of report references. Advantages of bottom-of-page placement are that the reader can more easily see the footnotes than if they are on a later page, especially when the document is recorded on microfilm. They are also not so distracting as when inserted within the text. In addition, an arrangement other than the traditional bottom-of-page placement seems to some readers somewhat less than formal and professional.

Shortened subsequent footnotes, with or without a bibliography, are also used at the bottom of a page, as illustrated by the actual footnotes that accompany this chapter. If you are not sure of the arrangement preferred by your readers, you are wise to use bottom-of-page footnotes in complete form the first time a particular reference is cited, whether or not you include a bibliography. If you are not sure whether to include a bibliography, you are wise to include it.

A great number of footnotes can be distracting regardless of where they are placed, although they must be used when they are necessary for proper credit to the original author. If you find that you are using an excessive number, to the extent that much of your report consists of bits and pieces of others' works, perhaps you are doing too much citing and not enough analysis and interpretation of your own. (An unusual number of footnotes are included in this chapter because the chapter itself is planned to serve as an example of the various uses of footnotes.)

Suggested Style Manuals

If you are requested to use a particular style manual as a guide, or if you are asked to use the format previously chosen for your organization, make sure that you follow the suggested methods exactly. A variation may distract or annoy your reader to the extent that it interferes with the reception of your intended message. In addition, ability and willingness to follow instructions is a necessary part of communication within organizations.

According to Barzun and Graff,[8] if no particular manual is stipulated, you are wise to choose one of two widely used manuals: *The MLA Handbook*[9] or *A Manual of Style,* University of Chicago Press, commonly referred to as the *Chicago Manual of Style.*[10] A digest of the University of Chicago system has been published by Kate L. Turabian.[11] Another widely used guide is *Form and Style: Theses, Reports, Term Papers,* by Campbell and Ballou, which includes illustrations from other style manuals.[12] Another guide is *Publication Manual of the American Psychological Association.*[13]

The rule for spacing between main headings and subheading is to use consistency throughout the report. The APA style uses endnotes rather than footnotes.

As many lettered levels may be used as necessary, typically, only A, B, and C-levels are used unless the paper is extremely detailed. As mentioned above, differentiation of levels is made by placement, font changes, or the use of a combination of uppercase and lowercase letters. The rule for subheading differentiation is consistent use throughout the report.

Footnotes with Corresponding Bibliographic Entries

The examples of footnotes and bibliographic entries that follow, as well as actual footnotes and bibliographies shown in this textbook, are based on *A Manual of Style,* 13th ed., University of Chicago Press. This manual is the one used by most publishers. It is appropriate for any manuscript unless you are directed to use another arrangement of documentation.

In the following examples, *F* indicates footnote and *B* indicates an

---

8. Barzun and Graff, p. 359.

9. *The MLA Handbook for Writers of Research Papers, Theses, and Dissertations.* 2nd ed. (New York: Modern Language Association, 1984).

10. *A Manual of Style,* 13 ed. rev. (Chicago: University of Chicago Press, 1982)

11. Turabian, *A Manual for Writers.*

12. Campbell and Ballou.

13. *Publication Manual of the American Psychological Association,* 3d ed., rev. (Washington, D.C., 1983).

```
                              TURABIAN STYLE
        The title is typed as an all-capital spread heading and is placed on the
   thirteenth line from the top of the paper. A triple space follows the title.

                                Main Heading
        The main heading, or second-degree heading, is centered, uppercase and
   lowercase, underlined, and preceded and followed by a triple space. Alternatively,
   the main heading may be followed by a double space. For detailed writing, another
   level of headings (centered, uppercase and lowercase heading without underlining)
   may be used between the main heading and the third-degree heading.

   Third-Degree Heading
        The third-degree heading is flushed left, uppercase and lowercase, preceded
   by a triple space, and followed by a double space. For detailed writing, another
   level of headings (flushed left, uppercase and lowercase heading without
   underlining) may be used between the third-degree heading and the paragraph
   headings.
        Fourth-degree heading. This heading—called a paragraph heading—is indented,
   underlined, and ends with a period on the first line of the paragraph. No extra
   spacing precedes it in addition to the double spacing used throughout the paper.
```

Figure 12–1. *Typewritten arrangement of report—Kate L. Turabian,* A Manual for Writers of Term Papers, Theses, and Dissertations

entry in a bibliography. Indentations in the finished report are five spaces for footnotes and seven for bibliographies.

For a book with one author:

F   [1]Malra Treece, *Successful Communication for Business and the Professions*, 5th ed. (Boston: Allyn and Bacon, 1991), p. 500.

B   Treece, Malra. *Successful Communication for Business and the Professions*. 5th ed. Boston: Allyn and Bacon, 1991.

For a book with two authors:

F   [2]Treece, Malra and Larry D. Hartman, *Effective Reports for Managerial Communication*, 3d ed. Boston: Allyn and Bacon, 1990.

B   Bonner, William N. *Communicating in Business: Key to Success*. 4th ed. Houston: Dame Publications, 1986.

```
                American Psychological Association Style
    The title is centered and typed in uppercase and lowercase.


                              Main Heading
        The main heading, or second-degree heading, is centered, uppercase and
    lowercase, without underlining. For detailed writing, another level of headings
    (centered, uppercase and lowercase heading with underlining) may be used between
    the main heading and the third-degree heading.


    Third-Degree Heading
        The third-degree heading is flushed left, uppercase and lowercase, and
    underlined.
        Fourth-degree heading. This heading–called a paragraph heading–is indented,
    underlined, and ends with a period on the first line of the paragraph.
```

Figure 12–2. *Typewritten Arrangement of report—Publication Manual of the American Psychological Association Style*

```
                       The Chicago Manual of Style
    The title is centered and typed in uppercase and lowercase.


                            A-LEVEL SUBHEADING
        The main heading–called an A-level subheading–may be typed as an all-capital
    spread heading and centered. Differentiation of levels, however, is made by
    placement, font changes, or the use of a combination of uppercase and lowercase
    letters.

        B-LEVEL HEADING
        The B-level heading may be indented in all-capital letters.
        C-level heading. The lowest subheading is typically presented as a paragraph
    heading. This subheading is generally indented, may or may not be underlined, and
    ends with a period on the first line of the paragraph.
```

Figure 12–3. *Typewritten Arrangement of report—The Chicago Manual of Style*[1]

1. Editorial Staff of the University of Chicago Press, *The Chicago Manual of Style* (University of Chicago Press, Chicago, 1982), p. 411.

```
                                                              Ervin 1

Timothy B. Ervin
Professor Hardin
English 312
May 3, 1990

                MLA Handbook for Writers of Research Papers
     The title is centered, uppercase and lowercase, without underlining. Double
space before and after the title.
     Also, double space the entire text and leave a one-inch margin around all
borders of the page. Pages are numbered by indicating the person's last name who
is writing the report and is flushed right 1/2 inch from the top of the page.
```

Figure 12–4 *Typewritten Arrangement of report—MLA Handbook for Writers of Research Papers*[2]

For a book with three authors:

F   [3]Gretchen N. Vik, C. W. Wilkinson, and Dorothy C. Wilkinson, *Communicating Through Writing and Speaking in Business,* 9th ed. (Homewood, Ill.: Richard D. Irwrin, 1989), pp. 22–24.

B   Vik, Gretchen N., Wilkinson, C. W., Wilkinson, Dorothy C. *Communicating Through Writing and Speaking in Business,* 9th ed. Homewood, Ill.; Richard D. Irwin, 1989.

For a book with more than three authors:

F   [4]Robert J. Kilber et al., *Objectives for Instruction and Evaluation* (Boston: Allyn and Bacon, 1974), p. 153.

B   Kibler, Robert J.: Cegala, Donald J.; Miles, David T.; and Barker, Larry L. *Objectives for Instruction and Evaluation.* Boston: Allyn and Bacon, 1974.

For an edited book or one revised by a person other than the original author:

F   [5]Richard C. Huseman, Cal M. Logue, and Dwight L. Freshley, eds., *Readings in Interpersonal and Organizational Communication,* 3d ed. (Boston: Holbrook Press, 1977), pp. 1–2.

B   Huseman, Richard C.; Logue, Cal M.; and Freshley, Dwight L., eds. *Read-*

2. Joseph Gibaldi and Walter S. Achtert, *MLA Handbook for Writers of Research Papers* (New York: The Modern0Language Association of America, 1988), pp. 185–90.

ings in Interpersonal and Organizational Communication. Boston: Holbrook Press, 1977.

F   [6]H. W. Fowler, *A Dictionary of Modern English Usage,* 2d ed., rev. Sir Ernest Gowers (Oxford: Oxford University Press, 1965), p. 157.

B   Fowler, H. W. *A Dictionary of Modern English Usage.* 2d ed. Revised by Sir Ernest Gowers. Oxford: Oxford University Press, 1965.

For a book with no author given:

F   [7]*The Chicago Manual of Style,* 13th ed. rev. (Chicago: University of Chicago Press, 1982), pp. 42–44.

B   *The Chicago Manual of Style.* 13th ed rev. Chicago: University of Chicago Press, 1982.

For a chapter of a collective work:

F   [8]Merwyn A. Hayes, ''Nonverbal Communication: Expression Without Words,'' in *Readings in Interpersonal and Organizational Communication,* 3d ed., edited by Richard C. Huseman, Cal M. Logue, and Dwight L. Freshley (Boston: Holbrook Press, 1977), pp. 55–68.

B   Hayes, Merwyn A. ''Nonverbal Communication: Expression Without Words.'' In *Readings in Interpersonal and Organizational Communication,* 3d ed., edited by Richard C. Huseman, Cal M. Logue, and Dwight L. Freshley, pp. 55–68. Boston: Holbrook Press, 1977.

For a book in a series:

F   [9]James A. Smith, *Creative Teaching of the Language Arts in the Elementary School,* Allyn and Bacon Series in Creative Teaching, vol. 2 (Boston, 1967), p. 30.

B   Smith, James A. *Creative Teaching of the Language Arts in the Elementary School.* Allyn and Bacon Series in Creative Teaching, vol. 2. Boston, 1967.

For an unpublished work:

F   [10]Myrena Sue Jennings, ''A Comparison of Middle Managerial Written Business Communications Practices and Problems and Collegiate Written Business Communications Instruction'' (Doctoral diss., Georgia State University, 1974), p. 271.

B   Jennings, Myrena Sue. ''A Comparison of Middle Managerial Written Business Communications Practices and Problems and Collegiate Written Business Communications Instruction.'' Doctoral diss., Georgia State University, 1974.

For an article in a periodical:

F   [11]Robert Gunning, ''The Fog Index after Twenty Years,'' *Journal of Business Communication* 6 (Winter 1968): 3.

B   Gunning, Robert. ''The Fog Index after Twenty Years.'' *Journal of Business Communication* 6 (Winter 1968): 3.

F   [12]Fred T. Allen, "Ways to Improve Employee Communication," *Nation's Business* (September 1975), pp. 54–56.

B   Allen, Fred T. "Ways to Improve Employee Communication." *Nation's Business*. September 1975.

F   [13]"The Mail," *Atlantic Monthly*, February 1979, pp. 28–32.

B   "The Mail." *Atlantic Monthly*, February 1979, pp. 28–32.

For an article in a well-known reference book:

F   [14]*Encyclopaedia Britannica*, 1987, s.v. "Printing."

B   *Encyclopaedia Britannica*. 1987, s.v. "Printing."

F   [15]*The Concise Oxford Dictionary of Current English*, 7th ed. s.v. "Communication."

B   *The Concise Oxford Dictionary of Current English*. 7th ed., s.v. "Communication."

For a newspaper article:

F   [16]*Los Angeles Times*, 28 January 1988, p. 1.

B   *Los Angeles Times*, 28 January 1988, p. 1.

For government publications:

F   [17]U.S. Congress, House Committee on Business, *Operating Small Businesses*, 79th Cong., 2d sess., 1946, H. R. 1888, p. 63.

B   U.S. Congress, House Committee on Business. *Operating Small Businesses*. 79th Cong., 2d sess., 1946. H. R. 1888.

F   [18]Social Science Research Council, *Adjustment to Physical Handicap and Illness: A Survey of the Social Psychology of Physique and Disability*, Bulletin 55 (Washington, D.C., 1953), p. 245.

B   Social Science Research Council. *Adjustment to Physical Handicap and Illness: A Survey of the Social Psychology of Physique and Disability*. Bulletin 55. Washington, D.C., 1953.

F   [19]U.S. Small Business Administration, Office of Advocacy, *Your Business and the SBA*, February 1987, p. 9.

B   U.S. Small Business Administration. Office of Advocacy. *Your Business and the SBA*. February 1987.

F   [20]U.S. Congress, Office of Technology Assessment, *Effects of Office Automation on the Public Sector Workforce: A Case Study*, (Washington, D.C., 1985), p. 23.

B   U.S. Congress. Office of Technology Assessment. *Effects of Office Automation on the Public Sector Workforce: A Case Study*. Washington, D.C., 1985.

For interviews:

F   [21]Personal interview with James X. Tennyson, Manager, Conrally Company, Midland, Texas, 19 November, 1990.

B   Tennyson, James X., Manager, Conrally Company, Midland, Texas. Personal interview, 19 November 1990.

F   [22]Telephone interview with Mary Key, Supervisor, Raven Corporation, Dayton, Ohio, 19 November 1990.

B   Key, Mary, Supervisor, Raven Corporation, Dayton, Ohio. Telephone interview, 19 November 1990.

For letters or memorandums:

F   [23]Letter from Marjorie Jacobs, President, X-View, Inc., to Richard Rayner, 19 November 1990.

B   Jacobs, Marjorie, President, X-View, Inc. Letter to Richard Rayner, 19 November 1990.

Footnote and bibliography formats of materials not illustrated above, such as leaflets, brochures, manuals, speeches, minutes of meetings, or radio or television programs, should be arranged similarly to one of the examples shown. A titled brochure or leaflet with no author given is arranged similarly to an interview or a letter.

If you cannot find examples or instructions for primary or secondary data that you wish to document, simply give all necessary information in a logical, readable order, as much as possible like the arrangement of other footnotes or bibliographic entries. It is better to give too much information than too little. If expected information is not available—for example, date of publication—show in footnotes and bibliographic entries that the data was omitted in the source you are quoting.

Shortened Footnotes at Bottom of Page

Shortened forms of footnotes are used for subsequent references. A simplified footnote consisting of the author's name, with page numbers, is usually preferable to the older, hard-to-remember Latin forms, although at times the term *Ibid.* may save unnecessary repetition of long titles, such as government publications with no author shown. Use of standard reference forms, including *Ibid.*, is explained below. Unless you see a real need to use Latin abbreviations, however, prefer the simpler, modern arrangement.

For example, in a subsequent reference to a book by Edward T. Hall, you may use this footnote:

```
Hall, p. 217.
```

If you refer in the same paper to two or more works by the same author, the title must be included in all footnotes:

```
Hall, The Silent Language, p. 217.
```

If you use materials written, for example, by both Jane Hall and Edward T. Hall, complete names must be included in all footnotes. Assume that you use two books by Edward T. Hall and one by Jane Hall. The shortest form of the footnote would be as follows:

```
Edward T. Hall, The Silent Language, p. 217.
```

Latin abbreviations have long been used as subsequent footnote references. The most commonly used ones are these:

Ibid. (*ibidem*). This term means "in the same place." It is used to refer to the immediately preceding footnote: Ibid., p. 12.

The following series of footnotes illustrates the use of *ibid*.

```
1. Joanna Brown, Reflections (Boston: Allyn and Bacon, 1981),
   p. 8.
2. Ibid, p. 142. [Brown's work, but another page]
3. Ruth Kemp, ''Tomorrow,'' Reader's Digest, March 1982, p. 14.
4. Brown, p. 147. [Brown's book, different page]
5. Kemp, p. 14. [same article, same page as footnote 3]
```

If your report or other written work includes a bibliography, the footnote form, including the first time a reference is cited, may be shortened. It is also correct, and often considered preferable in formal reports, to show complete information in the first footnote reference to a work, even when a bibliography is included. To do so is essential if no bibliography is included.

With a bibliography, shortened footnotes, even when used only once or for the first time, include only the author's surname, title of publication, and page number. If no author is given, the title and page number suffice, as shown in the third example below:

```
Hall, The Silent Language, p. 44. [book]

Swenson, ''Relative Importance of Business Communication Skills for
the Next Ten Years,'' p. 16. [article in periodical]

Essays on Research in the Social Sciences, p. 5. [no author or editor
given]
```

These shortened bottom-of-page footnote forms are permissible because complete information is shown in the bibliography. Do not use shortened forms if the complete documentation is not adjacent in the report.

Reference Citations in Text of Report

Shortened footnotes may be inserted into the text of a report that includes a bibliography. For example, reference to page 22 of a book by Brown could be shown in this way: (Brown, 22). If more than one work is listed by one or more writers named Brown, adequate information must be given in each note to enable the reader to find immediately the cited source. Another method is to number the references in the bibliography; thus, if a work by Brown is the second one listed in a bibliography, the reference would be: (2, p. 220) or (2:220). Shortened footnotes consisting of author's name, title of publication, and page number can be inserted into the text, within parentheses that set the reference off from the text.

A widely used method of reference citations within the text is referred to as the APA style.[14] Because this arrangement is easy to type and also convenient to the reader, it is often the choice for articles and reports of various kinds, including business writing. The citation is woven into the text in such a way as to be part of the text and avoid unnecessary distraction. For example:

```
Caraway (1990) analyzed the relationships of cost-of-living raises
to . . .
```

The preceding reference is to a complete study. When quoting a particular page or pages, appropriate citations are still made in the text rather than in a footnote at the bottom of the page or at the end of the paper. Occasionally you may refer to a chapter, rather than to a page, as when discussing ideas or topics presented throughout the chapter. For the most part, however, page numbers are necessary, as when using footnotes. For example:

```
In a study of the cost-of-living raises (Caraway, 1990, p. 20) . . .
```

A current trend in the *Chicago Manual of Style* (13th ed.) eliminates **p.** or **pp.** to refer to page numbers. In choosing the format and placement of footnotes, consideration for the reader should be the determining factor.

Bibliographies

The bibliography is considered as a supplement to a formal report. It may come before or after appendices, depending upon the material in-

---

14. *Publication Manual of the American Psychological Association*, p. 58.

cluded as appendices. Page numbering is often simplified by placing the bibliography first. The Arabic numerals used in the report proper continue in sequence throughout all supplementary parts.

Example of a Bibliography from a Business Report

A suggested form for a bibliography suitable for business reports is shown in Figure 12–5, which is headed by the term *References.* Some writers prefer *Bibliography;* others do not wish to describe as a bibliography a list that contains material other than written work, such as interviews. Either usage is correct if one definition of bibliography, ''a list of references,'' is accepted.

The Annotated Bibliography

An annotated bibliography briefly describes each listed reference, as in these examples:

> Gunning, Robert. *New Guides to More Effective Writing in Business and Industry.* Boston: Industrial Education Institute, 1964.

REFERENCES

DeClercq, Neill; Meiklejohn, Alec; and Mericle, Ken. ''The Use of Microcomputers in Local Union Administration.'' *Labor Studies Journal* X (Spring 1985), 3-25.

Durbin, Harold C. *Word Processing Glossary.* Easton, PA: Durbin Associates, 1984.

Langman, Larry. *An Illustrated Dictionary of Word Processing.* Phoenix: Oryx Press, 1986.

Lewis, Peter H. ''Advice for Shoppers.'' *New York Times* CXXXVII 20 October 1987, p. C3.

Pardoe, Blaine L. ''The Right Way to Select Word Processing Software.'' *The Office* CV (May 1987), 38-41.

Pepper, Jon. ''Word Processing Vies with Desktop Publishing.'' *PC Week* IV (November 24, 1987), 135-138.

Stafford, Paul M., and Alsop, Stewart. ''PFS: Professional Write, Great for Personal Use.'' *PC Magazine* V (November 25, 1986), 33-35.

Figure 12–5. *Example of a reference format.*

Gunning, best known for the development of a readability formula, offers help to the business and technical writer toward the clear expression of ideas. The theme is that clear expression is based upon exact thinking and understanding.

Dohan, Mary Helen. *Our Own Words.* New York: Alfred A. Knopf, 1974.

The story of the making of the American language, from its Anglo-Saxon roots and its beginnings among the earliest settlers and pioneers, through its development during periods of immigration and social change. The book includes an introduction by Alistair Cooke.

Summary

When a writer uses material first written or spoken by someone else, credit must be given to the originator of the material.

Documentation is usually in the form of reference notes and bibliographies, which differ slightly according to the style manual being used as a guide.

Reference notes are of two kinds, *source* or *content* (or discussion). Source references only cite. Content references explain, comment, or supplement.

Footnotes are placed at the bottom of the page on which the cited material appears, Notes also may be placed at the end of a written work or within the text itself.

Reference notes may be used without a bibliography. Occasionally a report may correctly include a bibliography but no reference notes. If both are used, all sources cited in notes must also be included in the bibliography. A bibliography may include sources not cited through reference notes if these sources contributed to the report.

Shortened forms of footnotes or other reference notes are used for subsequent references. Shortened forms may be used for all footnotes when a bibliography is included. Most business and professional writers prefer simplified, shortened footnotes instead of Latin abbreviations.

Bottom-of-page footnotes included in this chapter (apart from those shown as illustrations within the text) are used for these purposes: to give proper credit; to explain or comment; to strengthen discussion by citing authoritative writers and reference books; and to serve as examples of the various ways in which footnotes are used. In other words, the fourteen footnotes used in this chapter each illustrate the rules and usages discussed. Review these footnotes according to the principles and usages they illustrate:

Footnote 1. First footnote, book by three authors.
Footnote 2. A shortened form used as subsequent footnote.
Footnote 3. Content (discussion) footnote. Such comments would be

irrelevant if inserted into the text. (Some people will think that such comments are irrelevant, regardless of where they are placed.)

Footnote 4. Short, direct quotation of no more than three lines incorporated into the text.

Footnote 5. Quoted material of more than three lines, single spaced and set off from the text.

Footnote 6. Same as Footnote 5 except that quoted passage is indented to indicate the beginning of a paragraph.

Footnote 7. Same as Footnote 5 except that it does not include an ellipsis.

Footnotes 8, 9, 10, 11. This passage presents an unusual situation in that material paraphrased from Barzun and Graff includes mention of three style manuals, which also must be footnoted. Footnote 8 is placed after the authors' names instead of at the end of the sentence.

Footnote 12. This reference was first given in Footnotes 1 and 2. In this instance, reference is to the complete book. In addition, the full form of the footnote could have been used here, as in Footnote 11.

Footnote 13. This reference contains no mention of the author or title; none is given on the Manual.

Footnote 14. Subsequent reference.

Questions and Problems

1. Construct a bibliography that lists the textbooks you are using this semester, including this one; three journal articles in your major field of study; and three journal articles on the subject of communication in management.

2. Construct footnotes for references shown in the bibliography prepared for question 1. Include specific page numbers for passages that you assume you are including verbatim or in paraphrased form.

3. Construct a bibliography based on the bottom-of-page footnotes used in this chapter.

4. Construct an annotated bibliography of the textbooks you are using this semester.

5. Write a memorandum to your assistant, Harvey Coleman, who prepared reports based on secondary data. Summarize the two ways in which quoted material may be placed within the text of a report. Harvey has been using quotation marks regardless of the length of quoted passages.

6. Explain the form and use of an ellipsis.

7. Discuss this statement: Writers in business and the professions should spend their time more profitably than in exact construction of bibliographies and footnotes.

8. Interview a reference librarian in your college or university. Ask for his or her recommendations for a style manual. Also ask for opinions about bottom-of-page footnotes versus end-of-manuscript notes. Report your findings in the form of a short memorandum. (See Chapter 3.) Remember that the interview itself is a source of information that must be documented.

9. Investigate why you may prefer to use an ''Endnotes'' section or a ''Sources Available'' section in preference to a bibliography section.

CHAPTER **13**

Using Computers to Prepare Reports

Chapter Outline

Computer Technology and Communications

Business decisions are complicated. Making correct decisions are the keys to success for a business. To make correct decisions, businesses must learn to identify and organize useful data into meaningful reports that will improve the decision-making process at all levels of an organization.

Computers have increased businesses' ability to access, process, transmit, and store data. Consequently, organizations that fail to adapt and utilize computers to the best advantage are unable to operate as efficiently as competitors who generate more timely reports that facilitate decision making.

For example, executives and managers use computers to access data files on which reports are based; to organize data in the forms of charts, tables, or other illustrations; to facilitate the writing and editing process; to research industry statistics; to share files and applications with both local and remote offices; to improve service and product quality through design techniques; and to provide up-to-the-minute information about stocks, prices, and margins.

Let's analyze the development and progress of the use of computers and discuss the computer hardware and computer software that are commonly used to prepare business reports.

The development of computer technology evolved through five development epochs—called generations. Each generation highlights significant breakthroughs in technology and is characterized by the increased computer "user-friendliness," a term meaning ease of use. Further, the levels of computer languages have evolved from "low level" machine language (a combination of 0's and 1's that represent on/off switches) to "high level" English phrases—which the computer then interprets back into machine understandable form.

First-Generation Computers

First-generation machines were very large, used punched cards, and required extensive climate control due to the enormous amount of heat generated by their vacuum tubes. These computers were run by machine code. That is, programs and data had to be coded as 0's and 1's signaling the electronic states of on or off to the computer.

248

Second-Generation Computers

The transistor generation was in 1947, 1948, and 1949 and the solid state era was in the 1960s. Heat-generating, expensive, power-inefficient vacuum tubes were replaced by cooler, cheaper, less power-consumptive transistorized circuits and semiconductors. Second-generation computers used magnetic cores to supply up to 16,000 bytes (groups of data) of internal memory; magnetic tape and removable disk packs replaced magnetic drums and cards as primary means of external storage.

Third-Generation Computers

By 1967 the transistor circuits era moved to IC (integrated circuit) chips. These new circuits, housed on a tiny silicon wafer, were smaller, faster, and more reliable than predecessor circuitry—greatly improving processing capacity while reducing computer size. Third-generation computers began to make extensive use of video display monitors, supported multiprocessing, multiprogramming, and time sharing.

Fourth-Generation Computers

Semiconductor designers discovered ways to pack many thousands of circuits into the small silicon IC chips by using a process that first came to be known as large-scale integration (LSI), then very-large-scale integration (VLSI), and then ultra-large-scale integration (ULSI). These new chips replaced magnetic core media as means of memory storage, permitting main memory capacities to increase drastically, exploding from 16,000 bytes to over 16 million bytes of main memory storage. Costs decreased to a fraction of a cent per byte as well. This new circuitry permits processing speeds to increase to over one million instruction per second.

Microprocessor chips, invented in the early 1970s, contain all the processing functions necessary to run a computer. This invention reduced the general size (footprint) of computers and resulted in the development of the first microcomputers by the mid 70s.

Fifth-Generation Computers and New Developments

The fifth-generation trends include improved speed and capacity, distributed processing, and Artificial Intelligence (AI). Currently, very-high-speed integrated circuits (VHSIC) are in the early stages of development. The objective of this new development is to house the power of today's supercomputers on a single chip.

Another trend in advanced computers is the use of multiple processors to control peripherals (other machines such as printers, modems, etc.), logic, arithmetic, and user traffic. By the year 2000 some computers may contain as many as 1 billion processors—each performing a specialized function—providing technical capabilities approaching some of the power of the human brain and called ''artificial intelligence.''

Artificial intelligence (AI) research involves trying to develop machines that hear, see, move, and think. Expert systems are the main branch of AI needed by businesses. Expert systems are information-processing systems that attempt to capture and duplicate or simulate the reasoning and decision processes of experts in a given field. Less experienced personnel can use expert systems as consultants to help solve new or complex problems when the actual expert is unavailable because of time or cost constraints.

Business Communication and Data Processing

Capturing data is one of the first activities of processing. Information system designers give special attention to creating the best possible means for identifying and gathering data for processing—whether it be via paper documents or computer programs.

Effective decision naming depends on accurate data. Information managers need to identify the exact data needed for decision making and to take steps to ensure that only essential data are gathered in order to avoid wasting company resources. Industry dilemmas now are the result of too much data.

Data must be entered into the system before it can be processed. Once the processing is completed, the data leaves in the form of printed or monitor screen output. Most data pass through several phases of processing before conversion into final form for managers.

Transporting and Sending Data

Transmission lines or cables, over which data pass, can be sent to a printer for output or another screen for reading. Manual printouts are hand-delivered to either the end user or to data entry personnel for further processing. Other data are transmitted via direct cable, satellite, microwave, or fiber optic cable. Whether by wire, by wave, or by hand, the more transmission links per system, the higher the potential for error caused by human or machine.

Storing Data

Intermediate storage points occur frequently throughout any data processing system; key storage locations include points of data collection, of data input, of data output, of files, and of databases. The key point is that storage points are potentially numerous; moreover, like transmission links the more storage points in a given system, the more room for data error.

Using Sending and Storing Systems to Prepare Reports

Microcomputers were originally designed to function as a complete, miniature processing system. Today, many application packages like word processors, spreadsheets, and databases allow you (a single user) to input, organize, manipulate, and review data for decision making while the computer handles the storage, processing, and transmission of the data. These processing systems provide great advantages, especially when it comes to analyzing ''what-if'' scenarios before making recommendations to other departments or to superiors.

Business Correspondence Networks

Centralized processing systems (systems that consist of one mainframe used as the central processor linked to various on-site or remote terminals) switch back and forth among users so fast that they appear to be serving the users simultaneously.

Distributed processing systems are alternatives to centralized processing. Distributed processing is a network of computers that are linked to a centralized computer via cables or telephone lines. The remote computers have access to files, databases, and programs of the central computer and can preform the processing needs of the branch office or company in another city. These processors can be microcomputers, mainframes, or minicomputers connected to printers, plotters, modems, etc. Breaking up the system's processing activities into several sub-processing stations can enhance flexibility, increase processing/response (throughput) speed, and better share hardware and software resources.

Possible combinations of network configurations are endless. In choosing a network system, management must evaluate its current and future needs (computer systems become obsolete about every five years), regarding reliability, speed, storage capacity, and cost.

The next section of this chapter lists and describes some of the most common types of software available for business use today and the hardware devices used to interact with the computer.

Computers and Information Technology

Hardware Devices

Keyboards and ''mouses'' are the most commonly used devices for direct data input. Touchscreen devices that access computer memory or allow data input by touching the appropriate menu box or icon (video display symbol representing the action to be chosen) are also becoming more commonly used. However, these input devices are relatively slow when compared to the internal processing capacity of the computer and are susceptible to human error.

Business operations are commonly "input/output" bound, meaning that data entry and printing devices are slower than the internal processing of data by the computer. Consequently, faster sources of data entry and output are constantly needed. *Source data* automation is a rapidly developing field that creates devices to increase the speed of data input while reducing data input errors. Source data automation absorbs input data directly from the information source to avoid errors that easily arise from converting data from one form to another. *Optical scanners* are an example of source data automation. Optical scanners read and convert printed or written numeric representations into digital input form. Scanners may come in the form of a light pen or light wand and may be used for optical character recognition (OCR) detecting actual numbers or may be used to read numbers encoded in bar code form (i.e., the Universal Product Code). Bar code scanners are commonly used in retail stores to record sales and inventory data.

Software Devices

The software industry is one of the most rapidly changing of all computer-related industries. Due to low start-up costs, many companies have sprung up over the past few years, each producing its own brand of software. Most computer hardware systems require unique operating systems. Thus, one operating system generally cannot operate another type of computer system without some modification. Further, not every processing package works with every operating system; application packages must be specifically designed to utilize the specific operating system commands. For example, WordPerfect, a popular word-processing package, comes in different versions for PC (personal computer), DOS, Unix, Data General, MacIntosh, and various other operating systems.

Processing Software. Processing software includes accounting, inventory, bookkeeping, tax, and checkbook management application programs, to list a few. Myraids of applications are available on the market today and provide users with a wide selection of features and prices. Word processing, electronic spreadsheets, databases, and graphics packages are the most commonly used general purpose application programs. Let's discuss the uses of these application programs in report writing and identify popular packages that are currently used in businesses.

Word Processing. Word processing software packages relieve typists of much of the tedium associated with preparing letters, memos, and reports. Word processing packages assist you in creating, editing, and printing documents that contain business reports and letters. This increased efficiency is accomplished by the basic capabilities of word processing packages, which allow the user to move phrases and words around inside the document, inserting or deleting text, or rearranging entire blocks of words. In addition to these basic features, most word processing programs contain some or all of the following features that help you produce professional reports:

FEATURES	USAGE
Spell Checker	A spell checker automatically checks for spelling errors and facilitates easy correction of errors.
Thesaurus	If the computer system is using a hard disk, the user can readily select synonyms by using the on-line thesaurus.
Insert or Transfer Data	This feature allows data to be inserted from one file into another file or to transfer text files to other spreadsheets or database programs.
Macro	Macros allow frequently used words or formats to be assigned to a few programmed keystrokes. A macro library saves user time by providing frequently used formats or block paragraphs.
General and Print Format	These features allow the user to underline, boldface, italicize, center, flush right, indent, and super- or subscript text. Further, the users can automatically choose the number of columns and adjust column widths. Finally, users can easily adjust tabs, margins, spacing, pitch and print fonts, lines per inch, and right justification.
Page Format	Page format features allow the user to automatically position page numbers, renumber pages, center the page, adjust the top margin, include headers and/or footers, and prevents widow/orphan features.
Footnotes or Endnotes	The footnote and endnote feature inserts the footnote automatically, calculating the number of lines to save for the footnote at the bottom of the page. Also, the word processing program keeps track of the next footnote or endnote number.
Search	The search feature allows the user to find a

FEATURES	USAGE
	specific set of characters or software command function. Then, at the user's option, the string of characters or the software command can be replaced with a new character string or a new command. Searching and replacing names in a form letter could be a useful application of this feature.
Windows	At times the user may want to view portions of two separate pages at the same time. Windows allow the user to do this.
Switch	The switch feature allows the user to work on two documents at the same time, switching back and forth between documents as desired. The switch feature also allows the user to select a group of letters and instantly change them from lower to uppercase letters or vice versa.
Merge	The merge feature helps the user automate office procedures, such as forms, labels, reports, contracts, and memos. Often the merge feature is used to personalize mass correspondence; that is, each letter is prepared with each reader's name and address and sometimes with individual names within the letter.
Math	The math feature allows the user to use the word processing application to simulate a spreadsheet.

Other word processing features also speed the preparation of reports. Even more important, word processing features improve one's ability to produce professional and timely reports.

Word processing packages also speed up written communication in businesses by using electronic mail. Electronic mail allows a user to write a letter or memo and instantly send the message to several locations without making photocopies and mailing the messages. Some of the more common word processing packages include Microsoft Word, WordPerfect, Word Star, Multimate, Easy Writer, Perfect Writer, and others.

Electronic Spreadsheets. Electronic spreadsheets packages help users by electronically "crunching" numerical data. Electronic number crunching (calculating) means that mathematical and statistical computations are automatically performed by the computer. Electronic number crunching can save managers and employees a tremendous amount of time, especially if complicated formulas are used.

A frequent business use of spreadsheets is found in the preparation of financial analyses, especially "what if" analysis. For instance, by changing one or two input variables, such as cash payment or cash flow timing, analysts can see the resulting effect on company profits without having to perform dozens of time-consuming calculations manually. Because of the added capabilities that spreadsheet packages provide, reports that formerly required too much time and equipment are now generated routinely.

Computer spreadsheets are developed in a grid made up of horizontal rows and vertical columns. Today, most spreadsheets packages contain from 2,000 to 20,000 rows and 256 or more columns. The intersection of rows and columns are called cells, so the normal spreadsheet contains from 500,000 to 5,000,000 cells (rows times columns). Since most spreadsheets are too large to fit entirely on the display screen, the use of various key commands or a mouse allow the user to move rapidly throughout the spreadsheet to manipulate the data. Most spreadsheet commands are accessed through a menu (a guide to program operating procedures) either by a mouse or by keystrokes from a computer keyboard.

A **template** is a spreadsheet that contains formulas, functions, and appropriate headings. After the template is created it can be reused to evaluate similar operations by simply changing key dollars or amounts within the problem. The following are some other frequent spreadsheet features:

FEATURES	USAGE
Split Windows	This feature allows the user to see two different parts of the spreadsheet at the same time. Also, in connection with this feature is "synchronization," which allows the windows to move together or independently.
Freeze Titles	With this feature, the user can prevent the titles from scrolling off the screen as the user moves around in the spreadsheet.
Format Numbers	Formatting numbers can be applied to a specific cell or the entire worksheet (global format). The user may specify numbers to be displayed with or without commas, in currency, as percentages, in scientific notation, or as $+/-$ symbols.
Copy, Move, Insert, or Delete	The copy and move commands allow the user to duplicate or move cell formulas, numbers, and text from one cell location (or a range of cells) to another cell location (or range). The insert and delete commands allow the user to add or remove rows or columns as needed.

FEATURES	USAGE
Cell Protec-tion	This command is useful to prevent the accidental erasure of a cell. Often this feature is used in templates (to be discussed later) and allows unexperienced users to enter data in only unprotected cells.
Function Commands	Built-in formulas allow the user to compute complicated financial, mathematical, statistical, and date-and-time formulas by entering a simple command. Logic functions allow the user to program the spreadsheets using macros to make decisions based on prior calculations. Other special functions instruct the spreadsheet to rapidly look up data contained in a table that may then be used for further computations.
File Combine	This feature allows the user to combine ranges from worksheets or entire worksheets together.
Data Tables	The data table allows the user to generate tables that show the different values a formula computes each time one or two variables is (are) changed in the formula.
Data Fill	By using this feature the user can instantly fill a range with numerical data.
Macros	Macros are a powerful addition to any spreadsheet as they allow the user to automate the spreadsheet. That is, a series of keystrokes can be entered and saved on the worksheet and later invoked by a single keystroke. Macros are similar to programming languages like BASIC, PASCAL, and FORTRAN but are used to program specifically within the spreadsheet. Some worksheet macros have an especially powerful feature that allows the user to create his/her own menus.
Word Proces-sing	All spreadsheets contain at least some word processing features. However, the extent of these features varies from full capabilities to very limited single-cell edit functions.
Database	Databases housed within a spreadsheet package, like Lotus 123, have the advantage of being extremely fast—since the entire database is housed in the computer's internal memory. However, this form of a database faces the problem of limited storage capacity.

FEATURES	USAGE
Graphics	Spreadsheet packaged graphic capabilities are convenient, in that spreadsheet data can be accessed and displayed graphically without having to exit the system and access a graphics application program. Further, if graphics are built into the spreadsheet, then "what if" analyses can instantly be viewed by the user, often improving the user's decision-making abilities.

Other spreadsheet features are extensive; however, this discussion provides an overview of major spreadsheet features you may use as a report writer. Several popular spreadsheets available today are Lotus 123, Symphony, Excel, Framework, Oracle, Enable, Multiplan, and PlanPerfect.

Databases

In a database structure, information is listed in tables, called relations, made up of rows called tuples (similar to records in purpose) and separated by columns called domains (similar to fields). Domains contain information specific to a particular tuple. Databases help in creating, updating, and deleting records in a file. The following is a list of database features and uses of those features that may aid you in preparing your reports:

FEATURES	USAGE
Format	Format features enable the user to specify page breaks and provide titles for each printed page. Further, the user may specify the location for a report to be printed on a page.
Merge	The merge feature helps the user automate office procedures, such as forms, labels, reports, contracts, and memos. Often the merge feature is used to personalize mass correspondence.
Sort	The sort feature of a database allows the user to rearrange the records of a database according to one or more sort keys.
Query	The query command feature enables the user to search for and either highlight records or extract records that meet criteria—specified by the user. This feature helps the user quickly compile related information to be combined in various types of reports. Also, the query

FEATURES	USAGE
	command may be used to list and delete any duplicate records.
Math functions	Built-in formulas allow the user to perform financial, mathematical, statistical calculations on a database by entering a simple command.

The following are a few of the most popular databases on the market today: dBase II, III and III plus, Condor III, Data Star, MDBS, FYI 3000 plus, R:Base, R:Base 5000, Knowledgeman, and others.

Graphics. Graphics add variety to report writing, improve the reader's comprehension, and transmit detailed data in less time and space than can be done through written discussion. Not only are data easier to understand when presented graphically, but also the data repeats and reinforces information in an appealing written form, as discussed in Chapter 11.

The following is a list of graphic package features, especially those features that are useful in writing reports:

FEATURES	USAGE
Image Format	Several format features are available to help the user select the sizing, scaling, and positioning of the graph on the printed page. Normally, the graphics package offers preset full- and half-size scales, although the user can adjust the margins, the width, the height, and the rotation of the graph.
Labels	Different graphics packages offer a variety of means to label graphs. Most contain main titles, X and Y axis labels, data-point label, notes to the graph, and legends (to identify various symbols used in the graph). Some graphics packages have fixed locations for these labels, whereas other packages allow the user to decide the location.
Graph Types	A wide variety of graph types is normally available with any graphics package. The following is a list of the more common graph types: Line, bar, stacked bar, clustered bar, overlapping bar, XY, point, pie, expanding pie graphs. Some graphics programs also provide for organizational charts, flow charts, and three-dimensional graphs.

FEATURES	USAGE
Fonts and Styles	Users may enhance the appearance of the graph by selecting from a variety of fonts, pitches, colors, and line widths.
Freehand	The freehand feature provides the user with the ability to draw by freehand, using input devices such as a mouse or light wand.
Library	Some graphics packages offer picture libraries that contain pictures, maps, and geometrical designs.

Some of the more common word graphics packages include Microsoft Chart, Lotus 123, Chart Master, Diagram Master, Energraphics, PC Draw, PC Paintbrush, Harvard Graphics, and others.

Summary

Executives and managers use computers to facilitate their generating reports that improve their decision-making abilities. In order to benefit from the report writing capabilities of the computer, you must be familiar with the computer hardware and computer software that is commonly used to prepare business reports. Being aware of the computer's hardware and software abilities permits you to choose the equipment best suited for your needs and helps you select new equipment as your needs change. Further, if you know the abilities of the computer and how to use them, then you can access those abilities to improve your written reports. Word processing, electronic spreadsheet, database, and graphic application packages are important tools that a business report writer (you) will use on the job.

CHAPTER **14**

Drafting and Editing Reports

Chapter Outline

Change in Organizations

Personnel advisors estimate that you will change your job at least five times and that there will be major retraining or skill training in three of those job changes.

As an example, farmers today are using mechanized farming equipment, soil appraisers, computerized crop or animal rotation schedules, and market forecasting device. Dentists are using databases to organize appointments, order inventory, complete billings, assist research, project taxes, monitor investments, and complete government reports. Managers in manufacturing firms, chemical firms, food product firms—all businesses—appreciate the available stock market quotes or other necessary information for running a business, but using these data means learning to use software programs, telex services, modems, computers—an array of business systems and tools.

Career consultants, company on-site trainers and educators know that in this age, you will learn continuously. You must not be afraid to adapt on your job or change jobs.

Change in Communication Approaches

As procedures change in business, so will the types of messages business people use. So will creating and composing business reports change. Earlier business ages needed information, and this information was composed usually with a pencil and paper or with a boss dictating messages to a secretary. And for the era, these tools and skills worked, but for your era you must be prepared to adapt to numerous "voice based" tools and "computer or electronic based media."

Electronic Business Offices and Communication Processes

As little as four years ago, 50,000 micro, personal, or home computers were produced and sold in one year. Today, more than 50,000 personal or home computers are sold each day. Most of you have already played video games, generated a short report for your work assignment, used a word

263

processing system to write letters or reports, or used a database to control and appraise data.

You live in a most important electronic era and the communication messages and systems for creating those messages exist and are used today. But more important is "what must you use in business and how will you send and receive vital business information?"

Reporting in the Future

Terms and definitions of existing and futuristic systems and media are introduced late in this chapter. But you are already learning about "Hypermedia" and integration of voice-directed media; use of disk-based written and graphic media, screen or touch controlled media; use of charting and illustrations packages; and use of network media permitting interchange of messages, photographs, and dialogues.

Not many years ago, when you purchased groceries at your supermarket, you watched the checker enter the amounts on the register and add each item. A small window with a scanner now reads the UPC symbols (Uniform Pricing Codes). These symbols are bar codes found on almost all items. The codes identify size, weight, costs, etc. These codes also become an inventory device so that replacement merchandise can be ordered.

Magnetic Ink Character Recognition (MICR) permits processing machines to access your checking account and then directs the deductions from your account as well as the microfilming of your check for the bank's legal records. The zip codes on your letters and packages permit scanners to direct letters and business reports to the correct airport or post office and eventually to your home or office.

Drafting and Editing Business Reports

Organizations now demand that their employees, as well as their first-line supervisors and middle and upper-level managers, be proficient consumers and producers of business information and operating messages.

Small businesses, proprietorship or partnership businesses, may not have a desktop, laptop, or personal computer for all of the employees, but the supervisors will expect you to be able to use electronic equipment and systems.

Larger companies, particularly "electronic-based companies" such as telephone companies, banks, universities, churches, accounting and manufacturing firms, use numerous computers, and you must use the equipment and the systems. Business supervisors needing access to business information not only provide a desktop or personal computer for each of their employees but also have other centralized computer systems to support their handling of business information.

As discussed in Chapter 13, these electronic systems likely are linked together to form an electronic mail system—or a network of cables, microwave senders and receivers or satellite systems that permit employees to share information. In the same office you may be connected to a "local area network." You may be able to work in your office on the third floor and send messages to other colleagues on the twenty-second floor via cables built within your building or via existing telephone lines.

Area networks or worldwide networks may permit you to send to and receive messages from members of your company or clients or customers in other countries or other states. Photographs, charts, copies of text, can be transmitted through a "modem via computers and telephone lines or microwave routes," anywhere you have sending and receiving facilities.

Composing, Drafting, and Editing Reports on the Computer

Incident Case

Let's become employees of the Great Western Insurance Company. There are numerous employees and job responsibilities. Many business transactions occur each day—but we need to focus on your department. You work in the Claims and Reimbursement Department with about fourteen full-time employees, three supervisors, an assistant manager, and a manager. Also, because your company is located in a city where there are three universities, you hire from fifteen to twenty students. Some of the students work full-time during busy seasons and part-time when they are taking courses.

Scheduling becomes rather difficult during the summer, but full-time employees are able to take vacations when their families are out of school and the part-time workers are able to work more hours to handle the needs of the Claims and Reimbursement Department.

Of course, clients whose claims are paid are happy. Clients who do not qualify for reimbursement are unhappy, and so there is some pressure when it comes to communicating with unhappy customers. In some instances lawsuits occur, so that you also have to work with the corporation's attorney on occasion.

Lack of Cooperation and Communication between Part- and Full-time Adjustors

A major rain and hail storm caused serious damage in several Mid-western states. Your department is receiving around ninety major complaints and claims each day: this is a 70 percent increase in claims. You and your co-workers must handle this emergency, but the pressures are causing delayed decisions, much overtime work, and frayed nerves. Customers and clients are beginning to complain about delays. They are also complaining about abrupt and sometimes less than helpful attitudes by the adjustors.

You've weathered this emergency but would like to avoid these kinds of communication and service breakdowns should other crises occur. The manager, assistant manager, and supervisors are not certain, but they believe that working relationships are not as positive and helpful as they were before the crises.

Possible solutions may include having a meeting where all of you can "gripe" and get your complaints aired. But that seems like a rather short-term fix to what could be an important morale and operating behavior problem. After informally discussing what is needed, your manager decides to hire an outside consulting firm to come to your office and conduct interviews and studies that may help establish the once productive working teams.

Your Responsibilities

Because you worked as a part-time employee while you attended the university and are now a full-time employee with coordinating and supervisory responsibilities, you are being "deputed" from you full-time responsibilities to work with an outside consulting agency. Not only are you to work closely with the manager, assistant manager, and supervisors, but you are the liaison between the consulting firm and the Claims and Reimbursement Department.

It's a compliment to be given this assignment. Additionally it may provide you with an opportunity to use some of the other communicating and organizing skills you learned at the university. Essentially, you are asked to help organize the outside study, help gather the data, and help analyze the opinions and information.

After several meetings with representatives from the budget and allocations division in the home office, you've been authorized to hire a consulting firm at the rate of $120 per hour with a maximum expenditure not to exceed $9,500. Great Western Insurance has needed other studies completed and submits a list of four approved agencies. At the recommendation of your company president, you contact Victoria A. Nugent of Nugent

International Management Consultants, Rochester, New York. After initial telephone conversations, you, your manager, and the assistant manager meet with Ms. Nugent and agree to the schedules and tentative proposals for conducting the on-site interviews for completing the study of the Claims and Reimbursement Department.

All of you agree that Nugent must be given autonomy to conduct the study as their specialists suggest. You, however, are asked to work with Ms. Nugent as a liaison officer to facilitate information the consultants may need. Representatives from Nugent suggest that they come on-site to do their observations and identify the major problems and purposes of the study, then coordinate their work with you.

Your input is essential to Nugent Consultants' understanding of what is happening in the department so your boss suggests that you also develop a tentative outlining of the hypotheses and scope of the study. No other data are available that compare directly to your needs so you are preparing a study that assesses primary data and may be termed a primary research inquiry.

Get Organized and Get Started

Time is essential. If you had days you could do a thorough planning job—but you need to have your ideas in writing by tomorrow morning and you set a meeting with your supervisors and Nugent's representatives for 10:00 a.m. You have to hurry.

You load your "windows" package and your word processing packages into your personal computer and begin to make a rough planning outline. The windows are always available in the upper right-hand corner of your computer's video screen. Figures 1 and 2 illustrate your initial brainstorming and thinking notes. Fortunately, as you change ideas or think of new components, you can move these ideas into the planning windows and change the outlines as you begin to anticipate what you need to prepare for tomorrow's meeting.

Electronic Note Pad. Figure 14–1, your electronic note pad, lists the overall needs and objectives of the study.

Electronic Report Outline. Figure 14–2, also a part of your electronic outline, lists some of the decisions you think you should recommend to your supervisors and to Nugent's representatives. The report outline states:

Your notes helped in the meeting. You needed to make several modifications but Nugent and your supervisors agree that Nugent should prepare a questionnaire designed to assess workers' attitudes. Areas agreed as most important are (a) perceived openness or closeness of communica-

Figure 14–1.
*Electronic Note
Pad.*

NOTE PAD

1. Solve this problem.
2. Contact Nugent's consultants.
3. More success likely with outside specialist.
4. Telephone conversation w/ Nugent went well.
5. Agreed to do complete on-site consultancy.
6. Fees ok'ed--$120 per hour.
7.
8.

Figure 14–2.
*Electronic Report
Outline*

REPORT OUTLINE

1. POTENTIAL PROBLEMS
    a. Cooperation
    b. Supervisor's accessibility
    c. Delegation

2. PROCESS
    a. Interviews (No)
    b. Surveys--no names (Yes)
    c. Questionnaires (?)

3. SOLUTIONS
    a. Changes in supervision
    b. Successful services
    c. Improved profit line leads to increased employee morale.

tion lines, (b) worker's and supervisor's perceptions about job satisfaction and job responsibilities, (c) value statements about how committed the employees are to the company and how committed the company is to the employees.

You are asked to help Nugent's specialists interpret certain processes and job assignments. Ms. Nugent compliments you on your planning and help but indicates that now her specialists must draft the survey instrument, pilot the questionnaire, determine what kind of statistical analyses are appropriate to the data, and begin to visualize and predesign charts or tables for reporting the data they will get from your colleagues. For now, you can rest for a time, but you need to be available should the consultants have other questions.

The Study

Because your managers and supervisors do not want the problems to continue too long without attention, Nugent is asked to complete a draft of their survey instrument by the next morning. The representatives have helped other companies solve similar problems; suggest that they can have a survey by that time. They do. You are asked to clarify several definitions and job requirements during the day via telephone conversations, but by the next morning Nugent is ready to pilot study its first draft of the instrument.

You are not asked to read the instrument, but workers in another department read through the questions and make several suggestions that may help the readers understand the intent of the questions. Nugent's consultants believe that their tool, the survey questionnaire, is ready to administer to part- and full-time employees and to the managers and supervisors in Claims and Reimbursement. Since you are working so closely with the study, you do not complete the final questionnaire.

The Primary Data

The raw data are available, and Ms. Nugent takes the information to their office to enter it into their SSPS (Statistical Analyses Packages). The data appear useful and appropriate. Ms. Nugent indicates that they will begin drafting the report the following day, hoping to have a final draft by Friday.

The analyses progress well. But in the early afternoon you get a phone call from your boss asking you to meet in the seventh floor conference room. Ms. Nugent is there with the preliminary data. The results are interesting—but Ms. Nugent is having some difficulty drafting the final report. You are assigned to travel with her to their downtown office to serve as a writing specialist and to help the consultants edit their final report. Your company president, Douglas Madsen, wants the report to take on the plane with him on Friday afternoon. The report must be completed. Stay with the consultants until a final copy of the report is available.

In Ms. Nugent's headquarters you find the consultants working with their research findings. The data are grouped into facts and findings, and the significant responses to the questions listed as "values" are being plotted on a spreadsheet and adapted to computer-printed charts. There are five such charts. You study the printouts. The charts seem to be representative of what you thought the responses to the questionnaire would be.

Some of the data are more significant than others. The two writers and editor ask you to join them as they are writing sections of the report. The introduction, background, purpose of the study, scope of the study, limitations, methods and procedures sections are pretty clear-cut.

Problems exist with the facts, findings, and conclusions sections. You think the writers are repeating the facts or raw data too frequently and are not "explaining or grouping the raw data" into logical groups.

Too, you are certain that your company president wants an Executive Summary or a Synopsis since that is typical company writing procedure. After reading the ten pages of the final report and appraising the charts, data, and implications of the data, you have several suggestions to make about word choice and report format changes, but you are careful not to change the meaning of the findings, conclusions, or recommendations that Nugent's consultants will make to your president and managers. You do not want to bias or try to change the findings of their primary research.

You borrow a word processing system and quickly keyboard these recommended changes for the final report. You send a copy of the changes to Ms. Nugent.

1. Include an Executive Summary or Synopsis to present a brief summary of the findings and recommendations early in the report.
2. Include the letter of transmittal—no changes necessary.
3. Include the graphs and charts, making the charts larger as the numbers and titles on the charts are difficult to read.
4. Change some of the language style. The report is too formal, and the real messages are hidden or de-emphasized by filler and introductory clauses and phrases. Simplify, yet maintain the transitional features.
5. Provide a working draft of the report at this stage. Don't worry about binding and printing this initial copy.

Ms. Nugent likes your recommendations. The writers are a little frustrated because they believed their document was clear and easy to read. You show them one of the pages you edited. See Figure 14–3.

Purpose of the Study

This analysis was conducted in order to document the perceived separation between full-time and part-time employees at GWI, and the effect of this separation on the organization. The findings of this study are to provide insight into the problems at GWI and to provide possible solutions.

Scope

This study of GWI was limited to an individual needs analysis that focuses on the individuals of an organization and how they view their jobs and interpersonal employee relationships. The following three specific areas were targeted: commitment, perception of relationships, and communication.

Limitations and Delimitations

The study was limited because the survey was not taken in optimal conditions. First, an unexpected department meeting was called for all part-time employees in order to conduct the survey. Second, the survey was conducted during the busiest time of year for insurance companies. Consequently, the employees felt rushed to complete the questionnaire which may have effected the quality of the survey.

GWI's top management delimited the scope of the study to the targeted areas of commitment, perception of relationships, and communication.

Methods and Procedures

Using the three areas of commitment, perception of relationships, and communication as a base, Nugent's staff consultant committee formulated related survey questions.

Figure 14–3. *Sample edited page.*

The editor agrees with the changes you suggest and the writers quickly reboot their disk and load their word processing package. With several deletions and some moves, the changes illustrated in Figure 14–4, are made and the final page is printed. Figure 14–5 illustrates editing and drafting changes.

The changes consist of:

- Heading simplification
- Heading placement form transition help

Purpose

This analysis was conducted in order to document the perceived separation between full-time and part-time employees at GWI and to determine the effect of this separation on the organization. The findings of this study are to provide insight into the problems at GWI and to provide possible solutions.

Scope

The results of this study of GWI are based only on an individual needs analysis that focuses on the individuals of an organization and how they view their jobs and interpersonal employee relationships. The following three specific areas were targeted: commitment, perception of relationships, and communication.

Limitations

The survey was not taken under optimal conditions. First, an unexpected department meeting was called for all part-time employees in order to conduct the survey. Second, the survey was conducted during the busiest time of year for insurance companies. Consequently, the employees felt rushed to complete the questionnaire. These conditions may have influenced the accuracy of the survey.

Methods and Procedures

Using the three areas of commitment, perception of relationships, and communication as a base, Nugent's staff consultant committee formulated related survey questions.

Figure 14–4. *Corrected sample page.*

- Word choice for simplification
- Clarification of terms described limitations
- Clarification of terms describing scope and intent of the study
- Minor changes in punctuation to meet editor's request

You're also concerned about the charts. You suggest several changes.

- The titles are too brief and unclear.
- Increase the size of the chart—these are hard to read.
- Carefully label the y axis data. They are unclear.
- Document the statistical analysis used in the study—either on chart or at the end of the report.

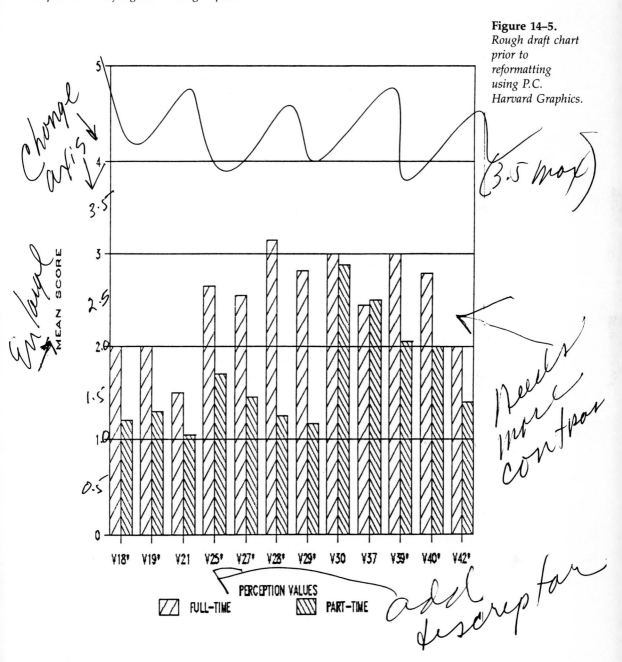

Figure 14–5.
Rough draft chart prior to reformatting using P.C. Harvard Graphics.

Printer: Note:
on page

The writers and editor agree that this would improve the report and immediately load their integrated spreadsheet and begin to work on the charts.

Figure 14–5 illustrates an original rough draft chart.

Figure 14–6 illustrates the edited and reformatted chart. Were the improvements helpful? Do the charts communicate the important data quickly and correctly?

The finalized report that was submitted to Great Western Insurance Company appears in Chapter 15. Note the attention given to writing, drafting, editing, proofreading, printing, and binding.

Writing in Business

The firm, Nugent Consultants, was paid professionally for this job, and the product must be useful. You also are paid for the reports, letters, and messages you write in the company.

Your payment comes from work carefully and thoroughly planned; research designs appropriate to the problems to be solved; and solutions and recommendations that remedy problems or permit you to manage more effectively.

So is business. You are given additional responsibilities and additional rewards as your supervisors understand that you contribute to the company or the organization. You create trust, and your ideas and positions are accepted as your work positively to contribute to the needs of the organization.

Effective reporting, writing, and meeting in groups are expected in business. Those employees and managers who learn progress in the company. Those employees who do not move on.

Electronic Communication in the 1990s

Current Technologies

Let's discuss the technologies currently being used to write reports and letters in the workplace and preview the future of business communication as it is enhanced by technology.

Electronic Mail (E-Mail).   Tremendous advances in computer technology occur yearly. These advances have had a dramatic impact on the way we communicate. Once limited by the postal system, we are now able to send messages coast to coast in a matter of seconds via Wide-Area Networks (WANs). These networks are similar to post office boxes that receive

Chart 2

Figure 14–6.
Reformatted chart.

**GWI Employees (Full- and Part-Time)
Analysis of Comparative Values
of Perception**

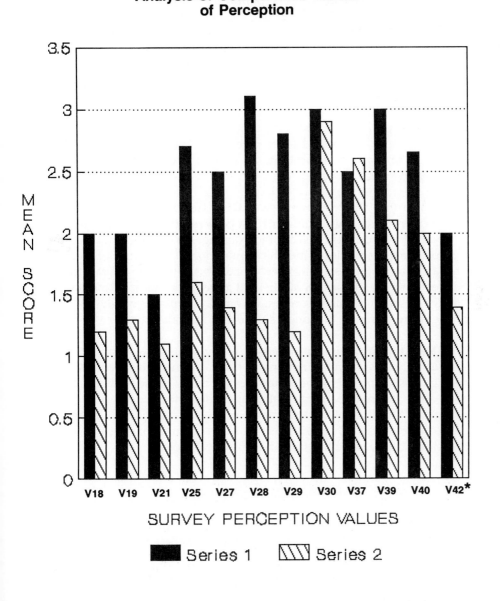

*See Survey: Report Appendix

and store mail for individuals. In this case, however, receipt of the message is almost instantaneous.

Another dimension of E-Mail is facsimile transmissions (FAX). FAX is the electronic transmission of paper documents. In other words, it is analogous to sending a photocopy of a document and having it received within minutes rather than the normal two- to three-day delay of the postal system.

Electronic Funds Transfer (EFT). The increasing use of automated teller machines that we see today is an example of EFT. This system bypasses the traditional paper-based system and allows individuals as well as major corporations to perform a number of banking services via computer or special automated teller machines. This service is becoming increasingly important as corporations strive to reduce overhead expenses and improve cash flows.

Electronic Data Interchange (EDI). Electronic data interchange is the electronic exchange of information between two or more parties. What separates EDI from other electronic exchanges is the highly structured nature of the transmissions and the elimination all rekeying of information once the original message has been sent. This technology is most common between buyers and sellers of physical goods; for example, manufacturers and wholesalers. Purchase orders, invoices, and payment advices are some of the more common documents used in EDI transactions.

Desktop Programs and Tools. Today's business managers perform increasingly diverse combinations of tasks, often simultaneously. Coordinating desktop programs provide access to many of the traditional desktop tools such as a note pad, calculator, appointment calendar, and phone directories. With the help of such desktop organizers, individuals are able to work more efficiently on a variety of tasks without having to waste time switching between applications and physical tools.

Future of Electronic Business Communication

Hypermedia. Hypermedia is one of the more exciting advances in computer technology in recent times. Hypermedia allows an individual to access information from a variety of sources and media. By integrating video, graphic, and written sources, Hypermedia allows the researcher to go beyond the boundaries set by traditional research methods and guidelines.

As an example, HyperPath, developed at Cornell University, enables students to obtain in one session volumes of information that would normally take days or weeks to track down. With HyperPath, the researcher is able to access textbooks, symposiums, lectures, visual aids, video presentations, and a host of other reference materials without leaving the den, office, or terminal.

Wide-scale use of the hypermedia technology provides two essential benefits. First, the research process advances. Second, Hypermedia enhances the researcher's ability to access relevant and up-to-date information. Both of these are keys to effective communication in the "Information Age."

Simulations. Simulation programs are generalized software packages that allow professors and students to design their own "make believe-almost real" business simulations. Much of the experimenting and learning that takes place today is in the form of static pictures and representations. Simulation replaces this static environment with dynamic people and life-like experiences.

Artificial Intelligence. Artificial intelligence (AI) combines Hypermedia and Simulation and is designed to approximate the thought process of the human brain. AI may enable the computer to recognize patterns, to draw conclusions from incomplete or ambiguous information, and to learn by experience. Once this is achieved, computers may become more powerful tools in research and problem-solving.

An impressive example of AI is Alias, built on HyperCard at Stanford University. Alias provides a dynamic learning experience as it models a given culture or period of history. This is but one example of how the traditional research process can be enhanced by linking and integrating materials.

There are a number of AI applications in use today that promise to provide tremendous rewards for the future. First is the use of AI in the development of expert systems. Expert systems combine a knowledge base with analytical procedures to solve problems that normally require human expertise. These systems are currently being used in the medical field but pilot projects are beginning to emerge in the business environment.

Another application of AI is Natural Language Processing (NLP). People do not have a natural spoken or printed language they can use to communicate with a machine. NLP is designed to create a more user-friendly language between man and machine through the use of a more natural language, such as English. Both voice recognition and printed matter recognition research is in progress.

Finally, AI is being used extensively in conjunction with robotics. Through intricate computer programming, robotic manipulators are able to perform many routine and repetitive physical activities. This technology will have a tremendous impact on businesses as humans are taken out of boring, repetitive functions and are allowed to focus on creative contributions.

Today's Reporting

To summarize, new technologies are developing and will not be ready for wide-scale implementation for a number of years. Today, however, we already have a number of powerful tools at our fingertips. Let's take a look at some of these tools and then discuss how they will affect the future of the workplace.

Word Processing. Word processing is revolutionizing the office and helping report-writing functions. Whether dedicated word processors or word processing packages such as WordPerfect are used, the preparation of letters, memos, and reports will never be the same. And, as Optical Character Readers (OCR) and Voice Recognition become more fully utilized, this process will see even greater improvements.

Executive Workstations. Using Local-Area Networks (LANs), individual terminals are linked to the company's central computer. This provides concurrent access to multiple applications such as spreadsheets, word processors, and database managers to an entire office or selected individuals.

Electronic Storage and Retrieval. Most of you are already familiar with a number of electronic storage mediums. Some of the more common mediums are magnetic disks and tapes, microfiche, and microfilm. Two technologies that have very bright prospects for the future are Computer Output Microfilm (COM) and optical disks. COM offers instant retrieval of data at less than half the cost of traditional computer printouts. By converting paper documents to laser-engraved images, optical disks provide high-volume storage capacities that require significantly less physical space than the other methods currently being used.

Data Management. Businesses are dealing with enormous amounts of information every day. To handle this flow of data, businesses are turning to database management systems to collect, organize, and distribute this information to the various departments and managers within the company. Once this information is distributed, spreadsheets are used to analyze the data by asking "What if" questions. Finally, reports and presentations are enhanced through the use of graphics packages that provide visual illustrations of numerical information.

Audiographic Teleconferencing. As businesses expand, so does their knowledge base. Unfortunately, this base of information may be located in Los Angeles, Denver, Chicago, and/or New York. Through tele-conferencing, the individuals in each of the cities can be brought together without their leaving their respective cities or offices. Audio teleconferencing simply proves oral communication links either through telephones or microphones and speakers for the participants. Audiograhic teleconferencing adds the physical dimension by incorporating document transmissions such as FAX. Finally, audiovideo conferences include voice, graphic, and video mediums to enhance and improve communication.

Summary

Computers are dramatically changing the way we look at communication, especially in the context of business reports and business messages. Reports that once took weeks to compile can now be prepared in just a night or a few days. As the technology continues to advance, this timeline could be reduced to a matter of hours.

In the years to come, computers and source availability will continue to play an increasingly important role in our business activities. This information enables businesses to exchange greater quantities of information faster and more efficiently than ever before. To succeed in this dynamic environment, businesses and people need to become more skilled in managing not only the workers but also the information that these individuals produce.

CHAPTER 15

Formal Analytical Reports

Chapter Outline

The word *formal*, in reports and elsewhere, is relative. Nevertheless, a report that contains numerous preliminary and supplementary parts is considered formal, at least in format.

The Report Package

The following list of report parts is not intended to be used for all formal reports, regardless of length. *Few reports will need all the authorization documentation and preliminaries.* Preliminary parts not shown in this list are desirable for some reports.

The preliminary and supplementary parts preceded by a check are the ones that are most often used. The others may be included or omitted depending upon the particular report situation. An index is likely to be omitted from all kinds of business reports.

Authorizations:
Report Plan
Proposal

Preliminaries:
✔ Cover
Title fly
✔ Title page
Letter of authorization
Letter of acceptance
✔ Letter of transmittal
✔ Table of contents
List of charts and tables
✔ Synopsis

Body of the report:
Introduction
Text of the report, usually divided into several major sections
Conclusions and recommendations, which are usually combined into one section

Supplements:
✔ Appendix (or appendices)
✔ Bibliography
Index
(The bibliography may precede other supplements.)

Authorizations

The terms *proposal, research proposal,* and *proposal report* are used to denote a longer and more formally written presentation requesting autho-

282

rization to conduct a study. Funding, time, and personnel need to be approved in advance of a research study. A *report plan*, particularly a plan for a class report or a short, informal business report, is less comprehensive than a proposal.

A Report Plan

Before beginning research to find the answer to a business problem, consider preparing a report plan, even though it must be a tentative one. Such an outline of procedure, although it will perhaps be changed during the research process, provides a far more efficient method of approach than no plan at all. This preliminary plan, which should be specifically worded and prepared in written form, may be referred to as a proposal if it is to be presented to another person or persons for approval.

This preliminary step to the research and reporting process is referred to here as a report plan, not a proposal, for you will need such a plan whether or not it is presented for approval of others outside the organization. When preparing proposals, which may be for business, government, professional, or educational research, you may find that a specified format and arrangement are required, including an estimate of cost.

When a specified format is expected, it is most important that you follow it exactly, just as you adhere to a particular and specified format for the report itself. Basically, though, a report plan or proposal is likely to consist of the types of information discussed here, which are in turn based on the steps to a solution of a research problem.

The report plan should include:

1. A specific statement of the purpose of the report, including, if necessary, subcategories. Try to word the statement of purpose so that the scope of your research is apparent. If you cannot do so, include a separate statement (or paragraphs, as needed) to make clear exactly what you intend to do.

2. Methods of finding information to lead to a solution of the problem. A tentative bibliography may be included in this section.

3. Methods of organizing, evaluating, and interpreting the data in order to reach a solution. Although this step will not be necessary for all report plans and proposals, it is essential in some situations. If the methods consist only of looking at the data, determining what they mean, and putting them into report format, then these duties can logically be assumed without a definite statement in the report plan. If the data are to be analyzed statistically, or in any special or unusual manner, these methods should be stated.

4. A tentative presentation of the report. This step, like the one preceding, will not be required of many proposals or report plans but is helpful to you for your own planning and is also useful in class assignments. Although you cannot determine the exact outline until you have completed the research or even later, a beginning outline keeps you from going too far astray in your thinking and in working toward a solution.

This tentative outline is also a tentative table of contents, with the headings of the main divisions of the report based on the subdivisions of the problem statement. In a report about Countrywide Insurance and career apparel, the divisions of the problem statement (benefits, disadvantages, costs, etc.) are logical divisions of the final report.

In addition to the preceding items to be included in the report plan, state specifically in written form, if only for your own use, the answers to these questions:

- Is this report to be analytical or merely informational?
- Is is to be formal or informal, in both the format and the writing style?
- Is it to be written in the personal or impersonal tone?

A Proposal

The parts of a report plan discussed and illustrated earlier in this chapter are also parts of a research proposal (using the term in its more formal sense), but the proposal usually requires additional information. The word *proposal* is used as an offer to supply services, such as a consultation or a bid on a contract.

A statement of purpose and a description of proposal methodology are essential in the written presentation of any report project. Other categories of information often necessary for complete research proposals include an estimate of costs, perhaps with a long, detailed budget; qualifications of researchers and other personnel involved in the work; necessary equipment and facilities; a summary of previous research in the area to be studied, including a bibliography and perhaps a summary of all previous investigation; a detailed work schedule, including a date when the project is to be finished; provision for evaluation of the entire project; and suggestions for continuing research.

The physical appearance of many proposals is somewhere between a simple letter or memorandum and a short formal report. Proposals are illustrated by Figures 15–1 and 15–3. A long proposal should begin with an abstract, which is similar to the synopsis discussed in Chapter 15 and

LETTERHEAD SAMPLE

March 6, 19--

Mr. Neilson E. Donaldson, President
All American Software Distributors
1988 N.E. 191st Avenue
Seattle, WA 98104

Dear Mr. Donaldson:

Please study this proposal and determine that it contains the services and
charges we agreed to in our March 3, 19-- meeting at your office. This
engagement document becomes effective upon your signature. Note that four copies
are signed and are enclosed. Because my convention planning staff are proceeding
as though the contract is signed, please telephone 801-489-3389 for other
information you may need.

The report plan was forwarded to you on Friday. The report plan outlines the
deadlines and schedules as well.

Introduction

All American Software Distributors contracts with West Conventions, Inc., to plan
and conduct its first but to become its annual DEVELOPERS USERS GROUP CONFERENCE.
Current developer clients, as well as prospective clients, are invited. Twelve
thousand (12,000) invitations are being printed for distribution to your customer
list as well as to our potential customers list of software distributors. The Mt.
Olympus Hotel in Seattle has been reserved for the conference to be held August
21-23, 19--. Approximately seven hundred (700) distributors are expected to
attend.

Research Requested

All American Software requested that West Conventions, Inc., and its marketing
team assess:
1. reasons for attendance and non-attendance at development conferences.
2. successes of conferences by software distributor competitors.
3. growth potential and product development to include:
   a. newWARE and world and local system networks.
   b. integration of newWARE and existing systems.
   c. development schedules and technology status.

Procedures

West Conventions, Inc., will assess similar developers' conferences and report
attendance, demographics of attenders, new products introduced, and emerging

Figure 15–1. *Sample of an engagement letter or business proposal* technology. Primary data, completed questionnaires, will assess competitors' meetings and results reported by April 23, 19--, assessing developers' conferences in the Midwest and the western United States. Two instruments will be prepared and submitted for your approval: one instrument sent to developers who have attended other seminars and one questionnaire sent to prospective developers.

After receiving the data, West Conventions, Inc., will appraise the results and submit their findings and recommendations in a written and an oral presentation no later than May 5, 19--.

Schedules

Proposal completed	March 6, 19--
Questionnaire instruments completed	April 2, 19--
Questionnaires mailed	April 7, 19--
Follow-up questionnaires mailed	April 21, 19--
Telephone follow-up as necessary	
Analysis completed	April 21, 19--
Written and Oral Report Presentation	April 23, 19--

Budget

Consultant's Services	$12,000.00
Postage and Paper goods	660.00
Printing	130.00
Travel	4,900.00
Presentation Materials	180.00
Misc.	150.00
Total	18,020.00

Agreement Statement

West Conventions, Inc., agrees to perform the outlined research, analysis, and presentations according to the proposed schedules. Schedules may be modified with agreement of both parties. All American Software Distributors agrees to pay all expenses incurred, not to exceed $18,020.00. West Conventions, Inc., accepts full responsibility for the stated research, reports, and presentations and will confirm all hotel facilities and space arrangements. Confirmation of registration and collection of registration fees will be conducted by All American Software. Conference programs and instructional and developmental sessions will be conducted by All American Software Distributors.

West Conventions, Inc.

_____ President
_____ Date

All American Software

_____ President
_____ Date

Figure 15–1. *continued*

286

WHAT IMPROVEMENTS SHOULD BE MADE IN THE PHYSICAL
ASPECTS OF THE GOLD BOND DISTRICT OFFICE
TO IMPROVE EFFICIENCY AND MORALE?

A Proposal
Prepared for

Richard Lunner, District Manager
Gold Bond Building Products

by

Sue Richardson, President
Business Consultants, Inc.
6600 Poplar Avenue
Memphis, TN 38119
(901) 685-5624

July 5, 19--

Figure 15–2. *Example of title page.*

shown with a formal report. Like a synopsis (sometimes the terms are used interchangeably), an abstract summarizes the main idea of the report or proposal, with emphasis on the overall purpose and expected results. An abstract provides an immediate answer as to what the longer proposal is about and thus increases readability.

Solicited and Unsolicited Proposals

Proposals are solicited or unsolicited. Solicited proposals are submitted in response to requests for such proposals, which are often in the form of printed announcements. Unsolicited proposals are originated by the person or persons who submit them.

Requests for proposals come from government agencies, educational institutions, foundations, business and professional organizations, and many other groups and individuals. Announcements that request proposals may include detailed, specific instructions as to how the proposals are to be submitted, arranged, and written. These instructions should be followed exactly.

Unsolicited proposals differ little from solicited ones, although they may be more difficult to prepare because of the lack of guidelines. Organization, conciseness, and readability are of particular importance. As in all communication, your ideas are most likely to be accepted if your readers are convinced that what you propose will meet their needs and desires.

Suggested Contents of a Research Proposal

The sequence of information shown in Figures 15–1 and 15–3 can be adapted and expanded to serve as a research proposal. Such a proposal might contain the following areas of content:

1. A cover sheet showing the title of the proposal; the name of the person, with position and organization, to whom the proposal is submitted; any necessary identifying numbers or phrasing to show that the proposal is in response to a particular announcement or set of specifications; the name, position, employing organization, address, and telephone number of the person or persons submitting the proposal; and the date the proposal is submitted. An example of a title page is shown in Figure 15–2.

2. An abstract that summarizes the entire proposal.

3. A table of contents if the proposal is long enough for a table of contents to be helpful.

4. An introductory or background section, provided such information is necessary before going directly to the statement of purpose.

5. A specifically worded statement of purpose with necessary subcategories.

6. A summary of related research.

7. Procedures, which may be described as methodology or sources of data.

8. Personnel to be involved in the project, with a summary of their background and qualifications.

9. Facilities and equipment to be used in the project.

10. Cost estimate, which may necessitate a long, detailed budget and a firm contractual maximum.

11. Provision for reporting results.

12. Provision for evaluation of research.

13. Provision for putting results into effect.

14. Suggestions for probable further research.

The suggested topics given above can be modified in various ways according to the purpose of the research, kind of readers, overall length and complexity, and specified format. Many proposals will be shorter than the one suggested by the preceding list of parts or sections, with some omitted or combined.

Proposals are arranged in various formats, including letters and memorandums, which are appropriate for short, simple proposals.

The basic principles of report writing apply to all kinds of reports, whether they are of minor, limited nature or extensive in coverage.

The researcher must understand the problem and be able to state it exactly. The next steps are to find the necessary information, evaluate and interpret this information, and organize it in the most readable and appropriate form. This procedure remains the same although the finished report may be presented in one of several forms: the complete, formal arrangement, a more informal report arrangement in that some or all of the preliminary and supplementary parts are omitted, a letter, or a memorandum.

A complete formal report, by its very nature, requires more time, effort, and instruction than shorter, more informal arrangements. You are likely to present reports in this formal arrangement much less frequently than in the shorter and more informal formats. By learning how to prepare a complete formal report, however, you will also be learning to prepare shorter ones, or those with differing formats.

Your ability to do an outstanding job on an extensive report project, which would likely be presented in a rather formal arrangement, could be an aid to the advancement of your business career. Even more important are your increased confidence and sense of accomplishment.

Preliminary Report Parts

The following paragraphs describe the usual preliminary report parts. Figures 15–4 and 15–6 are taken from the same report. Figure 15–5 is from a different report. In addition to the illustrations in this section, other examples of preliminaries are included later when discussing the remaining portions of a formal report.

The Cover

The *cover* is used to protect and to hold the report together, as well as to add to its attractive appearance. A cover also shows that you are careful enough about your report to present it in a neat manner. Don't force your reader to open the cover to find the title and author; this information should appear on the cover itself or through a cutout section.

The Title Fly

The *title fly* is a full page. It shows only the title. This page serves no useful purpose and may be omitted unless the particular handbook you are following tells you to include a fly page.

The Title Page

The *title page* includes the title of the report, the complete identification of the report writer and the person to whom the report is submitted, and the date.

Work for a concise but descriptive title. Although some titles are unnecessarily wordy, short ones are likely to be vague, nondescriptive, and overly broad, promising more than the report includes.

A specific title indicates the nature, purpose, and limits of the research. The title is the major heading of the entire written work. Like all other headings, it must describe the contents that come under it. The title should rule out what does *not* come under it, at least to the extent that a reader could reasonably expect to find such information.

If you have stated the purpose in a concise, appropriate form, you should have no difficulty writing a suitable title. In some instances, the statement of purpose may be an appropriate title, which, unlike the title, may be worded to show the results of the investigation. For example, a problem statement worded in this way:

```
''Should Dillard Enterprises Move to Commerce Square?''
```

may be stated in a title in this way:

```
''Why Dillard Enterprises Should Move to Commerce Square.''
```

This title could also correctly remain in question form. An example of a title page is shown in Figure 15–2.

To repeat and emphasize: *Make sure that the title is stated specifically.* The same considerations that apply to a specific problem statement, as discussed in Chapter 7, apply to the final title of the report.

Proposals

Proposals request authorization for projects and allocate schedules, staff, equipment, and budget.

The Letter of Authorization

The *letter of authorization*, as the name indicates, is written by the person who authorizes the report. It may not be a letter at all but a memorandum. In addition, some authorizations are given orally.

When you receive a written authorization, either a letter or a memorandum, include it in the finished report. This authorization serves as a reminder that the report was prepared and presented according to specific instructions. If the report is to be read by persons other than the authorizer, the letter or memorandum of authorization adds dignity and importance to the work, especially if the report is authorized by a person in a responsible position in the organization.

The Letter of Acceptance

The *letter of acceptance* is written by the researcher near the beginning of the report process as an acknowledgment of the letter of authorization. It makes clear that the report writer understands the problem and any specific instructions given orally or in the written authorization. Like the letter of authorization and the letter of transmittal, this message may also be in memorandum form. The letter arrangement has the advantage of being slightly more personal, yet more formal, as this important situation merits.

DIAMOND RESEARCH ASSOCIATES
1917 Catbird Court
Memphis, TN 38119

September 20, 19--

Mrs. Helen Rockwell, Owner
Rockwell Bookstore
397 Grove Park
Memphis, TN 38117

Dear Mrs. Rockwell:

This is the written proposal you requested in our conversation on September 16.

The Problem and Purpose

Before you can safely invest time and money in an additional bookstore, you must
have objective evidence about the probability of success. The purpose of this
research study is to determine whether the Kirby-Keswick community, Memphis
Tennessee, is likely to be a profitable location and whether a bookstore should be
established in this community at the present time.

Methods of Research

I plan to study the community and to make recommendations based on published
information, primarily the latest available Census data; personal and telephone
interviews with people experienced in the retail book industry; and my own
observations, experience, and analysis.

This gathered information will be compared to similar information about the
location of your presently owned bookstore at 397 Grove Park. Recommendations will
then be made based on all this gathered data.

I understand that I will not consider the feasibility of locations in any other
area of the city or the possibility of expanding your present bookstore.

The Final Report

Results of the research study, with detailed recommendations, will be presented in
a formal report arrangement, as you requested, suitable for presentation to
bankers, investment counselors, accountants, or other financial analysts. The
report will be neatly and accurately prepared using word processing equipment and
the best quality bond paper.

Figure 15–3. *Example of a proposal in letter format.*

Mrs. Helen Rockwell   2   September 20, 19--

My Qualifications

My educational background consists of a Bachelor of Business Administration degree from New Orleans University, with majors in finance and real estate, and a Master of Business Administration degree from Columbia University, with specializations in finance and investments.

I was employed for seven years as an officer in a bank in St. Louis. For the past five years I have been self-employed, working as a business consultant and financial counselor, in addition to handling my own investments. A list of individuals and corporations for whom I have prepared studies similar to your proposed one will be furnished upon request.

Cost

Your cost will be based upon my actual time spent, with an upper limit of eighty hours. The charge is $60 an hour, plus expenses. I estimate that the study can be completed in no more than forty hours. No extra charge will be made for typewriting or for five complete copies of the report. Additional copies can be obtained for only the cost of photocopying.

Time of Completion

The research and the final report can be completed within two months from the date of our agreement.

Mrs. Rockwell, I believe this proposal answers all your previous questions. If you have additional ones, telephone me at 901-685-0000.

The attached form, which will remain with this proposal, serves as our contract. I am enclosing an additional copy of this proposal, also with an attached sheet. I have already signed both copies. Please sign one of the copies and return to me. I will begin work on your project immediately.

Sincerely,

Blair Diamond

Ms. Blair Diamond, Consultant

Enclosures

Figure 15–3. *continued*

The Letter of Transmittal

The *letter of transmittal,* as the name indicates, transmits the finished report. It may be used for helpful and informative comments about the research process, particularly those that do not seem to fit into the report itself. It should include some reference to the authorization and to the purpose of the study.

Other information that may be included in the letter or memorandum of transmittal are suggestions for follow-up studies or other side issues of the problem. It may mention special limitations or difficulties encountered in the research or in the report-writing process, as well as the highlights or other details of the research process. Do not include in the letter of transmittal a synopsis or statement that sums up the findings and recommendations if you also prepare a separate synopsis.

If there is no need for a separate synopsis, the transmittal letter will serve both purposes. Often the synopsis included in a letter of transmittal can be adequately presented in a paragraph or two. The letter of transmittal and synopsis should not be combined if doing so will make the letter longer than one page.

An example of a letter of transmittal that does not include a synopsis is shown in Figure 15–4.

The Table of Contents

The *table of contents* is the report outline, or the tentative table of contents, in its final revised form, with the addition of page numbers.

A table of contents is helpful in many reports that would not be described as formal from the standpoint of arrangement or format. If a table of contents is well made, it serves as a summary of the entire written work and shows the flow of thought from beginning to end. It indicates the topics covered in the report, the sequence of those topics, and the relative importance of the divisions and subdivisions. It also gives the page number where each of the topics can be found. It is helpful to readers who are especially interested in particular sections of the report, or those who wish to reread particular sections.

As mentioned in previous chapters, it is essential that all headings and subheadings of the table of contents agree exactly with the headings and subheadings in the report itself.

Outline symbols may be used before the various captions of the table of contents. The relative importance of various headings is shown by choice of type and by placement. The reader should be able to see immediately the level of each heading and its relationship to all other headings. Major headings should stand out clearly from lesser ones, and subheadings of lesser weights should be clearly placed under each main heading.

April 13, 19--

Mr. Yancey Rowland, President
Rowland's of South City, Inc.
4515 Poplar Avenue, Suite 330
South City, FL 33505

Dear Mr. Rowland:

The accompanying report contains projected figures and actual test results of the
Salesmaster sales program as it would be used in your stores.

The material was compiled in order to determine whether the program would be an
effective sales tool as an addition to your current and future point-of-purchase
marketing efforts.

The program is presented on the basis of additional gross profits versus the cost
of ownership and operation of the machines.

Additional factors such as customizing of the cabinets to match store interior
colors, logo applications, and financial arrangements are mentioned briefly. I
would be very happy to discuss these with you at any time. Please telephone 701-
489-3097.

Sincerely,

Stuart Levine

Stuart Levine
Sales Manager

Figure 15–4. *Illustration of letter of transmittal.*

Avoid a complicated breakdown of headings. In most business reports,
two or three levels adequately describe the contents.

The page is headed with the caption *Contents* or *Table of Contents*. An
illustration of a table of contents is given in Figure 15–5.

Lists of Charts and Graphs

A list of charts and graphs may be headed: *Table of Illustrations, List
of Illustrations, Table of Charts and Illustrations,* or *Table of Figures.* The report
may also include separate lists, as a *List of Tables* and a *List of Charts.* This

TABLE OF CONTENTS

Figure 15–5. *Example of table of contents.*

report part should be headed by the most descriptive term for the illustrations used. It can be a continuation of the overall table of contents or shown on a separate page.

The Synopsis

A *synopsis* is a much condensed review of the entire report, including the introduction and the conclusions and recommendations. In order to stress results, the synopsis is often arranged in the direct order even if the report itself is presented in the indirect order. Usually two-thirds to three-fourths of the synopsis should be devoted to the final results. The remaining portion of the synopsis contains a very brief statement of the purpose, scope, methods, and, perhaps, the background and need for the study.

Many synopses that accompany reports arranged in the inductive order are similarly arranged. The synopsis must be brief, no more than one-tenth of the length of the entire report. For a very long report, the proportional length of the synopsis is even shorter. At its longest, the synopsis should fill no more than two typewritten pages, single-spaced. Some company and government officials insist that all synopses, regardless of the length of the entire report, be limited to one page.

You may be able to write an acceptable synopsis by condensing each major division of the report into one paragraph. Thus a report consisting of an introduction (Part I), four sections of findings (Parts II, III, IV, and V), and the conclusions and recommendations (Part VI) could be condensed into a six-paragraph synopsis.

If the direct order is used for a synopsis, the first paragraph sums up the conclusions and recommendations section of the report. The second paragraph sums up the introductory section, and the four remaining paragraphs summarize the four middle sections of the report (Parts VI, I, II, III, IV, V).

Headings used within a synopsis are optional. The goal is to present the results and management recommendations precisely. Headings may assist transition or visual and reading organization.

Neither of the preceding arrangements is necessary, but a synopsis should truly sum up the entire report. *Because emphasis is on results, more space is often given to conclusions and recommendations.*

The use of the synopsis, in effect, presents the report package in the direct order, although the report proper (beginning with the introduction and continuing through the conclusions and recommendations) is arranged in the indirect order. Because giving the "answer" before the presentation of reasons can be a psychological disadvantage, some report writers prefer to omit the synopsis unless it is an expected and traditional part of the formal report as used in the employing organization. Usually the synopsis should be included, even in reports with disappointing recommendations, because it is likely to be an expected part and, even more important, because it is an effective aid to readability. (This question is also discussed in Chapter 2 with the explanation of the direct and indirect order.)

The synopsis is sometimes reproduced and distributed to people who do not read the entire report, or it may be printed in professional journals or company publications. A written synopsis is also useful as the basis for a condensed oral presentation.

Illustrations of synopses are shown in Figures 15–6 and 15–7.

Terminology differs for the part usually described as a synopsis; for

---

SYNOPSIS

The purpose of this report is to determine the profitability of using Salesmaster
Moving Message sales display machines in all nineteen stores of the Rowland's
South City chain.

Information was obtained from manufacturer's sales representatives: from
literature distributed by the manufacturer; from reports of results obtained by
other users, as published in trade magazines and described in interviews; and,
most important, from results of actual tests in restaurants similar to Rowland's
in South City.

This report concentrates on the direct point-of-purchase usage of the
machine: that is, the advertising of featured items or special prices that change
from day to day. Other uses of the Salesmaster include goodwill and civic
messages, supplemental advertising for national or regional advertising campaigns,
and local promotions.

The machines have been tested in several different restaurants, including
five Krystal stores in Atlanta and two Rowland's in Blytheville, Arkansas. Results
have been extremely favorable when the machine is in a restaurant with a high
traffic volume, such as Rowland's. In Blytheville, a tape advertising sundaes,
shown on a Salesmaster for four weeks, increased sales of sundaes by 67 percent.

Results from these tests provide a basis for the estimate that installation
of the Salesmaster program in all nineteen stores should result in annual
additional gross profits of more than $60,000 a year. Results from the actual
testing program in Blytheville support ths estimate, which is also supported by
the reports of other users.

The program, if utilized in all nineteen stores, would cost $12,973 for
equipment, plus an annual cost of $3,268 for the 115-character message tapes. The
machines are guaranteed by the manufacturer for three years. The anticipated
return for the second and succeeding years should remain fairly constant.

Salesmaster Moving Message sales display machines should be installed in all
nineteen stores of the Rowland's South City chain.

Figure 15–6. *Example of a synopsis.*

example, *epitome, précis,* or *abstract.* The term *abstract* is often used to describe a very short summary of a dissertation or scientific study.

One variation of a synopsis is described as an *executive summary,*
which tends to be longer than the usual synopsis. This term is used to
describe a customary part of all reports prepared in some organizations.

SYNOPSIS

The cost of general purpose computer systems should be distributed to the users. Even though the users may be diverse and many and the problems in assigning costs complex, users of a service should be charged for that service.

This recommendation is based on a review of current literature on costing practices of general purpose computer systems and on past personal experience as a user of general purpose computer systems.

The major costs of a general purpose computer are hardware, software, machine maintenance, and personnel expense. These costs may be large and out of the control of the users.

Accepted cost accounting practices require that direct cost in the production of a good or service be shown as a part of the total cost of that good or service. Alternative suggestions such as establishing a computer operation cost outside the good or service or allocating these costs to overhead are not acceptable treatment of the cost of services rendered. Therefore, the distribution of computer cost should be made to users even though it is not, in practice, satisfactory to all users.

Figure 15–7. *Example of a synopsis.*

An example is shown with other portions of the report written by a researcher with Federal Express and illustrated in Figure 15–10.

Other Preliminary Parts

A preliminary part not shown in the list at the beginning of this chapter, which may be desirable for some reports, is an acknowledgments section. Acknowledgments may also be included in the letter of transmittal unless they are so numerous that the letter would be longer than one page.

Another preliminary part that is useful in some reports is a list of definitions of specialized terms used in the report itself. Definitions may also be placed in the introduction, if the list is fairly short—for example, no more than half the page. Another choice of placement is in the supplementary section of a report, where it is usually described as a *glossary*.

Pagination of Preliminary Report Parts

Preliminary pages (everything up to the first page of the report itself, which is the first page of the introduction) are numbered with lower case Roman numerals, if they are numbered at all. These Roman numerals are centered about one inch from the bottom of the page. Preliminary pages are counted beginning with the title page.

The title page is not numbered. The letter of transmittal and table of contents may be numbered or correctly left unnumbered. The synopsis is usually numbered, although it and all other preliminary pages may be left unnumbered unless to do so disagrees with the particular handbook you are using as a guide.

Thus, if a report contains a title page, a letter of transmittal, a one-page table of contents, and a one-page synopsis, these pages are counted in the numbering process as *i, ii, iii,* and *iv.*

Arabic numerals are used for the rest of the report, beginning with the first page of the introduction.

The Body of the Report

The body of the report, or the "report proper," begins with the intro-duction and continues through the conclusions and recommendations—if the report is arranged in the indirect (inductive) order. In a report arranged in the direct order, which is less likely to have preliminary parts, the report body begins with the gist of the message, which is ordinarily the recom-mendations section.

The Introduction

To review and summarize, the introduction may include these sec-tions:

1. Authorization. (Not necessary if you use a letter of authoriza-tion.)
2. Purpose. (Essential.)
3. Scope. (Essential if it is not obvious from the title and statement of purpose. Scope may be combined with limitations.)
4. Limitations. (Use only as needed—and with caution. Limitations often appear as excuses for a poor report.)
5. Historical background. (Also described as background, back-ground conditions, history, or in other terms.) This section should be included in the introduction only if it can be kept brief. In some reports this information deserves a complete division, often as Part II of the report body.
6. Sources and methods of collecting data. (Essential.) In a few long reports for which detailed and complicated methods of collection or analysis are used, these methods can be reported in Part II of the body of the report.

An example of an introduction is shown in Figure 15–8. This information is based on the tentative report plan shown in Chapter 7 as Figure 7–1.

The Text

The *text* of a report is used to mean the divisions of the report that come after the introduction and before the conclusions and recommendations section. This is not a completely descriptive term, for in a sense the

PURPOSE, SOURCES AND METHODS
OF RESEARCH

Purpose
      The purpose of this report is to explore the possibilities of word processing and administrative support operations for the Chickasaw Branch of Countrywide Insurance Company and to determine the feasibility of converting to a word processing system. The study is necessary because of rapidly increasing costs in administrative operations, as well as an increased volume of typewriting and related printing.

Scope and Limitations
      This study deals primarily with the potential for a word and information processing system to cut secretarial administrative costs by increasing the productivity of each secretary because of specialization. Not included in this research is a complete analysis of the most desirable equipment, as presently owned equipment will be adequate at the beginning of the operation and possibly for some time to come. Another aspect of the problem not considered is the exact nature of the training to be provided to secretaries and executives. Also excluded is consideration of the increase or decrease in morale because of the conversion to word processing.

Sources and Methods of Collecting Data
      Secondary sources provided information about the use of data processing systems by other firms. Interviews with management and the secretarial staff of the Chickasaw Branch were conducted to learn the general functions now being performed and the percentage of time being spent in each function. The work was broken down into two major categories: word processing and administrative functions. IBM sales representatives provided consultations as to the advisability of establishing an information and word processing center. Professional consultation is not readily available on needs except from vendors of equipment.

Figure 15–8. *Introduction of a formal report.*

entire report is the text. These middle sections are also referred to as the "findings" portion of the report. (Terminology as it concerns different sections of reports differs slightly according to the handbook or textbook you are using as a guide.)

The text of the report presents the data you have gathered and upon which you base conclusions and recommendations. *For the most part, this is the only kind of information you should present in the text of the report.* Leave your interpretations and recommendations for the concluding section or sections. For clarity and completeness, however, you will at times need to state an analysis of the meaning of some of your findings as they are presented. In addition, each section of a very long report can be treated as a separate report, with findings stated in each major section, followed by conclusions and recommendations that pertain only to those particular findings.

Conclusions and Recommendations

Conclusions and recommendations are based upon the findings presented in the middle section of the report. *Do not bring new information into these concluding sections.* Conclusions and recommendations may be presented in two sections or, occasionally, shown as two separate parts of the report. In the conclusions you present an analysis of what the findings, presented in the earlier sections of the report, mean to you.

Even though these are your conclusions, if you are writing the report in the impersonal tone, do not switch here and include the use of *I*. You can present your conclusions and recommendations without the use of *I*, as illustrated in some of the examples shown in this chapter. Avoid using the term *the writer*. Since you have collected and analyzed the data, obviously the conclusions are yours unless you state otherwise. Be as objective and impartial as possible in presenting the conclusions and recommendations.

To repeat and emphasize: Conclusions and recommendations are made upon the basis of the findings presented in the earlier sections of the report. If you use the conclusions and recommendations section or sections merely as a means of expressing your unsupported beliefs and ideas, then you had no reason to collect and analyze the data upon which these conclusions and recommendations were not based.

Supplementary Report Parts

The *appendix* section is used for supplementary material. (Both "appendixes" and the Latin "appendices" are now correctly used as the plural form of *appendix*.)

If a questionnaire has been used to gather information, a complete copy of the questionnaire must be included as an appendix; otherwise the reader cannot judge the validity of the reported information. The covering letter, or letters, that accompanied the questionnaire should also be included as an appendix. Sometimes statistical formulas or computations are appended, as are computer printouts. Extensive tables, large maps, diagrams, or other long materials are placed in the appendix section if they are too bulky for inclusion in the report itself.

The main consideration as to whether materials should go in the report itself or in the appendix section is whether the material relates directly to the text of the report or can be considered as additional and supplementary.

The *bibliography* lists secondary sources used in gathering data and in writing the report. A list of interviews or similar materials may also be included with the secondary sources; to be strictly correct, however, do not include interviews under the heading *bibliography*. *Reference sources* is a descriptive term that includes both secondary and primary research. Illustrations of bibliographies are shown in Figure 12–5 and Figure 15–11.

An *index* is unnecessary in almost all business reports; it is used only for very long, extensive reports.

Illustrations of Reports

Great Western Insurance Study

The formal report shown in Figure 15–9 is a report prepared by Nugent International Management Consultants. Sections of the report illustrated in the textbook include all preliminary parts: title page, letter of transmittal, table of contents, and synopsis. Also included are the complete introduction, the discussion of needs by full-time and part-time employees as they interact with their supervisors and with each other, and their responses indicating their opinions about the openness or closedness of the communication channels in the company. An appendix is also illustrated.

Notice in the table of contents that in this particular report recommendations are included early in the report in the synopsis and at the conclusion of the report as a summary.

When opinionnaires, questionnaires, and surveys are completed by consultants or their agencies, they may elect to develop and test their own survey instruments and to complete their own statistical or computer anlyses. This was the case in this report. Had Nugent consultants used other experts' materials, then documentation and bibliography information would be required.

GREAT WESTERN INSURANCE COMPANY
MANAGEMENT SURVEY
AND
CONSULTANT REPORT

Prepared for

Douglas Madsen, President
Great Western Insurance Company
1359 Vermillion Avenue, Suite 1450
Rochester, NY 31606

by

Victoria A. Nugent
Management Consultant

December 22, 19--

Figure 15–9. *Portions of a long, formal report, Turabian style*

CONTENTS

Figure 15–9. *continued*

SYNOPSIS

Recommendations

A structured training program should not be implemented at this time. Instead, we recommend the following:

- Hold integrated meetings for employees of all levels.
- Review objectives monthly and set new goals.
- Hold informal activities that allow both part-time and full-time employees to help plan and implement their work activities.
- Conduct additional studies to examine the relationships between supervisors and management.

Methods Used in Analysis

A questionnaire was prepared and used to gather data from the part-time and the full-time employees at each Great Western Insurance branch office. In a departmental meeting, these questionnaires were completed by part-time employees and then collected by a consultant. Full-time personnel received the questionnaires through department mail, and then returned the questionnaires to their respective department secretary. The response rate was 100 percent among the 48 part-time employees surveyed. Ninety-six of the 115 (84 percent) full-time employees returned surveys.

Conclusions

The full-time employees rated Great Western Insurance Company less favorably than the part-time employees even though they did not express a great deal of dissatisfaction. The areas of communication and perception of relationships with their superiors is of particular concern for full-time employees and should be the focus of further study.

Figure 15–9. *continued*

Nugent International Management Consultants

6449 North Ferger, Suite 1110
Rochester, NY 31516
(701) 489-3097

December 22, 19--

Mr. Douglas Madsen, President
Great Western Insurance Company
1359 Vermillion Avenue, Suite 1450
Rochester, NY 31606

Dear Mr. Madsen:

Here are the suggestions collected from the personnel questionnaire that was used
to evaluate the possible working differences between full-time and part-time
employees.

As you requested, the questionnaire focused on commitment, perception of
relationships, and communication. The findings of this study provide insight into
the employee problems at Great Western Insurance. The added insight should help
management improve the relationship between full-time and part-time employees and
between GWI's administration and its other employees.

Please telephone me at 701-489-3097 when I can be of further help.

Sincerely,

Victoria A. Nugent

Victoria A. Nugent
Management Consultant

bpj

Enclosure

Figure 15–9. *Cover/transmittal letter of a formal report*

INTRODUCTION

Nugent International Management Consultants conducted an individual needs analysis for Great Western Insurance Company. This analysis examines the commitment, the perceived relationships, and the communication among Great Western employees. The following summarizes the activities and findings of the study.

Background

Great Western Insurance Company (GWI) is an entity that mainly provides hospital malpractice insurance, group and individual medical insurance, life insurance, and property insurance.

GWI Management began to pay closer attention to interaction between full-time and part-time employees and noticed certain trends. Part-time employees approached full-time employees only with work-related matters. GWI management found no hostilities or obvious problems between the two groups, except for a feeling of uneasiness or intimidation among the part-timers.

Management came to the conclusion that perhaps different experiences or values were influencing the attitudes of the two groups and that this was the source of separation between the two groups.

Purpose

This analysis was conducted in order to document the perceived separation between full-time and part-time employees at GWI and to determine the effect of this separation on the organization. The findings of this study are to provide insight into the problems at GWI and to provide possible solutions.

Scope

The results of this study of GWI are based only on an individual needs analysis that focuses on the individuals of an organization and how they view their jobs and interpersonal employee relationships. The following three specific areas were targeted: commitment, perception of relationships, and communication.

Limitations

The survey was not taken under optimal conditions. First, an unexpected department meeting was called for all part-time employees in order to conduct the survey. Second, the survey was conducted during the busiest time of year for insurance companies. Consequently, the employees felt rushed to complete the questionnaire. These conditions may have influenced the accuracy of the survey.

Figure 15–9. *continued*

Methods and Procedures

Using the three areas of commitment, perception of relationships, and communication as a base, Nugent's staff consultant committee formulated related survey questions. Nugent's top management then reviewed these questions, adding to them and refining them until the precise questions were agreed upon. A copy of the questionnaire with the code booklet is included in Appendix A, p. --.

The survey was distributed to two different groups in GWI—full-time and part-time employees. The part-time employees were given the questionnaire, to fill out confidentially, during an unexpected staff meeting. The surveys were then collected while the supervisors were out of the room. The response rate from the part-time employees was 100 percent. All 48 part-time employees surveyed completed and returned the questionnaire. The full-time employees received the questionnaire through department mail and were asked to return the questionnaires to the Department Secretary. Ninety-six of the 115 full-time employees (84 percent) surveyed returned the questionnaire.

The questionnaire (see Appendix A) is coded to facilitate entering the data into the computer. As indicated by the questionnaire, a score of 5 means the question or statement was strongly disagreed with whereas a score of 1 indicates the question or statement was strongly agreed with. Central tendencies, correlations, and t-tests were then calculated to facilitate the comparison between full-time and part-time employees.

Findings and Analysis

Commitment

Chart 1 compares the mean scores of the five values that relate to commitment.

Insignificant Commitment Values

The following are insignificant commitment values since the means of these values are relatively equal between the part-time and full-time employees: In general employees *agree* that they enjoy working at GWI, that they are receiving valuable career experience at GWI, that they are giving more than is expected, and that they feel a strong concern for the success of the company (Values 23, 31, 35, and 41).

Significant Commitment Value

On a t-test only the query ''I take pride in being associated with GWI'' (Value 43) is significant. Value 43 indicates that part-time rather than full-time

Figure 15–9. *continued*

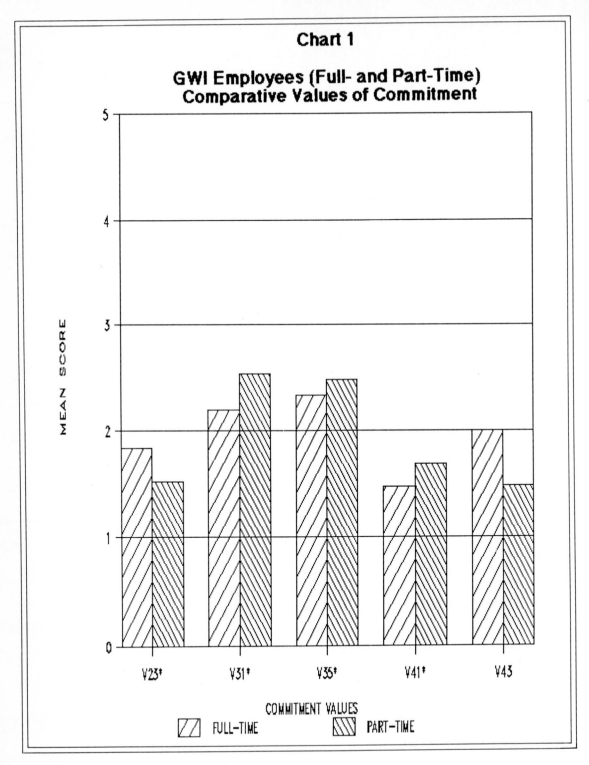

Figure 15–9. *continued*

employees take more pride in being associated with GWI (See figure 1 in Appendix B), p. --.

Perception of Relationships

Chart 2 compares the mean scores of the twelve values from the personnel survey (see Appendix A) that assess perceived relationships between the full-time and part-time employees. On a t-test the values indicated by an asterisk in graph 2 are insignificant.

Insignificant Perception Values

The following are insignificant perception values since the means of these values are relatively equal between the part-time and full-time employees: First, the majority of employees *strongly agree* that they are happy to encourage or help those they work with (Value 21). Second, most employees are *neutral* in feeling that GWI management relates well with part-time employees and that upper management has confidence in their ability to perform (Values 30 and 37).

Significant Perception Values

The following perception values are significant since the means of these values vary significantly between the part-time and full-time employees: First, the full-time employees *agreed* whereas the part-time employees *strongly agreed* concerning the following queries: (1) I work well with my superiors (Value 18); (2) I have a comfortable relationship with my superiors (Value 19); (3) My direct supervisor values my work (Value 27); and (4) I have confidence in the people I work with (Value 42).

Second, the full-time employees were *neutral* whereas the part-time employees at minimum *agreed* on the following queries: (1) Those I work with readily accept me and help me feel important (Value 25); (2) GWI management values my work (Value 28); (3) My suggestions are appreciated and wanted (Value 39); and (4) My full-time superiors show an interest in my success. Third, the full-time employees were *neutral* whereas the part-time employees *strongly agreed* that their full-time supervisor relates well with part-time employees (Value 29).

Chart 3 is a line chart of the significant values relating to the perception of relationships. This graph shows that GWI's part-time employees consistently perceive relationships to be better than do full-time employees.

Figure 15–9. *continued*

Figure 15–9. *continued*

312

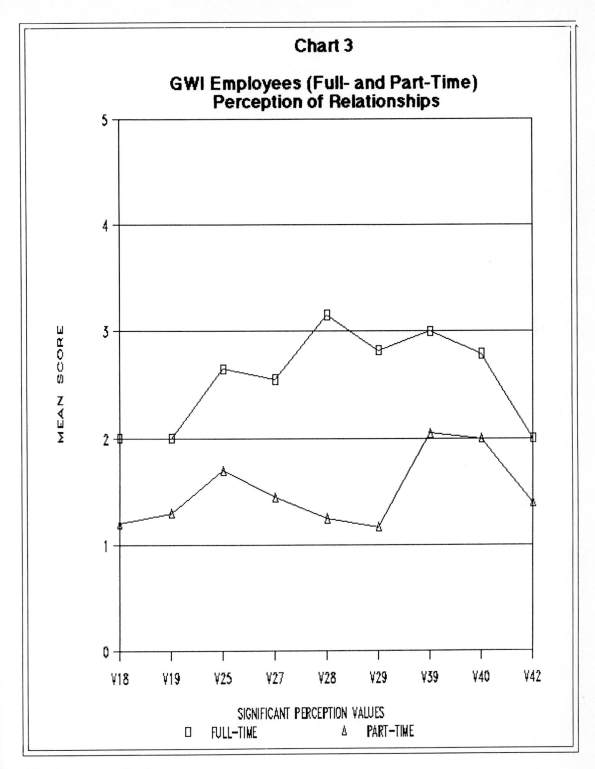

Chart 3

GWI Employees (Full- and Part-Time) Perception of Relationships

MEAN SCORE

SIGNIFICANT PERCEPTION VALUES

□ FULL-TIME   △ PART-TIME

Figure 15–9. *continued*

313

Communication

The survey indicates that full-time employees rely mostly on newsletters and meetings to receive information concerning their job performance and departmental policy, whereas part-time employees receive most of this information from their peers (Values 8 through 17).

Chart 4 compares the mean scores of the eight values from the personnel survey (see appendix A) that deal with the effectiveness of the communication between the full-time and part-time employees. On a t-test the values indicated by an asterisk are significant.

Insignificant Communication Values

The following became insignificant communication values since the means of these values are relatively equal between the part-time and full-time employees: First, the employees *agree* that they are familiar with their job description and know what is expected of them at GWI and that they have a clear understanding of their duties (Values 33 and 38). Second, the employees are *neutral* in feeling that GWI management relates well with part-time employees and has confidence in upper management's confidence and ability to perform (Value 30).

Significant Communication Values

The following communication values are significant since the means of these values vary significantly between the part-time and full-time employees: First, the full-time employees only *agreed* whereas the part-time employees *strongly agreed* concerning the following queries: (1) I can go to a superior with a work-related problem without feeling overly uneasy or hesitant (Value 20); and (2) I am approachable and open to work-related suggestions (Value 22). Second, in regards to the following queries, the full-time employees were *neutral* whereas the part-time employees *agreed:* (1) My efforts are recognized by others (Value 26); and (2) My suggestions are appreciated and wanted (Value 39). Third, the full-time employees were *neutral* whereas the part-time employees *strongly agreed* that their full-time supervisor relates well with part-time employees (Value 29).

Part-time employees seem to view their communication with people in the department better than do full-time employees. This difference in how employees view communication is demonstrated in Chart 5, a line chart, which shows that part-time employees consistently rate their communication higher than do full-time employees.

Figure 15–9. *continued*

Figure 15–9. *continued*

315

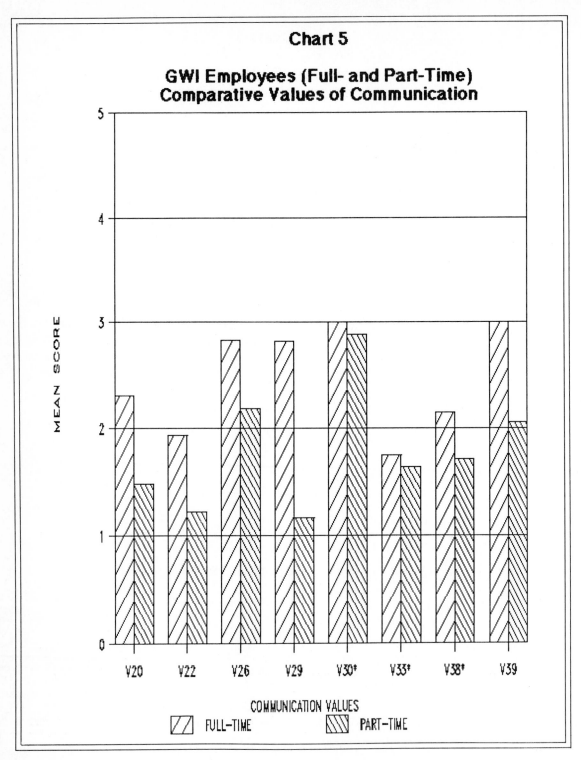

Figure 15–9. *continued*

316

Summary and Conclusions

The individual needs and analysis survey and results document GWI management's concern about the perceived separation of commitment, relationships, and communication between full-time and part-time employees.

In the area of commitment, both full-time and part-time employees feel strongly about their commitment to the organization. However, part-time employees apparently take more pride in being associated with GWI than do full-time employees.

With regard to perception of relationships within the organization, part-time employees consistently demonstrate more positive attitudes about their relationships with other employees than do the full-time employees.

Full-time employees and part-time employees describe differences in how organizational information is communicated. Full-time employees usually receive communication through formal mediums such as newsletters and meetings. Part-time employees, on the other hand, receive such information through the ''grapevine,'' from their peers. Even though part-time employees receive information in an informal manner, they feel more positively about the communication than do the full-time employees.

Overall, full-time employees rated the organization less favorably than the part-time employees even though they did not show any significant amount of dissatisfaction. The areas of *communication* and *perception of relationships with their superiors* is a particular concern for full-time employees and should be the focus of further study.

Recommendations

Consider the following actions:

- Hold integrated meetings for employees of *all* levels.
- Review objectives monthly and set new goals.
- Hold informal activities that allow both part-time and full-time employees to help plan and implement their work activities.
- Conduct additional studies to examine the relationships between supervisors and management.

(No bibliography is necessary for this report. Nugent consultants prepared the questionnaire, attained the results, analyzed the data, and presented the report and charts. Had the report quoted other reports or used sources from other questionnaires, documentation would be necessary.)

Figure 15–9. *continued*

```
                            APPENDIX A

                           CONFIDENTIAL                          VALUES

Time at GWI _____ (years) _____ (months)                    (1)

Marital Status [ ] Single [ ] Married (optional) married=1 single=2  (2)

DEPARTMENT                                                        (3)

[ ] SALES LEADS                  sales leads=1

[ ] INSURANCE AGENT              insurance agent=2

[ ] ADMINISTRATIVE               administrative=3

EMPLOYMENT STATUS                                                 (4)

[ ] Full-Time [ ] Part-Time      full-time=1 part-time=2          (5)


What do you perceive as the purposes for GWI? _____(6)
_____(7)
_____

Where do you get most of the information for your job performance?

Please rank from 1 to 5

_____ A) Peers                                                (8)

_____ B) Supervisors                                          (9)

_____ C) News Letter                                          (10)

_____ D) Meetings                                             (11)

_____ E) Other (please specify)
```

Figure 15–9. *continued*

Where do you get most of your information about department policy?

<u>Please rank from 1 to 5</u>

_____ A) Peers   (13)

_____ B) Supervisors   (14)

_____ C) News Letters   (15)

_____ D) Meetings   (16)

_____ E) Other (please specify) _____   (17)

                                                                   VALUES
I work well with my superiors   (18)

Strongly Agree 1 2 3 4 5 Strongly Disagree

I have a comfortable relationship with my superiors   (19)

Strongly Agree 1 2 3 4 5 Strongly Disagree

I can go to a superior with a work-related problem without feeling
overly uneasy or hesitant.   (20)

Strongly Agree 1 2 3 4 5 Strongly Disagree

I am happy to encourage or help someone I work with.   (21)

Strongly Agree 1 2 3 4 5 Strongly Disagree

I am approachable and open to work-related suggestions.   (22)

Strongly Agree 1 2 3 4 5 Strongly Disagree

I enjoy working at GWI.   (23)

Strongly Agree 1 2 3 4 5 Strongly Disagree

Figure 15–9. *continued*

I can think of people at GWI who do important work that goes unnoticed.   (24)
Strongly Agree 1 2 3 4 5 Strongly Disagree

Those I work with readily accept me and help me feel important.   (25)
Strongly Agree 1 2 3 4 5 Strongly Disagree

My efforts are recognized by others.   (26)
Strongly Agree 1 2 3 4 5 Strongly Disagree

My direct supervisor values my work.   (27)
Strongly Agree 1 2 3 4 5 Strongly Disagree

GWI management values my work.   (28)
Strongly Agree 1 2 3 4 5 Strongly Disagree

My full-time supervisor relates well with part-time employees.   (29)
Strongly Agree 1 2 3 4 5 Strongly Disagree

GWI management relates well with part-time employees.   (30)
Strongly Agree 1 2 3 4 5 Strongly Disagree

I am gaining valuable career experience at GWI.   (31)
Strongly Agree 1 2 3 4 5 Strongly Disagree

I often ''go above and beyond duty'' in my work at GWI.   (32)
Strongly Agree 1 2 3 4 5 Strongly Disagree

I am familiar with my job description and know what is expected
of me at GWI.   (33)
Strongly Agree 1 2 3 4 5 Strongly Disagree

Figure 15–9. *continued*

Communication between full-time and part-time employees could
be more effective.   (34)

Strongly Agree 1 2 3 4 5 Strongly Disagree

I feel I give more than is expected of me at GWI.   (35)

Strongly Agree 1 2 3 4 5 Strongly Disagree

Upper management is effective at GWI.   (36)

Strongly Agree 1 2 3 4 5 Strongly Disagree

Upper management has confidence in my ability to perform.   (37)

Strongly Agree 1 2 3 4 5 Strongly Disagree

I have a clear understanding of my duties.   (38)

Strongly Agree 1 2 3 4 5 Strongly Disagree

My suggestions are appreciated and wanted.   (39)

Strongly Agree 1 2 3 4 5 Strongly Disagree

My full-time superiors show an interest in my success.   (40)

Strongly Agree 1 2 3 4 5 Strongly Disagree

I am concerned with the success of GWI.   (41)

Strongly Agree 1 2 3 4 5 Strongly Disagree

I have confidence in the people I work with.   (42)

Strongly Agree 1 2 3 4 5 Strongly Disagree

I take pride in being associated with GWI.   (43)

Strongly Agree 1 2 3 4 5 Strongly Disagree

Figure 15–9 *continued*

As occurs in business, when problems need to be solved, rarely are there current sources or references in university or community libraries—so empirical research is completed—that is new discovery research and new discovery data. In this form of research, footnotes, endnotes, and bibliographies are not necessary. Where other references or materials are quoted or paraphrased extensively, it is essential that they are referenced properly.

Remember, personal opinions, management decision grids, and preference inventories frequently are classified as behavioral or participative sciences and require on-site solutions rather than library and historical solutions.

Analysis of Federal Express Airport Requirements, Detroit, Michigan

Figure 15–10 (only the beginning portions are shown) is based on an actual report prepared by an airport engineer at Federal Express, Memphis, Tennessee. It is used with permission of the writer and Federal Express.

Parts of the report shown in this chapter are the title fly, title page, letter of transmittal, table of contents, list of figures, list of tables, and executive summary.

Feasibility Study for Retail Bookstore

The following feasibility study (analytical report) answers the question of whether a retail bookstore should be opened in the Kirby-Keswick community, Memphis. Much of the data are based on information from the Census Bureau.

Compare the method of documentation used for this report with the method shown for Figure 15–9.

```
                   ANALYSIS OF FEDERAL EXPRESS
                     AIRPORT REQUIREMENTS


                      DETROIT, MICHIGAN






                        Prepared for

                        James Weaver

                  Manager, Airport Planning






                        Prepared by

                       David Bourland

              Airport Engineer, Airport Planning











                   Properties Department
                  Federal Express Corporation

                     March 24, 19--
```

Figure 15–10. *Portions of a report prepared by an airport engineer.*

March 24, 19--

Mr. James Weaver
Manager, Aiport Planning
Federal Express Corporation
Box 727
Memphis, TN 38194

Dear Jim:

As you requested, I have examined the airports within the Detroit, Michigan
metropolitan area in order to determine the best airfield facility for the
company's short and long range aircraft operations. The attached report is the
culmination of my analysis.

This report evaluates three airports in the Detroit area and subsequently
evaluates two alternative parcels of property for a Federal Express facility. The
report includes preliminary designs of the potential development of the properties
plus cost estimates. The Executive Summary condenses the information in the form
that you requested.

If this project is accepted for further development, I will be pleased to assist
you during the design and construction phases.

Sincerely yours,

David W. Bourland

David W. Bourland
Airport Engineer

Figure 15–10. *continued*

TABLE OF CONTENTS

Figure 15–10. *continued*

LIST OF FIGURES

LIST OF TABLES

Figure 15–10. *continued*

EXECUTIVE SUMMARY

Situation
    Federal Express is currently serving Detroit, Michigan, with one 727 aircraft
through the Detroit Metropolitan Airport. The aircraft parking site is on an
abandoned runway and is subject to a one-year lease which expires on August 31,
1989. The Wayne County Road Commission will not allow FEC to continue using this
site and consequently will not renew the lease. There is no other developed ramp
area on the airport for Federal Express to lease either from the airport or from
other airlines. Federal Express must act immediately to construct its own ramp
area at Detroit Metropolitan Airport or obtain satisfactory facilities at another
airport in the Detroit area.

Mission
    The immediate objective is to acquire an airport facility that will handle
the FEC aircraft operations at the expiration of the current lease. These
operations include the regularly scheduled 727 flight from Memphis, a Saturday 727
charter flight, and two Falcons or supplementals that serve the two cities of
Battle Creek/Kalamazoo and Saginaw/Bay City. In addition, passenger charter
flights are scheduled to begin in Detroit in January, 1990. The FEC facility will
handle the conversion of the aircraft and store the associated equipment. All
passengers will be boarded at the terminal building.
    With adequate room for expansion, long-term FEC requirements may be met.
These requirements include an increase in the number and/or size of aircraft
operating in Detroit. A city station may be located on the site to replace the
existing Romulus station at the expiration of the station's lease in September,
1989.

Execution
    The best alternative for Federal Express is a long-term lease on a 350,000
square foot parcel at Detroit Metropolitan Airport with the intent of ultimately
constructing 300,000 square feet of aircraft pavement, a twenty-truck city
station, and a 9,600 square foot ground-support equipment storage building. This
facility will accommodate two 727's and eight Falcons/supplementals at an
estimated total cost of $2,118,000.

Figure 15–10. *continued*

The construction of this project may be divided into two phases to reduce the initial capital outlay of the company. The first phase will be constructed in fiscal year 1989 and will satisfy the short term FEC airfield requirements at an estimated cost of $1,484,000. With the construction of the city station during the airport fiscal year 1990, the remainder of the site may be developed as proposed.

It is recommended that the Board of Directors of Federal Express Corporation approve a fifteen-year lease with the Wayne County Road Commission for the proposed site plus the proposed construction program at a cost of $1,484,000 in fiscal year 1989 and $634,000 in fiscal year 1990.

Administration

The Properties Department will be responsible for the overall administration of the project. Facilities Planning will coordinate the general and specific requirements of all Federal Express departments with the consulting engineer who is retained to produce the construction drawings. The Regional Properties Admininstrator will work with the consulting engineer to supervise construction. A completion date of November 16, 1993, has been set in accordance with the schedule shown in Figure 6 of this report. Since the completion date is approximately two months past the expiration date of the current lease, the airport authority has agreed to allow Federal Express to continue using the present parking site until construction is completed.

Control

Three significant progress points for this project are:

1. The completion of the design and the construction documents with FEC approval.
2. The receipt of bids and the award of construction contract.
3. The completion of the construction.

Facilities Planning and the Regional Properties Administrator will maintain a close contact with the consulting engineer and the contractor to provide proper control and coordination. These departments will also review any requests for partial payment with respect to the progress of the project. The Accounts Payable Department will review all payment requests for conformity with the terms of the contract.

Figure 15–10.   *continued*

SHOULD A RETAIL BOOKSTORE BE ESTABLISHED
IN THE KIRBY-KESWICK COMMUNITY?

Prepared for

Mrs. Helen Rockwell, Owner
Rockwell Bookstore
397 Grove Park
Memphis, TN 38117

by

Blair Diamond, Consultant
Diamond Research Associates
1917 Catbird Court
Memphis, TN 38119

December 14, 19--

Figure 15–11. *Feasibility study.*

❖ *Diamond Research Associates* ❖

1917 Catbird Court	Memphis, TN 38119	(901) 685-5624

December 14, 19--

Mrs. Helen Rockwell, Owner
Rockwell Bookstore
397 Grove Park
Memphis, TN 38117

Dear Mrs. Rockwell:

Here is your report on the feasibility of establishing a retail bookstore in the Kirby-Keswick community.

As you requested, I concentrated on in-depth data concerning both the industry and the community. According to your instructions, I have carefully documented all data except that derived from my personal observations, which are described as such. The report is arranged in a format that should be acceptable to the bankers from whom you planned to request a loan.

Comparisons emphasize the similarities and differences between the Kirby-Keswick community and the Laurel-Meade community, where your presently owned store is located. Although the neighborhoods are similar in many respects, their differences could affect the success of your proposed bookstore.

The information included here should enable you to make a wise decision. Please telephone me when I can help further. My home phone is (901) 683-1144.

Sincerely,

Blair Diamond

Blair Diamond, Consultant

dw

Figure 15–11. *continued*

CONTENTS

Figure 15–11. *continued*

SYNOPSIS

The Kirby-Keswick community should not be considered a feasible location for a bookstore under current conditions.

Information about the community and the bookstore industry was obtained from published sources, including latest U.S. Census data; from personal observation and analysis; and from people experienced in the retail book industry. These sources were also used to obtain information about the Laurel-Meade neighborhood, the locale of the bookstore now owned by Mrs. Rockwell, in order to predict the probable success of the proposed bookstore in Kirby-Keswick.

Overall, the Kirby-Keswick community is less desirable for a retail bookstore than the Laurel-Meade community. It is a younger neighborhood, with fewer persons of retirement age or near retirement age and far more children under age 15. Although it has somewhat more college-age individuals, it is a great distance from all Memphis colleges and in a rather isolated residential area, although an affluent one. Because of location and age of residents, Laurel-Meade is better able to attract college-age and older customers, the two groups that are assumed to buy the greatest number of books. In addition, the present Rockwell store is in the Laurelwood shopping center, a larger center than Ridgeway, the proposed location of the second store.

Although the Kirby-Keswick community has no other bookstores within its boundaries, at least eight other bookstores, including large chain outlets in shopping malls, exist within a five-mile radius. In addition, paperback books are sold throughout Kirby-Keswick and the entire city in grocery stores, drugstores, and other outlets.

The retail book industry as a whole, although improved since 1986, is still weak. Competition continues to intensify, especially for paperbacks, which increase in number as hardbacks decrease.

A new bookstore in the Kirby-Keswick area would face extraordinary challenges.

Figure 15–11. *continued*

SHOULD A RETAIL BOOKSTORE BE ESTABLISHED

IN THE KIRBY-KESWICK NEIGHBORHOOD?

Overview

Before time and money are invested in establishing a business, predictions based on objective evidence should indicate that the venture will be successful. Although no prediction is conclusive, decisions can be wisely made on the basis of accurate and complete information.

Authorized, Purpose, and Scope

This report was authorization by Helen Rockwell, owner of Rockwell Bookstore at 397 Grove Park, Memphis, Tennessee, on November 1, 19--. She is considering establishing a bookstore near her home in the Kirby-Keswick community in East Memphis, in addition to her present store.

The purpose of this report is to determine whether the Kirby-Keswick neighborhood is a feasible location for a new bookstore and whether such a store should be established at the present time.

Excluded from this study are the questions of whether Mrs. Rockwell should open an additional bookstore in some other area of the city or expand the one on Grove Park.

Sources and Limitations

Information about the community and bookstore industry was obtained from published sources, including latest Census data; from personal and telephone interviews with people experienced in the book industry; and from personal observations and analysis. These sources were also used to obtain information

Figure 15–11. *continued*

about the Laurel-Meade community, the location of the bookstore now owned by Mrs.
Rockwell, in order to predict the probable success of the proposed store in Kirby-
Keswick. (These sources are documented by use of a simplified system; for example,
the citation (4:51) refers to Item 4 in the bibliography, page 51.)

A major source of published data used in this research study is a new release
of the Bureau of the Census described as the Neighborhood Statistics Program (NSP)
report, which classifies information according to neighborhoods within cities. For
the first time, data are available by neighborhoods rather than by census tracts,
which often contain parts of several neighborhoods. (Census tract information is
still available, but it is not used in this report.) The NSP report was released
in January, 1988 (5), based on 1984 data. (A limitation of census reports is that
they are several years old before they are available for use.)

Officials of Memphis and Shelby County asked all established neighborhood
groups, about 150, to participate in the statistical program. Areas without
established associations with clearly defined boundaries were eliminated from the
statistical program. All areas continue to be included in census tract data
(3:A1).

Regardless of government classifications, no particular boundaries would
specifically apply to customers of any retail store, a fact that is discussed
later in relation to bookstores.

Feasibility of the Kirby-Keswick Community

The Kirby-Keswick community of Memphis, Tennessee, reported by the Bureau of
the Census as Neighborhood 40 (5) lies between and slightly to the south of the
heart of East Memphis and Germantown (3:A1). It is a fairly new development, with
most of the houses and commercial buildings constructed within the past twenty years.

Figure 15–11. *continued*

It is bounded by Southern Avenue on the north, Ridgeway and Quince on the east and south, and Kirby Road on the west.

The total population reported by the most current Census was 3,258, with 1,034 households.

Based on personal observation, the Kirby-Keswick community is heavily populated by mobile executive families. Homes are sold, the owners move on, and other highly paid families move in.

The community is in a rather isolated position from major thoroughfares except that its northern boundary is fairly close to Poplar Avenue. The neighborhood is quiet and well kept, almost exclusively residential except for Ridgeway Shopping Center at its outmost boundaries. Except for groceries and incidentals, it is safe to assume that residents do most of their shopping outside their own neighborhood, possibly in the shops in Germantown and other areas of East Memphis.

Age of Residents

Age groups influence book sales. A great number of avid readers in the United States are within two age groups, according to managers and owners of Memphis bookstores (7, 9, 11). These two groups are people of college age, or near college age, and retired individuals, or those nearing retirement age.

The Kirby-Keswick community does not have a high percentage of individuals in either of the two age groups that are assumed to buy the most books, although the college-age group may increase during the next few years. If the families now remain there or are replaced by families of similar age, the number of students in the college age group is expected to increase proportionately with the national trend, as shown in Chart 1. Because the residents are mobile, however, families

Figure 15–11. *continued*

Chart 1
U.S. school and college age population (in millions)

Source: U.S. Department of Education National Center for Educational Statistics

may be replaced with even younger families; they are unlikely to be replaced with older families.

As shown in Chart 1, the number of college-age individuals is expected to remain about the same until about 1991, when the number will begin to increase. Although this expected increase may make a slight difference to book sales overall, it would be unlikely to have a major effect on the Kirby-Keswick area because of its location, as will be discussed later.

Figure 15–11. *continued*

Table 1

CERTAIN AGE GROUPS IN THE KIRBY-KESWICK COMMUNITY, 1984

Age	Number	Percent of Total Population
Under 5	125	3.8
5-9	246	7.6
10-14	408	12.5
15-19	369	11.3
20-24	175	5.3
55-64	171	5.2
65 and over	138	4.2

Source: Bureau of the Census

The median age of the neighborhood is 35.2 (5:4). Further analysis of certain age groups is given in Table 1, which shows that older residents (age groups 55 to 64 and 65 or older) total only 309, or 9.4 percent of the total population. The 779 children under 15 make up 23.9 percent of the total population.

Economic and Educational Factors

As reported by the most recent Census, the mean annual household income in the Kirby-Keswick neighborhood was $40,217; the median household income was $31,897 (5:36). This mean income is the fifth highest of all reported Memphis neighborhoods (5, 3:A1). In addition, Kirby-Keswick is adjacent to the Greentrees community, which has a mean annual household income of $51,971 (5:36).

Of the 1594 employed persons age 16 and over, 636, or 39.9 percent, are employed in professional and managerial positions; 632, or 41 percent, are in technical, sales, and administrative support positions (5:28).

As could be expected, residents are well educated; 95.1 percent of the adults

Figure 15–11. *continued*

aged 25 and over have completed high school, and 47.4 percent have completed four

or more years of college. School enrollment for persons 5 through 18 is virtually

100 percent (5:40).

Other Variables

Although no other bookstores are now in the Kirby-Keswick area, a number of

stores, including large chain outlets, are already well established in nearby

communities. Eight bookstores exist within a five-mile radius, with three in the

Mall of Memphis and one in Hickory Ridge Mall. In addition, books, particularly

paperbacks, are sold in drugstores, grocery stores, and numerous other outlets in

Kirby-Keswick and nearby areas.

Another disadvantage is that the Kirby-Keswick community is located at least

eight miles from all Memphis colleges. Regardless of the number of students in the

community itself, many students are likely to buy books from their college store

or from another outlet near their school. Because of the residential nature of the

community, it is not on a direct route to any Memphis college, except for students

living in the community itself.

Although Mrs. Rockwell has never stocked textbooks as such, related books and

material used by college students constitute a considerable portion of the sales

of the present Rockwell store, according to Jason Harrison, Assistant Manager (8).

Mary Donnelly, owner of a bookstore near the campus of Shelby State Community

College, agrees that sales of books and materials are important to overall

bookstore sales (7).

Concerning the question of a possible site, a desirable store in the Ridgeway

Shopping Center, at the corner of Quince and Ridgeway, offers ample space and a

Figure 15–11. *continued*

reasonable price. The store, now vacant, will be redecorated to meet the specifications of the renter.

Financial Strength of the Retail Book Industry

Bookstores, as a group, have not prospered during recent years, as described in Publishers' Weekly:

The American Booksellers Association financial profile of its membership, specifically the independent bookseller segment, shows a decline of net profits for book retailers over the past four years. . . .

This most recent survey (based mainly on 1984 statistical data) matches the major findings of ABA's earlier financial survey, based on fiscal year 1980, conducted in 1981. (4:15)

Sales of hardcover trade books for adults—fiction or non-fiction sold in bookstores—totalled almost 10 percent less in 1986 than in 1985, as discussed below.

Demand for such books is becoming increasingly price sensitive, a recognition of the public's unwillingness to pay $18 to $25 for hardcover works whenever the possibility exists that such titles may appear later in less expensive paperbound format. (6:7-8).

According to a report in Standard and Poor's Industry Survey, textbook sales increased steadily, although not dramatically, from 1970 through 1984, the last year for which data were available. (Textbooks sales are discussed here because of their relationship to other books sold to college students.) The amount of dollar sales increased from about 700 million dollars in 1970 to about 1,800 million in 1984. Much of this increase, however, can be attributed to inflation. In addition, increased dollar sales do not guarantee increased profits (2:C74).

Conditions in the book industry have improved since 1984. According to the U.S. Industrial Outlook, 1988:

A return to consumer confidence led the way for more book sales in 1987, with both individual and institutions increasing their purchases. After adjusting for

Figure 15–11. *continued*

inflation, sales were up 1.4 percent from 1984. . . . The number of retail outlets increased, reflecting in part the industry's belief that the general public was ready to buy more books. (2:7-8)

The U.S. Industrial Outlook, 1988, also reports thus:

Book publishing in the United States is undergoing a number of changes. Priced considerably below hardbound, paperbound books now occupy more than 75 percent of the display space of most bookstores. (2:8)

A further prediction from the same source is for a 2.1 percent increase in book sales from 1987 to 1988. (2:8). Another prediction, stated in the U.S. News and World Report, June 18, 1988, is this: ''The Commerce Department predicts that book sales will increase almost 10 percent this year to 9.2 billion dollars'' (1:64). (This figure is evidently an updated prediction, as the U.S. Industrial Outlook is also a publication of the Department of Commerce.)

As these preceding statements indicate, the retail book industry is improving. It is important to remember, however, that percentages of increase are based on years when sales were much lower than in previous years, indicating that the book industry has not yet fully recovered.

Comparison of the Kirby-Keswick Community
with the Laurel-Meade Community

Similarities or differences between Kirby-Keswick and the Laurel-Meade community, the location of the present Rockwell bookstore, could affect the success of the proposed store.

The Laurel-Meade neighborhood is comparable in educational backgrounds, occupations, and income. The residents are older, with a median age of 54.8 (5:5).

Figure 15-11. *continued*

The number of college-age individuals is fewer. The number of people of retirement age, or near retirement age, is much greater (5:5).

Age groups in the two communities differ, as shown in Table 2, along with comparisons of certain other factors.

Table 2

COMPARISON OF CERTAIN FACTORS OF KIRBY-KESWICK
AND LAUREL-MEADE NEIGHBORHOODS

Characteristics	Laurel-Meade	Kirby-Keswick
Total population	1,756	3,258
Households	817	1,034
Mean size of household	2.5	3.15
Mean household income	$46,347	$40,217
Median household income	$26,184	$31,897
College graduates	641	939
Median age	54.8	35.2
Residents 65 or over	532 (30.2%)	138 (4.2%)
Residents 60-64	162 (9.2%)	135 (4.1%)
Residents 15-24	200 (11.3%)	544 (16.7%)

Source: Bureau of the Census

The Laurel-Meade community has an unusually large percentage of older persons, who are assumed to be good customers of bookstores. In addition, although not shown on the table, the rather small Laurel-Meade neighborhood is surrounded by other communities that are similar in age, income, and occupations (5).

Another important difference is that Mrs. Rockwell's presently owned store is in the Laurelwood Shopping Center in Laurel-Meade. This center is much larger than the Ridgeway center, the proposed location of the additional store. In addition,

Figure 15–11. *continued*

the present Rockwell store is approximately one mile from Memphis State University and one block from Poplar Avenue, a heavily traveled thoroughfare for students and many other residents of Memphis and outlying areas.

Recommendations

The Kirby-Keswick community should not be considered a feasible location for the establishment of a retail bookstore at this time. This recommendation is based on the following factors:

1. The Kirby-Keswick community, although affluent and well-educated, contains a relatively low percentage of individuals in the age groups that are assumed to buy the most books.

2. The Kirby-Keswick community is a rather isolated residential area, relatively far from all Memphis colleges and most major thoroughfares.

3. The retail book history as a whole, although improved since 1984, is still weak. Competition continues to intensify, especially for paperbound books, which increase as hardbounds decrease.

4. Residents of Kirby-Keswick already have access to numerous book outlets within a few miles of their homes, although no bookstores exist in the neighborhood itself.

5. Overall, the Kirby-Keswick community presents fewer opportunities for success than Laurel-Meade, the location of the present Rockwell store.

REFERENCES
Published Sources

1. ''Book Publishers Turn to a Happier Chapter.'' <u>U.S. News and World Report</u>, June 18, 1988, p. 64.

Figure 15–11. *continued*

2. ''Book Publishing.'' <u>Standard and Poor's Industry Survey</u>, January 1987, p. C74.
3. ''Neighborly Memphians Put into Statistical Focus.'' <u>The Commercial Appeal</u>. January 30, 1988, Section AI, pp. 4-5.
4. ''New ABA Financial Study Shows Bookstore Profitability Down Again After Four Years.'' <u>Publishers' Weekly</u>, January 29, 1986, pp. 51-54.
5. U.S. Department of Commerce, Bureau of the Census, <u>Current Census of the United States: Neighborhood Statistics Program</u>, Memphis and Shelby County Office of Planning and Development.
6. U.S. Department of Commerce, Bureau of Industrial Economics, <u>U.S. Industrial Outlook</u>, 1988, pp. 7-7, 7-8.

Interviews

7. Donnelly, Mary, Owner, Midtown Bookstore, 918 Union Avenue, Memphis, Tennessee 38111. Personal interview, November 21, 1988.
8. Harrison, Jason, Assistant Manager, Rockwell Bookstore, 397 Grove Park, Memphis, Tennessee 38117. Personal interviews November 2, 5, and 10, 1987.
9. Johnson, Matthew, Manager. Books and Such, 2211 Winchester, Memphis, Tennessee 38118. Telephone interview, December 2, 1988.
10. Rockwell, Helen, Owner, Rockwell Bookstore, 397 Grove Park, Memphis, Tennessee 38118. Personal interviews November 10, 14, 22, and 24, 1988.
11. Rogers, Ruby, Owner, Books and Books Shop, 1911 Poplar Avenue, Memphis, Tennessee 38111. Personal interview, November 29, 1988.

Figure 15–11. *continued*

Complete formal reports are comprised of preliminary parts, the report body (or text), and supplementary parts. The complete report, consisting of preliminaries, the report body, and supplementary parts, is known as the report package. **Summary**

Even when reports are correctly described as complete, formal reports, their content and arrangement often differ, as illustrated by the reports shown in this chapter. Many other variations also occur; for example, recommendations and conclusions may be given first (although not so often as in informal reports), and various other preliminary parts may be used.

The executive summary illustrated in Figure 15–10 seems to be increasing in use. It is longer than the synopsis illustrated in Figures 15–9 and 15–11.

As with all report-writing situations, the writer must use judgment and discretion in choosing the most appropriate format and arrangement for complete formal reports.

Cases   No cases are included at the end of this chapter because of the great number included in Appendix C. These cases are planned to accompany Chapter 15 and preceding chapters that pertain to analytical reports, but some also apply to informational reports. The cases in Appendix C are based on principles discussed throughout this textbook.

CHAPTER **16**

Oral Reporting in Groups

Chapter Outline

In this chapter, the term *oral reporting* is used in its broadest sense to include oral presentations of many kinds. Much of public speaking in general is some form of oral reporting, planned especially to inform or to convince.

Defining an Oral Report

The word *report*, like *oral reporting*, is also a broad term. It applies to and includes much of business and professional communication. Remember the definition given in Chapter 1, "A report is a written *or oral* message planned to convey information or to present a solution to a problem." Another definition, stated by C. William Emory, applies to both written and oral reports: "What is a report? It is a statement of results, events, conditions, progress or interpretation of information in communication; if written, it provides a record."[1]

Although reports are thought to be basically the imparting of information, other purposes of communication, including persuasion and conviction, enter into various kinds of speaking for business and the professions. And there is no reason that oral reports should not entertain, also using this word in a broad sense.

The three often-stated purposes of communication—to inform, to persuade, to entertain—cannot be separated. Although the reporting of factual information differs from an after-dinner speech planned primarily for entertainment, all elements of communication are interrelated and do not exist as separate entities. All communication, even that which seems to be only routine and factual, is influenced by the individual emotions of the sender and receiver of the message. The intellect does not function separately from the emotions or without regard to physiological conditions.

All intentional communication is persuasive in the sense that the speaker or writer wants the reader or listener to understand the message and to accept and be influenced by the message. Thomas Leech states: "The most brilliant idea is worth little until it is expressed. How well it

1. C. William Emory, *Business Research Methods* (Homewood, Ill.: Richard D. Irwin, 1976), p. 416.

is expressed or communicated can be as significant to its acceptance and implementation as the idea itself.''[2]

The third purpose of communication, entertainment, is not necessarily excluded from the presentation of most business and professional reports, although in some instances a light approach is completely out of place, as in serious or somber situations. In most other oral presentations, a light, humorous touch is to be preferred to an overly serious one so long as all remarks are related to the general subject matter.

The three purposes of human communication according to Lee Thayer apply to all forms of reports. These purposes are:

1. To affect one's own or another's knowledge of or thinking about something in some way—by attempting to alter a present conception, to add to it, to establish a new conception, etc.
2. To affect one's own or another's attitudes or orientation toward himself, others, or some aspect of his (or one's own) environment in some way; or
3. To affect or influence one's own or another's behavior in some way.[3]

An oral or written report can accomplish all three of Thayer's stated purposes. A report planned for the purpose of gathering information from which to make a decision (1) affects the reader's or listener's knowledge of the situation; (2) affects the reader's or listener's attitudes or orientation from the standpoint of how the information shown in the report relates to sales, location, personnel, publicity, or any other aspect of the organization; and (3) motivates the reader or listener to take the steps necessary to implement recommendations given in the report.

In simple terms, successful communication has occurred when:

1. The message received is approximately the same as the one that is sent;
2. The message obtains a favorable response, although this response is not always apparent, and what is considered favorable differs according to the sender, the receiver, the message, and the environment;
3. The sender and the receiver of the message maintain favorable relationships.

2. Thomas Leech, *How to Prepare, Stage, and Deliver Winning Presentations* (New York:. American Management Association, 1988), pp. 4–5.

3. Lee Thayer, *Communication and Communication Systems* (Homewood, Ill.: Richard D. Irwin, 1968), p. 145.

Notice that in this discussion about the purposes of communication, emphasis is upon the receiver of the message. When sending written or oral messages, keep the receiver constantly in mind. This is a restatement of the you-attitude.

Some oral presentations are referred to as *briefings*. A briefing involves the presentation of long, complex bodies of information in a condensed oral summary. These briefings may be given for the purpose of presenting recommendations to an audience for approval or disapproval or may be merely informational. Some briefings and other oral reports are based on previously written reports; others are presented only in oral form.

You as the speaker, or the "briefer," should be considered the most knowledgeable person on the subject, at least insofar as you are presenting the results of your own research. You should exhibit confidence, yet remain open to the suggestions, questions, and criticisms of other people.

The audience at a briefing is likely to consist of executives, department heads, professional people, or others whose time is valuable. The speaker is obligated to present information in a concise, well-organized way. Briefings may be as short as fifteen or twenty minutes, plus additional time for questions and discussion. Some briefings run for more than an hour, or, conceivably, for a much longer time. You as a speaker should plan your talk with extreme care so as to present the desired material in the allotted time period.

Comparing Oral Reports with Written Reports

The principles of effective communication through written reports discussed in preceding chapters also apply, for the most part, to effective oral reporting. Precise use of language, clarity, empathy, knowledge of subject matter, appropriate emphasis and organization—all these qualities are necessary for the successful transmission of a message in either written or oral form.

Both written and oral reports must be preceded by careful and thorough research and an objective analysis of data. As in other forms of communication, a speaker must consider the probable reactions of the audience to ideas and suggested recommendations.

The principles of effective writing, as well as of competent research, apply to effective oral reporting, although there are certain differences that must be taken into consideration. The speaker need not worry about spelling, paragraphing, punctuation, and typewritten arrangements. Neither is the speaker benefited by these factors, which, when effectively used, are aids to immediate understanding of the written message.

The same principles that apply to objective interpretation and presentation of data in written reports apply when making an oral presentation. Emphasis must be on data, and what the data seem to indicate, not upon the writer or speaker. Evidence is more important and convincing than the writer's or speaker's beliefs and desires.

Like written reports, oral reports can be presented in the *direct* or the *indirect order.* A report arranged in the indirect (inductive) order begins with the introduction, followed by a discussion of findings, and ends with conclusions and recommendations. In the direct (deductive) order of arrangement, recommendations are presented first, followed by supporting details. When presented in the direct order, however, an oral report should have a specific, emphatic ending, often in the form of a short summary.

A written report may become the basis for an oral report. The synopsis can be distributed before the oral presentation for the purpose of informing listeners of the overall picture. This procedure is not advisable, however, if the audience can be expected to have adverse reactions before the research and circumstances are thoroughly explained. In addition, distributing a synopsis or any other written material immediately before an oral presentation distracts listeners' attention from the spoken message.

Many people find oral reporting much easier than preparing written reports. For others, facing an audience is terrifying. The best way to build confidence in yourself, as well as to make your report convincing and informative, is to know your subject thoroughly and to take the attitude that your purpose is to inform and to convince—and perhaps to entertain—but not to impress.

If you are completely familiar with all aspects of the problem, even though you don't know all the answers, and if you sincerely want to pass this knowledge on to your listeners, you are likely to express your ideas clearly and convincingly.

As advantage of oral communication over written communication is that you have instant feedback. Another advantage is that your facial expressions, tone of voice, and gestures help to make your words clear, convincing, and effective.

Graphic illustrations are used in oral reports as in written reports. They can be used effectively or, as in written reports, they can be misleading, distracting, or unnecessary. The principles of graphic illustration discussed in Chapter 11 apply to reports of all kinds. An additional consideration when using illustrations in an oral presentation is that every member of the audience must be able to see the illustration, easily and completely. As in written reports, the illustration should not be expected to convey the most important elements of the presentation, but to supplement the information presented in words.

Another important difference between written and oral reporting is the extreme importance of nonverbal communication in oral messages of all kinds.

Determining the Purpose and Content
of an Oral Report

A *statement of purpose,* as the term is considered in planning an oral report, is used in two ways.

First, make sure that your audience understands exactly, early in the presentation, why you did the research study on which the report is based. If this purpose is not made clear immediately, your message will be even less understandable than a similarly organized written report would be because the reader has the opportunity to turn through pages in order to find explanatory information that should have been given earlier. Your listening audience does not have this opportunity.

The second way in which the *statement of purpose* should be considered early in the planning stages of an oral presentation is this: In addition to making sure that your audience understands the purpose of your research study, consider the purpose of your presentation to the audience. In other words, exactly why are you speaking to the group? What do you want to accomplish? What are some likely barriers to the accomplishment of your particular goal?

Often the purpose is to provide information, in condensed form, so that listeners will know basically what you have found in a research study. Perhaps you have the further purpose of convincing your audience to accept your recommendations. Even if this is the case and you have decided beforehand that your purpose is to bring the audience to your way of thinking, you should not interpret this approach as being manipulative. You do not convince by giving only one side of a story; to do so is perhaps the surest way to convince your listeners that you are less than open in your approach and that you cannot be believed or trusted. As in a sales letter or oral sales message, you convince by giving specific reasons, supported by evidence, why your recommended course of action is the most beneficial one to your listeners and to the organization as a whole.

Write a Statement of Your Exact Purpose in Specific Words

As when you are beginning a research project, you should state the purpose of your oral report in specific written words. This purpose should include the desired response from your audience.

This statement of purpose describes what you want to accomplish by your oral presentation. For example, you may wish to evoke one or more of these responses from your audience:

1. The acceptance of a recommended course of action;
2. A realization that your organization is contributing to the welfare of the community;

3. A feeling of pride in the organization and of self-confidence in their own abilities.

Write Your Central Idea in Specific Words

The central idea is the gist of what you want to *say*. The central idea, as described above, is what you want to *accomplish*. Both the purpose of your oral report and the central idea are related to the purpose of a previously prepared written report—if the oral presentation is based on the written report. The purpose of your oral report, however, is not the same as that of the previously completed research study.

If you cannot state the purpose and the central idea in specific words, you are not yet ready to proceed with the planning of the oral report.

Estimating Listeners' Reactions

As with all communication, predicting the probable responses of your listeners will enable you to express your ideas more persuasively and diplomatically. If your listeners are likely to be pleased with your findings and eager to follow your suggestions and recommendations, your presentation will be far easier and more enjoyable than if you expect opposite reactions.

Estimate the knowledge and background of your listeners about the subject of the report. Your listeners' interpretation of everything you say will be influenced by their past experience, especially as these experiences pertain to the content and approach of the report.

Consider your audience as a group, as well as a collection of individuals who make up that group. What characteristics do your listeners have in common? Do the members of your audience think of themselves as part of the group, subject to group values, goals, and standards of behavior? Do the members of the group have a common motive or goal? Do they like and accept one another?

Some groups contain individuals whom other members recognize, sometimes unconsciously or informally, as leaders. If you can identify these leaders, perhaps you should direct a portion of your message directly to them, although this approach must be used with extreme caution and should not be noticeable to the rest of the audience.

Understand the Occasion and the Environment

Communication of all kinds is affected by the environment in which it occurs. You as a speaker can do much to control that environment or to adapt the presentation according to the setting and the situation. The acceptance of your remarks, of your ideas, and of yourself will be influenced by the setting in which they are presented. As you plan your report or other oral presentation, make sure that you have the answer to these questions:

1. Why is the meeting being held? Is it a regularly scheduled meeting or one called for a special purpose?
2. What is the relationship of your report to the presentation of other speakers?
3. What is the sequence of oral presentations?
4. How will listeners be affected by the time your report is presented?
5. How much time do you have available for your presentation, and can you expect to have your listeners' undivided attention for this period of time?
6. Where is the meeting to be held?
7. Is the room small or large, and will listeners be crowded together or scattered over a too-large area?
8. Will you need and have available a public-address system?
9. Is a speaker's stand available?
10. Is equipment available for the use of transparencies or other graphic aids?
11. Will there be enough light for you to read your notes without hesitation?
12. Will the room be heated or cooled to a comfortable temperature?
13. Will the room be free from outside noises?
14. Will your listeners be comfortable in all other repects?
15. Is the room of a size and arrangement that all members of the audience can hear your words and see you? Can you see all members of the audience?

If possible, examine the room and equipment well in advance of your talk. If it is not possible to do so, at least arrive early on the day of your presentation and consider the relation of the environment to your talk. An early examination of the setting may result in a modification of your planned presentation. For example, if you have planned to use transparencies and find that they cannot be easily seen by every person in the room, you are wise to omit them altogether or to enlarge them.

Even the most thorough preparation and planning cannot prevent all distractions or disturbing elements. Although you should do everything possible to arrange for the environment most conducive to the acceptance of your talk, an outstanding, interesting, convincing presentation will do much to atone for unfavorable aspects of the setting in which the talk is given. The most pleasant room and conditions will not compensate for a mediocre presentation.

Planning and Preparing an Oral Report

As you proceed with the preparation of an oral report, keep in mind your specifically stated purpose and central idea.

Analyze Your Subject to Decide What to Include

Expressing your central idea in a few words enables you to see the subject in its entirety and to understand the relationship of each part of the report to the central idea. Only when you look at your topic in this way can you decide upon the best way to present your topic so as to achieve the desired results.

If a report is to be given for the purpose of helping your listeners make a decision, consider carefully the issues involved. Does the recommended action provide a solution to an existing problem? What benefits will accrue from your suggested solution? Are your recommendations practical and realistic? Is the topic a controversial one about which you are not likely to obtain agreement? Will your recommendation, although beneficial overall, result in undesirable side effects? Most important of all, does your report supply sufficient evidence, provided by objective and reliable methods of research, to convince your listeners of its credibility?

Decide upon the essential information and explanation to be included, then decide how to present it in the available time. Always work for simplicity. Be interesting and clear. At times you must also be convincing. A multitude of details is not simple, interesting, clear, or convincing.

Write an Outline of Key Ideas in the Order of Presentation

After you have stated specifically the purpose you hope to accomplish through your oral report and your central idea, estimated your listeners' reactions, considered the occasion and the environment, and analyzed the subject in terms of what must be included, you are ready to prepare an outline of how you will express and expand upon the central idea. This planning process is similar to preparing a tentative table of contents for a written report.

The outline is the skeleton of your entire speech; it contains your main ideas in the sequence you will present them. Other helpful, interesting, or perhaps amusing details will be added as you progress in the planning of your talk.

Even though you are giving an oral presentation based on a previously prepared written report, do not assume that your oral report should follow the same outline. For one reason, you are not likely to have enough time to discuss each subdivision in the same order and detail as in a complete written report. In addition, you may need to include some information not in the report itself. And, from the standpoint of emphasis and interest, you may wish to spend more time on conclusions and recommended actions than on detailed findings, as you often should do when preparing a written synopsis.

Consider Time Limitations

It is absolutely essential to plan oral presentations in order to ensure that the desired material is given in the allotted time. The best way to plan your time exactly is to practice your speech with the aid of a tape recorder, a home video recorder, or a more professional video recording in your school or in your firm's recording studio. Even this timing will not be exact, except in the case of a speech that you read word for word, because of unintentional departures from the planned sequence of topics and unforeseen interruptions.

Oral presentations should not be read unless your speech is to be recorded or published in your exact spoken words. In such a situation, do everything you can to avoid possible misinterpretation. In most business and professional presentations, reading the report is much less desirable than the more casual and usual method of "telling" or "talking" the report.

Even without the use of a tape recorder, you can estimate time fairly well by estimating the number of words in a planned talk. Although speaking rates vary somewhat, the average rate is 110 to 150 words a minute. If you do not have interruptions because of questions or periods of presenting graphic aids, your average speaking rate can be used to determine how many words you can speak in, for example, a 25-minute period.

You should work to make the report or other oral communication no longer than it needs to be to convey the desired information and to achieve the desired results. As with written communication, however, too much concern with brevity often results in lack of understanding, acceptance, and conviction.

Even more important than length is quality, although from the standpoint of courtesy and consideration speakers should stay within their specified time periods. It is extremely inconsiderate to run on into the time allotted for a following speaker. You are also being inconsiderate of your audience when you are unnecessarily slow and repetitious. Such an approach is not likely to build favorable listener response.

Talk with People and Look at Them

You are talking with *people*, not with a vague, collective *thing*. Although it is true that individuals within a group may react to your talk, and to you, in relation to the reactions of other members of the group, you are communicating with *individuals*, with people like yourself.

When you talk with people, look at them. In a pause just before you begin speaking, look out over the room and see somebody—then look at other people. Let your eyes meet theirs, briefly. Make sure that you include members of the audience at far edges of the group. This action is a form of greeting, perhaps even more important than your spoken words of greeting. In addition, the pause prepares your audience for your opening remarks by getting their attention. Otherwise, if you rush too quickly into your spoken greeting, some of your words will be lost to some of your listeners. By your glances, you invite your audience to enter into a conversation with you.

The audience's part of the conversation, when you are speaking without verbal responses from your listeners, is communicated through facial expressions, nods or frowns, posture, and actions. As will be discussed further in regard to nonverbal communication, your listeners provide vivid, instant feedback without saying a word.

An opening pause (do not extend it too long) relaxes you because it takes your mind away from yourself, the speaker, so that you can concentrate on your audience. When you think of your audience instead of yourself, your stage fright will decrease.

After you have prepared your listeners and yourself, start talking with them. Speak rather slowly at first until your listeners have had time to become accustomed to your voice. Every person has unique voice qualities and speaking characteristics. After a few sentences, speak at your natural rate, making sure that each word is distinct. (If you have not listened to your recorded voice, preferably as rehearsal of the particular talk you are preparing, you are not yet ready to give that talk.)

As in the initial eye contact with your audience, continue to include your listeners in all parts of the room. Avoid directing your attention to one part of the room or to only a few individuals. Do not look very long at any one person.

Make sure that everyone in the room can hear you. If you are not sure, ask. If necessary, adjust the public address system or project your voice.

Speak conversationally with a relaxed voice. If you shout or strain, or assume the pose and gestures of an orator, you are not being conversational.

As mentioned earlier, the use of a recording device is of immense help toward improving your tone of voice, gaining a conversational approach, as well as being a check on pronunciation, logic, appropriate use of emphasis, conciseness, timing, and all other qualities of effective speech. A tape recorder or video recorder is almost as essential as a pen or typewriter in preparing yourself to give an outstanding oral presentation. Video equipment does record both sight and sound.

Understand the Importance of Nonverbal Communication

Nonverbal communication occurs constantly, whether we are speaking to groups or engaging in conversation. It is impossible not to communicate with other people around us, even when we do not speak.

Nonverbal communication includes gestures and other bodily movements, facial expressions, posture, clothing and overall appearance, use of time and space, and various other methods of expressing meaning. We communicate by tone of voice, rate of speech, the "oh's" and "ah's" that we insert into speech, pauses, hesitations, and silence. We communicate through what we omit from our spoken words.

Like all other forms of communication, nonverbal messages should be sincere. Planned gestures and body movements usually appear to be just that—faked. They are also silly. Gestures should be used naturally, reinforcing the meaning being expressed through words. Too much hand movement is distracting and annoying.

Videotape equipment is helpful in determining whether your gestures and other forms of nonverbal communication are appropriate and effective. If such equipment is not available, ask friends to evaluate your speech from all aspects, with special attention given to the use of gestures, posture, and overall movement. It may be dangerous to try to "spice up" your talk by adding gestures, even if you are now using none. In case you are using too many hand movements, however, make an effort to avoid these distracting movements.

Be sincere, enthusiastic, and knowledgeable, with a well-planned presentation, and your sincerity, enthusiasm, knowledge, ability, and consideration of your audience will be apparent to your listeners. You will exhibit confidence and develop belief and trust by the overall excellence of your presentation.

Enthusiasm is contagious. If you are not enthusiastic about your subject, you cannot expect your listeners to be.

You communicate more through your nonverbal messages than with words. Authorities in the field estimate that about 70 percent of the communication that occurs in oral messages is through combined methods of nonverbal communication. Much of nonverbal communication is unplanned; thus, it is a sincere form of communication. Your nonverbal messages are influenced by your feelings about your listeners, your subject, and yourself. Nevertheless, some nonverbal communication is unlike your real feelings. For example, if you frown because you are nervous or afraid you will not be understood or accepted, the frown may be mistaken for dislike of your listeners. Even if the frown is correctly interpreted, it results in a negative impression and is a form of distraction.

Suggestions for effective nonverbal communication are these:

1. Sincerely like your audience.
2. Know your subject thoroughly in order to appear confident.
3. Be well dressed, but not overdressed.
4. Look your listeners in the eye (but not too long at any one person) and talk with them.
5. Avoid excessive, meaningless gestures and nervous movements.
6. Keep calm.
7. Remain objective. Do not let your anger show, no matter what the provocation.
8. Speak clearly and pleasantly. Make sure that you can be easily heard throughout the room. But don't shout.
9. Make sure that you have an excellent command of language usage. (Yes, it's a little late to start if you must give a speech next week and still are not sure whether it's *for my wife and I* or *for my wife and me*. But do what you can, including study of an English handbook.) This suggestion may seem to apply to verbal communication, but not to nonverbal messages. Actually, it applies to both. Obvious and repeated errors (we all slip now and then) tell your audience far more about you than you could put into words. Recording your talk and listening to yourself on tape serves as a check for lack of clarity, slurred pronunciation, and tone of voice, as well as occasional grammatical variations.
10. Relax. You can't if you're unsure of yourself. That's why the nine preceding suggestions are important.

Also use your knowledge of nonverbal communication to analyze the feedback you receive from your audience. Nothing is more satisfying to a speaker than to notice a look of intense interest on the faces of the listening audience. After a few speaking engagements you will soon learn to recognize sincere interest and approval. Even if your listeners are only pretending to be interested in your remarks, you can soon recognize simulated approval and agreement. If your listeners are sitting straight in their chairs and looking you in the eyes steadily and directly, beware. This is a pose of faked attention. Watch for listeners leaning toward you. If you are sure that they are having no difficulty in hearing, this action is a sign of sincere attention.

Notice such telltale signs of boredom as fidgeting, random glances around the room, and looking at watches. (If they are pretending to be interested in your remarks, they will not look at their watches. At least you will know that frequent checkers of time are honestly telling you to move on.)

You can tell by facial expressions, to a great extent, whether or not your audience agrees with you. You can tell when they do not understand or when they are disappointed or annoyed. You can always tell when your audience is pleasantly surprised that you are doing such a good job.

Build Self-Confidence

Remember that you will naturally feel somewhat nervous before you are to make an important oral presentation, or maybe an unimportant one, if you are inexperienced in public speaking. Some speakers of long experience state that they continue to have stage fright before they actually begin speaking but that it disappears as they address the audience. Some people believe that this stage fright is beneficial as long as it is not so severe as to be paralyzing. They say that when they are not nervous at all they know that they are too complacent—and that they will not give an enthusiastic presentation.

Nevertheless, your nervousness should not be so extreme as to result in shaking hands or a trembling voice, which are embarrassing not only to yourself but to your listeners. As a word of comfort, though, most of the terror you feel will not be apparent to the audience. A slight touch of shyness is more appealing, to some people, than the opposite approach of being extremely confident and overly aggressive. On the other hand, being ill at ease indicates that you are more interested in making a good impression than in bringing a message to your audience or in talking with them.

Some techniques that may help build confidence are these:

1. Try not to be afraid in advance. Worrying or being afraid won't change anything, but only make matters worse. Use the time you would spend in being afraid in preparing your talk.
2. Be complete and thoroughly prepared. After all that preparation, you'll be an expert on the subject. And why should an expert be nervous?
3. Unless you are positive that your listeners are actually hostile, an unlikely situation, assume that they are friendly and supportive. This assumption is likely to be correct whether they are friends, acquaintances, or strangers.
4. The audience is made up of *people*. Don't think of your audience as a mass of faces. Speak to your audience as you would to one friend or a small group of friends.
5. Look at people and notice their reactions. As you see your audience accept and respond to your words and actions, your confidence will increase.

6. You are likely to make a few mistakes. So do all the other experts.
7. After the presentation, when you are complimented, say "Thank you," "I'm glad you liked it," or something else that indicates you also think you did a good job. Don't say "Oh, that was terrible" or "I was absolutely scared to death."

Consider the Use of Graphic Aids and Other Illustrations

Graphic aids, such as charts displayed on transparencies, can add to the clarity and interest of an oral presentation. They can also weaken the oral presentation and detract from the spoken words. Use illustrations only if they are needed to supplement your talk. Do not assume that your most important goal is to comment on the information presented in the graphic aids, but that the illustrated material supplements your spoken words.

Graphic illustrations such as bar or line charts express relationships much more quickly and accurately than spoken words. The same advantages that graphics bring to written reports apply to oral reports; in many instances, these aids are even more necessary.

Two-inch slides are ideal for presenting photographs, charts, or tables where the projection facilities are appropriate. Large audiences can see illustrations more clearly when a large screen and projector with sufficient lamp power are available. Avoid using a slide presentation in a small room where you have to darken the room. Your audience cannot see or hear you if the projector is humming in their ears and the room is dark.

Duplicated handouts also serve as a form of visual aid. Some speakers believe, though, that the use of such material distracts from the immediate proceedings. Avoid distributing several pages at one time, some of which do not apply to what is being discussed at the moment. Members of the audience, instead of looking at the speaker or participating in discussion, may spend their time reading the handouts.

Graphic aids and other illustrations, wisely planned and used, are helpful in presenting an interesting, informative oral report. To be effective, however, they require the same careful planning and organization as the remainder of the report.

Be careful not to "lose" yourself in the illustrations being presented to the extent that you lose your audience. You are communicating to your listeners through the *use* of graphic aids. Talk with the audience, not to the illustrations. The illustrations are not telling the story; you are.

Avoid Distractions

In addition to distractions previously discussed, various other actions and mannerisms hinder the understanding and acceptance of your intended message. Although you cannot eliminate all distractions, careful planning will do much to prevent them.

Avoid the annoying, time-consuming practice of shuffling sheets of paper that contain your notes, particularly if you are using a public-address system. The sound may be greatly amplified.

Also avoid moving the microphone unless it is necessary to achieve a desired volume of sound. Many speakers move the microphone unnecessarily, resulting in distracting noise.

Prefer note cards, approximately 5 by 8 inches, to sheets of papers. They are easier to handle without shuffling and noise. You can turn them less obviously. Put the cards into a notebook designed especially for the size cards you are using.

Make sure that your notes are large enough for you to see as the notebook lies on the speaker's stand so that you will not be forced to lower your head or hold the notebook in your hands. If you have thoroughly prepared yourself for the presentation, you will have no need for constant use of your notes, but having them available will add to your poise and confidence. Do not write your notes in great detail; they will be harder to refer to and will require more cards and thus more turning of the cards than if only major ideas are listed. Do not take the risk, however, of omitting important information from your talk because you do not have it in your notes.

Another distraction is frequent glances at your watch or at a clock in the room. Although you must keep close track of time, you should do it inconspicuously. A solution that you may find helpful is to tape a wristwatch with an easy-to-read dial to the inside cover of the notebook containing your note cards, opposite the cards. If you are standing, with the notebook placed on a speaker's stand, you can look at the watch so unobtrusively that your viewers will never guess it is there.

In addition to taking your listeners' attention away from your spoken words, distracting action and mannerisms indicate lack of confidence. They result in a rather negative approach, not a cheerful, positive one.

Speaking and Interacting in Groups

Of course you may present or speak to groups! More often, however, in your initial positions, you will meet with small groups in planning meetings, client's conferences, or problem-solving meetings. It is important to be prepared for any kind of a discussion or a presentation. You can do it well. To build confidence, do not concentrate on the terms *public speaking or meeting leader*. Think in terms of talking with your listeners—sharing or presenting information.

Consider your talk or discussion as a planned conversation with a group of friends. Do not think of yourself as a performer but as a communicator. You are conversing with the audience, not acting a part. As in all effective communication, consider the interests of your audience and present your material in a positive, listener-oriented approach.

Conference Tabletop Meetings

There are numerous kinds of conferences or meetings. Titles such as buzz session conference, brainstorming session conference, seminar session conference, and symposium session conference are used in businesses. Other conference sessions may include a panel discussion or a panel of expert witnesses reporting in a conference session.

Depending on the need of the meeting, the agenda may be planned as a presentation where an "expert" or "company authority" wants to present information without discussion or without questioning.

The lecture conference session or presentation may be a speech. A lecture or speech does not encourage questions or answers. In companies, lectures or speeches give general information, and the messages are directed down-the-line to subordinates and employees. Bosses usually do not want to hear alternative views in lectures. Limited feedback may be permitted but a lecture-style meeting primarily gives information. Delayed feedback in the form of follow-up memos or a second or third conference session may permit responses.

A more frequently used conference session is termed "tabletop conference or problem-solving meeting." This style of meeting may have a prepared agenda but often is called with little notice or preplanning. The primary objective of a tabletop conference session is to solve problems or a series of related business or personnel problems.

In your business position, you should have some information concerning the problems to be discussed, but you seldom will have time to prepare a speech or to gather necessary data or financial statistics.

Charts, graphs, tables enhance decision making in tabletop conference meetings, but are more appropriate to preplanned meetings.

A tabletop conference meeting permits all to exchange ideas, weigh pros and cons and compromise opinions until a common decision is reached, or until the executive tells the participants what the decision is and what actions to take. Such a conference setting permits all to share ideas, express options, encourage teamwork, develop pride and commitment to a project, and plan actions and schedules. Too, when decisions are made, all in the meeting hear the decision. Communication barriers are limited and fewer misunderstandings about the action and responsibilities occur.

Helpful Tabletop Conference Skills

Planning problem-solving meetings and leading tabletop conference skills are important communication skills you may need to use in your daily business meetings. Meeting atmosphere or room facilities, climate skills—nonverbal language skills and spoken language skills—are tested constantly—tested in meetings you direct or in meetings you attend.

Climate skills consist of your ability to plan meeting agendas as well as to arrange meeting atmosphere and physical facilities. Your *nonverbal language* skills communicate feeling about both your visual and verbal messages. Follow these techniques in your tabletop conferences:

1. Establish your position at the conference table quickly.
2. Sit close to or far from the leader as your position permits—or your inclination suggests.
3. Support for the meeting is evident by your nearness to the leader of your "position" or your "side."
4. Opposition to the problem or the leader is evident by your distance and your lack of enthusiasm or verbal support of the "leader or the issue."
5. Provide reinforcement clues—nod head yes, frown a disagreement, or indicate problems visually and verbally.
6. Use papers and note pads to establish your belonging.
7. Take notes to indicate acceptance of data and belief in and acceptance of facts and information.
8. Sit up straight and be attentive as a sign of support.
9. Relax, lean back, push your chair from the table to express boredom or lack of acceptance of ideas.
10. Be intense or interested in a "vital" meeting.
11. Dress for the role of the meeting.
12. Lack of dress and lack of supportive body language are negative or combative signals—use them sparingly.

Your *verbal comments* may appear to sound casual and spontaneous, but be informed and be alert to the tempo of the conversations and decisions. "Face" and acceptance are particularly essential to new employees. Should your comments be not complete or your language phrased poorly, you lose face and eventually employee and employer trust. You can be less than fully informed but do not take strong positions or state strong preferences until you have data or the position to back you up.

Listeners have a right to hear pertinent information. The conviction of your delivery or your bravado may authenticate your data, but it is best not to bluff.

All too often a meeting leader may ask your preference or opinion.

Don't be daydreaming—stay with the meeting and with the conversations, even if you are tired. You can relax later in your office or when you are at home.

Summary

Principles of effective communication through written reports also apply to effective oral reporting.

Determining the purpose of an oral report is essential early in the planning stages. The statement of purpose, as for a written report, should be expressed in a few specific words. The central idea should also be put into specific words. The purpose of an oral report is what you wish to accomplish. The central idea is the core of the message.

Predicting the probable response of your listeners will enable you to communicate more persuasively and diplomatically. The environment, as well as the speaker and other members of a group, influences listener response.

Careful planning of all phases of an oral presentation is necessary for success. This planning should include an analysis of which items of information must be included, how to present necessary information in a specified time, the sequence of presentation, and control of the environment.

Questions and Problems

1. Give an oral report to the class based on a written report you have prepared earlier in the course. Adhere strictly to your allotted time as assigned by your instructor or as agreed upon by you and your classmates. If appropriate and practical, use audiovisual aids to illustrate and emphasize. Allow time for questions from your audience.

2. Prepare an outline of a speech on a subject with which you are thoroughly familiar. Prepare your report and present it to the class.

3. Prepare a short talk to be presented to your classmates. Plan the time according to your instructor's specifications as to the amount of time available. Choose some subject that is related to communication but preferably one that is not discussed in this book. For example, discuss the use of graphic aids in oral presentations, perhaps limiting your talk to the use of one particular kind of graphic aid. Other possible suggestions include recent developments in technology that speed the process of communication; the choice of a word processor; differences between language usage in Great Britain and America; regional differences in pronunciation or word usage.

    All these topics are broad enough for long presentations. If you attempt to cover them in a short talk, you will of necessity be giving a broad overview. Perhaps you can limit your topic to some particular aspect of these subjects; for example, a few examples of extraordinary word usage in the Ozarks or from any other section of the country that you know well. In addition to these suggested topics in communications, you can think of many more.

4. Tape-record a speaker on television or on the radio. Evaluate the performance according to principles presented in this chapter.

5. Members of the class are to form into four- to six-person groups. Assume that the members make up a panel on a convention program. Each group is to select a topic similar to the one described in problem 3. One member of the panel is to act as both chairperson and master of ceremonies. On the day of the class presentation, each member is to be allowed a specified time, according to the total time available, in which to present a report on one aspect of the overall subject. The chairperson is to introduce the panel members to the class before they make their presentations. After all presentations have been made, allow time for questions from the audience, which may be directed to any member of the panel.

6. Experiment by giving short presentations while you sit around a conference table in a simulated business meeting. Solve a problem, resolve a miscommunication, discuss conflict management, or practice small-group leadership skills in making presentations while seated at a conference table.

7. Use one or more of the many topics suggested in Cases in Appendix C, as the basis for an oral report.

CHAPTER **17**

Planning the Search for Career Employment

Chapter Outline

Chapters 17 and 18 are planned to help you communicate effectively in order to secure employment. Chapter 17 emphasizes the research phase of the job-seeking process and the preparation of the resume. Chapter 18 presents a consideration of the application letter and other letters about employment, plus a discussion of the employment interview.

An outstanding letter of application, with a well-organized, attractive, and convincing resume, can make the difference as to whether you find the kind of employment you are seeking. Although no writer, presentation will get a job for you, it can provide an opportunity for an interview, at which time you continue the process of convincing the interviewer that you are the best possible choice for the position.

The most important factor in the search for employment is that you are qualified for the job for which you apply. The most creative, attractive, and appropriate letter and resume will not substitute for having something valuable to sell, just as a cleverly worded sales letter must be written about a good product if it is to be truly effective on a continuing basis.

Methods of Obtaining Employment

Consider the various ways in which employment is obtained. Some of these methods are more effective than others, depending upon the applicant's background and goals and upon job requirements and hiring policies of the potential employer. You should decide upon the approach that seems to be best for your particular situation, but you should also use all other appropriate methods.

Regardless of your outstanding qualifications or of a favorable job market, you should take the initiative in your job search instead of waiting for an employer to offer a position or even to advertise one. Taking the initiative has several advantages. You become aware of differing opportunities and are able to compare prospective employers and employment opportunities. You are more likely to find a better job when you actively seek one, instead of waiting for one to come your way, because you learn about more openings. You are better able to consider your particular strengths in relation to the needs of differing employing organizations.

Another obvious advantage is that your initiative in looking for a job tells the employer a great deal about you, including the fact that you have enough energy and ambition to plan and conduct a thorough, organized campaign to place yourself. The quality of your work after being hired, with resulting opportunities for advancement to a higher position, is likely to be similar to your efforts in finding and obtaining the job.

In addition, as you survey employing organizations, you will no doubt find one or more in which you are especially interested. Your special interest in a particular organization, which will be apparent in your written application and interview, is a definite positive factor from the standpoint of the employer. An applicant who very much wants a job with a particular organization has a definite advantage over one equally qualified who just wants a job—anywhere.

Solicited Application Letters and Resumes

A solicited letter of application, with or without an accompanying resume, is written in reply to advertisements, announcements, or other requests for applicants. Ordinarily, you should use the two-part application (letter and resume) for job openings of all kinds.

You may find advertisements in your local newspaper for the kind of work you are seeking. Another place to find announcements of openings in a specialized field is professional journals, although these openings may require moving to another part of the country. Many advertisements, particularly for executives and engineers, appear in *The Wall Street Journal.*

Writing a solicited application letter differs little from writing a solicited sales letter. You must convince the reader that the product you are selling—yourself—is the one that should be selected. As in all sales messages, the reader is convinced by specific evidence not by a high-pressure approach.

The opening section and all remaining sections of the application letter and data sheet should be built around a central selling point. The central theme, based upon the central selling point, tells how your most important qualification, or perhaps a group of related qualifications, can benefit the particular employing organization. Emphasize the strength or strengths you believe will be most applicable to the particular position, but include other positive factors as well. The employer looks at your entire background, personality, ability, attitude, and, especially, potential value to the organization.

Unsolicited Application Letters and Resumes

Unsolicited applications can be considered a form of direct-mail advertising, similar to messages planned for direct-mail campaigns to sell a product or service.

Prepare a mailing list of organizations for which you would like to work. This mailing list should consist of the names of the organizations and the names, titles, and addresses of people responsible for receiving and reviewing applications. Try to find the name of the person who will be responsible for hiring you instead of sending your application to the personnel department. This person is likely to be a department head or the manager of the office or division where you would be employed.

Make absolutely certain that the individual's name is spelled correctly and that the company title is correct. Preparing your mailing list will require a great deal of research in order to select the organizations and individuals to receive your application.

Some books and consultants on the job-seeking process advocate sending out several hundred letters and data sheets. If you attempt such a broad-scale mailing, you lose any hope of tailoring your approach to individual companies, to say nothing of the great amount of time and expense involved. You are better advised to be more selective in your choice of organizations.

Remember, however, that you are not likely to receive favorable replies from all the applications you mail. Depending upon current employment conditions in your area of specialization and upon your background and qualifications, you may receive a request for an interview or for further information from only a small percentage of your total list.

The two-part application consisting of a letter and resume should ordinarily be sent as a unit. Some applicants, however, send only a prospecting letter and offer to send a complete resume upon request. If you decide to use only the letter, include enough convincing, specific details to make the reader want to know more about you. An example of a letter that combines the functions of an application letter and resume is illustrated in Figure 17–7. All the other data sheets shown in this chapter are intended to be sent with the application letters illustrated in Chapter 18.

Each letter you send should be individually typewritten or prepared on a word processor or letter-quality printer. To do otherwise is to suggest that the letter is only one of many, that you are looking only for a job, any job, that you are not especially interested in the organization to which the letter is addressed. Letters that are prepared by the use of automatic typewriters or word processors, of which there are several kinds, retain their individually prepared appearance.

Resumes are also printed or reproduced by some process, such as photocopying, that results in attractive copies. Resumes, whether individually typewritten or reproduced, should be on bond paper identical to that used for the accompanying letter. Videotaped resumes are appearing frequently in selected jobs. Videos complement written and printed applications.

As a practical matter, if you send out many unsolicited applications the resume should be duplicated in some way. If you are applying to organizations that are similar in nature and supposed needs, a resume can be made to "fit" all of them, although not so exactly as one especially written for each organization.

Placement Service

The college placement office, for graduating college seniors, is often one of the best means of securing career employment. The services of these offices are available also to graduate students, alumni, and students who are discontinuing college for one reason or another.

Placement offices, in addition to arranging interviews with company representatives, usually maintain a library of brochures and literature about employing organizations, including various government agencies. The number of employing organizations that hire through college placement offices changes from year to year, depending upon the economic situation and upon other varying factors.

If you find employment through a college placement office, you may not use an application letter or resumé as they are discussed in this chapter. You will almost certainly make a written application of some kind, however, even if it consists only of filling in the standard application form of the particular organization. In addition, you will probably write follow-up letters and a thank-you letter after the interview.

Some organizations ask the applicant to prepare a letter of application and a data sheet, similar to those discussed here, after the applicant has been interviewed. This instruction may be given to test the communication ability of the applicant or perhaps in order to determine whether there is a sincere interest in the job. Usually, however, the purpose of an application letter and a resume is to obtain an interview. Hand-written application forms are used by many firms.

Private and government employment agencies place thousands of persons each year. Government agencies are free. Placement fees are paid to privately owned employment agencies, either by the individual who is hired or by the employing organization, or the fee may be divided between the employer and the employee. Although these fees to private agencies seem high, if you can find a better job through an agency than you could find on your own, your actual value received exceeds the cost. You are wise, however, to check with your local Better Business Bureau before signing a contract with an employment agency.

Jobs are also obtained through the simple process of going to personnel offices and placing applications or by making telephone calls. Although these methods may constitute a satisfactory approach to some kinds of jobs, including those that college students find as part-time work as they complete their schooling, they are not usually the best approach to full-time career employment.

An unsolicited two-part application, based upon research into the company to which the application is sent, shows more care and preparation and more actual interest in the organization. In addition, your letter, resume, and sample materials can be read when time is available. A telephone call may come at an inopportune time and result in a hasty ''no.''

Analyzing Your Qualifications

When planning a sales campaign, one of the first steps is to make a product analysis. You look at the product, test it, and compare it with competing brands. Then you decide upon your central theme, or the most important selling feature, also called the central selling point.

As you plan a job-seeking campaign, you make this analysis about yourself. You analyze the ''product,'' compare it with competing ones, and note how the product fits the market for which you are preparing your application. Although this analysis is for your use only, it will be far more beneficial and complete if it is in written form.

You will have several features to stress, but the main theme of your presentation will depend upon the kind of work for which you are applying, as well as upon the type of organization. Because the emphasis will differ according to these factors, an individually tailored application letter, as well as an individually planned resume, is more likely to be effective than using the same two-part application for organizations with varying needs.

Because you will not always be sure of these varying needs, you will not always be exactly correct in your choice of the central selling point. Usually the central selling feature will be either your education or your experience. For most persons completing a college degree, especially young college graduates with limited experience, the central selling point is some facet of the educational background, ordinarily the major field.

After people have been out of school for several years, experience is likely to become the most important selling feature if it is similar to the kind of work for which they are applying. People with diversified experience should stress successful experience in a job similar to the one being sought.

In certain instances, extracurricular work or an avocation will be the most convincing central theme. For example, a football star may be hired as a sporting goods salesman. In this case, the football experience is of more value than is the student's major in, for example, journalism. If the student is applying for a job as a newspaper reporter, the academic major should be stressed to the extent that the application is built around it. The football experience should be mentioned but given only limited coverage.

As when selling a product, do not stress the central selling point to the extent that other selling features are omitted or overly subordinated. You cannot be completely sure that you are choosing the most logical central selling point. In addition, you are likely to be hired on the basis of total qualifications, consisting of education, experience, personality, attitude toward work, and the ability to grow and develop in usefulness to the employing organization.

As you analyze yourself, you will no doubt find that you have weak and strong points. As you present yourself to the prospective employers, stress strong points and subordinate or leave unmentioned those factors that you consider to be weaknesses. *Never misrepresent in any way.* The positive approach, as in other communications situations, "accentuates the positive and eliminates the negative." What you consider to be a weakness can often be presented in positive terms. For example, instead of saying, "I have no experience except for part-time work in a grocery," say

```
My four years' experience as a checker and office employee with A&P
Grocery Company were valuable in that they gave me experience in
working harmoniously with other employees and in courteously serving
the customers. I worked an average of twenty-five hours a week during
the entire four years of attending college, yet maintained a grade
point average of 3.2, a score that qualified me each semester for the
Dean's list.
```

Other examples of points to emphasize and subordinate will be given later in this chapter as you learn to prepare the application letter and resume.

Education

If you are completing college or a graduate program, your education to be considered in your self-analysis consists especially of work leading toward a degree. Other educational preparation consists of high school subjects, technical or business courses, and other specialized schooling, as well as educational experiences obtained in military service. Consider courses that apply to the job you are seeking, including those within your major field and any others that especially relate.

Consider also your scholastic standing overall and in your major field. Whether or not you mention your scholastic standing depends upon what it is. According to the principle of the positive approach, you are not obligated to emphasize a negative aspect. If you have an average only equal to that necessary to obtain a degree or very slightly above, emphasize the degree and leave unmentioned the actual grade point average.

The degree is a real accomplishment even if other persons have surpassed you in A's and B's. But if you are asked for your exact standing, be truthful. By being truthful, according to an old adage, you are not forced to remember what you said. Some organizations immediately disqualify any applicant who is discovered to have misrepresented even the slightest bit of information.

You may wish to give your grade point average only in your major field, not the overall average, as the standing in your major field is likely to be higher. This performance in your major field should be of most concern to the employer. In some instances you should mention research projects or papers that are particularly relevant. After you have completed graduate work, mention of a thesis or dissertation or published articles is considered an essential part of your educational preparation.

Remember to include specific skills and abilities developed in your educational program, such as ability to work with computer, software systems, or various office machines, especially if you are likely to use these in your future work. If you have used these machines in previous employment, the mention of this ability should be listed in the section on experience. If you have not actually used them in employment but have had training in their use, mention your ability in the educational section of your data sheet.

As you complete the analysis of your educational preparation, you will probably find that it should be your central selling feature. From a standpoint of emphasis, as you have already learned, a description of your education in terms of how it will benefit the reader should be described in more detail than other factors. Also from the standpoint of emphasis, educational preparation should be presented before other less important factors.

Work Experience

Work experience is ordinarily one of the two most important factors of career preparation, although a few college students complete degrees with no work experience whatsoever. If you have no work experience, educational preparation must be stressed to an even greater extent. You should also show how participation in professional and social organizations has provided experience in leadership positions and in working with other persons.

Some applications have the idea that only related work experience should be mentioned in the application letter or on the data sheet. This approach is unwise. Work experience of any kind, as long as it is legal and honorable, is better than no experience at all. Any job, even the most menial, indicates that you have the energy and initiative to seek and hold a job.

Remember to include work experience acquired in military service. In many instances this will be your most important and relevant experience, or even the central theme of your entire application.

As you continue with your self-analysis, remember to make a note of accomplishments, such as exceeding a sales quota, earning a promotion, or receiving certificates of recognition for unusual achievement. Begin to think of the best ways to present these successes to show how you can benefit the prospective employer. You also have the problem of presenting these successful experiences without appearing egotistical.

Activities, Achievements, and Personal Characteristics

In this portion of your analysis, list extracurricular activities in school; social and professional organization, including membership and offices held; and any other meaningful activity or accomplishment. Include honors, awards, publications, and other recognitions. (Scholastic awards are usually presented in connection with your other educational achievements.) Foreign language abilities, computer programming abilities, hobbies, personal business ventures, and many other facets of your total experience may have a bearing upon your ability to fit into the particular organization to which you are applying.

Check yourself in these and similar areas:

Ability and willingness to assume responsibility	Ability to make decisions
	Ability to persevere
Ability to adapt to changing situations	Ability to think logically and creatively
Ability to communicate in oral and written form	Courtesy and diplomacy
	Emotional and physical health
Ability to work with other persons	Maturity
Leadership	Dependability
Judgment	Promptness
Self-confidence and poise	Ambition and enthusiasm
Appearance	
Sense of humor	
Neatness	

Most important, ask yourself if the field of work being considered is in line with your real interest and ability. What do you want from your career? To prevent the resume from becoming extremely long, as well as from the standpoint of presenting only necessary and relevant information, use discretion as you present this type of somewhat supplementary information. As you remember from the study of emphasis, when you attempt to emphasize a great many things you succeed in emphasizing nothing. On the other hand, you are not presenting the best possible picture of yourself if you omit favorable data that may show your ability to be a good employee. After you have made a complete and objective self-analysis, you should have a realistic approach to the job-seeking process. You still have the task of choosing the best method of presenting qualifications and determining which factors to stress and which to subordinate. In order to answer these questions, you need to know something of your prospective employer.

Analyzing the Employment Market

The market analysis is the next step in the job-seeking process. You must know your employer and the job requirements in order to show how your qualifications meet the employer's needs. Although many items of information cannot be obtained until the interview, or perhaps not until you actually begin work or have worked for a considerable time, much information will be available if you diligently look for it.

First of all, what information will you need? You will need enough information to indicate that an organization is one that will offer you sufficient opportunity, provided you are hired, to justify your accepting this employment. Although this statement may seem obvious, it is the most important answer you are seeking. As you make this investigation, you will also gain enough information to help you intelligently plan your presentation to the specific organization.

You should not take the attitude that you must accept a job that offers little opportunity for growth or for the kind of work you prefer. You may be forced to accept an offer that is less than ideal, but at least you should aim high. On the other hand, remember that you are not stuck forever in any job. Although frequent changes do not look good on your record, many if not most persons change jobs several times during their lifetime.

Although you may not stay with your first full-time job, it should be chosen with care. In one way or another, it will affect your entire career. In addition, the employing organization will spend time and money in hiring and training you—perhaps a great deal of time and money. If you do not enter into the employment contract with the sincere desire to succeed and to remain with the organization, you are not being completely fair to the employer or to yourself.

Another purpose of research into potential employing organizations is to obtain information about how to sell yourself intelligently. If you can determine your possible duties, you can choose the particular qualification or qualifications to emphasize.

Another advantage (as well as an obvious necessity) of doing research into the job market is to know which organizations have openings for persons like yourself. You can assume that many large organizations will periodically employ persons with widely used specializations, such as engineering, accounting, or sales. For positions such as these, unsolicited letters of application are appropriate and useful. You can, in fact, use unsolicited letters for all possible openings, but you will be less sure of receiving a favorable reply.

Even if an unplanned "hit-or-miss" approach seems to succeed, it is still far from being the best method. You are not able in this way to fit your qualifications to the particular employer. You are also likely not to find the organizations for which you would most like to work.

Where will you find all this information? Printed sources will provide some of the information you seek. Annual reports of the firms in which you are interested include far more information than the financial statement. They also tell something of the product or services, as well as the location of the home office and branch offices. They may give information about management policies.

The *College Placement Annual* is especially applicable to persons graduating from college, including graduate school. A copy of this book is often available through your college placement office. Employing organizations are listed alphabetically and also by occupational specialties and geographic locations. Other information includes brief notations as to the kinds of openings, the educational background of the applicants being sought, and the proper person in the organization whom you should contact.

Moody's Manuals of Investments, although intended primarily to provide information to potential investors, also provides information essential to the potential employee. Information included in these manuals consists of a summary of the history of each organization, method of operation, location, products or services, and the financial structure. These books are available in most libraries.

Standard and Poor's Manuals are also planned primarily for investors. They contain information similar to that contained in *Moody's Manuals*. Another publication of this corporation is *Poor's Register of Directors and Executives, United States and Canada*. This directory may be useful in finding the name and title of the person to whom you should send your application for employment.

You may be able to find a specialized guide to employing organizations, with a listing of their management personnel, for your own particular city. Check with your college or public library. Such a guide will contain information about local companies that are not included in national reference books, as well as information about branch offices of national companies. This kind of guide will be your most likely source of exact names and titles of people to whom you wish to address your applications. In addition, if you wish to send applications to organizations in cities other than your own, you may find similar guides to these cities in your local library.

The Business Periodicals Index, the *Wall Street Journal Index*, and other indexes are useful in locating magazine articles that have been written about particular business organizations in which you are interested.

Many government and professional organizations issue publications of their own planned to describe employment opportunities and the necessary qualifications for employees. Much of this literature is available through college placement offices and public and school libraries. You can also learn about job openings from professional journals in your field.

Perhaps the best way of all to learn about prospective employers is to ask other persons who are employed in these organizations doing work similar to the kind you would be doing. As in any other survey, however, the more people you ask, within limits, the more valid your data are likely to be.

Advantages of the Two-Part Application

A two-part application enables you to use the letter to present highlights of the detailed information included on the resume. These factors are stated in light of what your qualifications will do for the reader. As in other sales messages, the letter is more coherent and emphatic when it is built around a central theme.

Prepare the resume, then choose from it important elements to be included in the letter. The letter can be considered as an interpretation of your most important qualifications of all those shown on the resume in terms of reader interest—much as you present important elements of a product as you write a sales letter to be sent with leaflets and brochures. Both of these parts of the two-part application are prepared after you have made a detailed analysis of your qualifications and researched the companies in which you are interested.

Your Resume—A Report on Yourself

The resume (also described as a data sheet) can be the deciding factor in getting the interviewer's attention. It can also continue the sales presentation throughout the interview and the negotiation process.

A well-prepared resume should be a truly superior expression of your talents and background. It should be a credit to your creativity and ability to put ideas into convincing words. The most effective resumes sell ability, talent, and potential, as well as education and past experience.

You should not understate your qualifications, but you also must not misrepresent in any way. Two or three hundred applicants may also want the job for which you are applying; now is no time to be modest.

A resume, like the letter that accompanies it, should be striking in appearance. It should be absolutely perfect in typewritten form and arrangement. Use good paper, a good typewriter, and a typewriter ribbon that gives a clear copy or word processors and quality printers. Special paper, such as a heavy bond in a light cream or buff color, may make your application stand out from all the rest. A correctly prepared copy, however, with correct punctuation and exact wording and spelling, will be superior to many others, even if it is on plain white paper of good quality. Why anyone would sent out unattractive and incorrect applications is difficult to understand, considering the importance of the message. Make sure that you do not leave in such obvious errors as strikeovers, misspelled words, messy erasures, and uneven margins.

Every resume should contain certain basic parts, although the format may and should vary according to the aspect to be emphasized. Each should contain the employment objective (this may be included in the heading), education, and work experience. You may or may not wish to include a list of references and a personal data section.

The Heading

The heading should include your name, address, and telephone number. Sometimes these items of information, used alone, make up the entire heading without some kind of descriptive title such as *Resume, Data Sheet, Vita,* or *Qualifications of.* Your objective may be included in the heading instead of being listed in the first section of the data sheet; for example, *Sherry Clara Aldridge's Qualifications for Accounting Work with Arthur Andersen and Company.* Another method of showing the objective in the heading is to follow your name with a description of your occupation, provided you are applying for similar work; for example *Joe Lee Cole, Industrial Psychologist.*

To list "accounting work" in the heading or in the section of the data sheet entitled *Objective* is too vague and general if you are aware of a particular opening that can be described in more specific terms. Avoid being overly specific when you are not exactly sure of the kind of work available to you; on the other hand, don't be so general that you say nothing at all. "I'll do anything, and I can do everything" is not usually a good approach when seeking career employment—although being a generalist is often more advantageous than being able to work only in a narrow specialization. You are likely to have much competition. Don't eliminate possible opportunities by a too specific description of the job you seek.

Perhaps you should give two addresses and telephone numbers in the heading of the data sheet, especially if you expect to change your address soon. Providing a daytime and an evening telephone number is a thoughtful consideration for an interviewer. Students often give their school address and their home or permanent address.

Employment Objective

If you do not state the employment objective in the heading of the resume, it should be stated in the first section of the resume. Although the objective is sometimes omitted, the resume is much less readable without it. The reader must look through other sections, or at the accompanying letter, in order to determine your employment goals. This factor alone could result in your application being discarded when many other more complete and readable resumes are on the reader's desk.

As a truly qualified candidate, you will be able, with training and experience, to handle a variety of responsibilities related to your educational background and past experience. Even if you begin in a specialized area, you must be able to assume additional duties if you are to be truly valuable to the employing organization, to say nothing of reaching a higher level of responsibility for your own benefit. In addition, few organizations want an applicant who will be content to remain in an entry-level position. Thus your objective may indicate, without appearing presumptuous or obvious, that you are looking for employment with opportunities for growth. For example:

```
Objective: Beginning accounting and auditing work with eventual
           managerial responsibilities.
```

Even if the heading of your resume refers to your employment objective, you may also include an employment objective section as long as you avoid exact repetition. Such an arrangement emphasizes the objective.

The Introductory Summary

The objective may be included in a section of the resume referred to as an *introductory summary, summary, overview,* or a similar term. The summary includes an abstract of the overall capabilities of the applicant. Such a summary is especially beneficial in a long resume, one of several pages, but it may be used in one of regular length.

An introductory summary serves the same function as the *synopsis* or *executive summary* of a report. The most important and relevant elements are given first, in a very much condensed form, followed by supporting details. As with a synopsis of a report, the reader knows immediately what the entire resume is about and the outstanding qualifications of the applicant. A resume long enough to benefit from the use of an introductory summary is more likely to be one of a person with considerable work experience, not a person with little experience who is about to finish college, although such a summary is an aid to readability in any resume.

The introductory summary may be used in addition to, and immediately following, the objective section. Often the two sections should be combined to make the data sheet concise.

Education

An important section of most data sheets is entitled *Education, Professional Training and Education, Professional Education, Academic Experiences,* or some similar designation. Choose the most appropriate, simple heading that best describes the educational experiences that come under it. The section on education should often come after the objective section, or after the summary if included. Place the section you want to emphasize first. If you are a young graduate with little work experience, education is probably your central selling point, as mentioned previously in this chapter. If you have extensive work experience, even though you are just now completing college, related work experience is likely to be more important than your degree. After you have been out of school a few years, work experience is almost sure to be the major qualification for work in the same field, although education remains important. Sometimes you will not be sure which is more important. In any event, give sufficient emphasis to both experience and education to convince the reader of your qualifications.

Use care in the wording of the education section of the data sheet. Ordinarily, if you mean education say *Education*. When you word headings, use the same simple, direct, straightforward, specific approach that is best for all business and professional communication. You need not and should not work for a "cute" or "clever" approach. If you are qualified for the opening, say so in simple, concrete language.

The content of the section on educational experiences, whatever you call it, is discussed earlier in this chapter under "Analyzing Your Qualifications."

To repeat and emphasize: give specific, concrete details (which are of necessity incomplete), interpreted in the light of how these particular educational experiences have prepared you for the job for which you are applying.

Work Experience

This heading, like that for education, is entitled in various ways. Although you are not limited to *Work Experience, Present and Past Employment,* or any other exact phrases, the reader should know immediately that you are describing your past employment, including any self-employment, in terms of how this employment relates to the job you seek.

Much of the content of the employment section of a data sheet is discussed earlier in this chapter under "Analyzing Your Qualifications." As mentioned earlier, this section should often precede education, especially when you consider your experience more valuable for a particular application than your education.

Your present or most recent experience is ordinarily the experience that is most relevant to your application. In the usual course of events, the most recent experience is the most relevant. In addition, from the standpoint of a potential employer, what you are doing now is of far more concern than what you did five years ago.

At times, however, a period of employment other than your present or most recent becomes the period you should emphasize or even build your entire application around. For example, if you worked for seven years in sales, decided to try teaching, then gave up teaching to apply for another sales job, you should stress your sales experience even though it is not the most recent.

The traditional method of arranging periods of work experience on the resume is in *reverse chronological order.* (Another resume arrangement, described as the *functional,* is discussed and illustrated later.)

Ordinarily your present job is considered to be the most important, the second most recent next in importance, and so on. If you are using the reverse chronological arrangement, be consistent even when you consider your present job to be one that does not deserve major emphasis, as in the illustration of teaching and sales work. In such a situation, emphasize by giving more details about your sales experience. In addition, you may be able to interpret your teaching experience in the light of how it applies to sales work.

Continuing with this hypothetical application for employment, teaching experience could be the most important factor of your overall experience and the major field to be emphasized. For example, if you have been a high school teacher and are now applying for a job with a publisher that distributes high school textbooks, your teaching experience is likely to be far more valuable than previous experience in selling real estate. If you are now applying for a job that is related to real estate, you should stress your experience in real estate, whether or not it is the most recent.

All these considerations of how to present your qualifications, and determining which qualifications are most relevant, are examples of the *you-attitude* in action. Present your qualifications from the standpoint of how the employer will benefit from hiring you. To do so, emphasize your experiences that seem to be the most advantageous to the successful handling of the job.

When using reverse chronological order, account for all periods of time since you began work. Or, if you have many years of experience, account for the past ten years if you prefer. When you have had many short-time or part-time jobs, it is not essential to give exact dates of employment, with names and addresses of all employing organizations. You can summarize some work experience: ''1986–1987, part-time jobs at service stations, grocery stores, and drugstores while attending college full time.''

A *functional* resume groups items around four to seven key job functions. This arrangement is particularly appropriate for a ''job-hopper'' whose frequent changes would receive unwanted emphasis if presented in reverse chronological order. The functional arrangement can be beneficial for other reasons, as it emphasizes important and impressive capabilities and accomplishments, not years of experience.

The functional arrangement can also be used to avoid mention of dates, names, and places that might be considered undesirable in a resume but would be necessary if you used the reverse chronological order, in which you must account for all time periods.

Examples of both chronological and functional resumes are shown in this chapter.

Other Appropriate Sections of a Resume

You are free to choose headings to best describe your qualifications, accomplishments, and abilities that do not fit under headings of experience or education. Some examples of often-used sections are *Professional Affiliations, Publications, Activities, Community Work,* and *Interests and Hobbies.* A section described by such a heading as *Personal Data,* which includes age, height, weight, marital status, and other such bits of information, is no longer included in most resumes. At one time the inclusion was so customary that it was almost mandatory. Now this information is more likely to be omitted.

The question of whether to include age and some other personal data with your application is still debatable. Photographs, statements of sex, race, and religion are termed ''discriminating'' and should be omitted.

Most people who work in placement or personnel departments agree that you are free to omit completely all personal information if you choose to do so, including hobbies and special interests. On the other hand, there is nothing to prevent you from giving information that you feel will be to your advantage, although you should not imply that you feel you will be hired because of these factors.

Some items of personal data almost always should *not* be mentioned, including national origin and political party. Even these kinds of sensitive information, however, may belong on some data sheets. For example, if you wish to be an assistant to a congressman or congresswoman who is a Democrat, you should mention your activities in the Democratic party.

In some instances, experiences in church work, religious organizations on campus, or political organizations may be relevant to a job for which you are applying. Such work may show leadership ability and assumption of responsibility. If you have spent a great deal of time in these activities, perhaps you have few other outside interests to report. You must use your own judgment whether to show these items in your employment application.

References

References are not always listed on a resume. This section, ordinarily the last section, may be replaced by a statement similar to this one: "References will be furnished upon request," or you may omit the section entirely. Whether or not to include specific references is another debatable question. If you are applying to only a few employers and you have been given permission to use as references people whose names may favorably impress the employers, list these names. Some employers still expect references, or the mention of references, as an essential part of all data sheets.

When you are sending out a great many unsolicited applications, you are wise to omit the names of people who will recommend you and offer to send further information later. Although potential employers are unlikely to contact the persons you name until after an employment interview, they could do so. You then run the risk of having the persons who have agreed to recommend you bothered unnecessarily by many inquiries.

If you do include references, always state the individual's full name, title, business organization or occupation, address, and telephone number.

Illustrations of Resumes

Illustrations of resumes are shown in Figures 17–1, 17–2, 17–3, 17–4, 17–5, and 17–6. Letters to accompany these data sheets are shown in the next chapter, Figures 18–1, 18–2, 18–3, 18–4, 18–5, and 18–6.

The "letter resume" shown in Figure 17–7 is an illustration of a letter combined with a data sheet. This letter, sent in reply to an advertisement, contains information that should *not go* in a letter of application that is sent with a separate resume, for example, personal data and a chronological listing of positions. On the other hand, the letter does not include some information that would ordinarily be given, such as the name of present employer. Although this letter does not give complete information (evidently Frank Scott did not want to chance, at this stage of the job search, that his present employer would be informed), the letter contains convincing details. It is a good choice for this individual's particular situation.

REBECCA S. ROSENBERG

1472 Tutwiler Avenue   Cincinnati, Ohio 45208   513 272-3625

Objective

A position in Sales Training/Development in a business setting, preferably with Electronic Data Systems Corporation, and to use ability to help others increase sales effectiveness through positive personal relationships.

Work Experience

October, 1984–Present. Sales representative, Checks, Inc.
    Responsible for establishing and increasing sales through direct personal contact at approximately 200 banks in northern Kentucky.

    Conducted and aided cross-selling and security training programs for bank personnel in more than 30 banks. Now writing training programs for all branches of Checks, Inc.

    Perform cost analyses of banks' operating procedures. Develop and implement cost-saving programs tailored to meet the particular needs of each bank.

    Have maintained healthy growth in sales each quarter, often reaching highest sales per quarter in company.

November, 1978–October, 1984. Customer service representative, Checks Inc., Cincinnati, Ohio.
    Responsible for phoned-in questions or problems from bank customers.

    Promoted and established goodwill through written and telephone communications.

    Served as support representative between salespersons and production.

June, 1978–November, 1978. Sales clerk, Gold's Appliances, Cincinnati. Supervisor, Harris Gold. 513 282-333.

September, 1978–June, 1979. (Part-time). Seating hostess, cocktail hostess, bartender, Steak & Ale Restaurants, Cincinnati. (Supervisor is no longer there; address is unavailable).

Figure 17–1. *Example of resume emphasizing work experience, with secondary emphasis on education. Accompanying letter is shown in Figure 18–1. (Based on resume prepared by Rebecca Rosenberg.) (Larger print form with times roman print.)*

Rebecca S. Rosenberg   Page 2

Education

Completing Bachelor of Business Administration degree at University of Cincinnati at end of Spring semester, 1991. Have completed entire college program while attending classes at night and working full-time.

Double major in marketing and industrial psychology. Minor in education.

"A's" and "B's" in the following courses related to sales training and development:

Basic Marketing	General Psychology
Sales Fundamentals	Psychology of Personality
Consumer Behavior	Public Speaking
Business Communication	Human Relations in the Organization

"A's" in all six education courses required for minor.

Completed Motivation Sales workshops by Zig Ziglar (1989) and Don Judson (1988).

Completed Dale Carnegie courses in Human Relations and Sales (1984–85).

Other Facts

Excellent health . . . enjoy sailing, backpacking, jogging, reading, gardening, and the challenge of helping people learn to increase their sales ability.

References

References will be furnished upon request.

Figure 17–1. *continued*

HARWOOD E. LOGAN
4784 Craigmont Avenue
Salt Lake City, Utah 84103

Telephone: 801 386-4108

OBJECTIVE:	Telecommunications Management
SUMMARY:	Experience in the operational control and management of communication systems, using a wide variety of transmission means and terminal devices. Retired major, Marine Corps. Bachelor of Business Administration degree, 1988. Speak three languages.
SYSTEMS MANAGEMENT:	Managed operation of European portion of worldwide communication system comprised of data, teletype, and voice networks. Directed corrective action to restore disrupted service. Presented system status briefings to top-level management. Wrote procedures manual for internal functioning of operations center.
CUSTOMER SUPPORT:	Determined requirements; planned, installed, and directed operation of communication systems designed to support the needs of customers. Trained customers in use of systems. Identified, isolated, and resolved system operation problems. Provided advice and information to customers.
NETWORK DEVELOPMENT:	Performed administrative duties related to the installation and activation of an automated-switching voice communications network in Europe.
OTHER EXPERIENCE:	Taught electronics. Maintained digital computer and peripheral equipment. Maintained electronic control equipment.
EDUCATION:	Bachelor of Business Administration degree, University of Utah, completed May, 1988. Bachelor of Liberal Arts, 1967. MBA degree in process, 1991. Electronics and engineering courses throughout military service.
REFERENCES:	References will be furnished upon request.

Figure 17–2. *Example of functional resume. Application letter shown in Figure 18–2. (Based on resume prepared by Albert E. Harwood) (Printed by letter-quality printer, this resume would fit on one sheet.)*

MARIE P. BROWN, CPA

Current: Permanent:
728 West 1720 North   1004 Patrick Henry Drive
Apartment #320   Suite 6
Cambridge, Massachusetts 02215   Falls Church, Virginia 22044
508/377-2003   804/240-5101

EXPERIENCE   Brown & Brown, Certified Public Accountants (January 1984–Present)
              Founder and Managing Partner of CPA firm with three professionals and two
              offices (metropolitan Boston and Hammond, Virginia). Provide full range
              of financial management services including audits, corporate tax returns, tax
              planning, deferred compensation plans, buy-sell agreements, incorporations,
              bank financing, system development, etc.

              Eastern Associates—Management Consultants (March 1981–January 1984)
              Manager. Performed management study to determine the service charge for
              municipal users of a major water and sewer utility for the city of Baltimore
              Department of City Services. Also assisted with budgets and five-year plans.

              Bests Corporation (March 1980–August 1981) Senior Financial Analyst and
              Internal Auditor. As Senior Financial Analyst in the Restaurant Division,
              responsibilities included:
                * Analyzing economic viability of all financial projects including acquisi-
                  tions and divestitures,
                * determining pricing for disposition of major segments,
                * preparing disaster plan scenarios,
                * calculating economic effect of tax law changes on modeling scenarios,
                  and
                * assisting in determination of hurdle rate structure.

              As Internal Auditor performed a variety of operational and financial audits
              for senior management.

Figure 17–3. *Resume prepared by graduate with extensive experience and education. Application letter is shown in Figure 18–3. (This resume would fit on one page if printed on a desktop laser printer.)*

Alexander Graham CPA's (December 1977–March 1980) Senior Accountant. Audited a wide variety of firms including large and small manufacturing companies, multinational and local banks; savings and loan association, airline, university and not-for-profit concerns. Also worked in the Tax Department and prepared corporate tax returns for Fortune 1000 firms.

EDUCATION   Master of Business Administration, Harvard School of Business, Cambridge, Massachusetts, Class of 1991.

Master of Arts—International Studies, David M. Kennedy Center of International Study, Brigham Young University, Class of 1988.

Bachelor of Science, University of Tennessee, School of Business, Accounting Major. Graduated with honors in December, 1977.

AWARDS AND
ACTIVITIES   Certified Public Accountant
Leader—Girl Scouts of America
Delegate—Republican Party of Virginia
Outstanding Young Women of America
Member of Chamber of Commerce—Burke Area, Virginia

Figure 17–3. *continued*

Juan O. Hermanas

1999 North University Ave #147, Springfield, Missouri, 65844-0094   (417) 373-4108

Objective: International sales and financial operations leading to foreign subsidiary management in 3–5 years.

Education: **MBA,** Graduate School of Management, University of Texas, El Paso. Emphasis: International marketing and finance. To be awarded April, 1990.

MA, International Studies, David M. Kennedy School of International Study, Brigham Young University, Provo, Utah. Emphasis: Asian Studies. To be awarded December, 1989.

BS, Marine Engineering, United States Merchant Marine Academy, Kings Point, New York. Minor: Management, Specialty: International Trade, June, 1977.

Experience: Sycamore Consultants, Erie, Pa., **Management consultant** to industrial clients, March to July, 1987.
- Feasibility studies—financial analysis of cogeneration proposal
- Training Seminars—for control integration of cogeneration power plant
- Marketing problem solving—industrial domestic and international sales staffing

Maritime Marine Motors, Erie, Pa., **Marine Engineer, Group Manager, Divisional Marketing Manager, Divisional Manager,** July 1982 to Feb. 1987.
- Improved domestic and export sales from 300,000 to 3.3 Million in 3 years
- Managed engineering, sales, and marketing functions, staff of 4–6
- Increased output of custom-built heavy machinery product by 200 percent
- Negotiations and sales with clients in Western and Eastern bloc countries
- Supervised 20 to 24 domestic and international sales reps, 40 percent travel

Figure 17–4. *Data sheet of graduate with outstanding experience and two masters degrees. Letter is shown in Figure 18–4. (This resume may not fit on one page, but when experience is extensive and complementary to the job, include a second page.)*

Maritime Industry, various US shipping companies. Sailed as **Engineer Officer** in charge of operations & maintenance on oceangoing ships of the American Merchant Marine. Voyages occurring throughout 1979–1982.
- Supervised technical operations of vessel power plant and maintenance
- Worked with high degrees of autonomy and responsibility.
- Extensive international travel in Far East, Near East, Europe, 90 percent travel

Idaho Engineering, Boise, Idaho, **Mechanical Engineer,** July 1979 through April 1980.
- Wrote specifications, computer programs
- Inspected quality and completion of new construction for food processing plant

U.S. Ship Works, Bangor, Maine, **Test and Trials Engineer,** July 1977 through September 1978.
- Completed 18-month training program in 13 months
- Worked extensively with MIL SPEC and Ingalls quality assurance programs

Personal: Married, 2 children, interests include Karate, tennis, and computer models. Willing to relocate internationally.

Figure 17–4. *continued*

MONROE J. WALDRON

2745 Elmwood Avenue
Berkeley, CA 94705

415 527-9233

SUMMARY OF
QUALIFICATIONS
AND OBJECTIVES

Aggressive and capable manager with nine years of experience in manufacturing
management. Presently Assistant Packaging Manager for division of major
corporation. B.S. degree in manufacturing technology. Good promotion history.
Looking for position in manufacturing management where future opportunity will be
based on performance and results. Particularly well qualified as production department
manager.

EXPERIENCE

Assistant Packaging Manager, Conrad Division, Rivley, Inc. Responsible for packaging
drugs and cosmetic products; direct and control 18 salaried employees and 251 union
personnel; develop, maintain, and coordinate production scheduling for 38 production
lines; responsible for maintaining quality control standards and assuring that products
are in compliance with CGMP and FDA guidelines; enforce applicable OSHA
regulations; represent management in union-related activities. March 1984 to present.

Major accomplishments include:

* Selected by upper management to correct reject problems on major product lines.

* Instituted new sanitation and operating procedures.

* Assumed leadership of weekly production committee that regularly makes significant
  contributions to plant efficiency.

* Increased production efficiency of seasonal pre-packs, resulting in a cost saving of
  $50,000 annually.

* Trained supervisors in safety program that resulted in decrease in accident frequency
  rate by 51 percent and severity rate by 22 percent.

* Decreased absentee rate by 3.5 percent in one-year period.

Figure 17–5. *Resume prepared by applicant with three jobs in one company. Emphasis is
on accomplishments. Letter is shown in Figure 18–5. (Based on material by W. J. Hughes)*

Compounding Section Supervisor, Conrad Division, Rivley, Inc. Was responsible for the production of emulsions, suspensions, creams, ointments, powders, and tablets. Responsibilities included direction and control of three salaried employees and fifteen hourly personnel. Responsibile for ensuring that compounding of formulations was in strict accordance with established procedures and formulas. Developed, maintained, and coordinated schedule with packaging and inventory control; advised and assisted in adapting procedures from laboratory to actual production conditions and requirements. May 1980–March 1984.

Major accomplishments included:

* Installed a product transfer system which resulted in improved sanitation of production lines.

* Effectively supervised production area during period of major expansion. Assumed total responsibility for hiring and training personnel. Specified equipment needs to increase production.

* Updated majority of manufacturing procedures to bring into compliance with CGMP standards.

Packaging Line Supervisor, Conrad Division, Rivley, Inc. Was responsible for production of assigned packaging lines. Trained and supervised personnel. June 1976– May 1980.

MILITARY SERVICE

Progressed from private to captain in twelve years of active service with Army National Guard. Completed five phases of Command and General Staff School. Commanded company during period of major reorganization which required special skills to assign, train, and develop officer and enlisted personnel; simultaneously reduced company readiness time by 50 percent. President of 30th AR Bde Officers' Association.

EDUCATION

B.S. degree in manufacturing technology. San Francisco State University, 1976. Various job related courses, workshops, and seminars, including a sixteen-week Management by Objectives program for manufacturing management.

Figure 17–5. *continued*

WILLIAM THOMAS KING'S QUALIFICATIONS
FOR AIRFRAME AND POWERPLANT MECHANIC

Home Address   School Address

3931 Meadow Lane   Memphis Area Vocational-
Olive Branch, MS 38654   Technical School
601 895-2066   Aviation Complex
                                          2752 Winchester Road
                                          Memphis, TN 38116

Available to begin work on July 1, 1991

Education

Diploma and Powerplant License, Memphis Area Vocational–Technical School, Aviation
Complex, 2752 Winchester Road, Memphis, TN 38116 (June, 1991)

Diploma and Airframes License, Aviation Structural Mechanic H, Hydraulic A. Marine Aviation Training Support Group–90, Naval Air Technical Training Center, NAS, Millington,
TN 38054 (1988)

Diploma, Hillcrest High School, 4184 Graceland Drive, Memphis, TN 38116 (1984)

Work Experience

Attendant/Mechanic, Roy's Chevron, 7144 Old Highway 78, Olive Branch, MS 38654 (Part-
time) Supervisor: Roy Collier (January 1990-Present)

Aircraft Hydraulic/Pneumatic Mechanic, United States Marines, VMAT–102, MCAS, Yuma,
AZ 85369 Supervisor: GynSgt. H. A. Omach (December 1984-July 1989) Honorably
discharged as E-5 Sergeant. Major duties included inspecting, repairing, and performing
preventive maintenance on the Douglas A-4M/TA-4F hydraulic and pneumatic systems and
components and wheel braking assemblies.

Maintained power control packages, used specifications, blueprints, and necessary tools and
test equipment. Requisitioned supplies, equipment, and special tools required in missions.
Performed and supervised technical training of personnel, maintained records and reports,
inspected shop maintenance as a Collateral Duty Inspector for Quality Assurance.

Attendant, Guidry's Texaco, 1315 Winchester Road, Memphis, TN 38116 Supervisor: Joe
Guidry (August 1982–November 1984)

Figure 17–6. *Resume of graduate of technical school. Military experience is an important
qualification. Accompanying letter is shown in Figure 18–6.*

Organizations and Licenses

Aviation Maintenance Foundation, Inc., From 1987–Present

Airframes License December 4, 1987

Powerplants License to be completed on July 1, 1991

Qualified to Operate the Following Equipment

AHT–63/64 Hydraulic Test Stand	MMG–1a/2MG–2 Electric Power Unit
TA/JG–75 Aircraft Tow Tractor	NAN–1/1a/2/3 Nitrogen Servicing
Cornice Brake	Unit
Oxyacetylene Welding Equipment	Microfiche Maintenance/Parts Reader
Maintenance Info. Automated	Retrieval System Machine (MIARS)

Own a complete set of hand tools for airframe and powerplant maintenance

Personal Data

Health: Excellent
Hobbies: Woodworking and RC Airplanes

References

Mr. John Litterer	Mr. Jack Doty
Machinist	Instructor
4601 Gwyck	Memphis Area Vocational–
Olive Branch, MS 38654	Technical School
601 895–3325	2752 Winchester Road
	Memphis, TN 38116
	901 354–1955
Sgt. Earl Combes, USMC	Mr. Roy Collier, Owner
Instructor, F–18 Program	Roy's Chevron
860 E. Grangeville	7144 Old Highway 78
Apartment #68	Olive Branch, MS 38654
Handord, CA 93230	601 895–6676
209 584–9436	

Figure 17–6. *continued*

1987 East Mexicali Drive
San Diego, CA 92123
February 22, 1990

Mr. Henry C. Cotton
Personnel Manager
First National Bank
8047 West Loma Boulevard
San Diego, CA 92107

Dear Mr. Cotton:

Three years of banking experience and a college education in marketing should enable me to be successful as the Trust Department Officer for whom you advertised in the San Diego Times.

I am now employed full-time in the Trust Department of a San Diego bank. Past experience in banking includes two and one-half years at Mercantile Bank in Long Beach, California. This experience would be helpful to First National, as the Mercantile Bank is similar in size and organization. In addition, I spent nine months there in the Trust Department.

In early 1985 I began work at the Mercantile Bank as a clerical employee. In May of 1985 I was offered a full-time position as a supervisor of three other persons. Later that year I moved to my present position in the Trust Department in a bank in San Diego. (My employers will recommend me highly, I feel sure, and I will give you their names at our interview. In the meantime, however, I ask that you keep this application confidential.)

As I have always worked toward high goals, I will continue my education after graduation from San Diego State University in May of this year. While working full-time and going to college at night, I have also attended four American Institute of Banking seminars in finance and international investment banking.

Previous experience includes seven years of sales experience (automotive parts and industrial paper) and four years in the U.S. Navy.

Please write me or telephone me at 714-458-2514—in order to arrange an interview. I can begin work two weeks after notifying my present employer.

Sincerely,

Frank B. Scott

Telephone Messages:
  (714) 455-2202
  (parents)

Figure 17–7. *Frank B. Scott's letter. Example of a "letter resume"—a letter that serves the purpose of the usual separate application letter and resume.*

When looking for employees, most organizations consider these fac- **Summary**
tors: related experience, related education, dependability, the ability to cooperate with others, and a willingness to work.

When looking for employment, the use of an unsolicited application
letter and resume is an advantage in that you show a special interest in a
particular organization, a plus factor in the evaluation process. This approach also shows that you have the initiative and ambition to research
employing organizations and to make an intelligent effort to place yourself.
Another advantage is that you are more likely to find the kind of work for
which you are best suited and that offers the opportunity you are seeking.

In order to plan an effective search for employment, analyze your
qualifications and the employment market. After these analyses are completed, the letter and data sheet are planned and written to show how your
qualifications meet the needs of the employer.

The application letter is a kind of sales message. The accompanying
resume is a report on yourself and is also a form of sales presentation. Like
other sales messages, these materials are most effective, as well as concise,
when they are built around a central selling theme.

For most young college graduates, education is the most appropriate
central selling point. Other factors that may be central selling themes are
work experience, and, in special circumstances, extracurricular activities,
hobbies, or special interests.

Like other business messages, the two-part application should make
the most effective use of the you-attitude and the positive approach.

1. Prepare a self-analysis, similar to that discussed in this chapter. Include all **Problems**
   aspects of your education, experience, hobbies, personal characteristics, or
   anything else that will affect your success throughout a career, as well as
   your success in obtaining employment. Make this study complete. Ordinarily it will be more detailed than your resume but by making a thorough
   self-analysis, you will be better able to decide which items to include and
   which to emphasize on your final data sheet. This analysis is for your own
   use only, not to be prepared as a classroom assignment, so be complete
   and objective.

2. From your detailed self-study, make a list of the kinds of employment for
   which you are qualified and in which you are interested. Approach this
   study from one of two ways:
   a. Assume that you are near graduation and that you are looking for full-
      time career employment. This assumption is probably the more valu-
      able one if you expect to graduate within a year or, regardless of your
      standing in college, if you now have in mind definite career objectives.
   b. Prepare a list of various kinds of work in relation to part-time or sum-
      mer jobs. If applicable, include only the kind of work in which you are

sincerely interested and which offers opportunities for career employment.

3. After you have made your self-analysis and listed the kinds of work that
you prefer and for which you are qualified, make a study of employing
organizations that seem to offer the opportunities you are seeking. Use the
sources described in this chapter and another other appropriate and useful
ones. Write a short report, in the format that your instructor direct, of how
you proceeded in the investigation. List the three organizations toward
which you plan to direct your efforts and the reasons for these choices.

4,5,6. Prepare a resume from the detailed studies you have made so far. You are
to send the letter and a resume to each of the three organizations that you
have chosen. Perhaps you should prepare three different resumes; or, if
the organizations are similar, you may be able to use the same resume for
all three.

CHAPTER **18**

Completing the Job-Finding Process

Chapter Outline

After you have analyzed your qualifications and the job market, and after you have completed a resume, you are ready to write the application letter.

This chapter includes discussions and illustrations of application letters, the employment interview, and related letters you may write as you complete the job search. After you begin work, you may write letters to other persons about aspects of employment; such letter are also illustrated here.

The Letter of Application

As you plan your letter of application, keep in mind the following guides:

1. Use the positive approach. Emphasize strengths and subordinate weaknesses, but do not misrepresent.

2. Use the you-attitude in that you stress what you can do for the reader. Do not use a "hard-sell" method, but state your work experience and educational background in specific and positive terms, especially as they relate to the work for which you are applying.

3. Show that you are definitely interested in the position, but don't sound as if this is your last chance.

4. Do not copy a letter written by some other person—or one from this book or any other book. This warning applies to all material. Such copying, even with changed details and paraphrasing, is almost certain to result in stilted, unnatural writing. In addition, sometimes personnel managers learn to determine exactly the book in which the letter originally appeared.

5. Although you will of necessity use *I*, try not to use the word to excess. Avoid starting several sentences with *I*.

6. Don't ask for sympathy. This is not the you-approach or the positive approach. You will not be hired because your baby needs shoes, but because you can do a good job and earn more for the employer than you are paid. (You *must* earn more, or you are not a profitable investment.) Even if a job should be filled because of sympathy, the applicant begins work at a disadvantage and not on a businesslike basis.

7. Don't be unduly humble, and don't apologize for taking the reader's time. Remember that the employer is not doing you a favor by hiring you. If you are qualified and a hard worker, the employing organization will benefit from the employment.

8. Don't complain about past or present employers. Even if you have real grievances, your discussion of these things almost always sounds as if you are to blame. If you find it necessary to explain why you are leaving, and this explanation is because of a real dissatisfaction that must be stated, at least *do not mention it in the letter or data sheet.* Save this discussion for the interview and present both the advantages or the areas of growth you wish to attain and cannot attain in the present position.

9. Don't boast or sound overly aggressive or presumptuous—although it is just as important not to sound unsure of your abilities. A straightforward, businesslike approach will let you take the middle road between egotism and a doubtful, overly humble tone.

10. Don't lecture or waste time stating the obvious.

11. Don't mention salary, fringe benefits, or working conditions in the application. To do so will emphasize the I-approach, not the you-approach. Such information will be given to you during the interview. If it should not be, ask at that time for information you must have before making a decision.

12. Don't try to be overly clever, at least for most jobs. If you are being considered as an advertising copywriter or for similar work, your application letter and resume may be in a more original or unconventional form. Regardless of the position, you have the problem of making your letter stand out from all the others, but you could work so hard for attention that you receive the wrong kind, even to the extent that your application is eliminated from consideration.

13. Work for original phrasing and eliminate trite, unnecessary stereotyped wording. Avoid such phrases as these: ''May I present my qualifications?'' ''Please consider my application for the position of . . .'' ''This is my application. . . .'' An aptly worded letter will make this fact clear without stating it obviously. As in other communications situations, however, you are wiser to be clear than to be completely concise, if there must be a choice. The reader should recognize that your letter is an application without having to read halfway through it. To leave a letter in this state is much worse than saying ''This is my application,'' ''I am an applicant,'' or ''Consider me as an applicant for this position,'' although you can usually find more original wording.

Illustrations of Letters of Application

Examples of application letters are shown in Figures 18–1, 18–2, 18–3, 18–4, 18–5, and 18–6. These letters accompany the resumes illustrated in Figures 17–1, 17–2, 17–3, 17–4, 17–5, and 17–6.

1472 Tutwiler Avenue
Cincinnati, OH 45208
April 22, 19--

Mr. Ray Flemming, Director
Sales Training/Development
Electronic Data Systems Corporation
7171 Forrest Hill Lane
Dallas, TX 75230

Dear Mr. Fleming:

Three years of experience in sales and a degree in marketing should enable me to contribute to your Sales Training and Development Department. In addition, I have experience in sales training and a record of growth in employment responsibilities.

As a sales representative for a bank supplier, Checks, Inc., I conduct training classes in cross-selling and security for bank employees. My ability to work with others, as well as to lead, is established by the success of these programs.

My education has been directed toward sales and training. While working full-time and going to college at night, I have also completed several Motivation/Sales seminars. To supplement the requirements in the College of Business Administration at the University of Cincinnati, I completed courses to fulfill requirements for a second major in industrial psychology, in addition to marketing, and a minor in education.

My present employers will substantiate the information in my application. After I have talked with you and am being seriously considered for employment, I will ask you to get in touch with officials at Checks, Inc.

The enclosed resume provides further information about my skills, abilities, and interests. Please contact me at the address shown above—or telephone me at 513 272-0000 to arrange a time to discuss my career with your firm.

Sincerely,

Rebecca S. Rosenberg

Rebecca S. Rosenberg

Enclosure

Figure 18–1. *Application letter to accompany data sheet illustrated in Figure 17–1. (Based on material by Rebecca Rosenberg)*

4784 Craigmont Avenue
Salt Lake City, UT 84103
March 10, 19--

Mr. Harrison McCullar, President
Modern Communications, Incorporated
4824 West Williams Boulevard
Denver, CO 80218

Dear Mr. McCullar:

Congratulations on your amazing success in building Modern Communications in only ten years. May I help you in the area of communications management?

My twenty-three years of military experience spent mostly in the field of communication systems, plus two years of civilian experience in the same field, should be specific and complete preparation for leadership in your corporation. In addition, I am fluent in the French and Japanese languages and am eager to expand your operations abroad.

I have thoroughly research your organization—products, people, progress, and you. Of the many other organizations studied in order to determine where to build a career, yours seems to be the one that offers the greatest challenges.

Will you let me know when I can talk with you about your organization and its future? I can be reached at 801 386-0000 or at the address shown above.

Sincerely,

Harwood E. Logan

Harwood E. Logan

Enclosure

Figure 18–2. *Letter to accompany functional resume illustrated in Figure 17–2.*

728 West 1720 North
Apt. #320
Cambridge, MA 02215
February 17, 19--

Commissioner Janice B. Propst
City Equity Funding Study
City of Cambridge-5442 East Wing
Cambridge, MA 02215

Dear Commissioner Propst:

Dean Alton P. Moon encouraged me to forward my appointment application and statement of *agreement to serve when appointed* to your village study committee assessing project equity funding. Dean Moon is also nominating me for the appointment but indicated that you and the commission need a resume and an agreement.

The attached resume explains my years of supervisory and administrative experience and education. Before establishing my company, I was most interested in organizations that contribute to the welfare of youth and to community and governmental groups responsible for upgrading the village's libraries, parks, and recreational facilities.

As an advisory member of District #221 Girl Scouts of America, I want to assist young women and their leaders in their training and recreational programs. Note also that I've contributed as a program coordinator for the Burke Area Chamber of Commerce and am an active delegate to a political party.

My business and graduate studies prevent me from assuming the leadership of a committee, but I am willing to serve the committee as a member. Upon completion of the MBA degree, should you and other members of the council wish, I will be happy to chair and lead one of the committees. While salary is not expected, I understand that the village does reimburse traveling expenses, office expenses, and mailing expenses.

A Tuesday evening interview and orientation meeting would certainly be pleasant. Or, another day and time is agreeable. May I phone you on Thursday to discuss an appropriate time and location? You may telephone me in the evenings at 508-377-0000 or you may leave a message for me at my Boston, MA office. The phone number is 804-240-5101.

Yes, I'm excited about associating with you. I'll telephone you Thursday.

Best wishes,

Marie P. Brown

Marie P. Brown, CPA

Figure 18-3. *Marie P. Brown's application letter. Resume is shown in Figure 17-3.*

1999 Plaza Diaz 147
El Paso, TX 77905
February 24, 19--

Mr. James B. Farnsworth
Personnel Officer
Farnsworth International Electronics Corp.
St. Louis, MI 65301

Dear Mr. Farnsworth:

Your advertisement in the February 23d *Wall Street Journal* indicates your need for electronic engineers with specialties and/or experience in marine products. My language abilities, managerial experiences, operations and maintenance on oceangoing vessels, and management degrees certainly qualify me for consideration. Please accept my application.

Your assistant, Raydeen Manning, indicated in our telephone conversation yesterday that I should forward an application and resume to you immediately. Ms. Manning is forwarding a formal application form and I understand that I am to complete the form in my handwriting. Also, you require three letters of recommendation and the handwritten form before my application is reviewed.

You are correct, many electronic firms are establishing manufacturing divisions in other countries. The quality of the marine electronic products being manufactured in Korea, Ceylon, Hong Kong, and Taiwan are excellent. Too, the labor costs are lower.

My resume is detailed. Note that I have consulted and conducted business in numerous Far Eastern, Near Eastern, and European countries. I speak Chinese. My wife is also bilingual, but our children have not lived in other countries.

Computer programming skills, computer languages skills, network and word processing skills are tools I use easily. Also, I communicate comfortably in small groups or large groups.

My technical background and engineering skills are too extensive to note here. Wouldn't it be desirable for us to meet? My schedule permits me to interview on Thursdays, Fridays, and Saturdays. I can meet you at your convenience. May I telephone next week to arrange a time we can meet? My telephone numbers are 505-373-4108 at my home. Or, my university telephone number is 505-373-0000. I'm anxious to become a member of your supervisory and engineering team.

Sincerely yours,

Juan O. Hermanas

Juan O. Hermanas

Figure 18–4. *Juan O. Hermanas, extensive experience, graduate, previously employed. Not an entry or beginning job—note coordination from letter to resume shown in Figure 17-4.*

2745 Elmwood Avenue
Berkeley, CA 94705
July 24, 19--

Mr. William J. Hughes
Vice-President, Manufacturing
Snyder-Plover, Inc.
P. O. Box 377
Memphis, TN 38109

Dear Mr. Hughes:

For the position in manufacturing management advertised in the *Wall Street Journal,* I offer twelve years of progressively responsible experience with a drug and cosmetic manufacturer, a company similar in many respects to Snyder-Plover.

Since 1976, when I completed a B.S. degree in manufacturing technology at San Francisco State University, I have devoted my entire career to the Conrad Division of Rivley, Inc. My efforts have resulted in cost savings and increased efficiency from several standpoints, as explained in more detail on the enclosed resume.

The president of Conrad Division and other management personnel will recommend me, but please do not contact them at this time. In addition, I can furnish other business and personal references and any further information you require.

I have done thorough research into the manufacturing division of Snyder-Plover. Some of your problems are of the same type as those I successfully solved for my present employer. I also know that you offer opportunities for increased responsibility based on a record of successful accomplishment. This increased opportunity for growth is the only reason that I would consider leaving my present employer.

Please schedule an interview at your convenience—but will you let it be soon? I have two weeks' vacation beginning November 2. Then, after I am hired, I will give two weeks' notice to my present employer.

You can reach me at my home telephone, 415-527-0000, any evening after 6:00 p.m.

Sincerely,

Monroe J. Waldron

Enclosure

Figure 18–5. *Letter of application to accompany data sheet shown in Figure 17–5. (Based on material by W. J. Hughes)*

3931 Meadow Lane
Olive Branch, MS 38654
April 30, 19--

Mr. Thurston Drew
Maintenance & Engineering Department
Federal Express Corporation
P.O. Box 727
Memphis, TN 38194

Dear Mr. Drew:

Mr. Jack Doty suggested I contact you about your opening for an aviation mechanic in your Memphis Maintenance & Engineering Department. Mr. Doty is an instructor at Memphis Area Vocational-Technical School, where I will soon complete a 22-month training program in aviation mechanics.

Military training, as described on the enclosed data sheet, provided actual experience in performing preventive maintenance inspections and repairs on aircraft hydraulic and pneumatic systems. While supervising the training of technical personnel, I coordinated maintenance records and allocated tools and materials.

In December, 1988, I received an Airframes License. I will receive a Powerplants License in June of this year. I have the tools necessary for airframe and powerplant maintenance. I am willing to travel or relocate and can begin work on July 1.

You can reach me by telephone (601 895-0000) most evenings after 7:00 p.m. Please call to arrange a time when we can talk about putting my maintenance and repair skills to work for Federal Express.

Sincerely,

William Thomas King

Enclosure

Figure 18–6. *Letter from aviation mechanic to accompany resume shown in Figure 17–6.*

The Employment Interview

When your resume and application letter accomplish their purpose, you will be asked to come for an interview. A successful interview is crucial to your obtaining the employment you wish.

Except in unusual circumstances, more than one person is interviewed for a single opening. This necessary and desirable competition requires that you continue the sales presentation throughout the interview, presenting the superiority of your qualifications and potential for service and development.

Preparation for an Interview

Much of your life has been spent in preparation for an interview for employment in which you are interested and for which you are qualified, although you may not have been consciously making this preparation. Your educational background, your avocational interests, your work experience—all these have prepared you for the work for which you are now applying, as well as for a favorable presentation on your qualifications during the interview.

Research to enable you to decide upon the organizations to which to submit your written application will also enable you to participate in a pleasant and successful employment interview. Your knowledge of the organization, as well as your interest in it, can favorably impress the person or persons with whom you talk. This knowledge will be even more beneficial because it adds to your self-confidence and enables you to ask necessary and intelligent questions.

From your detailed self-analysis, as discussed earlier in relation to beginning a job search, and from your study of the particular organization to which you are applying as well as of related organizations, you have accomplished a major portion of your preparation for a successful interview. Review your self-analysis and a copy of the letter of application and the resume before you go for the interview. Make sure that the details are firmly in your mind. Giving conflicting information will cast doubt upon either your integrity or your memory.

You and the Interviewer

You may wish to take with you to the interview two or more copies of your resume, even if you have previously submitted one to the employing organization. The interviewer is not certain to have a copy, although, ideally, the person with whom you talk has recently reviewed a copy of both letter and resume. In some cases you will go for an interview with organizations to which you have not submitted a resume, especially when the interview has been arranged through college placement offices. In such interviews your bringing along copies of the resume can save a great deal of time that would otherwise be spent in giving information that can be concisely stated in a well-organized resume.

Moreover, your additional effort, interest, and consideration for the interviewer or interviewers—many firms now use interviewing teams—are points in your favor as you are compared with other applicants. Your carefully prepared resume continues your sales approach in an orderly manner that may not be possible in the half-hour or so exchange of information.

The interviewer will ask you, perhaps, to expand upon the information you have shown in written form, which is of necessity presented in condensed wording. You may be asked, for example, to give more details about your work experience.

You may be asked to explain why you left a position or positions, to describe the type of work that you liked best and least, to state what you feel you accomplished on each job, and to express your opinions as to whether your supervisor and co-workers were capable and cooperative. Be careful when commenting on this topic; your interviewer is not really asking about your co-workers and supervisors, but about yourself. But, as in all other situations, do not be untruthful. Remember, though, that your own competence and spirit of helpfulness and dedication will usually result in your finding the same qualities in other persons.

Principles of communication you have studied previously apply to your attitude toward the interviewer and your approach to the interview. You have learned, as in written communication, to enter into all business interpersonal situations on a straightforward basis of equality. Although you may have much to gain or lose according to the outcome of your search for employment, or upon the outcome of a particular interview, the representative of the employing organization also has a purpose essential to the welfare of the organization—that of finding the best person for the job.

If you sincerely believe that you are this person, and can convince the interviewer of this fact without building resentment because of your egotism or an overly aggressive approach, both you and the employing organization will have benefited from the relatively short time spent in talking about your professional future.

Questions to Ask

What questions will you ask? Don't be in a hurry to shower the interviewer with questions, many of which will be answered in the course of the conversation. On the other hand, don't merely sit and wait for information to come your way, and do not answer in monosyllables. Although you should not try to take charge of the interview, seize the opportunity to present yourself in the most favorable light. If you cannot communicate well enough to do so, you may leave the impression—probably an accurate one—that your communication skills will be less than ideal for your career. At some time you are likely to be asked if you have questions, or if you have further questions. Inexperienced applicants have been known to blurt out rather odd questions or statements at this time, such as "Where did you get that tie?" (an actual question) and, from a twenty-one-year-old, "Most of all, I am interested in your retirement plan."

If you have done adequate research into an organization, along with other organizations, you already know something about the company, including its offices and branches, products, and services. You can also find its recent growth and earnings. By reading company brochures, you will know a great deal about training programs and employee benefits.

One area of vital concern will be your opportunities for growth and responsibility. Are you likely to become "locked in" regardless of your hard work and ability? You will also need to know the company policy on promotions, whether higher positions are filled from the outside or whether you will need to count on moving within a few years to an organization that offers greater opportunity.

Most of all, you will want to know whether the work is the kind for which you are especially well prepared. Is it the kind in which you can excel and maintain a sincere interest? Is this an organization in which you can feel that your work matters and of which you can be proud, not only for the benefit of the employing organization but for yourself and your family? If you cannot feel a sincere pride in the organization that you are joining, you as an idealistic person will not be satisfied, regardless of the salary. Conversely, a good income is essential for most persons as a symbol of competence and accomplishment—to say nothing of its being necessary for comfort and security.

Remember that if you are not fitted for the job for which you are being considered, or if it is not a job in which you can be content to spend a portion of your life, the real benefit to be derived from an interview could be the fact that the job is given to someone else.

Your Appearance

Careful attention to your appearance, including neat and appropriate dress, favorably impresses most interviewers and adds to your own self-confidence. A dark business suit, with a dress shirt and tie, is appropriate dress for male applicants. Care in your appearance shows that you have a sincere interest in both the job and the organization.

Women applicants are appropriately dressed, according to the opinion of most executives, in a conservative dress or a matching or coordinated jacket and skirt. All applicants should choose conservative, attractive, flattering, and appropriate clothing and then forget about their appearance and concentrate on the conversation.

Ending the Interview

You are not likely to be offered a job during the first interview, although often you can tell whether or not you are being given favorable consideration. Before you leave, you will need some kind of commitment as to when the interviewer will let you know the decision.

Ordinarily you will not need to inquire about salary, but if the interviewer does not tell you, you will be forced to ask.

The basic principles of communication—the you-attitude, the positive approach, consideration, conciseness, completeness, and courtesy—added to your self-confidence and your attractive appearance, will make your interview successful if you apply for a position for which you are qualified and one in which you are interested.

Remember that communication throughout your interview, like all other communication situations, will be less than perfect and complete. Remember that nonverbal communication, including such things as your arriving and leaving on time, your posture and facial expressions, your dress, and your voice, will tell the interviewer as much or more about you than your words can do.

Following Through in the Employment Search

Thank-You Letters

Within a day or two after your employment interview, mail a thank-you letter. This letter is a matter of courtesy; you should send it whether or not you feel that you are being favorably considered. The thank-you letter is ordinarily short because you have little to say. It is a form of good-will message. Sincerity and a natural, conversational tone are the major requirements (see Figure 18–7).

Many applicants do not send thank-you letters after an interview, perhaps because of a mistaken idea that to do so is presumptuous, or, more likely, because of simple procrastination or lack of effort. That few persons send these letters is a point in your favor that may make you stand out from other applicants. It serves as a reminder as to who you are. After a few days of interviewing, many personnel interviewers are not sure who is who. Samples of your work or other appropriate materials help reinforce your original application materials and remind the interviewers of your conversations and your qualifications.

At times you will have additional information to convey in the thank-

November 20, 19--

Mr. Henry W. Samuels
Yohanak Corporation, Vice President
Manitowoc, WI 54220

Dear Mr. Samuels:

Thank you for a most pleasant and informative interview last Wednesday.

After your discussion of the opportunities for growth as a sales representative
with the Yohanak Corporation, I am even more eager to go to work for you.

I will be glad to supply any information you may need in order to make sure that I
am the best choice for the job. My telephone number is 312-409-0000.

                                        Sincerely,

                                        John Clifft

                                        John Clifft

Figure 18–7. *Example of a thank-you letter.*

you letter. For example, perhaps you have been asked whether you would
move to another city and you have requested time to think it over. If you
have made up your mind in the day or two before the thank-you letter
should be mailed, your decision may be stated in the letter. Or perhaps
you have read the brochures that were provided for you, or you have been
asked to submit the names of persons to recommend you, if these names
were not included on the data sheet.

Additional information is not a requirement. Send a thank-you letter
even if you have no new information to convey.

Follow-Up Letters

Follow-up letters, in addition to thank-you letters, may be helpful
when you have not heard from the employing organization within a reasonable amount of time after the interview. The exact time varies; some
college seniors are interviewed near the beginning of their senior year and
notified within a month or two of graduation. Usually, the applicant is
notified within a few weeks or even within a few days.

Follow-up letters are also used after the submission of the application letter and data sheet if too much time seems to elapse before the applicant is called for an interview.

Follow-up letters, provided they are well written and used at the proper time, accomplish several purposes. They show that you are still interested in the organization and that you are diligent in your efforts to obtain employment. These letters may also report additional information not included in the application letter and data sheet or reported in interviews—for example, the completion of related courses, additional work experience, or special scholastic honors or other accomplishments.

Avoid a demanding or hurt tone, and don't indicate surprise that you have not been asked for an interview. But don't apologize for writing.

Job-Acceptance and Job-Refusal Letters

Job-acceptance letters, like other good-news and routine informational letters, are usually best arranged in the direct order, with the acceptance in the first sentence. Adapt your job-acceptance letter to include any additional information that the employing organization may need or to ask questions of your own.

In job-refusal letters, remember to express appreciation for the employment offer. As in other negative messages, your letter will be more psychologically convincing and acceptable if reasons are given before the refusal.

Do everything you can to keep the goodwill of the reader and of the organization as a whole.

Summary

The application letter, although sometimes sent alone, is ordinarily a covering letter for the data sheet. In addition, it is a sales letter that should be built around the most outstanding qualifications of the applicant in relation to the position sought.

The purpose of the application letter and the resume is to obtain an interview. As in other letters requesting action, the request for an interview should be stated specifically, but diplomatically, near the end of the letter.

The tone of the application letter should be straightforward and businesslike; the applicant must show confidence in his or her ability but refrain from appearing egotistical or overly aggressive.

A thank-you letter should be sent after an employment interview. Other letters written in the search for employment are follow-up letters, job-acceptance letters, and job-refusal letters.

Inquiries about prospective employees and replies to these inquires, like other routine inquiries and requests, are best arranged in the direct order. Job-refusal letters are best arranged in the indirect order.

Problems

1. Write a letter of application to accompany the resumes you prepared for problems 4, 5, and 6 in Chapter 17. These letters should vary according to the organization to which you are applying.

2. Mail these letters and resumes, especially if you are applying for part- or full-time work. (Make sure that the envelopes you use are of good quality and of standard business length so that the letter can be folded in approximate thirds. The envelopes should match the paper in weight and quality.) Or, if you still have considerable time left before you complete your degree or your occupational preparation, or if there are other reasons that you do not wish to mail your letters and data sheets at this time, complete some or all of the following assignments as your instructor directs.

    If you do mail the application letters and resumes, follow through with your interview or with follow-up letters, thank-you letters, acceptance letters, or whatever is appropriate to complete your job search.

3. Assume that three weeks have elapsed and that you have not heard from the organization that you considered to be your first choice. Write a follow-up letter indicating your continued interest and asking again for an interview. Avoid sounding hurt, doubtful, or demanding.

4. Assume that you have received a letter from the second organization asking you to come to their local office to talk with Mrs. Helen Woolner, the district manager. The time set is 1 P.M. on Wednesday of the following week. (Use exact date.) You are asked to write to Mrs. Woolner to confirm the suggested time. Do so.

5. You received a letter from the third organization on the day after you have mailed your reply to Mrs. Woolner. You are surprised that Mr. Harry B. Hicks and Mr. John Jerry, who are identified only as being from the personnel office, wish to see you at 1:30 P.M. on the same day that you are planning to talk with Mrs. Woolner. Write an appropriate reply. Suggest another time for the interview.

6. You receive a letter from the organization that you had considered to be your first choice. You are told by Ms. Rachel Welsh, Personnel Director, that the organization is not now hiring anyone with your particular background but that she will keep your application on file. Although her letter does not necessitate a response, you decide to write a short letter that will perhaps be placed in your file. Decide what you want to say in this letter. Write it.

7. You go for the scheduled interview with Mrs. Helen Woolner. You are favorably impressed. You believe that you have a good chance to be hired. Write a thank-you letter for the interview. Assume reasonable details.

8. You receive a letter from Mr. Harry B. Hicks in response to your letter written for problem 5. He wishes to talk with you at 10 A.M. on Monday of the following week. You have a final examination scheduled at this hour. You talk to your professor, who refuses to give you the examination at any other time. Because this is the second time you have been unable to come for the interview, you realize that you must convince Mr. Hicks that you

are still sincerely interested. (He has not mentioned the date you suggested in your last letter to him, which is now more than two weeks past.) State that you will complete your final examinations on Thursday of the following week, at which time your college work will be finished.

What should you say in this letter? You wish to make it clear that you are still interested in the organization and that you are not giving him the runaround. It has now been six weeks since you mailed your application letter and data sheet. Should you mention that you have already been interviewed by Mrs. Woolner? Should you write or telephone? If you decide to telephone, make detailed notes as to the information and ideas you intend to convey.

9. You receive from Mrs. Woolner a letter offering employment beginning four weeks from next Monday. The salary is about $300 a month less than you expected, and you are to begin work in a district more than 500 miles from your home. You believe that the company offers growth opportunities and, although you do not want to move, you realize that mobility is often necessary in order to avoid limiting opportunities for success. You might suggest a relocation allowance or some moving expenses.

What will you say in your reply? Will you want to ask for more time in order to investigate further the possibilities of beginning work with organization number three? Plan or write your letter according to your decision.

10. At last you go for an interview with the third organization on your list and talk with Mr. Harry B. Hicks, Personnel Manager; Mr. John Jerry, District Manager; and Mr. H. D. Blackburn, Assistant Vice-President. You are given a tour of the offices and plant.

Write an appropriate thank-you note to all three of these persons. The actual choice of the person to whom you should send a thank-you letter will depend upon circumstances, including the consideration of the person who seems to be the one most directly responsible for making the decision. When in doubt, write to each person who spends time with you or who helps you in any way.

11. It is now two weeks later. You receive from Mrs. Woolner a letter stating that she must have your decision immediately. (For this assignment, assume that in problem 9 you ask for more time in which to make your decision.) In the same mail you receive a letter from Mr. Hicks who offers you work in the local office. He has told you that there is a possibility of transfer within a year or two when you are ready for a promotion, but there is also a possibility that you can be promoted and remain in your home city. Your beginning salary is $200 a month greater than that offered by Mrs. Woolner's organization. You decide to accept Mr. Hick's offer. Write the letter of acceptance.

12. Write to Mrs. Woolner. Keep her goodwill.

13. You receive a letter from the organization which was originally your first choice. They ask you to come for an interview and to telephone and arrange a time that will be convenient for both of you. Plan what you will say in the telephone conversation.

Composing Business Messages

Using Word Processing or Computer Systems

Composing Messages Using Word Processing or Computer Systems

Composing messages on a computer or word processor in business writing is fast becoming a necessity. The tremendous advantages and efficiency of word processors are quickly making other forms of data origination outdated. In addition, many business managers and workers already have access to and some familiarity with a keyboard, computer, monitor, and printer. Managers can ask their assistants to rewrite/edit their memorandums, letters, or reports by simply giving them the disk or by transferring their files to the assistant's word processor through local-area networks. After the manager reviews the assistant's draft, the document is ready to send or, if necessary, additional changes can be added.

Composing data with a word processor provides several benefits over handwriting or dictating documents to an administrative assistant or secretary. Composing at a word processor permits:

1. Immediate feedback.
2. Reviewing content and word style of messages for acceptance or rewriting.
3. Writing and composing messages rapidly.
4. Multiple proofreading and/or editing of drafts.
5. Saving the dictator's time and the transcriber's time and not inputting additional errors.
6. Page format drafting and editing ease (move text, delete text, insert text, format text, add headings to text, check spelling in text, insert footnotes, and other editing commands).
7. Ease in preparing printed copy for editing or review.
8. Accessibility of messages for reuse or rewriting.

Learn composing and word processing skills by composing at the keyboard. You may want to enroll in an introductory word processing course or you may use a programmed learning textbook or a tape or disk video text. All word processing packages are sold with programmed instructions using tutorials or simulations to help you learn. Start with the basics (indent, delete, save) and then later incorporate more advanced processing features.

Although at first you may feel awkward as you enter ideas on the

416

keyboard into the computer, as you continue **"keyboard writing"** becomes remarkably natural and much faster than handwriting messages. Specialists recently reported that keyboarding ideas gives a freedom and an ease with words not previously realized. Writers can keyboard spontaneously knowing that if they don't like their style or their phraseology, they can delete the text and begin again.

Composing messages on a word processor is an efficient way to originate written communication. Since you will eventually need to study financial spreadsheets or create databases, you can advance your writing and business skills through composing on your computer. Learn the skills necessary to use the new integrated software packages available to your employer.

APPENDIX **B**

Analyzing Cases

(Techniques and Working Papers)

Business Simulations

Solving problems and making correct decisions are essential to operating businesses successfully. Managing or being an effective manager suggests that you have data or reasons for making decisions and solving problems. Your decisions may involve employees you supervise, clients you serve, products you manufacture, or services you provide.

Experience in one or more companies permits you to compare operating procedures or to weigh rationales for decisions. Teachers may discuss procedures and suggest appropriate manager or worker behavior in their courses, but rarely are circumstances, problems, or decisions identical, and it is impossible to predict how you must act and think as a manager in your jobs. You must learn to trust your judgment and to make decisions.

On-the-job problems are real. Needs are urgent and time is essential. Decisions are based on your interpretation of data or communicated messages that at the moment seem logical—or you believe the facts and the messages to be real. So you communicate, you act, you make decisions, you delegate, you order, you manage—and you are managed.

Using Cases and Simulations

While real experience is best, it is impractical to think that you can work in businesses full-time and also attend a university or participate in company-sponsored training programs full-time. Management training, communication training, and writing training courses must then permit you to role-play or make believe and to practice your decision-making and communicating skills as realistically as possible.

Case Analysis

Business cases simulate business needs and procedures. Cases differ in their philosophy and approach—depending on what selected business principle needs to be taught or reviewed in a training session. Finance cases teach budgeting, forecasting, market analysis, etc. Organizational behavior cases assess people needs, company or group structure variations, supervision styles, etc. Writing and communication cases teach message organization, word choice, language style, etc. Integrated cases attempt to involve the many facets of businesses and endeavor to simulate a function-

419

ing business. Many instructional cases are printed, studied, and discussed. However, electronic-based cases are also used.

Electronic Case Analysis

Integrated cases are used extensively in management training programs today and may be called management games. These cases are programmed for computers in software packages that permit you and your management teams to "simulate operating a business." Integrated cases usually compare "management teams" as they make financial and operating decisions about a business providing services or selling products. Often team members with accounting, finance, marketing, production, shipping, and other essential specialties are assigned a particular worker or manager role.

As your team operates your business, your many business and product decisions are analyzed by computers and you receive "cost of goods sold" reports, "salary expense" reports, "inventory on hand" reports, "shipping and transportation" reports, "marketing and sales reports," and many other reports—essential operations feedback that permits you to make a profit or to sustain a loss in your company.

Though not real, the thrill of succeeding and the excitement of being managers make these business simulations seem real and are valuable learning experiences. Too, it is great to be the winning management team.

Artifically Intelligent Electronic Cases

Selected artificially intelligent electronic cases exist in some companies and at several universities at the present time. These revolutionary simulation or case analyses are becoming more available as AI and Hypermedia technology develops. Publishing companies and software development companies will provide new games and new software in this area. You will no doubt experience an AI Electronic Case in your business training.

"What if" possibilities are entered into the computer and the system analyzes what happens, given the circumstances and the financial and operational decisions you make. You then assess the outcomes, remember and use successful business practices, and avoid failures or questionable business practices.

Identifying Different Case Components

Written cases are used in most training programs today. Occasionally a case is dramatized and videotaped, but due to cost and because of availability, you need to learn to read cases quickly and to identify the essential facts in the case.

Cases are researched carefully and written, tested, and rewritten, but it is impossible to provide all of the "situational" data in written cases. You do not know all of the office politics surrounding the incident, you cannot hear the verbal messages, or gauge the nonverbal messages critical to specific incident cases.

You are able to read the case, and based on your knowledge of business operations, your biases, your wishes, your interests—you make decisions based on your interpretation of what is best and what needs to be done. You manage.

Techniques for Analyzing the Case

Cases identify conditions of a business setting. The conditions may include staff conflicts, supervisory deficiencies, production restraints, product testing, sales needs, and other pertinent information. Cases are designed and written carefully. There is obvious information that appears as truths. These are labeled as *givens* or *knowns* and are case facts. In reality, the apparent givens or knowns may be only partial truths. Case writers may introduce disinformation or information that appears important but is not vital or maybe incorrect.

Because business operations are complex, you cannot read a case once and presume you understand the conditions of the case. *Suppositions* or *unknowns* are inferred and are communicated so carefully that "nondata" assume the power of facts or knowns. You must study cases thoroughly. Working in groups becomes important as you analyze cases because the group provides the biases and perspectives of other "managers" in your analyses of the case.

Use the following cases techniques:

1. Speed-read the case quickly, using a highlight marker to identify major givens or knowns.
2. Study and read the case again for other knowns you may have missed and make marginal notes about conditions or circumstances that influence "what is going on" in the case.
3. Define fundamental problems and list the problems on your working papers.
4. Determine the cause or apparent cause of the problems.
5. Identify important people and personalities and list these data on your working sheets.
6. Select plausible compromises or alternatives and list these solutions on your working sheets.
7. Recommend appropriate solutions or courses of action.

8. List expected implementation of your action with dates and times of implementation.
9. Establish lines of feedback and expect a report about the solution or the partial solution to the case.
10. Report your decisions and actions to your supervisors.

Sample case analysis working papers are illustrated in Figures 1 and 2 of Appendix B.

Reporting Your Decisions and Actions

Reports written for a professor in the classroom differ from the reports you prepare for a boss or a supervisor. In a classroom or training program setting, your instructor needs to understand that you not only are capable of analyzing a case but that you have identified appropriate working conditions and financial facts that support or explain the problems or needs of the case. Consequently, a short formal paper format may be apropriate. An executive may wish you to draft your case report in the form of an executive summary, a synopsis, or a manager's action memo. Refer to Chapters 3, 4, and 15 for a review of report formats.

Writing and communication courses using business cases emphasize your ability to think logically and to organize your reasons and actions in consistent formats using appropriate words to communicate clear meanings. Your analyses demonstrate that you identified appropriate needs of the case and suggested solutions that are sound.

In economic- or finance-related cases you obviously emphasize the money and business conditions of the case. Numerous tax, financial, and comparative reports assess your ability to study costing and accounting information. Cases requiring these analyses emphasize the financial appraisals. Tables, charts, and graphs explaining your conclusions and recommendations become important in these cases. Appropriate writing skills complement your writing reports for instructors or executives and managers.

Executive Decision Reports

While teachers and executives appreciate a report that illustrates your analyzing skills and your writing skills, both are more interested in your solutions and the corrective actions you order.

Let's discuss three managerial decision reports you may use on your job.

An Executive Summary   contains the decision and action statements of your recommendations. Extensive data and reasons for your decisions

''Knowns and Unknowns'' Analysis Approach

''What is Going On?''

<u>Givens/knowns</u>

  1.
  2.
  3.
  4.
  5.
  6.
  7.
  8.
  9.
10

<u>Suppositions/unknowns</u>

  1.
  2.
  3.
  4.
  5.
  6.
  7.
  8.
  9.
10.

<u>Action/Course/Recommendations</u>

Name Groups Involved
Name Individuals Involved
Elect a Communication Media
Elect a Communication Psychological Approach
Assume a secondary communication in writing is sent—use an informal report or
   letter report
What elements of Persuasion are involved?
Outline your processes for gathering data
List the components you would use in your argument—both oral and written
Prepare a three- or four-stage outline for review by your group and the instructor

<u>Notes:</u>

Figure 1, Appendix B: *Sample case note and analysis sheet emphasizing known facts
and unknown suppositions about business operations.*

```
CASE ANALYSIS                          ''Solving the Major Problems''

Characters/Issues      Evidence            Alternatives         Action
Involved
_____       1.                  1.                   1.

Characters             2.                  2.                   2.

                       3.                  3.                   3.

                       4.                  4.                   4.

                       5.                  5.                   5.

                       6.                  6.                   6.


_____

Issues/or Problems     1.                  1.                   1.

                       2.                  2.                   2.

                       3.                  3.                   3.

                       4.                  4.                   4.

                       5.                  5.                   5.

                       6.                  6.                   6.


Recommended Action:
```

Figure 2, Appendix B: *Sample case working paper emphasizing facts, alternative actions, and final decision or business action.*

are contained in the body of your report, the facts and findings sections, and are again summarized in the conclusions and recommendations sections of the report. A possible dialogue in an executive summary may read:

> *Send the replacement shipment to Oklahoma City on overnight air express. Send me a memo tonight on my private electronic mail overnight line. Itemize the additional costs, the reason why an incomplete order was sent earlier, and the name of our loading supervisor who initialed the original shipment.*

A Synopsis provides an executive decision statement at the beginning of the synopsis in addition to other facts explaining the recommendations or the orders. While an executive summary may be a few paragraphs long, a synopsis provides the decision and action statement but then summarizes the remainder of the conclusions and recommendations. A professor or a manager should be able to read a short one- or two-page synopsis of a twelve- or fifteen-page report and feel secure in the conclusions and recommendations you provided.

Annotated or abstracted writing emphasizes the action portions of information. Readers may return to the original reports with the facts, findings, tables, graphs, charts, etc., to read all of the "whys" or "why nots," but in the synopsis you carefully provide the essential information necessary to substantiate your actions or to provide reinforcing information so your supervisor also is secure about your business decisions.

A Manager's Action Memo is an in-house message drafted in a memo format. Messages sent to colleagues or workers you supervise in a company are written quickly. Typographical mistakes, incomplete sentences, and specific memo formats are emphasized less than a precise explanation of what the problems are, the actions taken, and the feedback necessary. Messages forwarded up the channels are edited carefully and communicated correctly and represent what you would want your boss to read. Messages sent to clients or customers outside the firm are most carefully edited for meaning and liability.

You will experience business simulations in your training. The majority of your cases are printed and you will develop good case analytical skills. As you continue your education or your on-the-job training, you will also experience integrated cases as well as electronic incident cases. Use the suggestions in this appendix to help you polish your abilities to determine problems within businesses, assess financial and economic data, and communicate appropriate business decisions.

APPENDIX C

Instructional Cases

Instructions

In the following cases, except where additional research is required, much of the necessary information is given. You are free to make reasonable assumptions and to add minor details. Retain the overall content and meaning of the problem to be solved and do not change facts and instructions given with each case.

The names of individuals and organizations are fictitious. Addresses given are not actual ones. If real names of individuals or organizations are used, the use is completely coincidental. Some cases are intentionally poorly organized, with sentences and phrases that need improvement, in order to provide practice in organization and phrasing.

Unless you are given specific instructions in the case itself, or with a group of cases, use the format and arrangement you consider best for the particular infomation and situation. Follow directions given by your instructor. For all cases, more than one format and order of arrangement is acceptable and appropriate. As in all writing, work for simplicity, clarity, and reader interest.

As you have no doubt assumed, far more cases are given here than you could write in one training program. The numerous assignments are included to provide choices for you and for your instructor. In addition, you can benefit by reading all the problems and thinking about appropriate ways to approach the solution of each. Perhaps some of the cases will be used as a basis for class discussion even though you do not prepare written solutions.

Certain problems apply to particular educational majors or professional fields. You may be more interested in these problems than in those outside your field. Do not think, however, that you should restrict yourself to these problems. Good reports in all professional fields are far more similar than they are dissimilar. A few problems should be undertaken only by those of you who already know something about the subject matter; for example, one case requires some knowledge of computers, databases, and computer networks. A person experienced in these fields should be able to do a better job with this case than an inexperienced person.

Other short problems follow preceding chapters, especially Chapter 3.

Cases That Require No Further Research

Case 1.   Installing an Office Computer Network (Persuasion)

You've been hired by Pugh-Wentworth, Ltd. and sent to one of its branch offices in the outskirts of St. Louis. There are eleven employees who work in the office. (You will eventually become the office manager, but will work for about three months as Assistant to Robert Worley, who is going to retire).

You are responsible for supervising the eleven employees now—and with your recently completed MBA you are well prepared. No other employee, including Mr. Worley, has an advanced degree. In fact, four of the employees do not have degrees but have been efficient support personnel for the company for many years.

The home office in Chicago is now installing computer networks. They will base their reporting needs on software packages being specially designed by the home office.

However, to keep track of sales, orders, and salesperson services you elected to install Oracle or Surpass integrated database. Decide how to help train your eleven employees, devise a rotation schedule, implement the appropriate software on the ten new IBM-compatible computers (with the necessary printers and plotters), and communicate to your employees.

Write a short memo report including an introductory memo, a schedule, and a training sequence.

Case 2.   Changing Employee's Attitudes (Persuasion)

You work for Jun Niccki Associates. You are being pressured by your executive vice president to improve your employees' attitudes so that service is improved and so that customers sense that the company does want to help them solve import/export problems.

One of your account managers wrote the following message to a valued distributor. The distributor is reducing the order for the quarter because of your not getting the proper number of units to the company's warehouses in time for them to be distributed to the sales offices.

Outline the correct Psych for this message:

I.

II.

III.

Rewrite your assistant's message in a managerial-service style. Choose appropriate service-oriented words.

I can't understand how you expect me to guess at size and numbers of advertising materials you need—let alone interpret the quarterly product orders. We've always tried to help you but this time I just couldn't take the time to follow up with each of your sales offices to confirm their orders. The computerized inventory and sales systems we've set up for all of our other distributors, throughout the United States and Canada, is working just fine and we know you can reduce your costs and problems if you will just get your people using the system. We'll wait to send out this quarter's specs and proportional shipping schedules until you confirm what you really need in the way of advertising materials and products.

Case 3.   Remodeling of Offices

You are the office manager. Remodeling of offices is scheduled to begin on Monday of next week. This remodeling will require rearrangement of desks and other furniture, sharing of offices, and other changes, some inconvenient, as work proceeds from one floor of offices to the next. The entire remodeling process is scheduled to last three or four months.

All loose paper and files need to be secured inside the desks before the furniture can be moved. All books on shelves and personal items must be packed and labeled. Packing material will be available in your secretary's office tomorrow. Several of the offices look as if they have never been straightened. The sales representatives always say they are too busy to do housekeeping chores. You believe that this packing will require quite a bit of time, but some people are likely to find things they thought lost forever.

You fear that there could be problems in sharing offices, even temporarily, because of some personality conflicts.

Assume that all details, such as the remodeling time schedule (tentative) and temporary office assignments, are on a separate sheet attached to your written message. Refer to this schedule. You need not prepare it.

Individuals who want to pick the colors of the walls of their remodeled offices should pick the color from the seven choices available; these colors are illustrated in a folder in your secretary's office. Her name is Mrs. Helen Brown. If they have not made their choice by Friday of next week, their offices will be scheduled to be painted an off-white—really a kind of soft cream. This color is one of the seven colors shown in the folder.

Write a memorandum to the group of employees on the floor that is to be remodeled first. Choose an appropriate arrangement and approach for your memorandum.

Case 4.   A Christmas Bonus

You are the personnel manager. Write *one* letter to *all* employees based on this information. Make any reasonable assumptions.

1. All employees are to receive a Christmas bonus—although this does not apply to those who have worked for less than six months.
2. The amount of the bonus is two weeks' base pay. No overtime, commissions, or any kind of extra pay will figure into the amount of the Christmas bonus.
3. The bonus will be added to the paycheck of December 11.
4. Some employees have been working extra hard because of the end-of-year rush.
5. All employees will receive a food basket containing a turkey or ham, fruitcake, and other food and gift items.

Assume that this is to be a form letter prepared through the use of your word processor or automatic typewriting equipment; that is, letters are typewritten automatically, then names and addresses are added.

For the purpose of this assignment, show the inside address and the employee's name in the usual way. (Letters prepared by this method cannot be distinguished from individually typewritten letters.) Use this inside address:

```
Mr. James T. Holloway
1967 Luzon Cove
Oklahoma City, OK 73077
```

Use your choice of the semiblocked, modified block, or full-blocked letter style. Why do you think that one letter, sent to *all* employees, is a better choice than different letters to the two groups?

Case 5.   *The Dungreen Townhouses: Asking to be a Part-time Manager*

You and your spouse live in one of the townhouses recently purchased by Mr. and Mrs. Melvin Hobbs. You are an employee of the University of Houston, where you work in the Information Systems Department. You attend classes part-time and are working on an MBA degree.

You believe that the townhouse is a good value. You felt fortunate to rent it, although it costs more than you can afford. Soon, though, your spouse will complete a bachelor's degree in education and go to work, you hope. But teaching positions are becoming scarce.

You believe that Mr. and Mrs. Hobbs will need help in managing the project. They are both busy professional people. He is a salesman who has recently come into money by writing inspirational books. (You don't like the books, but you don't dislike them to the extent that you will move from his townhouse.) She is a professor at the University of Houston.

You would like to offer your services as part-time manager, although you really don't have a lot of time to spare. You consider offering your services in exchange for the rent, but Bob Hutchinson, the CPA who handles their affairs, says they are tight with the dollar. (You realize that your friend, Bob, shouldn't discuss his clients, that to do so is completely unprofessional. But you are glad to get the information.) You are afraid that if you are paid the full amount of your rent, they might expect too much of you. You have little enough time as it is.

You are young, strong, and healthy, as well as good-looking and a near-genius. It is unfortunate that you don't have any money.

Your father, however, taught you how to work, an ability that will be to your advantage in caring for the townhouses. You know how to repair leaking faucets, mow the lawn, and change light bulbs. You also know how to use a hammer, paint brush, and screwdriver. Your spouse can't tell the paint brush from the screwdriver but can answer the telephone and mow the grass. There are only eight townhouses in the complex, including yours, but there is a large backyard.

Write a letter to Mr. and Mrs. Hobbs. Convince them to reduce your rent in exchange for work that you and your spouse will do in managing the townhouses. How much should you ask? What will you do to earn this amount? How can you convince Mr. and Mrs. Hobbs? (You were a little late with your rent this month, which is the first month they have owned the complex.) Assume necessary details, but do not misrepresent the facts in any way. After all, you hope to keep on living in the luxury townhouses for a long time.

Cases That Require Further Research

Case 6. *Your Own Subject, Your Own Report*

Follow through with the report you began with your study of Chapter 7, the project for which you prepared a report plan. Present the results of your investigation in a complete formal report as discussed and illustrated in Chapter 15. If you did not prepare a report plan with the study of Chapter 7, at this time present a report plan or a proposal in some other form and submit it to your instructor for approval. Ideally, this problem is an actual one you have encountered in your business or profession. You can solve a real problem and complete a class assignment at the same time.

Case 7. *So Many Problems*

With your instructor's approval, prepare one or several short reports based on real problems or questions in your business or profession.

Case 8. Recommending Equipment

Assume that your office has need for one of the following items:

- a microcomputer, modem, monitor, printer
- a laser printer
- a photocopier (some models have both duplicating and photocopy features)
- a voice-writing and transcribing machine (or machines) for use in a private office
- an interoffice communication system
- a similar item of equipment or office furniture
- a voice mail system
- a network system with 18 user stations

Investigate the brands available and recommend your choice, considering the particular needs of your organization.

Case 9. Combining Your Efforts

With your instructor's permission and assistance, investigate some problem in your school or community. This research can be planned as a class project with individual class members investigating some phase of the problem and preparing individual reports. The total findings can then be combined for an overall report on the situation. Or the class can be divided into committees, each to assume special responsibilities in regard to researching and reporting a portion of the situation. If your topic has been investigated previously, try to obtain the results of these investigations. Test these results, or use the information to form the basis for further investigation of the problem. Present the results of your study in the form suggested by your instructor.

*Case 10. Determining Employment Opportunities in Your Career Field**

Examine the classified advertising section of five consecutive Sunday editions of your local newspaper. (If you do not live in a large city, examine issues of the Sunday newspaper from a nearby city.) Try to determine employment opportunities for people like yourself.

---

* This problem is adapted from one written by Dr. Ed Goodin, Associate Professor of Management, University of Nevada, Las Vegas. Used by permission.

For example, if you are a beginning accountant, look for openings that you feel capable of filling. The advertisements may include such terms as *staff accountant, entry-level accountant,* or *recent graduate.* If you are an experienced accountant, look for openings at a higher level. Examine advertisements carefully. Some do not have descriptive titles, yet offer employment opportunities in your field.

As other examples, if you are looking for a job as an executive secretary, look for this job description or such terms as *administrative secretary,* or *secretary to top executive.* Be as specific as you can. If you are a mechanical engineer, you need not be concerned with opportunities for chemical engineers. You can perhaps be even more specific and investigate, for example, opportunities for mechanical engineers in manufacturing or in whatever area you are experienced and interested. State exactly the purpose and scope of your research.

Determine from the advertisements answers to these questions: Which qualifications are most often listed? What is the average salary? How are you asked to apply? Do advertisements indicate opportunities for promotion? Is travel or relocation necessary?

Present the answer to these questions, plus others that you believe to be important, in appropriate report form. Charts or tables will be helpful to present your findings in the most readable style.

Case 11. Market Survey, Clothing

You have read news reports that sales of clothing are down. Is this true? Draw up a questionnaire that you will submit to at least twenty students or, if you prefer, persons who are employed in positions similar to your own. Limit your study to either women's clothing or men's clothing. In addition, interview at least three shop owners, managers, buyers, or others who are in a position to know the answer to your question. Summarize your findings. Use tables and charts as necessary for readability.

Case 12. Investigating Employment Opportunities with Differing Companies

Investigate two organizations for which you would like to work. Study their annual reports, recruiting brochures, and other secondary souces published by some individual or organization other than the organizations you are investigating. Talk with at least one present employee of each company. Also try to find past employees, who may be able to tell you more than present employees. Try to find people who are or were in jobs similar to the one you seek.

Consider all aspects that are important to you on the job, including whether or not relocation is likely and whether there are opportunities for promotion. In the concluding section, summarize the reasons you have chosen one company over the other.

Case 13. The Concerned Citizen

Look into legislation that you consider unfair to you or to some segment of the population. Write a report about this law, or these laws, and make recommendations for change, with reasons. Remember that you are most convincing when you give specific, definite evidence, not when you emote. Although your mind is made up before you start (you could decide that you are wrong), use an objective approach and wording. Be considerate of your reader. Make photocopies of your report and send to your senators and representatives.

Case 14. Feasibility of Implementing Word Processing Center*

Facts: You are the president of (your last name), O'Hara, and Feinstein, a legal corporation, with offices in the central business area of your hometown. Your firm and the firm of O'Hara and Feinstein have recently merged into one legal corporation to provide more and better legal services to the local community. Your company is growing rapidly. There are nine attorneys, including yourself, and five secretaries. Your leased suite of offices covers 2,600 square feet and is located at (you supply the exact address). Your company does not furnish parking space.

Because of the growth of your firm, you, O'Hara, and Feinstein have just concluded a staff meeting where the major topic was whether to install some type of equipment to set up a word processing center for the correspondence of your firm. Lately, the secretaries have fallen behind in finishing letters, reports, depositions, briefs, case reviews, annual reports, and the usual accounting and office documents that are necessary in an office like yours. More and more overtime must be paid and authorized, and Saturday morning work is getting to be a regular occurrence.

You decided at today's meeting to look into the possibility of installing word processing equipment. Both Robert J. O'Hara and James W. Feinstein are interested in this possibility. Data are needed to answer these questions to make a justifiable decision:

1. Should additional secretaries be hired?
2. Will productivity (output) increase with a word processing center?

* Case written by Dr. Jean W. Vining. Used with permission.

3. Will operating costs be reduced, increased, or remain the same?
4. What personnel changes would be needed?
5. Should the equipment, if installed, be leased or purchased?
6. What configuration of word processing equipment do many legal firms use?
7. Will special training or orienting be needed? If so, who will provide this training and at what cost to your firm?
8. What will the cost of the equipment be?
9. What kinds of equipment will be needed?

Case 15.   Reducing Expenses for John Lee and Company's Sales Personnel*

Facts: You are the administrative manager for John Lee and Company, an industrial company that is one of 33 branches located in the Southwest. The home office for John Lee and Company is Dallas, Texas, with regional offices located in Memphis, Houston, New Orleans, Tulsa, and Little Rock. For the last ten years the 135 sales representatives in the 33 branches have been supplied with a company-owned car with total maintenance provided by John Lee and Company. Each representative has paid an annual prorated portion of the liability insurance coverage for his or her company car and has been given a gasoline allowance not to exceed $400 per month. Generally, John Lee and Company has had a policy of replacing the sales representative's car with a new car every 18 to 24 months. Costs have increased rapidly during the last two years and the longtime practice of furnishing sales people with company cars is now being questioned. This policy is also being questioned by many other firms throughout the nation. Possibly management can arrive at a more economical plan without sacrificing sales.

Case 16.   Corporate Gift Giving as a Goodwill Policy*

Facts: You are the administrative assistant to the president of Delta Manufacturing Company, a manufacturer in the New Orleans area. At this morning's regular staff meeting, you were asked (authorized) to investigate the policy of corporate gift giving. The question to answer is this: Should Delta Manufacturing Company begin the practice of gift giving? The management and the company president, Frank R. Smith, have been thinking about giving presents to your firm's industrial customers, as

---

* Case written by Dr. Jean W. Vining. Used with permission.

many of Delta's competitors do. Corporate gift giving is a commonplace practice by many firms. Your company may want to become involved in this practice if the practice is legal and successful. Your management recognizes that such a policy can cause problems if mismanaged or if implemented haphazardly with no structured ground rules or policies spelled out before implementing the practice.

You are to research this problem. The practice of corporate gift giving generally consists of a company giving presents to selected officials of those organizations with whom the company does business on a regular basis. Usually the gifts have nominal value (limits which can be spelled out in any guidelines that you decide to map out) and most commonly consist of such items as food items, leather goods, office supplies, leisure items, or tickets for entertainment. These gifts are intended as goodwill gestures—as expressions of appreciation for the client's business. Most company officials look on the practice as ethical as long as the gift values remain low and as long as the gifts are uniformly given to all customers.

Directions: Your typed report should be submitted to Mr. Frank R. Smith, president of Delta Manufacturing Company, 1005 Poydras Street, New Orleans, Louisiana 70130. Your report should include a cover, title page, letter of transmittal, table of contents, and the findings and analyses section presented in the body of the report. You will recommend whether or not the Delta Manufacturing Company should implement a policy of presenting gifts to its customers, along with other recommendations for the policy to be implemented. Or you many decide to recommend against establishing such a policy. If so, give reasons that can be substantiated by the facts and figures presented in your report.

Findings should be justified by verifiable data.

Case 17. Implementing Matrix Management
(Group Writing Case)

```
Date:   November 11, 19--
To:     All Departments-Branch Managers
From:   E. Ralph Greenbaugh, Personnel Services
RE:     Matrix Management Teams


     Effective immediately we are initiating the matrix
''specialists'' concept that we've been discussing in our meetings
for the past four months. You've read the PM BULLETIN and heard the
input from personnel about the various issues, but in the last board
```

meeting the directors voted seven ''yes'' and two ''no'' to implement this structure.

Integrating the matrix or specialist team concept means that branches from within the region, or from within the company, may request other specialist and team members to be assigned temporarily to another city or region. Branch managers will need to negotiate transfers and assignments. We are especially concerned about utilizing our computer audit specialist effectively. We estimate that you will now work at your ''home base'' about every four weeks out of five.

Branch managers, submit your management plan no later than next Monday.

By Monday, forward to this office, your team organization for each of your nine staff members. Identify your three ''apparent'' team leaders, and attach a brief qualification statement. Indicate how you intend to organize your nine staff members into three matrix teams. Identify which of your nine staff members (regardless of tenure with the company) are likely to cooperate with this new team assignment and which of your staff may reject or not cooperate with the new assignments. We anticipate some apathy and resentment from ''old-timers'' but believe in the long run this matrix concept brings strength and flexibility to the entire company.

Should you anticipate training needs, facility needs, or other support equipment needs, please briefly outline these in your proposal (you have all of these needs).

My assistant, J. Arthur Ruff, is available to assist with questions you may have. Your matrix assignment may include procedural training efforts that are currently working successfully for you in your branches.

Management plan assignments are due Monday. Thank you.

(Assume you are managing three team groups in the business of your choice.)

1. Complete your matrix organization.
2. Identify team leaders.
3. Estimate kinds of equipment and changes in facilities you need (i.e., team leader's offices, larger working areas, multiple network stations, etc.).
4. List training programs in place.
5. Identify necessary training programs.

Prepare a short report. Preface your report with an executive summary or managerial action statement.

Case 18. Program Termination (Small Group Discussion Case with a short written report)

You are one of the members of an evaluation committee for your school. Your committee decides when a candidate for graduation will be terminated. Because there is a long waiting list of students wanting to enroll in the School of Management, your rules are strict and your committee meets frequently.

In a group of four persons, each assume a role. One member is a student's advisor. Another member is from the Registrar's Office. Another member is from the Records Office. The fourth member is the Graduation Review Officer. After discussing the conditions of the case, add other conditions you think may be appropriate to this case. Using these additional assumptions, write a letter of dismissal to the student, a report containing a list of courses uncompleted, and a detailed outline of the field project that is uncompleted.

Rothchilde Management Institute
28037 Mateo Drive
Mateo, CA 91800

Office of the Dean   (818) 661-2323

July 12, 19--

Dr. _____
Department Chairperson
Marketing and Advertising Department
(Your School)
(Your City and State)

Dear Dr. _____:
Ray L. Peterson is not completing his program of study. After each of the previous reviews, he was granted an additional semester to complete his course work, complete his field work and graduate.

As you know, he is now in his eighth year of study and our degree policies permit a six-year period of time for completion of a degree in the School of Management. Yet, again this semester there is no evidence of course work. He did register for an additional hour of independent study credit, but he has twelve now and four is the maximum accepted.

Mr. Peterson must be terminated from the program. Please forward the attached letter of termination. Also forward a copy of the short report that lists the uncompleted courses of study and the outline of the field study that Ray proposed nearly three years ago. Keep copies of the letter and the report for our legal records. Also forward the original letter and report via certified mail.

It's unusual to have to take this kind of action but the review committee agree that Mr. Peterson has had ample time to finish the degree or to indicate the reasons for the delay. He hasn't replied either way.

You may have other questions so please telephone me at _____ to discuss the questions. Forward the termination by next Friday.

Yours truly,

Ralph A. Warton
School of Management Committee
 for Graduation Review
Attached: letter, report
Copies to departmental advisor; Smith, Records office; Registrar's office

Case 19. *Employment Case (Learning Case Analysis Skills—* *use Appendix B)*

You are one of three members of your county employment commission. You interview applicants for the position of administrative assistant to the Dade County Manager. After the interviews, give the information about each interview along with your recommendations to Mr. Leonardo G. Begoni, Dade County Manager, in a short memo report. Base your recommendation on the following information:

1. Education Qualifications: graduation from an accredited college or university with a master's degree in public administration.
2. Previous Experience: necessary but negotiable.
3. Communication Skills: both oral and written skills necessary. Skills in working with groups helpful. Bilingual languages useful.
4. Personal Skills: ability to meet the public, ability to handle complaints, ability to manage office personnel and work with other county officials important.

Candidate Number 1   Spencer Howard
Candidate Number 2   Rudy K. Hernandez
Candidate Number 3   Virginia Foustein

Spencer Howard   Born in Ohio, 26 years old, married, one child.

Recent master's of Public Administration, graduate of Syracuse University (GPA 3.6), last year received a certificate entitled, Training in Municipal Association. Graduated from Ohio State University in Political Science receiving a bachelor of arts degree three years earlier.

Served one year as Planning Development Coordinator for a county in Ohio. Also worked as a research assistant for a professor at Ohio State University. One year as a sales representative for Encyclopedia Sales, Inc. His ability seems good in communicating orally. Some difficulty in English-related courses. Mature in his thinking and in his actions during the interview. Previous experience indicates that he has had substantial experience in dealing with the public.

Rudy K. Hernandez   Single, 24 years old, Mexican-American.

Univeristy of Georgia, master's degree in Public Administration, GPA 3.4. Bachelor of arts in Communications from Southwest Louisiana State College.

Some public administration experience as an administrative intern in the Personnel Department of the City of Atlanta for one summer. Student-body vice-president at Southwest Louisiana State College. Editor of *MPA Newsletter.* Teaching aide for a communications professor at SLSC.

Communicates very well in both oral and writing situations. Speaks Spanish and English. Enthusiastic person. Interacts favorably with people.

Virginia Foustein   36, three children.

1962, Northern Virginia University, bachelor of arts in English and Journalism (3.9), no graduate degree.

Four years administrative assistant to a senator in D.C. Three years as an administrative assistant to a mayor of a middle-sized town in Florida. Has functioned more as a private secretary than as an administrative assistant and is well organized.

Virginia has dealt relatively little with groups of people.

Communicative skills are excellent—both oral and written.

Main interest is creative writing—she has published three short stories.

Doesn't seem interested in obtaining a manager's position but needs the funds. Wants to move to Dade to be near retired parents.

Qualification factors (1 to 5 points each)	Howard	Hernandez	Foustein
Educational Background			
Experience in P.A.			

Communicative Skills
  a. Oral
  b. Written			

Personal Characteristics
  a. Maturity
  b. Personality			

TOTAL			

This memo report should be complete with background of problem, introduction of factors and alternatives, analysis, and decision of why you hired the candidate of choice and why you did not hire the other two candidates. Phrase your report diplomatically. You are an *affirmative action* and *equal opportunity* employer.

APPENDIX **D**

Disk-Based Guide to Basic English

Additional instruction and samples are provided without charge to students and teachers who purchase the textbook, *Effective Reports for Managerial Communcation,* 3rd Edition.

To receive your master copy of the IBM PC Compatible *Basic English Tutor,* please write either of the authors at the addresses provided in the beginning of the textbook.

Printed Student Handbooks titled *A Brief Guide to English Usage* are also available from the authors. Teachers may receive master copies ready for duplication.

Additional Reference Sources

Basic Principles of Effective Writing

Barzun, Jacques, *Simple and Direct: A Rhetoric for Writers*. New York: Harper & Row, 1984.

Bernstein, Theodore M. *The Careful Writer: A Modern Guide to English Usage*. New York: Atheneum, 1965.

———. *Do's, Don'ts and Maybe's of the English Language*. New York: New York Times Books, 1982.

———. *Watch Your Language*. Great Neck, N.Y.: Channel Press, 1965.

Corder, Jim W., and Rusziewicz, John. *Handbook of Current English*. 7th ed. Glenview, Ill.: Scott, Foresman, 1985.

Ewing, David W. *Writing for Results in Business, Government, the Sciences, and the Professions*. 2d ed. New York: Wiley, 1985.

Hodges, John C., and Whitten, Mary E. *Harbrace College Handbook*. 10th ed. New York: Harcourt Brace Jovanovich, 1986.

Zinsser, William. *On Writing Well: An Informal Guide*. 3d ed. New York: Harper & Row, 1985.

Business and Professional Speaking

Applbaum, Ronald L., and Anatol, Karl W. E. *Effective Oral Communication in Business and the Professions*. Chicago: Science Research Associates, 1982.

Ehninger, Douglas, et al. *Principles of Speech Communication*. 10th ed. Glenview, Ill.: Scott, Foresman, 1987.

Holm, James N., and Holm, James N., Jr. *Productive Speech Communication for Business and the Professions*. rev. ed. Boston: American Press, 1985.

Mudd, Charles S., and Sillars, Malcolm O. *Speech: Content and Communication*. 5th ed. New York: Harper & Row, 1985.

Rodman, George R. *Public Speaking: An Introduction to Message Preparation*. 3d ed. New York: Holt, Rinehart & Winston, 1986.

Samovar, Larry A., and Mills, Jack. *Oral Communication: Message and Response*. 6th ed. Dubuque, Iowa: William C. Brown, 1986.

Walter, Otis M., and Scott, Robert L. *Thinking and Speaking: A Guide to Intelligent Oral Communication*. New York: Macmillan, 1984.

Interpersonal and Organizational Communication

Berlo, David. *The Process of Communication*. New York: Holt, Rinehart & Winston, 1960.

Goldhaber, Gerald M. *Organizational Communication*. 4th ed. Dubuque, Iowa: William C. Brown, 1986.

Koehler, J. W., Anatol, Karl W. E.; and Applbaum, Ronald L. *Organizational Communication: Behavioral Perspectives*. 2d ed. New York: Holt, Rinehart & Winston, 1981.

Timm, Paul R. *Managerial Communication: A Finger on the Pulse.* 2d ed. Englewood Cliffs, N.J.: Prentice-Hall, 1986.

Timm, Paul R., and Peterson, Brent D. *People at Work: Human Relations in Organizations.* 2d ed. St. Paul: West, 1985.

The Job Search

Beatty, Richard H. *The Resume Kit.* New York: Wiley, 1984.

Biegeleisen, Jack I. *Make Your Job Interview a Success: A Guide for the Career-Minded Seeker.* 2d ed. New York: Arco, 1987.

Bolles, Richard N. *What Color Is Your Parachute?* rev. ed. Berkeley, Calif.: Ten Speed Press, 1988.

Bostwick, Burdette, E. *Resume Writing: A Comprehensive How-to-Do-It Guide.* 3d ed. New York: Wiley, 1985.

Corwen, Leonard. *Your Resume: Key to a Better Job.* 3d ed. Englewood Cliffs, N.J.: Prentice-Hall, 1988.

Holtz, H. *Beyond the Resume: How to Land the Job You Want.* New York: McGraw-Hill, 1984.

King, Normal. *The First Five Minutes: You May Never Get a Second Chance to Make a Good Impression.* Englewood Cliffs, N.J.: Prentice-Hall, 1987.

Rogers, Edward. *Getting Hired: Everything You Need to Know About Resumes, Interviews, and Job Hunting Strategies.* Englewood Cliffs, N.J.: Prentice-Hall, 1982.

Smith, Michael H. *The Resume Writer's Handbook.* 2d ed. New York: Harper & Row, 1987.

Report Writing

Baxter, Carol M. *Business Report Writing: A Practical Approach.* Belmont, Calif.: Kent, 1983.

Bowman, Joel P., and Branshaw, Bernadine P. *Business Report Writing.* New York: Dryden, 1984.

Brown, Leland. *Effective Business Report Writing.* 4th ed. Englewood Cliffs, N.J.: Prentice-Hall, 1985.

Lesikar, Raymond V. *Report Writing for Business.* 7th ed. Homewood, Ill.: Irwin, 1987.

Lewis, Phillip V., and Baker, William H. *Business Report Writing.* 2d ed. New York: Wiley, 1984.

Comprehensive Textbooks on Written and Oral Communication

Bonner, William H. *Communication in Business: Key to Success.* 5th ed. Houston: Dame, 1988.

Haggblade, Berle. *Business Communication.* St. Paul: West, 1982.

Himstreet, William C., and Baty, Wayne Murlin. *Business Communications.* 8th ed. Belmont, Calif.: Kent, 1987.

Huseman, Richard C.; Lahiff, James M.; and Penrose, John M. *Business Communication: Strategies and Skills.* 3d ed. New York: Dryden, 1988.

Lesikar, Raymond V. *Basic Business Communication.* 4th ed. Homewood, Ill.: Irwin, 1987.

——. *Business Communication: Theory and Application.* 5th ed. Homewood, Ill.: Irwin, 1984.

Murphy, Herta A., and Hildebrant, Herbert W. *Effective Business Communications.* 5th ed. New York: McGraw-Hill, 1988.

Sigband, Normand B., and Bell, Arthur H. *Communication in Management and Business.* 4th ed. Glenview, Ill.: Scott, Foresman, 1986.

Timm, Paul R., and Jones, Christopher G. *Business Communication: Getting Results.* 2d ed. Englewood Cliffs, N.J.: Prentice-Hall, 1987.

Treece, Malra. *Successful Communication for Business and the Professions.* 5th ed. Boston: Allyn and Bacon, 1991.

Wells, Walter. *Communications in Business.* 5th ed. Belmont, Calif.: Kent, 1988.

Wilkensen, C. W.; Wilkensen, Dorothy C. M.; and Vik, Gretchen N. *Communicating Through Letters and Reports.* 9th ed. Homewood, Ill.: Irwin, 1986.

Wolf, Morris Philip, and Kuiper, Shirley. *Effective Communication in Business.* 9th ed. Cincinnati: South-Western, 1989.

Research Methods and Techniques

Barzun, Jacques, and Graff, Henry F. *The Modern Researcher.* 4th ed. New York: Harcourt Brace Jovanovich, 1985.

Berdie, Douglas R., and Anderson, John F. *Questionnaire: Design and Use.* 2d ed. Metuchen, N.J.: Scarecrow Press, 1986.

Chase, Stuart. *Guides to Straight Thinking.* New York: Harper, 1956.

Clover, Vernon T., and Balsley, Howard L. *Business Research Methods.* 4th ed. Columbus, Ohio: Publishing Horizons, 1988.

Deming, W. E. *Sample Design in Business Research.* New York: Wiley 1960.

Edwards, Allen L. *Techniques of Attitude Scale Construction.* New York: Irvington, 1982.

Emory, C. William. *Business Research Methods.* 3d ed. Homewood, Ill.: Irwin, 1985.

Erdos, Paul L. *Professional Mail Surveys.* rev. ed. Melbourne, Fla.: Krieger, 1983.

Huff, Darrell. *How to Lie with Statistics.* New York: Norton, 1954.

Kerlinger, Fred N. *Foundations of Behavioral Research.* 3d ed. New York: Holt, Rinehart & Winston, 1986.

Kish, Leslie. *Survey Sampling.* New York: Wiley, 1965.

Spear, Mary Eleanor. *Practical Charting Techniques.* New York: McGraw-Hill, 1969.

Index